Legal Interpretation

Legal Interpretation

Perspectives from Other Disciplines and
Private Texts

Kent Greenawalt

OXFORD
UNIVERSITY PRESS

OXFORD
UNIVERSITY PRESS

Oxford University Press
2010
Oxford University Press
Oxford University Press, Inc., publishes works that further
Oxford University's objective of excellence
in research, scholarship, and education.

Oxford New York
Auckland   Cape Town   Dar es Salaam   Hong Kong   Karachi
Kuala Lumpur   Madrid   Melbourne   Mexico City Nairobi
New Delhi   Shanghai   Taipei   Toronto

With offices in
Argentina   Austria   Brazil   Chile   Czech Republic   France Greece
Guatemala   Hungary   Italy   Japan Poland   Portugal   Singapore
South Korea   Switzerland   Thailand   Turkey   Ukraine   Vietnam

Published by Oxford University Press, Inc.
198 Madison Avenue, New York, New York 10016
www.oup.com

Oxford is a registered trademark of Oxford University Press

Library of Congress Cataloging-in-Publication Data
Greenawalt, Kent, 1936–
Legal interpretation : perspectives from other disciplines and private
texts / Kent Greenawalt.
   p. cm.
Includes bibliographical references and index.
ISBN 978-0-19-975613-1 (hb : alk. paper)
1. Law–Interpretation and construction. 2. Law–Philosophy.
3. Comparative law. I. Title.
   K296.G734 2010
   340'.2–dc22

2010007433

ISBN 978–0–19–975613–1

1–3–5–7–9–8–6–4–2

Printed in the United States of America
on acid-free paper

In honor of the memory of J. Roland Pennock, John Plamenatz, H.L.A. Hart, and Sir Isaiah Berlin (four teachers who helped me develop a potential I did not realize I had)

Preface

This book, on how interpretation in other disciplines may bear on legal interpretation and on interpretation of privately created legal texts, is intended as the first of three volumes. It has been a long time in the making, with origins going back to a paper I delivered at a Cornell Law School conference roughly fourteen years ago. My interest in forms of legal interpretation has been continuously engaged by seminars and classes in jurisprudence for a superb group of Columbia Law School students over the years. The seminars and classes have involved study of statutory, common law, and constitutional interpretation. My hope is that books covering these important and controversial subjects will follow.

Some of the material in Chapter 2 is drawn from an essay on "Vagueness and Judicial Responses to Legal Indeterminacy," 7 *Legal Theory* 433 (2001). A section in Chapter 3 is based partly on "Variations on Some Themes of a 'Disporting Gazelle' and His Friend: Statutory Interpretation as Seen by Jerome Frank and Felix Frankfurter," 100 *Columbia Law Review* 176 (2000). The last section of Chapter 5 builds on "Interpretation and Judgment," 9 *Yale Journal of Law and the Humanities* 415 (1997).

Chapter 6 of this book is largely drawn from the paper I developed for the Cornell conference. It was published as "From the Bottom Up," 82 *Cornell Law Review* 994 (1997). Much of Chapters 1, 8, and 9 appeared as "A Pluralist Approach to Interpretation: Wills and Contracts," 42 *San Diego Law Review* 533 (2005), first prepared for a conference on Legal Interpretation at the University of San Diego Law School. My thoughts on topics of this book were greatly aided by comments at these two conferences, by participation in a conference on What Is Meaning in a Legal Text: A First Dialogue for Law and Linguistics (papers resulting from the conference were published in 73 *Washington University Law Quarterly* 769 (1995)), by various faculty workshops at Columbia Law School, and, this past spring, by a seminar on religious and legal interpretation at Princeton University, and by responses to a Leon Green lecture I gave at the University of Texas Law School.

Among the individuals who at one time or another gave me very helpful comments are Larry Alexander, Akeel Bilgrami, Vincent Blasi, Edward Blatnik, Peter Brooks, Patrick Cheng, Marvin Chirelstein, Deborah DeMott, Anthony Dillof, Michael Dorf, Elizabeth Emens, Allan Farnsworth, Robert Ferguson, Katherine Franke, Stephen Garvey, Alfred Hill, Paul Horwitz, Mark Hulbert, Avery Katz, John Manning, A. P. Martinich, Thomas Merrill, Bernadette Meyler, Curtis Milhaupt, Eben Moglen,

Arthur Murphy, Katharina Pistor, Joseph Raz, Carol Sanger, Robert Scott, William Simon, Adrienne Stone, Suzanne Stone, Peter Strauss, Susan Sturm, Stephen Sugarman, Robert Summers, Jeremy Waldron, John Witt, Lewis Yelin, Robert Young, William Young, and Benjamin Zipursky. I owe special thanks to Melvin Eisenberg, who reviewed several drafts of the chapter on contractual interpretation.

Among the students who have provided extremely valuable research assistance and comments on drafts were Michael Dowdle, Stephanie Duff-O'Brien, Caleb Edwards, Lisa Ells, Daniel Krockmalnic, Adam Kolber, Neel Maitra, Adam Mehes, Thomas Rosen, and Laura Swanson. In the later stages of the project, Matthew Guarnieri gave me astute comments on a number of chapters, as well as helping me update those chapters. Adam Hochroth provided extremely careful and valuable help in the process toward publication.

Katherine Bobbitt, who translated my writing into electronic form, used her superb editorial skills to catch missing or mistaken words and phrases and to improve the expression of ideas; she also discovered useful materials for research.

Once the manuscript was submitted to the publisher, David McBride made numerous valuable suggestions that led me to improve the organization and clarity of many chapters.*

---

* The note style in the book is an amalgam of that used in legal scholarship and that used in the social sciences and humanities. The only aspect that may require explanation is that the page number following an article citation refers to the first page of the article, and that is the only page indicated when the reference is to the article in general.

Contents

Chapter 1

Introduction

Dimensions of Inquiry

I. ILLUSTRATIVE QUESTIONS

After Dr. Rowland agreed in 1956 to work in the South Pacific Health Service, covering hundreds of islands, he and his wife, a nurse who was going with him, made wills. They knew they would be taking many trips from island to island in small ships. Using printed forms and without consulting a lawyer, each provided that the other would receive everything if he or she survived the writer of the will. In the event of Mrs. Rowland's death "preceding or coinciding with" his, Dr. Rowland left his property to his brother and niece. Mrs. Rowland's will, using the same language, left her estate to her niece. When a ship on which they were traveling in the Solomon Islands went down two years later, no one survived; the Rowlands had drowned quickly or been eaten by fish. Under English law, when the order of deaths was uncertain, the younger person was presumed to have outlived the older. The English courts had to decide whether the deaths of the Rowlands "coincided," in which case Dr. Rowland's property would go to his relatives, or their deaths did not coincide, in which event his property would pass to his wife and then on to her niece.[1]

Ivo Planić, a Croatian soccer star playing in a German league, signs a contract to play with the American Metro Stars "during its season." The Metro Stars agree to pay half of his $300,000 salary if he is unable to play with them because he is injured before he joins the team. During the last game of the German season, Planić suffers a severe fracture, which will take a year to heal. At the time of his injury, the Metro Stars had had a month of training and had begun to play exhibition games; the beginning of the regular schedule was three weeks away. To determine if the team owes Ivo $150,000, a court must decide whether he breached the contract by not joining the team during its training camp and exhibition schedule or whether the language "during its season" limited his obligation to the regular season.[2]

In 1964, as part of comprehensive civil rights legislation, Congress adopted Title VII, forbidding employers to "discriminate" against anyone because of his or her race, color, religion, sex, or national origin. A section of the statute inserted during deliberations in Congress provided that the

1

law should not be interpreted "to require" any employer to grant preferential treatment based on race, etc. As part of an employment contract for a plant in Louisiana where very few African-Americans held skilled jobs, Kaiser Aluminum Co. and the United Steelworkers Union agreed that some places in a craft training program would be reserved for African-Americans even if they had less seniority than white applicants. In a case that proved highly controversial as well as important, the Supreme Court needed to decide whether this form of affirmative action violated the statute.[3]

Law enforcement officials often plant electronic devices that transmit or record conversations on undercover agents and informants. Under the Fourth Amendment, government officers are not permitted to engage in "unreasonable searches." The standard requisites to make a search "reasonable" are that officers have a substantial probability of finding evidence of a crime and that they obtain a search warrant. If one person in a conversation uses an electronic device without the knowledge and consent of the other party, does that constitute a "search" within the meaning of the Fourth Amendment? Courts had to resolve this constitutional issue.[4]

II. INTERPRETATION IN LAW AND MORE BROADLY

In many respects these illustrations from a will, a contract, a statute, and a constitutional provision vary, but they share certain common features. Concentrating on interpretation undertaken to discern whether or not textual language applies, this study aims to identify the particular questions which any such approach to interpretation must answer (explicitly or implicitly), and to show how the considerations that bear on desirable interpretation shift as one moves from one kind of legal interpretation to another. Although the main focus is on the interpretation of texts, like those in my examples, we shall also look at legal interpretation to assess the significance of earlier judicial decisions.

Textual interpretation, and interpretation more generally, are not restricted to law; they characterize much of our lives, from ordinary conversation to our reactions to great works of art. One source of insight about interpretation in law is interpretation in other domains, and we shall explore just how much or how little commentaries about other forms of interpretation contribute to our understanding of legal interpretation.

The completed study will be in five parts. It begins, in this book, with the contributions of disciplines other than law and moves to legal texts created by private parties. Books to follow will concentrate on statutes, common law development, and constitutional law.

At the heart of much of this book is reflection on insights we may draw from disciplines and inquiries outside the law. Successive chapters address themselves to problems in the philosophy of language, literary interpretation and interpretation by musical and dramatic performers, religious interpretation, and general theories of interpretation. The scope of these chapters reminds us strongly that legal interpretation is not a kind of isolated island; it resembles in many respects forms of interpretation that reach other aspects of the rich variety of human life. Just as it would be foolish to disregard what these other forms of interpretation may possibly teach us, so also it would be misguided to assume that the conceptions and methods of other disciplines are susceptible to simple and easy translation into the legal domain. My basic aim in this part of the book is not to make the kinds of contributions to the other disciplines that one might expect from experts in those disciplines. It is rather to analyze just how far those within the law can draw from those disciplines and how far evaluations about legal interpretation need to rest on aspects of the law that are distinctive.

These five chapters provide a deepened understanding of legal interpretation by suggesting similarities or analogies between that and other forms of interpretation, and by indicating dissimilarities that limit the usefulness of outside disciplines for what does and should take place within the law.

Theories of interpretation, or hermeneutics, can be placed in two broad categories. The first is theoretical work or reflection on how interpretation of a particular sort should proceed. For many centuries of Western history, the subject of such reflections was biblical interpretation. In recent times, literary interpretation, and interpretation of art more generally, have become a major focus. But, of course, interpretation is hardly limited to these areas; it occurs in every domain of life. For our purposes, historical, anthropological, and psychological interpretation, among others, can be important, and these will be mentioned along the way.

Beginning in the eighteenth century, a different kind of theoretical work emerged. It was not about desirable methods in various disciplines, but about the nature of interpretation or understanding itself. Among the leading thinkers in this effort have been Hegel, Schleiermacher, Dilthey, Heidegger, Gadamer, and Habermas. Two crucial questions about any general theory of interpretation are how much it has implications for methods within disciplines and how much it has to learn from such methods. Needless to say, a general theory must draw (at least to a significant degree) on how people interpret; thus, the actual practices within particular subjects (if not the theorizing about the practices) must be relevant. Conversely, sound general conclusions about the nature of interpretation are likely to rule out certain methods as obviously misguided, or at least as standing in need of complicated justifications. In tackling general theories of interpretation, Chapter 5 relies primarily on a summary and analysis of the work of Hans-Georg Gadamer, the most influential proponent of a general theory of hermeneutics.

The exact division of the next five chapters, although it helps to make sense of our inquiries about law, is somewhat arbitrary. Philosophers of language have significantly influenced general views about interpretation; authors concentrating on one discipline or another have offered general theories of interpretation; and authors beginning from general theories have drawn conclusions about how interpretation should proceed within specific disciplines. Readers should be alert to the reality that the chapters are highly interconnected.

The study of other disciplines involving the meaning of language and interpretation, and of broad theories of interpretation, can relate to legal interpretation in at least five different ways. Conceivably, if one well understood the philosophy of language, literary criticism, religious hermeneutics, or general interpretive theory, one would be able to see that one form of interpretation in law (or a branch of law) is obviously correct, or that the proper form must include one particular set of elements.

More modestly, the insights drawn from other disciplines might be about limits, about demonstrations that certain proposed or imaginable approaches can be ruled out as untenable. Perhaps most obvious here is the insight that we can never see the past exactly as those who lived in that past saw it. Since we are incapable of such understanding, any theory that demands it is mired in error from the start. But the conclusion that we cannot see the past perfectly does not, alone, tell us whether an interpreter in law should try to recapture the past as closely as he can.

Beyond what it teaches us about limits, examination of other disciplines can also suggest approaches and provide analogies for legal interpretation. This is not only a question of making us aware of possible approaches, but also of suggesting that some approaches seem initially more promising than others. However, before we make any transference from non-legal to legal interpretation, we need to evaluate any approaches and analogies carefully in light of the nature and purposes of human law. To take one easy illustration, certain conclusions about religious interpretation may be inapposite for law if they rest heavily on assumptions about divine inspiration that have no analogue in the law of modern states.

Beyond these three specific connections with legal interpretation, other disciplines might shed light on its essential nature, that is, what interpretation in law really amounts to. In addition to its intrinsic value, such an understanding might have implications for desirable practice and for how we should regard disagreements about that practice.

A final possible lesson from other disciplines is insight into why people could be attracted to forms of interpretation apart from their merits. If we can identify reasons why interpretative approaches could prove attractive in this way, that can create suspicion about their actual superiority. Suppose Janice is convinced that a political leader is extremely able. It is pointed out to her that the leader's physical resemblance to a beloved uncle may have powerfully influenced her judgment. This, of course, does not prove the leader is less than extremely able, but it provides a basis for Janice to make a careful appraisal of relevant reasons for and against that conclusion. In a similar way, demonstrations of psychological inclinations toward interpretive approaches can engender more careful evaluations of their strengths and weaknesses.

A number of pitfalls await any attempt to translate conclusions drawn from other disciplines into law, even assuming that the conclusions strike one as highly perceptive for the subjects to which they are addressed. Often as a preliminary to their substantive discussions, writers on interpretation will draw a distinction between language in ordinary usage and language used in literature, or in scripture, or in some other special way. A somewhat related distinction is between language that is clear and language that is unclear. Unsurprisingly, if an interpretive theorist draws a conclusion based on a premise about non-ordinary language or unclear language, the conclusion may not apply to language that is both ordinary and clear in context. I shall insist that much language in the law *is* clear for particular applications.

Within other particular disciplines and general theories of interpretation, writers may give different senses to concepts such as interpretation, meaning, understanding, significance, application, and tradition. Nuances attaching to different senses become yet more difficult if one is dealing with a translation of a term used in a foreign language. When we assess the soundness of what a writer has said, we must try to take the terms as the writer is using them, not as we might use them ourselves. And when we evaluate its relevance for law, we must avoid assuming that a claim made about, e.g., "understanding" of Scripture, translates easily into what we would consider understanding in law.

Anyone who is looking at other disciplines for relevance to law must also keep in mind the rich variety of legal standards. Various techniques for discerning the meaning of particular texts can have strikingly different degrees of importance. Interpreting a will or a technical statute is not the same as interpreting common law; and within constitutional law, the extent to which the ordinary meaning of the text of the Constitution will dispose of a problem varies enormously. One need not go beyond ordinary meaning to figure out the minimum age of the president or the number of senators for each state, but standard meaning is only a halting first step in resolving a difficult issue about what is protected freedom of speech.

A corollary of the varieties of legal standards is that the relevance of conclusions from other disciplines can vary greatly for different legal standards. Suppose one finds a convincing account of what takes place when people engage in broad historical interpretation. Unless one comes up with reasons why history bearing on legal conclusions should be (or is) treated differently, these conclusions about historical interpretation would bear on interpretation of relevant history before and after adoption of the Constitution's Free Speech Clause; it would also bear on the common law understood as responsive to historical changes. History in that sense seems irrelevant for how to interpret a contract or recently enacted statute.

Despite all these cautions and caveats, an examination of other disciplines can be highly valuable. In each of them, the roles of writers (speakers), readers (listeners), and texts (utterances) take on overarching importance, and we can certainly glean insights from the controversies within these disciplines about a matter that turns out to be crucial for much legal interpretation.

One reason why an examination of other disciplines can be fruitful is precisely because of cautions and caveats. Reflection that includes these can counter the temptation to succumb too quickly to appeals that move from an interpretive methodology outside law to what those operating within the law should be doing.

As our study proceeds, we shall see, as legal scholars drawing from other disciplines have realized, that many of the insights drawn from those disciplines have greater relevance for broader forms of legal interpretation, especially the parts of constitutional law that involve general principles, than for interpretation of private documents such as wills and contracts, the subject of this book's second part.

III. BASIC ISSUES ABOUT TEXTUAL INTERPRETATION IN LAW

When legal interpretation involves discerning the meaning of texts and applying them, we can identify some basic dichotomies or possibilities. These reach across the various domains of law, from the privately created texts discussed in this book to ordinary statutes to vague generalities of the Constitution, covered in subsequent volumes.

With a degree of arbitrariness in categorization, we can discern seven dimensions of choice that characterize the interpretation of legal texts. How an interpretive endeavor in law should go forward depends on just how elements of these dimensions should be ordered or combined. These seven dimensions of choice arise for every kind of interpretation of legal texts, and thus are a basic key for virtually all that is contained in this book and the two to follow.

I begin with a quick summary of the seven dimensions of choice, before returning to examine some crucial aspects in more depth.

1. Writer or Reader?

Should interpretation rely on the perspective of the writer or that of the reader, or some combination of the two? Of course, the typical interpreter is a reader, but that does not settle whether the interpreter should try to adopt the perspective of the writer. Thus, a court might or might not interpret Dr. Rowland's will in accord with what Rowland probably wanted and understood.

2. Subjective or Objective?

Should an interpreter try to grasp how actual writers or readers have understood a text or should her focus be on what a reasonable writer or a reasonable reader would understand? One form of subjective interpretation is definitely not appropriate in law, as we shall explore in chapters that follow. An interpreter is not justified in merely settling on her personal reaction to a text, whatever others might think about the text (as the reader of a poem *might* be justified in doing). The interpreter tries to rely on bases that will be, or should be, persuasive to others.

3. Abstract or Contextual?

Are words and phrases to be interpreted to have a more or less uniform meaning across a range of situations or tied closely to specific context? To take the crucial word in the Rowland case, should "coinciding" mark out the same degree of temporal proximity, regardless of the occasions foreseen when someone wrote his will and the actual circumstances of his death, or should the term be treated flexibly in relation to particular situations?

4. Specific Aim or General Objective?

The apparent aims of a specific textual provision typically fit broader objectives. But sometimes an interpreter identifies a tension or conflict between the two. How then should she interpret the provision? To take our Title VII example, suppose that the statute's language forbidding employers to "discriminate" seems to bar all preferential treatment based on race, *and* that the statutory scheme is largely designed to prevent outright discrimination against African-Americans. Judges recognize that if they are forbidden to engage in voluntary affirmative action, employers will fail to correct much outright discrimination against African-Americans that is less than obvious, instead waiting to see whether anyone directs enforcement efforts against them. Because, given limited resources, public enforcement can be focused on only a small slice of discriminating employers, the consequence of reading the statute to bar voluntary affirmative action will be to perpetuate illegal discrimination against African-Americans.[5] How should the judges then interpret the significance of "discriminate" as it applies to affirmative action?

5. The Relation Between Textual Meaning and Ideas of Justice and Social Desirability

No one doubts that a substantial aspect of interpreting a text is discerning its meaning. How far should courts, and other interpreters who can make binding judgments about the significance of texts, take considerations of justice and social policies into account—even when they were probably not embraced by the writers of the text and might not figure in an ordinary reader's account of what the text means? One aspect of justice is seeing that one party to a case is not taking unfair advantage of the other, but in many cases broader issues, such as how to remedy racial discrimination, are also implicated. One social policy is the efficient use of resources: should courts hesitate to interpret wills, contracts, and statutes to mandate wasteful expenditures even if that is what they seem to say?

6. Inquiry Limited to the Document or Including External Evidence

A critical question in every area of interpretation of legally authoritative texts is how far outside the documents courts should go. If Ivo's contract with the Metro Stars is written, can judges hear testimony about what the parties said orally to each other, or should they limit themselves to the writing? Should judges consider the "legislative history" of statutes or restrict themselves to the statutory language? Exactly what outside sources judges should consult, and exactly when they should consult those sources, are controverted in major areas of modern American law.

7. Time of Writing or Time of Interpretation

Should interpretation focus on the time a legal document was written or the time it is interpreted? Of course, interpreters logically must act at the later stage, but they may or may not see their job as trying to figure out how things looked when a legal document was written. This question about time becomes critical if the authority of a statute or constitution stretches out over decades or centuries.

Let us now retrace our steps over the seven issues to deal with various clarifications and nuances.
1. An interpreter focusing on writers and readers must implicitly decide who counts and for how much. With wills or contracts, is it the understanding of the parties that matters or that of their lawyers? Within a legislature, do the views of an active sponsor of a law count more, or less, than those of a passive member whose vote is crucial to passage? Among possible readers of a statute, should an interpreter focus on experts in the field (say, atomic energy), on lawyers, or on ordinary people; on those who will be regulated by a law, on administrative officials, or on outsiders? In some instances, notably when one individual acts under the instructions of another, the person who later must make an authoritative interpretation may be mainly interested in how a particular original reader (the individual receiving the instructions) did (reasonably) understand them.

If an interpreter thinks the perceptions of both readers and writers matter, he must somehow order or weight or combine these. That may mean, as we shall discover in the chapter or contracts, giving conclusive force in particular respects to what a writer or a reader thinks; it may mean giving the views of each some vague, indeterminate weight; it may mean inquiring about writer understanding only if a reader would find a text unclear.

2. An interpreter seeking to discern the subjective view of writers or of readers must determine (at least implicitly) exactly what attitude or understanding matters. Three possible candidates in respect to writers are hopes, expectations, and sense of proper understanding. Ordinarily these will coalesce: The writer expects his words to be taken a certain way, he hopes that will happen, and he thinks that should happen. But these perspectives can split apart, in which event an interpreter must decide which to credit. Another question about appraisal of a writer's intentions concerns the place of hypothetical intentions: How far should an interpreter consider what a writer would have thought about matters the writer did not consider? Although the point is less obvious, similar questions can arise when the interpreter appraises reader responses to a text.

Interpreters who rely on writers or readers taken in some objective way must determine how to construct the "objective" person in that category. What information will he be assumed to have? Will the constructed person be the average person in a relevant category (say, expert, lawyer, or lay person), the reasonable person (free of some of the ignorance and irrationality of real people), or the most astute person (with capabilities exceeding those of ordinary people)? Almost any construction of an objective person requires an estimate of the responses of actual people, and, if we probe deeply enough, therefore entails at least an implicit decision about whether hopes, expectations, or sense of proper interpretation matter most *and* a decision about how to order, weigh, or combine different views held by different people.[6]

Many approaches to interpretation combine appraisal of subjective and objective responses. Exactly what ordering or combination makes best sense depends on the kind of interpretation that is involved.

3. Although human communication rests on individuals having linguistic competence about the meaning of words in a language, the exact meaning of words uttered in ordinary conversation depends on context. It follows that we have powerful reasons for also understanding words within legal texts in their full contexts; but there are some countervailing arguments. One is that ascertaining precise context is too difficult for judges and other interpreters. Another argument is that if the drafters of legal documents know how courts will understand particular terms, they can craft the documents with a greater degree of precision and confidence than might be possible were interpreters to inquire into detailed, disputable claims about context. Such arguments would be available to support the position that "coinciding," "during its season," and "discriminate" should be given standard, uniform legal meanings, despite their shifting coverage in ordinary conversation.

4. An appraisal of overall purposes can assist in identifying mistakes and in discerning the significance of a particular communication. Thus, if a law says that forms must be filed before December 31, we perceive that provision as keyed to the end of the year. We may conclude that the failure to say "before or on December 31" was probably a mistake.[7] If a contract fails to state a time for performance, courts will determine what time is reasonable given the purposes of the contract. But sometimes a specific provision, not the consequence of a mistake, will seem at odds with general purposes. In that event, courts must make a choice between the two (unless it concludes that the *real* general purposes included ad hoc compromises impossible to reconstruct).

5. In the way that the general purposes of a law or contract may help guide a judge who interprets a specific provision, so also may external policies. The government has a policy in favor of people providing for immediate family members in wills. If the language of a will is unclear on the point, a probate judge will interpret it not to exclude family members. Because this policy corresponds with common sentiments, it may be a fair assumption that a writer whose will has been unclear probably did not mean to exclude a family member. Thus the external policy fits with a common sense guide to what the writer intended. The serious issue arises when, despite whatever force the policy may carry about a writer's intent, he probably did aim to exclude *and* that is how the will's terms are most plausibly read. When an interpreter relies on an external policy to override apparent meaning and probable intent, *then* he relies on the policy to overcome standard techniques to discern meaning.

6. The idea of interpreters confining themselves to a document is a bit misleading. Any interpreter brings to bear her knowledge of the language and of general circumstances. For example, if a man has contracted to work in an office for ten hours on Friday in exchange for $400, an interpreter will not conclude he has broken the contract if he leaves after eight hours because the building has caught fire. Interpreters commonly consult dictionaries to learn the meaning of words they do not recognize, and when texts use phrases common in law, judges refer to the history of how those phrases are understood in law.

The significant questions about external sources concern various explanations, oral or written, that do not find their way into the text itself, such as indications in the legislative process of what a statute accomplishes, comments by writers of wills and contracts, and other "external" evidences of meaning, such as past relations of contracting parties.

7. When an interpreter focuses on readers, he may consider readers at the time a text was written or modern readers, or both. For statutes and constitutions that have stood the test of time, a modern reader may understand provisions differently than would have readers at the time of adoption.

For some relatively few cases, an intermediate period may be important. Suppose a statute is passed in 1800; a 1960 charter for a charitable group refers to the statute, the charter is interpreted in 2010. A court might ask how the statute's language would have been understood in 1960.

One might initially think that the time dimension does not arise with writers; they, after all, engaged in a performative utterance at one particular point in time. But one may ask how the writer of a will or contract subsequently regards its terms, or would now want its terms understood, or would now react to nonenforcement of certain terms. One *might* think of a legislature as a kind of writer in continuing session, reissuing or itself reinterpreting the documents it has adopted.

IV. NONTEXTUAL INTERPRETATION

Nontextual interpretation, which does not focus on a single text, could involve a practice or historical movement. In law, the distinction between textual and nontextual interpretation is clarifying but by no means sharp.

When judges render decisions about the common law—for example, a rule about a manufacturer's liability for a negligently designed product—they look to all highly relevant previous common law decisions and to settled practices, and they make judgments about fairness and efficiency. Although the decision of a case in the present does not rest on the meaning of a single text, the texts of prior opinions are extremely important. And, on occasion, a common law decision does turn almost entirely on the language of one authoritative opinion. (This is especially true for a court that is lower in the hierarchy than the court issuing the original opinion; the lower court has less flexibility in the way it treats precedents of the higher court.)

Interpretation of the meaning of vague constitutional texts often includes assessment of historical understandings of acceptable government action. What forms of interference with speech and press did the founders regard as illegitimate? What searches did people deem reasonable? Interpretation of the "text" requires reference to a much broader understanding of what things a government of free people could or could not do. More generally, when a judge decides to interpret a particular provision in light of "the whole Constitution," this is not so different from interpreting the nature of American government, a form of nontextual interpretation. Further, in both constitutional and much statutory interpretation, judges rely heavily on what earlier decisions have already settled, thus bringing elements of common law interpretation into what is formally textual interpretation. Thus, textual and nontextual interpretation are often interwoven, but, despite this, the distinction retains important significance, and some judges make it a centerpiece of their judicial philosophy.

The crucial questions about nontextual interpretation are not easily broken down. Clearly one aspect of that interpretation is discerning the significance of what has happened in the past—for example, what judges have decided about negligence liability or what people once took to be acceptable searches. But how far does such interpretation involve normative judgment? Does it involve evaluation of what law will be best for the future? And, even in respect to interpreting the past, does it involve choices that are inevitably normative, construals of the past in light of the interpreter's values or values he ascribes to a group of people in the present? Related to all these questions is the problem of how far nontextual interpretation may be reduced to the pursuit of social values, such as justice and economic efficiency.

According to many accounts, coherence is a crucial value for common law interpretation.[8] Judges should aim for coherence of the law in their decisions. This general approach raises critical narrower questions. In aiming for coherence, how far should judges concentrate on narrow "local" areas of law, how far on the law more broadly? How far should they worry about coherence within the common law, how far coherence of areas of the common law with relevant statutes and constitutional standards? And how far should a judge of a multimember court vote for the result she thinks would achieve the most coherence (even if she knows she will be outvoted), rather than aim for the most coherent approach her whole court might be willing to accept, even if the result is less than ideal?

V. CLARIFICATIONS ABOUT THE TERM "INTERPRETATION"

The scope of the term "interpretation" is by no means self-explanatory or uncontroversial. Interpretation can be given broader or narrower meanings. This is true within the law, as within other disciplines. Lawyers often regard whatever factors figure in a court's final decision about how to treat a particular case as involving interpretation; but some authors differentiate "interpretation" from discerning obvious meaning, on the one hand,[9] and from creatively filling in content by "construction," on the other. According to this understanding, "interpretation" falls between two poles; an interpreter is genuinely trying to discern a text's meaning, but meaning is not obvious.

"Interpretation" may also be distinguished from "application." Here the notion is that someone first interprets meaning and then renders an application to specific circumstances. Critics of this approach argue that applications are part of how one interprets, filling out the meaning of the text that is being applied.

If one employs these or yet more complex distinctions, one must recognize that in many actual cases, saying when interpretation gives way to something else, such as construction or application, will not be easy. More importantly, when judges ascribe meaning to legal texts, they rarely distinguish an exercise that is interpretation from more activist construction and more discrete application. In subsequent volumes, we will look again at possible limits of "interpretation" when courts apply statutes and constitutional provisions; but here unless I indicate otherwise, I employ a broad sense of interpretation that includes all efforts to discern meaning and to determine particular applications that depend on that meaning. None of my comparisons between law and other disciplines rest on the particular boundaries assigned to "interpretation," though some points would need to be reformulated if the term were given a narrow scope.

I do in this book, however, distinguish interpretation from something that is undeniably and explicitly more creative than interpretation. Courts may explicitly provide new terms, perhaps based on an interpretation of an entire document. Courts may also, on grounds of changed circumstances or public policy or constitutional restraint, explicitly revise the content of a legal text. Such revisions raise sharply the authority of courts. Although the line between interpretation and outright revision matters, interpretation that stretches or substantially disregards ordinary meaning is not easily distinguishable from revision. This is especially true if one is dealing with an area of law in which a court will not acknowledge that it is actually revising authoritative language.

A different kind of distinction is about the point of interpretation. One may "interpret" the Constitution not only in regard to what actions it requires and protects, but also as a representation of the values of American society. Much interpretation in other disciplines resembles that kind of interpretation more than the prosaic forms of legal interpretation; and the possible relevance of interpretation in other disciplines, for law depends significantly on which of the divergent aspirations of simple application and deep reflection of values is in focus.

A caution similar to that about interpretation applies to "meaning." People employ different senses of that concept. If one seeks to evaluate claims about meaning in any discipline, one needs to grasp the sense of meaning a person employs.

VI. COMMON LAW SYSTEMS

Our examination of legal interpretation is largely limited to common law systems, the systems of law that have developed in the English-speaking world. Many of the basic questions that we shall examine are also raised within civil law systems, whose heritage derives from the European continent and particularly the Napoleonic Code, but my references to these systems will be only occasional.

VII. TENTATIVE CONCLUSIONS

Much of this study descends to a degree of detail, but almost all of it is directed in one way or another at the broad questions I have sketched.

My general conclusions about legal interpretation can be summarized as follows:

A. General theoretical considerations about the nature of language and interpretation can be very illuminating, but they do not determine how courts do, or should, interpret texts that have legal force. On issues about which people can disagree, resolution depends heavily on normative assessments about how a legal system should work. Correlatively, the insights from other particular disciplines mainly highlight possibilities and suggest analogies and limits.

B. The desirability of a method of interpretation depends only partly on what method, perfectly applied, would yield the best results. For legal inquiries, the methods must be ones that fallible human beings can employ without undue inconvenience. The factual inquiries the methods require need to be ones judges or juries are competent to make. These methods also should not open up opportunities for intentional misuse and unconscious bias, so far as these can be avoided.

Any method should be one that is reasonably economical. It should not be too cumbersome. And officials should not have to apply it too frequently. For the most part, people should grasp their legal rights and obligations without going to court. Ordinary people should understand contractual terms without litigating, and without consulting lawyers. If many statutes need to be too complex to be grasped by ordinary people, at least lawyers and experts in the fields should understand them. An expert should be able to give confident advice about a statute's meaning. In short, official interpretation must proceed under the assumptions that initial interpretation will often be made by non-lawyers and that in most circumstances official interpretation will not be necessary. Unofficial interpretation is the crucial backdrop for official interpretation.

C. In general, subjective and objective elements should mingle in a desirable strategy of interpretation for legal texts. It matters what the people who use language and those who are the main audience of language believe the language accomplishes, but whatever sense the language itself conveys to a broader audience is also intrinsically important. Further, reliance on objective elements may be valuable in preventing fraud and in avoiding complicated tangles of inquiry. The exact mix of subjective and objective elements depends on the domain of law. Among the relevant considerations are the importance of the writer's intentions, the number of writers and of primary addressees, and the political authority of the writers.

For the most part, even when objective elements figure, they should be formulated in terms of specific contexts, not broad generalities.

D. Legal interpretation, textual as well as nontextual, is some mix of discerning the past and evaluating what will be best in the future;

the degree of each depends greatly on the domain of law and particular legal problem.

E. Counterfactual inquiries have an appropriate place in nearly all fields of legal interpretation, if not all, but they should be employed with caution.

F. Courts should adopt standards of proof and persuasion that make it difficult to overcome the "natural sense" of language that is used, but in general they should not bar otherwise relevant inquiries. Exactly what inquiries about meaning should be entertained depends partly on the kind of interpretation those who write authoritative words desire.

G. Considerations of justice and public policy play a significant part in the ways courts should understand legal texts. Of course, the aim to have a strategy of interpretation that is reliable and economical is itself one kind of public policy, but I refer here to more substantive policies, such as using resources efficiently, or promoting the welfare of children. Just when courts should make interpretations guided by justice and public policy is highly controversial, but two relevant factors are the specificity of the language that is interpreted (if interpretation is textual) and whether "the law" for the case is privately or publicly created. If relevant language is highly general, vague in its coverage, and designed to apply over long periods of time—as with many of the Constitution's most important standards—courts need to consider carefully how it may best apply in modern circumstances. In general, judgments about justice and policy should figure more prominently in the interpretation of constitutions and statutes and in common law developments than when courts determine the coverage of wills and contracts,[10] although such judgments are highly important for explicit judicial revision of terms of legal documents, the focus of Chapter 10.

Notes

1 In re Rowland [1963] Ch.1 (Eng. C.A.).

2 This is an imaginary case.

3 *United Steelworkers of America v. Weber*, 443 U.S. 193 (1979). The Court decided that the law did not bar such affirmative action.

4 *United States v. White*, 401 U.S. 745 (1971). A divided Supreme Court determined that no search was involved.

5 *United Steelworkers of America v. Weber*, 443 U.S. 193, 209-16 (1979) (Blackmun, J., concurring).

6 See Kent Greenawalt, "Are Mental States Relevant for Statutory and Constitutional Interpretation?," 85 *Cornell Law Review* 1609 (2000).

7 *Locke v. United States*, 471 U.S. 84 (1985).

8 See Ronald Dworkin, *Law's Empire* 224–312 (Cambridge, Massachusetts, Harvard University Press 1986).

9 Andrei Marmor, rather than focusing on obviousness, suggests that "one does not interpret that which is *determined* by rules or conventions." *Interpretation and Legal Theory* 22 (Oxford, Clarendon Pr. 1992).

10 This means that the main controversies over judicial determinations of what is desirable and just are reserved for subsequent volumes.

Part I

PERSPECTIVES FROM OTHER DISCIPLINES

Scholars have long aimed to dispel confusions and mysteries of legal interpretation by looking outside the law. In this part of the study, we shall focus on other disciplines to learn about the nature of language, communication, and interpretation, both to develop a sense of commonalities and differences among various endeavors in which interpretation plays a part, and to recognize much about what judges, and others, do when they interpret legal texts. Can we also obtain guidance about how legal texts should be interpreted—for example, whether judges should accord writer's intent or reader's understanding a dominant role?

We shall see that other disciplines and general theories about language and interpretation provide limited positive guidance for judges deciding what perspectives to employ. These disciplines can deepen our understanding of linguistic communication, reveal illuminating comparisons that help us to understand the efforts of those who interpret the law, instruct us about what is possible and what is not in human interpretation, indicate a range of possibilities, and suggest *some* reasons why particular approaches may be less promising than they appear at first glance.[1] They cannot tell us which among a range of plausible options legal interpreters should adopt. These crucial choices must be grounded in a practical understanding of the nature of law, of particular legal systems and forms of government, and of discrete branches of law, such as wills, contracts, statutory interpretation, and constitutional law.

Readers of these chapters should be aware that I have chosen to focus on matters that have special relevance for legal interpretation. My aim as a nonexpert in the particular disciplines is to explain and analyze how the basic positions I discuss may help us to understand the processes of interpretation within law.

Notes

1 Scholars can develop plausible general theories about interpretation, with legal interpretation being one branch, so long as these general theories are cast at a high level of abstraction and do not dictate just what the criteria of interpretation should be in law, or in its subparts.

Chapter 2

Speaker Intent and Convention;
Linguistic Meaning and Pragmatics;
Vagueness and Indeterminacy

Three Topics in the Philosophy of Language

I. INTRODUCTION

Our first inquiries involve the philosophy of language. One might hope that if philosophers of language could distill the essence of human communication and of meaning, or could reveal the methods by which all texts are understood, we could figure out what interpreters of legal texts do, and should do, when attempting to ascertain their meaning. Even if philosophers cannot provide judges and lawyers with ready-made formulas, they can illuminate many aspects of legal interpretation. This chapter considers related subjects about which scholars in the philosophy of language, and in the related discipline of linguistics, write. The first of these is reflection on the nature of linguistic and other human communication. The broad second subject includes standards of linguistic meaning and the pragmatics of communication—how listeners understand speakers, the relevance of context, and what is implied by what is expressed. I then turn to philosophic writing about vagueness, and its possible relevance for legal interpretation. A fourth general topic—the relation between language and how people understand themselves and the world in which they live—is reserved for subsequent chapters.

II. THE SOURCE OF MEANING IN COMMUNICATIONS

Among philosophers of language who have written about communications, some have focused on the intent of speakers and writers, others have concentrated on the place of conventions of language as enabling understanding. Given concern in law as to whether writer's intent or reader's understanding should dominate the interpretation of texts, this difference of emphasis warrants our examination for its possible relevance.[1] Without attempting a systematic examination of the field, I shall discuss the varying perspectives of three brilliant and prominent philosophers. For us, the main significance of this focus is (1) to inquire about the roles of speaker (or writer) intentions and listener (or reader) understanding in determining the meaning of communications, and (2) to perceive some bases why each of these might be regarded as having powerful significance in law. Although we need not understand each detail in order to grasp the possible import of the various positions for legal interpretation, it helps to have a sense of some nuances and complexities one finds in the literature.

As we consider competing positions, we should not lose sight of a large degree of common ground, much of which may be summed up in four propositions. First, the success of much human communication depends upon shared understandings within cultural communities that various words and phrases signify particular things. Although individual speakers and listeners may differ about the exact coverage of particular words, English speakers, by and large, realize that "dog" is not the word for large creatures with long trunks (what we call "elephants"); they also understand that "democracy" does not denote a single all-powerful ruler who automatically acquires authority upon his father's death (what we call an absolute, hereditary monarch).

Second, speakers and writers occasionally are attempting to convey something different from what their language in context would be taken by most listeners and readers to signify. Nothing prevents us in such instances from thinking about two different meanings, such as "speaker" meaning, and "sentence" meaning, and for many purposes other than law, we will not need to settle on either as *the* meaning.

Third, not all successful communication depends on shared understandings about language. Europeans landing on American shores were able to achieve minimal communication with indigenous peoples despite the absence of shared linguistic conventions.

Fourth, when persons communicate, their effort to transmit messages to their listeners will reflect what they believe their listeners are capable of understanding, and listeners will typically interpret messages in light of what they believe speakers are trying to convey.[2]

A. Utterer's Intentions

One important approach to meaning in communication is that the speaker's (or writer's) intent is what is central. Influentially defending his position over a period of forty years, Paul Grice proposed that a speaker's meaning can be understood in terms of intentions and the recognition of intentions, and that the meaning of communications can ultimately be understood in terms of speaker meaning.[3] Grice did not deny that linguistic convention matters for much communication or that sentence meaning may differ from an utterer's meaning, but he nonetheless claimed that the key to communication has to do with the intentions of the utterer. According to one account, the leading tenets of intention-based semantics are that a "notion of speaker-meaning can be explicated, without reliance on any semantic notions, in terms of acting with the intention of affecting an audience in a certain way," and that "expression-meaning . . . can be explicated without reliance on any semantic notion other than speaker meaning."[4]

In his various essays, Grice aims to provide a satisfactory account of what speakers "mean" when they communicate in terms of nonnatural meaning. Grice focused mainly on oral speech, on ordinary kinds of communications, and on the time the communications are made; he is not thinking about poetry and does not consider instances in which the force of a communication lasts (as with a continuing direction about how to behave) and for which the speaker's intention itself may alter as time goes by. The success of Grice's effort to explicate speaker meaning bears on the plausibility of his fundamental claim that speaker meaning is the core notion of meaning.

Grice contrasts nonnatural meaning with natural meaning, the close linkage of two natural phenomena having nothing to do with what human beings decide to mean, as in, "Dark clouds mean rain."[5] Sentences in the pattern of "U means something by x" are instances of nonnatural meaning. Trying to meet counter examples dreamed up by himself and critics, Grice moves from a relatively simple account of nonnatural meaning to ones that are increasingly complex.

Grice initially rejects a causal approach that for "x" to mean a particular thing, it must have a tendency to produce a certain attitude in the audience.[6] For example, if U (the utterer) says to A (the audience), "B is a professional basketball player," A will probably assume that B is tall;[7] but being tall is not part of the nonnatural meaning of "professional basketball player."[8]

Proceeding to a more promising line, Grice offers as a first shot about informative or descriptive utterances, "'x meant something' would be true if x was intended by its utterer to induce a belief in some 'audience' and to say what the belief was would be to say what x meant."[9] Grice then examines two kinds of counter-examples—ones in which his initial idea of inducing belief is satisfied but nonnatural meaning is absent, and ones in which nonnatural meaning is present without any attempt to induce belief. The counter-examples show the inadequacy of a simple "induce belief" approach; to meet them, Grice makes his definition more complex.

The first kind of counter-example involves circumstances that fit the proposed initial account of nonnatural meaning (that is, U "utters" something intending to induce a belief in x) but are not genuine instances of nonnatural meaning. (1) A leaves B's handkerchief near the scene of a murder, hoping the detective will believe that B was the murderer. (2) A (Herod) presents Salome with the head of John the Baptist. (3) A shows a friend a photograph of the friend's wife making love to B. In each instance, A wants to induce a belief in an audience, and except in the handkerchief example, A intends the audience to recognize his intention. But none of the instances involve nonnatural meaning.[10] For that, the audience must not only recognize the intention that A inform him (absent in the handkerchief example), he must also recognize that his being informed is partly *because* of A's intention (absent in the John the Baptist and photograph examples, in which the information the recipient receives does not depend on any assumption about A's intention). To exclude such counter-examples, Grice offers a revision that requires that the speaker attempt to induce a belief by means of his intention.[11] For example, if I say to you, "It rained last night after you went to sleep," I intend to induce in you a belief that it rained on the basis that you perceive my intention to induce that belief.[12]

A different kind of counter-example is troubling both for Grice's original suggestion and for the revision we have just examined. These counter-examples suggest that inducing a particular belief is not the key to nonnatural meaning. We are confident that some utterers do communicate nonnatural meaning but do not intend to induce a belief to that effect by their audience's recognition of that intention. When U is taking an oral exam (responding that the Battle of Waterloo was fought in 1815), she is not trying to induce a belief in her examiner about when the battle took place.[13] Nor is she trying to induce a belief when she merely reminds the listener of something he already knows.[14] On other occasions, knowing that her listener will disbelieve her, the utterer aims to induce a belief contrary to what she asserts—she says "Pete is honest," intending her listener to assume Pete is dishonest.[15] Her meaning nevertheless is that Pete is honest, the contrary of the belief she seeks to induce. Also, as Stephen Schiffer has pointed out, when one proposes to demonstrate something ("since there are icicles, it must have been below freezing"), or argues for a position ("the fall of communism shows the superiority of market economies"), the utterer aims to induce belief but not through recognition of his intention to do so.[16]

To respond to instances in which the utterer's intention is not to induce his listener to believe what she asserts (including the examples of the exam, reminding, and aiming to induce belief contrary to what one asserts), Grice revises his account to make the *speaker's* direct intended effect an indication that *she* believes something.[17] Therefore, if I say, "It rained last night," my direct intended effect is that my audience grasp that I am asserting a belief it rained last night. If I say, "Pete is honest," I want my listener to think I am indicating that Pete is honest, even while I hope and expect she will think I am lying.

A similar transposition takes place in Grice's treatment of imperatives and quasi-imperatives, which, typically designed to induce action, not belief, are closer analogies to most legal texts than are descriptive utterances.[18] Formulations in terms of an intended effect to produce an action in the audience[19] (or to produce an intent by the audience to do something)[20] through a recognition of the speaker's intention are subject to counter-examples like those we reviewed for descriptive communications.[21] As with those, Grice aims to distinguish the counter-examples from genuine instances of meaning by adding further levels of intentions and recognitions of intentions.[22]

Grice briefly recognizes the possibility for imperatives of someone who demands or requests action with the aim of inducing its opposite.[23]

To take a homely example, parents tell their children, "You are forbidden to eat Brussels sprouts," hoping that will make Brussels sprouts so attractive that the children will insist on eating them.[24] The *meaning* of the parents' statement is that the children should not eat Brussels sprouts, although they intend to produce the opposite effect.

One can meet this example by characterizing the speaker's direct intended effect as making the listener believe that the speaker intends the listener to do what the speaker says (i.e., not eat Brussels sprouts). Parallel with descriptive statements, the intended direct effect of the imperative has become a belief about the aims of the speaker.[25]

This revision alone cannot handle a more subtle situation that Grice does not address. The speaker, a sergeant, issues an order to soldiers beneath him that is in line with what his superiors want and expect: "Shine your shoes before going to bed." The troops realize that the sergeant is merely covering himself in case the lieutenant inquires whether he issued the order, and that the sergeant has no wish that they intend to obey the order; and the sergeant understands that the troops know both that he is indifferent about their shining their shoes and that he has made no attempt to conceal that indifference. Thus, the speaker is aware that the listener does not suppose that the speaker intends that the listener intend to perform the order.[26] Yet the order means that the soldiers should shine their shoes, whatever the sergeant actually intends about the shoes being shined (in this, the example is like the Brussels sprouts case) *and* whatever his listeners suppose about the speaker's intentions, so long as everyone recognizes that this is a regular order (not a joke or metaphorical expression), and that the order carries potential consequences about the respective responsibilities of the sergeant and those under him if the lieutenant is upset over unshined shoes.[27] (Various analogies exist within the law when detailed orders or contractual provisions call for actions that no one expects to take place.)[28] Grice could respond that the meaning depends on what the speaker would aim to have the listener perceive about his intent were the speaker fulfilling his role in the spirit the superiors expect.

The constant thread in Grice's accounts of nonnatural meaning is to place the utterer's primary intention at the center of what he means. If a listener is in doubt about what a speaker intends to convey, he will look at the context and ask what fits with a purpose he obviously has (e.g., a man who calls for a "pump" at a fire does not want a bicycle pump).[29]

In one article, Grice elaborates distinctions between what an utterer means and what his sentence means, between occasion meaning and timeless meaning, and between timeless meaning for the "idiolect" of an individual and that for a group or class of individuals.[30] If a speaker says, "Mickelsen gave Woods quite a beating," the sentence means that Mickelsen defeated Woods easily at golf; but if someone is speaking ironically, he may mean that Woods defeated Mickelsen easily, rather than the other way around.[31]

An individual's occasion meaning will usually reflect his timeless meaning, which at one point Grice suggests is a notion such as "having a certain procedure in one's repertoire."[32] Thus, a person might typically wave her hand in a certain way to show that she knows a route,[33] or she might typically use certain words to convey a particular message.[34]

Timeless meaning for a group of individuals, according to Grice, occurs when there is a general practice that an utterance means a certain thing.[35] His account clearly reveals the possibility that timeless meaning for any single individual may not correspond with group practice, since a person may consistently use certain words and phrases in idiosyncratic ways that diverge from general practice within his group.

Grice's intricate and fascinating efforts to elaborate a full account of a speaker's nonnatural meaning help to support his view that speaker meaning is the central notion of meaning. This conclusion, our main concern, might be thought to bear significantly on legal interpretation, and indeed, some legal scholars do think that the centrality of intent for all communication entails that the meaning of legal texts depends upon the writer's intent. The notion of timeless meaning for individuals and groups might also be thought to bear on how some legal texts should be understood.

Grice strongly resists the idea that "meaning is essentially connected with conventions," which are only one way of fixing what sentences mean.[36] An example of meaning not being fixed by convention involves a small girl who is learning French and thinks a sentence in French means "Help yourself to a piece of cake." The sentence, in fact, has an entirely different meaning. Nevertheless, if I, with full awareness of the sentence's standard meaning in French, utter it to the girl, wishing her to take a piece of cake, what I mean by the utterance is that she should help herself to a piece of cake.[37]

In a Retrospective Epilogue, Grice explains that one must "distinguish between a notion of meaning which is relativized to the users of words or expressions and one that is not so relativized; and, . . . of the two notions, the unrelativized is posterior to, and has to be understood in terms of, the relativized notion; what words mean is a matter of what people mean by them."[38]

One may wonder whether there is a serious tension between Grice's approach and the fact that the very intentions that we form are substantially influenced by the language (or languages) that is (are) part of the world in which we develop and live. The relation of language to life is an important subject in chapters that follow. It suffices to say here that a defender of Grice's approach can concede that language undoubtedly influences individual intentions while still maintaining that the *meaning* of individual communications depends on those intentions.

B. Convention

A significantly different emphasis is found in David Lewis's *Convention*, published in 1969[39] and in an essay published shortly thereafter.[40] After providing a detailed analysis of the elements of a convention, Lewis concludes that a population's use of a language like English is to be explained as a convention. He places convention at the center of communication and the meaning of linguistic expressions.

Lewis begins with a number of coordination problems, including situations in which two parties want to reestablish a telephone conversation that has been broken off, rowers of a boat wish to establish a rhythm, and drivers must decide whether to proceed on the right or left. Each person "must choose what to do according to his expectations about what the others will do."[41]

Certain combinations of actions are "equilibria: . . . each agent has done as well as he can given the actions of other agents."[42] Thus, all people should drive on the right or the left side, and when a telephone call has broken off, one party should call back and the other should wait. Lewis defines "a coordination equilibrium as a combination in which no one would be better off had any one agent alone acted otherwise, either himself or someone else."[43] If one person drives on the left while others drive on the right, no one benefits.

People are more likely to solve coordination problems if they have a system of mutual expectations.[44] One effective means of coordinating is by agreement—declarations of present intentions or promises—but agreement is only one source of concordant expectations.[45] Lewis describes a custom that grew up in Oberlin, where all local telephone calls were cut off after three minutes, that the original caller would call back.[46] Had I telephoned Lewis in later years and been cut off, I would have called him back, assuming his familiarity with that pattern and his awareness that readers of his book might expect him to behave accordingly. Yet we would have had no agreement. People who face familiar coordination problems without the ability to communicate often rely on precedents (i.e., how such problems have been solved in the past).[47]

A population's common use of language is a convention. A person in the United States uses English because he expects his neighbors to understand and use English.[48] Although not all features of language are conventional, the use of any particular language is, given the obvious possibility of using a different language. People observe a regularity in their utterances and responses to utterances in the expectation that their neighbors will act similarly.[49]

Having explained that a regularity is not a convention if there is no alternative way to proceed,[50] Lewis gives us his final definition in *Convention*: "A regularity *R* in the behavior of members of a population *P* when they are agents in a recurrent situation *S* is a *convention* if and only if it is true that, and it is common knowledge in *P* that, in almost any instance of *S* among members of *P*,

(1) almost everyone conforms to *R*;
(2) almost everyone expects almost everyone else to conform to *R*;
(3) almost everyone has approximately the same preferences regarding all possible combinations of actions;
(4) almost everyone prefers that any one more conform to *R*, on condition that almost everyone conform to *R*;
(5) almost everyone would prefer that any one more conform to *R'*, on condition that almost everyone conform to *R'*,

where *R'* is some possible regularity in the behavior of members of *P* in *S*, such that almost no one in almost any instance of *S* among members of *P* could conform both to *R'* and *R*."[51]

In "Languages and Language," Lewis's formulation of the relevant conditions differs somewhat. Most significantly, for condition (3), he writes "This belief that the others conform to *R* gives everyone a good and decisive reason to conform to *R* himself"; and he adds a sixth condition that the facts listed in the five conditions "are matters of *common* (or *mutual*) *knowledge* . . . ."[52]

We can see how Lewis's definition applies to language. (1) Almost everyone in many parts of the United States speaks English; (2) almost everyone expects others to do so; (3) almost everyone prefers that people speak English, and has a good reason to do so himself; (4) almost everyone prefers that any additional person speak English, so long as almost everyone is doing so;[53] (5) almost everyone would prefer that any additional person would speak French, if almost everyone spoke French; and (6) the facts embodied in these conditions are commonly understood.

In his article, Lewis emphasizes an aspect not to be found in his book. He claims that use of a language includes a convention of truthfulness and trust in the language. Speakers try to say what is true in the language, and hearers trust that what they hear is true in the language.[54] Thus, if someone says "I like dogs more than cats," the hearer trusts that the speaker is talking about the animals designated dogs and cats in English and means by "like" and "more" what those words ordinarily signify in English. The hearer also trusts that the speaker is truly describing her preference.[55]

Lewis thinks that many conventions may be called rules, but "not all so-called rules are conventions."[56] We should understand "rules of language" as tacit conventions.[57]

Addressing the view about nonnatural meaning Grice adopted in his first paper on the subject,[58] Lewis suggests that "the audience's response is produced by means of a conventional signal, given in conformity to a signaling convention."[59] Lewis does not claim that nonnatural meaning is *always* a consequence of conventional signaling.[60] In an example of an acquaintance who draws a picture of a wife and her lover in order to convey to the husband that his wife is having an affair,[61] Grice did not assume a conventional understanding to this effect (as opposed to the drawing indicating a dream or a wish), and Lewis himself later uses an example of someone putting a scarecrow in quicksand as an effective way to warn others not to walk in the quicksand, even though the others do not believe the scarecrow is a conventional warning signal.[62] Lewis apparently does not disagree with Grice that people can attempt to convey nonnatural meaning outside of existing conventions and that they will sometimes succeed.

How does Lewis differ from Grice? Grice does not deny a place to conventions of language. Lewis does not focus on the meaning of particular communications. He sets out to explain how people are able to communicate effectively and why the use of language proceeds as it does, resembling other conventional practices. Lewis may accept Grice's basic idea of how to discern an utterer's intention.[63] One could be persuaded by all that Lewis says and still maintain the idea that the meaning of any particular communication depends on a speaker's intentions. And various scholars have thought that Lewis's account of convention is invaluable in explaining how one moves from Grice's notion of speaker meaning to linguistic meaning.[64]

Nonetheless, Grice and Lewis adopt significantly different emphases. By placing convention at the center of communication in ordinary language, Lewis stresses not only speakers but the trust of listeners. He talks of rules of language[65] and treats the possibility that some sentences may be unambiguous on every occasion of their utterance.[66] His attention to what sentences conventionally mean might possibly matter for interpreting legal texts. One who is trying to fix the import of texts with legal consequences might focus on what terms would convey to most readers rather than what the writers actually had in mind, if the writers have strayed from conventional meaning through ignorance, a slip, or an aim to confuse.[67]

C. Doubts about Convention

Although speakers of a language may share many conventions about its use, nevertheless different people accord subtly different meanings to various words and phrases. When a speaker's expressed thought is simple and straightforward, the listener may be able to grasp the basic message precisely, and without reflection. A typical question among people walking dogs is, "Is your dog male or female?" One answer or the other is forthcoming. Although their senses of the significance of owning a dog of a particular gender may vary widely, everybody understands what it is to say a dog is male or female. But what other remarks convey is less clear.

Suppose you tell a friend, "John has a good sense of humor." Because you and your friend may have different notions of what is humorous, your comment may require reflection on her part and leave her with a slightly different idea of John than you intended.

The distinction between straightforward communications and those calling for reflection applies to imperatives as well as descriptive statements. "Please pass the salt" is (usually) simple but other imperatives have the vagueness and uncertainty of a remark about a sense of humor. A thirty-year-old woman tells an older man: "Treat me with respect." He may find it hard to understand just what behavior she regards as evidencing respect, given shifting attitudes about whether actions like opening doors are polite or condescending. Some theorists have suggested that imperatives or rules necessarily require interpretation because they must be translated into applications, but when it comes to discerning meaning, no plausible basis, as Chapter 5 explains, exists to draw a sharp distinction between imperatives and descriptive statements or between rules and individual imperatives.

In an essay entitled "A Nice Derangement of Epitaphs," Donald Davidson claims that our responses to malapropisms—misuses of words— significantly undermines any purely conventional account of meaning.[68] If a speaker says, "a nice derangement of epitaphs," the listener assumes that he means "a nice arrangement of epithets." Davidson says that when a speaker uses the wrong word, "the similarity in sound tips the listener off to the right interpretation."[69] This capacity threatens the distinction "between what a speaker, on a given occasion, means, and what his words mean . . . since here the intended meaning seems to take over from the standard meaning."[70]

I think it is helpful to recognize that when a speaker misspeaks, as in Davidson's example, it may be either because he has "slipped"—if quizzed, almost everyone would use "arrangement" (not derangement) for a collection—or because he actually misunderstands the standard meaning of a word—he may be confused about what "epitaph" means.

Davidson concentrates on *first meaning*, a term he uses in preference to the encrusted phrase "literal meaning"; the best way "to distinguish first meaning is through the intentions of the speaker."[71]

Addressing the suggestion of philosophers and linguists that speakers and hearers share a system that allows hearers to grasp novel utterances, Davidson examines three plausible principles: that (1) "First meaning is systematic. . . . (2) First meanings are shared. . . . (3) First meanings are governed by learned conventions or regularities."[72] The ability of hearers to interpret malapropisms threatens the sufficiency of these principles because these expressions cannot be interpreted according to abilities typically considered to constitute linguistic competence. For understanding, it is not necessary that the speaker and hearer use the same language, so long as they share an understanding of the speaker's words.[73] One fairly common illustration of such an understanding, which needs to be distinguished from malapropisms, is when two acquaintances have some-what different understandings of complex concepts like "liberal," "democracy," and "faithful" (or agree about their core applications but differ about what they cover at the edges). A listener may have a fair sense of what the speaker signifies although he would use the term differently.

Davidson distinguishes between a hearer's *prior theory*, with which he is prepared to interpret an utterance, and his *passing theory*, which is how he does interpret the utterance.[74] The prior theory is not shared by speaker and hearer and is not "what we would normally call a language."[75] The hearer's prior theory has all of the special features of the speaker's idiolect that the hearer is ready to take into account; a hearer will have different prior theories for different speakers.[76] The hearer's passing theory will differ from his prior theory insofar as the utterance causes his theory to change; that theory will include attempts to interpret words that deviate from ordinary usage on that occasion.[77]

What a speaker and hearer share, if communication is successful, is a passing theory; that "is not learned and so is not a language governed by rules or conventions known to the speaker and interpreter in advance."[78]

Davidson concludes on a skeptical note. We "have discovered no learnable core of consistent behavior, no shared grammar or rules. . . ."[79] There is "no such thing as a language of the sort conceived by many philosophers and linguists; we should give up the attempt to illuminate how we communicate by appeal to conventions."[80]

Davidson is right that we can recognize a speaker's meaning in ways more complex than competence in conventionally established rules of language. His account might seem to reinforce Grice's approach to speaker's intentions as the key to meaning in particular circumstances, although a rejection of the centrality of convention need not commit one to any particular alternative.[81]

Even if all Davidson says about how we understand each other is correct, widely shared senses about the meaning of words and rules of grammar may still be an extremely important part of interpretation, and these shared aspects may be well thought of as based on conventions.

D. Potential Relevance for Legal Interpretation

What is the relevance for law of discussions of intention-based semantics and the conventional aspects of communication? At a minimum, they explain in considerable depth our sense of the importance of what speakers and writers are attempting to convey when we reflect on their meaning, and they show the extent to which shared understandings make linguistic communication possible. They give us a powerful basis to reflect on the significance of intent and conventional understanding in the interpretation of legal texts.

Are the philosophic positions more determinative than this? Would the right approach to the issues they examine actually demonstrate how interpretation of legal texts should proceed, or at least create a strong presumption about proper methods, pointing toward interpretation that focuses on a writer's intention or on conventional meaning? Whether or not one can come up with a successful philosophic account of communication along one set of lines or another, or with some combination of intention and convention, turns out to be relatively unimportant for the best methods of interpreting various legal standards. (Without examining every conceivable philosophic account, I cannot *prove* that none would yield the correct technique for legal interpretation, but what follows here, and in subsequent chapters, is sufficient to establish the claim's substantial probability.)

Let us consider two oversimplified questions about "meaning" in law: (1) Should the law take a will to mean what the testator intended it to mean when she wrote the will, what the words she used were commonly intended to mean in her other communications, or what the words would convey to a competent reader of its language, unfamiliar with the writer's idiosyncrasies? (2) Should the meaning of constitutional language be understood as evolving over time? The answer to these questions is not resolved by the relative soundness of intention-based semantics or the centrality of conventions.

The wills question is the more straightforward. Suppose intention-based semantics is unsound: to put it crudely, Grice is wrong in making the speaker's intention *the key* to the meaning of communications. We might nevertheless believe that trying to carry forward the testator's actual intentions is desirable. Everyone makes mistakes in the language that they use, and perhaps judges should attempt to accomplish the wishes of a will's writer, whatever one would say about the ordinary linguistic meaning of what she wrote. If it were thought that determining intent on a single occasion is too difficult, perhaps a court should at least rely on the writer's common use of words over time, her "timeless meaning," to use a phrase of Grice's.

Suppose, to the contrary, that intention-based semantics is a persuasive theory, that the core of meaning does lie in a writer's intentions, *and* that a challenge, such as Davidson's, to the conventional account of communication in language is philosophically telling. Nonetheless, one may say that judges are not in a position to grasp the unstated intentions of a person who has died, that they would find it too difficult even to discern a person's peculiar timeless meaning, and that, in any event, a person's ordinary usage may not appear in a formal document like a will (even if she, rather than a lawyer, is the will's writer). One might conclude that reliance on the conventional meaning of the language found in wills is able to produce greater certainty and encourage carefulness when wills are written.

We can see quickly that neither the philosophic persuasiveness of intention-based semantics nor the degree of centrality of convention for understanding meaning determines how wills should be interpreted.

The philosophical literature helps to understand more fully the reasons why a speaker's meaning does not always coincide with the "ordinary" meaning of the sentences he utters, a divergence of which everyone is aware; but the relative power of theories from the philosophical perspective provides little help in resolving the essentially practical question of what to do about wills.

The question about constitutional interpretation is more complex. It is initially unclear what an approach based on a speaker's meaning might entail for "communications" issued by multiple bodies of individuals and meant to endure over time; but, in any event, the question about changing meaning is, for the United States, a practical one about the desirable interpretation of a written constitution that is very difficult to amend and that serves as a standard to determine the validity of ordinary laws. The questions that interest Grice, Lewis, and Davidson do not carry us far in deciding how to treat meaning in a constitution that lasts through time. (On this subject, the chapters that follow will explore whether theories about interpretation of other texts that endure, such as great literature and Scripture, yield more helpful guidance.)

Davidson's treatment of mistakes in communication may have more direct relevance for legal interpretation. Except for the parties to a contract who may settle terms according to corresponding passing theories that are not widely shared, the writers of legally binding language are writing mainly for judges familiar with established legal terms (as with wills), or for judges, administrators, and a general audience (as with statutes).

With wills and contracts, we can imagine simple misuses of words that are recognized fairly easily by readers who can identify what is wrong and see what was intended instead. Davidson does not tell us how the law should handle such slips, but he does give us one insightful way to conceptualize the issue. Rather than distinguishing between literal and intended meaning, we might perceive "first meaning" as including a correction of an obvious slip and thus contrasting with the standard meaning of the words that have been employed (if they have, unlike the phrase "a nice derangement of epitaphs," a standard meaning). This conceptualization may make a court's adoption of intended meaning seem attractive, but the administrative reasons to resist the approach are by no means undercut by Davidson's novel concepts.

Apart from mistakes in punctuation, mistakes in statutes more often involve a collection of words rather than a single word. A striking example I noted in the introductory chapter is a statute that provided that claims had to be filed before December 31.[82] Taken in the standard way, such words trap the unwary, because people will be surprised to learn that if they file on the last day of the month and year, they will be too late. Had this limit been announced orally by a single individual, we would say with confidence that he misspoke and almost certainly meant "before or on December 31." That those who drafted and voted on the actual statutory language meant to preclude filing on the last day of the year is unlikely, though conceivable.

A rather different kind of example was posed by a New York "whistle-blower" statute, which says that someone who has blown the whistle on misbehavior and is claiming statutory protection against retaliation shall not lose any rights "except that the institution of an action [under] . . . this section shall be deemed a waiver of the rights and remedies available under any other contract, collective bargaining agreement, law, rule, regulation or under the common law."[83] Anyone reading the language carefully would conclude, "This can't mean what it says." No legislator would want a worker who claims that she cannot be fired for reporting illegal activities to lose the right she would otherwise have to recover damages as a consequence of her boss burning down her house.

If we extend Davidson's comments on malapropism slightly, we might reason that in cases of absurdity, the first meaning would not be the absurd meaning but a reasonably discernible alternative meaning, if there is one. With the December 31 term, a natural first meaning would be "before or on December 31." An intelligent reader might discern no first meaning for the whistleblower law, because, lacking the device of follow-up questions we employ in ordinary conversation, he might be perplexed about exactly what the language would convey. On the fundamental questions of how the law should handle these matters in various domains, Davidson gives us no answers, although his conceptualization and his stress on how much the understanding of hearers and readers is based on their assumptions about what speakers and writers are trying to communicate is very helpful.

One other distinctive approach to meaning might be thought to have more direct implications for legal interpretation. Some writers have claimed that the meaning and reference of natural kinds, such as "gold" and "water," depends on the actual characteristics of those kinds, not any misconceptions that an individual, or most members of a society, may have at a particular time.[84] These "realists" claim further that many evaluative standards, including moral standards, are similar, in that their true meaning and application depends on correct evaluative judgments. One might suppose that when the law incorporates any such standards, their proper legal meaning depends on the best evaluation according to such a standard.

As Brian Bix has suggested, the status of authority and intention in law precludes any simple solution along these lines.[85] Suppose a testator's will leaves his "paintings by Rembrandt" to Adele and his "paintings by Van Gogh" to Bruce. Shortly after writing the will, he becomes incapacitated and unable to alter his will. Before he dies, it is firmly established that his "Rembrandt" paintings were not by that master but by his assistant. Nonetheless, the paintings that he and everyone else thought were by Rembrandt will go to Adele.[86] If a state legislature offers subsidies for growing vegetables at a time when virtually everyone assumed that tomatoes were vegetables (a natural kind), courts should not deny those growing tomatoes their periodic payments when experts finally persuade people that tomatoes are really a fruit. And if, when a constitutional or statutory requirement of "just compensation" is enacted, everyone conceives that such compensation is equivalent roughly to market value, judges who come to believe that really just compensation for the rich is much less than that should not implement their own conception of true justice in this respect. It is possible, of course, that constitution-makers *might* employ words with a moral meaning; e.g., "cruel punishment," with the hope and expectation that judges will aim for a correct moral evaluation in applying them; but we certainly cannot assume that is always how such language should be interpreted in law. The actual intentions of those who write legal documents, and the general understandings of the concepts that are included in constitutions and statutes, can complicate desirable legal appraisals in ways that distinguish these from simple moral judgments.

III. LINGUISTIC MEANING AND PRAGMATICS

We now turn to ordinary standards for understanding communications in language and various guides for drawing inferences beyond what a communication explicitly conveys, captured in the notion of Pragmatics.

Within law, as well as other domains of human discourse, interpretation depends largely on the understood meaning of single words and multi-word expressions and on standards of grammar. Lawrence Solan has written of a "code" that "linguists call a generative grammar, the set of internalized rules and principles that permit us, unselfconsciously, to speak and understand language with ease and with great rapidity."[87] If someone says, "He thought Fred had convinced the jury," we know that the "he" refers to some male other than Fred.[88] It is an obvious point that lawyers, judges, and other interpreters rely on grammatical principles when they construe texts. Whether one's ultimate focus is on a speaker's intentions or on conventional understanding, the ordering of words often leaves little doubt about what is meant.

But we also need to recognize more complex truths. On many occasions the placement of words leaves uncertainty about meaning. Sometimes a reading of the words apart from context will make two (or more) constructions equally plausible; on other occasions, such a reading will make one interpretation more plausible than another, but will leave room for the competing conclusion. An example of the latter is a provision that no employee would be dismissed except for (among other causes) "Conviction of a felony or of any crime involving moral turpitude."[89] This language seems to set out two categories—one of felonies, the other of crimes involving moral turpitude—thus including whatever felonies do not involve moral turpitude. Nonetheless, contrary to a general assumption that qualifying phrases attach to the last antecedent, a California court, faced with dismissal of a teacher who grew one marijuana plant at home, held that the language of moral turpitude limited "felony" as well as "any crime." Ruling that his behavior did not involve moral turpitude, the court reinstated the teacher.[90] The court had fully understandable reasons for not wishing the harsh consequence of dismissal to fall upon a teacher who had engaged in this behavior, but it failed to acknowledge that it was straining the ordinary sense of the language.

On numerous other occasions judges write as if their decisions are linguistically compelled when something else is going on.[91] Various canons of construction, such as the last antecedent rule, reflect to some extent how language is commonly to be understood, but judges may refer to those rules as if they are completely dispositive, rather than one guide to understanding meaning. In a case involving a death sentence, the issue before the Supreme Court was whether the jury had mistakenly been told to disregard mitigating circumstances. The trial judge instructed the jurors not to be "swayed by mere sentiment, conjecture, sympathy, passion, prejudice, public opinion or public feeling."[92] Chief Justice Rehnquist, with three colleagues, concluded that "mere" applied not only to sentiment, but also to sympathy (thus allowing weight to be given to sympathy that derived from factors rightly seen as mitigating). Justice Brennan wrote for four dissenters who concluded that "mere" did not apply beyond "sentiment" because it obviously did not apply to prejudice,[93] and if "mere" did not apply to all items, it should be limited to "sentiment," the word immediately following. Who knows how jurors took this language, assuming they were listening carefully? Conceivably they thought "mere" applied only to "sentiment," or only to the first three items on the list, those preceding "passion" and "prejudice," or only to any items for which "mere" would seem to them a sensible qualification. In any event, as Professor Solan points out, the justices voting for the broad reading of "mere," which tended toward rendering the judge's instruction permissible, all tended to uphold death penalty convictions in a range of cases; the opposing justices often found grounds for overturning death penalties. It seems much more likely that what was doing the real work in the opposing votes had to do with views about the death penalty rather than a subtly different sense of the trial judge's grammar.[94]

That judges frequently put greater weight on assertions about what the structure of language shows than is fairly warranted is easily explicable. That practice is one manifestation of judicial opinions being written to make issues sound more one-sided, more conveniently disposable, than they really are. Reference to "rules" that reflect linguistic practices appears to be a neutral way of dealing with cases, a way that does not involve highly controversial claims about social justice and desirable policy. As Solan has put it, "judges . . . frequently succumb to the temptation of using . . . linguistic principles to justify their decisions, without any explanation of why one principle was chosen instead of another, creating the appearance that it could never have been otherwise."[95] The use of linguistic argument "is frequently incoherent and idiosyncratic."[96] Just how far written opinions should clearly state the precise bases of judicial determinations is arguable. What is not arguable is that when they are reaching the decisions themselves, judges should give the appropriate weight, no more, no less, to standard linguistic assumptions.

During the past half century some linguists and philosophers of language have examined the ways in which context affects what utterances mean and what can be implied from utterances beyond their standard meaning. The boundaries of the field of Pragmatics have been variously understood, but for our purposes we may think of it as "the study of the relations between language and context that are basic to an account of language understanding."[97]

A good deal of study within Pragmatics concerns what may be implied from what is said. As Andrei Marmor suggests, sometimes an implication that is not directly expressed can be drawn from the language in every one of its contexts: "X is A but B" (an example is "Leo is fat but very handsome") implies that the conjunction of X being both A and B is somehow surprising or particularly interesting.[98] Marmor calls such implications "semantically encoded" because they are drawn from the semantic meaning itself.[99] In all likelihood, it will sometimes be arguable whether a particular implication is semantically encoded in this sense or depends on context,[100] but that question need not detain us. What matters for ordinary understanding and in legal interpretation is what implications may fairly be drawn, and undoubtedly this often depends on the context in which language is used.

Many of the basic principles of Pragmatics were sketched by Paul Grice, who provided an account of rational communication that helps explain why people say or do not say things, and how listeners draw inferences from what speakers do say.

Concentrating primarily on conversations, Grice posited a Cooperative Principle of rational communication.[101] "Make your conversational contribution, such as is required . . . by the accepted purpose and direction of the talk exchange in which you are engaged."[102] From this principle, he derived four categories, which yield more specific maxims.

The first category is Quantity; its maxims are to make one's contribution as informative as is required and not to make it more informative than is required.[103]

Under the category of Quality, one should make one's contribution a true one, which includes the more specific maxims of not saying what one believes to be false or that for which one lacks adequate evidence.[104]

Under the category of Relation, the sole maxim is "Be relevant."[105]

The category of Manner contains one general maxim, "Be perspicuous," and various more specific maxims to avoid obscurity and ambiguity and be brief and orderly.[106] In law as well as elsewhere, the maxims may conflict to a degree. Those writing legal texts often have to choose between brevity and trying to cover many possible contingencies.

A central assumption of Grice's approach is that meaning can often not be determined simply on the basis of the meaning of words and the structures of sentences. One must know the conversational context and what is probably in the mind of the speaker.[107]

Georgia Green says that the Cooperative Principle, and the maxim of relevance in particular, provides a basis for a natural account of how we discern coherence in texts.[108] Quoting a famous passage of Lieber's about a housekeeper telling a domestic to "fetch me some soupmeat" (an illustration that will occupy us in Chapter 6 on Informal Instructions), Green suggests that coherence is a function, not only of the text, but also of "the text-producer's estimate of his audience's beliefs and inferring capacity, and of his acting appropriately on this estimate."[109]

Grice realized that "usages which, taken at face value, appear illogical but are taken as rational contributions . . . typically convey much more than is said."[110] Violations of the maxim of quality may be used to express understatement, hyperbole, and sarcasm. And a speaker who evidently disobeys one of the maxims is often trying to convey information by what Grice calls implicature. Thus, if someone asked for a recommendation for a pupil who has applied for a job teaching philosophy, writes only, "Mr. X's command of English is excellent, and he has attended tutorials regularly," the implicature is that Mr. X is not very able at philosophy.[111]

Pragmatics can be an illuminating lens through which to view aspects of legal interpretation, among other things helping to explain how judges understand the import of language and why they may view a text as implying more than has been written or in a manner at odds with the ordinary sense of the writing. Geoffrey Miller has suggested that many maxims of statutory interpretation may be seen as embodying ideas embraced by Pragmatics. Thus, the principle that provisions will be understood not to be completely redundant of other provisions or of no effect, reflects the notion that communications should be apt in quality and perspicuous.[112]

We should be aware, however, of significant differences between legal texts and ordinary conversations that may limit the relevance of various pragmatic principles and affect the significance of those that are relevant. As Andrei Marmor has urged, legal texts are not themselves conversations, and insofar as one focuses on "conversations" related to statutes, one may think both of conversations within legislatures and conversations between legislatures and various audiences.[113] We have no guarantee that a statute, adopted after various compromises are hammered out, will have the coherence of a single speaker's conversation. Further, given broad disagreement about the respective roles of legislatures, administrative agencies, and courts, it may be much harder to fix on conventions that are agreed upon than in typical conversational exchanges.[114]

Among the aspects of pragmatic inferences that seem most applicable to legal texts are those that construe language so it will accord with normal principles of effective communication. If someone asks the time, and the response is "The milkman has come," one infers (or could have inferred when I was a child) that the speaker does not know the exact time, but that it is early in the day shortly after the usual time of the milk-man's arrival, which is regular enough to give a fair sense of the approxi-mate time.[115] (Unless one was being sarcastic, one would not say "The milkman has come" to a person rising in the afternoon after a late night party.) If a sign says, "No liquor will be served unless you are 21," a reader understands in social context that this means 21 or over, a conclusion that one would not reach about a notification that in a children's baseball league "players must be ten years old." In a legal context, a statute that specifies that "Persons over 18 years of age may vote" implies that no one under 18 may vote.[116]

When they interpret legal texts, courts will commonly give effect to unspecified presuppositions that apparently underlay the text. If some-one tells a driver running out of gasoline, "There's a gas station in the next town," the driver assumes the speaker presupposes that the station is open.[117] Similarly, if a statute assigns a task to an administrative agency, a court will normally assume that the agency can employ means necessary to carry out the task, although a statute could negate that inference by barring the use of particular means.[118]

We can point to pragmatic aspects of legal interpretation, but recogni-tion of these does not resolve matters when the implications of applying a pragmatic maxim are opposed to other criteria of resolution or when two maxims yield contrary conclusions. In the *Holy Trinity Church* case,[119] the law prohibited contracts with aliens outside the country to perform "labor or service of any kind" unless one of a list of particular vocations, such as singers and lecturers, was involved. Clergy were not included in the exceptions. If one assumes that ministry is "service of any kind," and that a minister is not a lecturer, clerics are covered by the general rule and are not exempted by any named exception. The usual pragmatic impli-cation if a number of exceptions are spelled out is that there are no fur-ther exceptions.[120] Yet, barring contracts with foreign clergy to come to American churches seemed seriously at odds with the overall purpose of the law—which was to prevent the importation of manual laborers at extremely low wages—and with American traditions. Having to decide how much weight to give to the plain implications of the specific statu-tory provisions as against the overall purpose of the law, the Supreme Court chose the latter. (This is a case to which we shall return when we get to statutory interpretation.)

The insight of Pragmatics that speakers often flout or apparently flout maxims of cooperative exchange to make points by implication (as with Grice's writer of a recommendation who says nothing about substantive abilities) has very limited relevance for law.

Writers of legal texts do not deliberately flout maxims in order to engage in sarcasm or irony, and they do not designedly leave conclusions to be drawn by implication that are in sharp contrast to the texts. We do not expect the writers of wills or contracts or statutes blatantly to fail to observe principles of rational communication.

I should note two possible exceptions to this last generalization. A writer of a contract may engage in intentional obscurity so that the other party will not be aware exactly what he is giving up; and drafters of a statute may cloak concessions to special interests in confusing language. In both circumstances the usual strategy is not to convey a message by implicature;[121] it is to bury language that is still sufficiently specific so a court will be able to recognize it and enforce the terms.

Drafters may also adopt unclear phrasing because they cannot resolve a problem. Although a court may say that such language is not dispositive, it will not typically conclude that a legislature was deliberately violating principles of rational communication.[122] Geoffrey Miller suggests that Grice's point about implicature has relevance for courts that interpret statutes to avoid absurd results.[123] Courts do then construe provisions to make sense, and they reach a conclusion that goes beyond, and against, the specific textual language, but they typically assume legislators made mistakes in formulation, not that they deliberately flouted ordinary principles of communication.

Perhaps the most fundamental lesson for interpreting legal texts of Grice's approach and of Pragmatics more generally is that, like other kinds of communications, such texts—whether provisions of wills, contracts, statutes, or constitutions—need to be understood in context and in light of their overall purposes. That is a truth that we shall see developed in various respects when we turn to interpretation within other disciplines and to general theories of interpretation.

IV. VAGUENESS AND INDETERMINACY

Ordinary language and the law are filled with vague words and concepts. Philosophers have considered how the application of these should be regarded.[124] Our inquiry is whether their conclusions have relevance for legal interpretation.[125] I shall suggest that certain competing philosophical theories of vagueness do not directly entail consequences for how legal texts should be interpreted, but some correlations may exist between a person's sense of what is generally involved in the application of vague concepts and of how judges should interpret legal texts.

Concepts like "bald" and "heap" are substantially vague.[126] It is impossible to say just when a man's loss of hair is enough to make him bald, or when the reduction of items on a pile renders it less than a heap. Indeed, there is a paradox about such vague concepts, called the "sorites" paradox,[127] with which philosophers struggle. Removing one hair does not affect whether someone is bald, but if enough hairs are removed one by one, a man who was not bald has become so. Although most simple concepts are not as vague as baldness, all, or nearly all, have some some degree of vagueness, in the sense that there actually are circumstances, or could be circumstances, in which it would be doubtful if the concept would apply. "Five o'clock" and "now" are relatively precise, but for exactly how many seconds or minutes before or after 5:00 is it correct to say "It is now five o'clock"? The answer is not clear, and will depend partly on context. Further, as Timothy Endicott has suggested, much vagueness is pragmatic rather than derived from linguistic terms. In some contexts "Come at 5:00" could mean exactly the same thing as "Come at about 5:00."[128]

Many concepts are vague at least partly because they incorporate diverse elements, or may apply based on "family resemblance" rather than any one set of necessary conditions. Whether a group of people is "a crowd" depends not only on the number of persons but also on how close together they are.[129] There may be examples of "games" or "religions" that share little, if anything, in common, and whether a particular exemplar containing some features of undoubted games or religions actually qualifies as a game or religion can be uncertain.[130] Terms like "democracy" and "freedom" are complex terms involving multiple features, ones whose application is, as Jeremy Waldron has emphasized, uncertain not only because of fuzzy borders but because what are the crucial elements are themselves fundamentally contested.[131] Among substantially vague concepts are many evaluative criteria, such as reasonable, fair, cruel, selfish, and generous; their application typically involves both contestation over which elements matter most and uncertain edges whatever one's view about critical elements.

The law is filled with vague terms, both simple terms and complex evaluative ones. These appear in particular legal texts, and in various standards judges employ to interpret and apply texts. (Jurors are also called upon to apply standards with some of those terms.) When judges draw on multiple standards to decide cases and develop more specific legal rules than they find in the constitutional and statutory provisions they are interpreting, these interpretive standards are commonly vague, and the manner in which they should be combined is also vague. In a great many respects, the vagueness problem in law is like that with more ordinary uses of language.

To oversimplify a great deal, some philosophers believe that there is no correct or incorrect answer to whether a vague concept applies at its borders (that is, about some people, there is no right answer to whether they are bald); some philosophers believe that there is a correct answer though one unknowable epistemically; some philosophers have more complicated intermediate positions.[132] For purposes of analysis I shall concentrate on the implications for law of the first two positions, which present a stark contrast.

Before undertaking that effort, and making clear that I am not aiming to develop a well-defended position about the true philosophical significance of vagueness, I shall mention that, for me, the plausibility of the competing positions depends a lot on what vague concept is involved. For "bald," I find the epistemic view that there is always a correct answer to whether someone qualifies as bald, to be implausible, bordering on ridiculous.[133] Different individuals have different notions of how much hair loss makes someone bald, and judgment may depend on context; but even if we focus on one person in one context, most people do not conceive of the existence of any sharp divide between the bald and the not bald. Even if we refined the categories to include terms such as "partially bald," people would still perceive no clear divide between the partially bald and the bald and the not bald. They simply do not understand the concepts to yield such sharply separate categories. For such concepts, Timothy Endicott's notion that they should be understood in terms of a similarity to paradigms seems persuasive.[134]

On the other hand, for concepts like just distribution, due process, and common good, it seems more arguable to me that people do imagine actual divides, impossible though it may be to perceive their exact boundaries. Suppose I am giving some money to my children and some to charity. I am aiming for a distribution that meets my sense of my responsibilities to my children and to the broader society. One might say, as with hairs and baldness, that a penny more for charity and less for children will not affect the justice of the distribution. But, of course, at some point of shifting pennies, too much will go to charity. Whether I use as a standard of judgment my particular sensibilities or imagine some more objective test of what should be done by a person in my circumstances, I might well conceive that some exact division (though not one I am capable of knowing) is the best, or most just possible, and that two other divisions (one with more to charity, the other with more to children) are exactly on the edge of what is needed to avoid injustice to one group or the other. (That is, I assume that some range of distributions is just enough to be not unjust.) In other words, I find it plausible to think there may be correct answers both to disputed issues of over what is just (as realists about moral concepts claim more generally) and to the exact edges between the most just and less just.

I now turn to the law. The analysis that follows does not depend directly on my own sense of plausible philosophic approaches. The most evident possible relevance of all the perplexity about vagueness is whether the law is indeterminate, but that perplexity may also have implications for how judges should go about interpreting the law.

If there are correct answers to the application of vague concepts, and that holds true for vague concepts in law, it follows that legal standards are not indeterminate in one important sense. If questions about how to apply vague concepts often lack answers in ordinary usage and in law, the law with which judges deal is sometimes indeterminate; and judges must *create* law rather than find it. The latter conclusion raises questions about how we should understand "the rule of law" if such indeterminacy is unavoidable. But how does all this bear on how judges actually interpret legal texts? What exactly is the connection?

Stephen Schiffer, a philosopher with his own complex and subtle theory of vagueness, provides a skeptical answer.[135] He offers four major claims. (1) Whether there are cases in which the law is indeterminate is a non-issue. All concepts are vague to some extent; vague concepts admit the possibility of *borderline* cases where it is *indeterminate* whether the concepts apply; there will be such vagueness and borderlines for laws, for legal principles, and for legal policies.[136] (2) "Logico-semantical theories of vagueness . . . have nothing to offer jurisprudential concerns about vagueness."[137] (3) The philosophical theorist of vagueness has nothing to say to judges who must decide what to do when it is indeterminate what they should do; the judges face a normative question for which vagueness theorists can provide no help.[138] (4) Because people are basically concerned with applying vague concepts, and they test theories that explicate vagueness in relation to those practices, "No correct philosophical account of indeterminacy can be expected to affect our applications of vague concepts . . . ."[139]

I agree with Professor Schiffer that philosophical theories of vagueness have no direct practical implications for how judges decide borderline cases; judges face a normative question of what to do. However, a judge who embraced a particular philosophical theory of vagueness might be influenced in how he conceptualizes determinations of difficult legal issues, and this conceptualization *could* affect the judge's method of decision. In other words, we might find a significant correlation between belief in a philosophical theory about vagueness and judicial method, although the former has no strict implications for the latter.

Professor Schiffer makes clear he is talking about all laws, principles, and policies. Since some of these are themselves complex, he is obviously not limiting himself to simple concepts like "bald" or "vehicle" or "employee." In legal cases, judges typically consider a set of principles and policies together; decision does not depend on elaboration and application of any single concept. Judges interpreting legal standards are influenced by the purpose of the standards, by the consequences of applying them, and by a whole set of background legal values. Let us imagine that we can roughly divide the population into those who are clearly not bald, those who are clearly bald, and those who are in the middle, the arguably bald.[140] A law provides that "bald people" who do not wear hats shall be fined. Applying the notion that criminal statutes should give fair warning, a judge decides that the arguably bald do not count as bald for this purpose. Another law provides public grants for bald people to pay for treatments to grow hair. Recognizing that the arguably bald and their loved ones are concerned about hair loss, and that many of the arguably bald will soon join the ranks of the clearly bald, a judge decides that the arguably bald should receive grants under this statute. This example shows that even when a legal decision requires application of a single concept, the scope of coverage and the area of borderline cases will depend on a set of relevant reasons; both coverage and borderlines may differ from what one would conclude about a concept viewed acontextually.[141]

If the correct resolution is still uncertain after one consults all relevant legal principles and policies, the proper legal result is indeterminate.[142] Schiffer's claims cover such situations.

A picture of the judges themselves applying vague concepts and resolving instances of uncertainty is accurate enough for many circumstances, but it fails to capture others. The legislature may adopt a vague standard that is to be applied in the first instance by an administrative agency. The agency determines applications of the standard. Courts may accept the administrative determinations so long as they are reasonable.[143] Judges do not decide exactly where they would draw the line, how they would deal with borderline cases; rather they accept the judgments of others so long as they are reasonable. Under this approach, the vague statutory concept, e.g., "fair rate," "employee," or "ordinary income," is filled in by a combination of administrative and judicial decision. The borderlines that judges determine are the boundaries of reasonable application.[144] Schiffer's claims cover these circumstances in which indeterminacy concerns the range of reasonable application.

When is a proposition indeterminate? We may speak of metaphysical indeterminacy if the proposition is neither correct nor incorrect. Epistemic indeterminacy may exist if highly reasonable people, as well informed as is practical, have an unresolvable disagreement about whether it is correct, or have no idea whether it is correct.[145] A claim that chocolate ice cream is best is indeterminate in the metaphysical sense; there is no correct answer to which flavor of ice cream is best.[146] A claim that it was raining on any part of the island now labeled Manhattan exactly 12,000 years ago to the moment is indeterminate in the epistemic sense;[147] there is a correct answer as a matter of historical fact, but that answer is not now knowable.[148]

If we think of indeterminacy as covering both the metaphysical and epistemic possibilities, no one doubts that the answers to many legal questions are indeterminate. Highly reasonable, very well-informed people disagree about many outcomes. Thoughtful people understand that either no outcome is really correct, or that they may be mistaken which outcome is correct.

Some theorists employ a more restricted sense of indeterminacy, one limited to situations of metaphysical indeterminacy, in which there really is no correct answer.[149] Either the subject is one that does not admit of correct or incorrect answers—what flavor of ice cream is best—or no answer to a particular question is better than every other answer. When legal scholars such as Ronald Dworkin claim that the answers to all (or almost all) legal questions are determinate, it is this sense they have in mind.[150] Well-informed lawyers may disagree about correct answers, and thoughtful lawyers may not be confident their views are right, but there really are correct answers.

When we ask whether there is a correct answer to how a judge should resolve a legal issue, we need to distinguish indeterminacy in law from indeterminacy about the best resolution, overall. I can draw this distinction clearly by imagining a legal philosopher, Jerry, who has the following views. The law has many gaps in which it fails to provide answers for judges. The most sound moral and political philosophy is a version of Benthamite utilitarianism, promoting the greatest average happiness. Judges left free by the law to decide in either of two ways should create new law by promoting the greatest average happiness in their resolution of the particular dispute and in the legal rule they establish to support the decision.[151] Jerry thinks "the law" is often indeterminate, but how judges should decide is not often indeterminate, since utilitarianism, properly applied, will resolve virtually all moral and political issues, including what law judges should create.

The indeterminacy that matters for legal philosophy is indeterminacy *in* law. The denial of indeterminacy is a claim that within the law (in some sense) a judge can find correct answers to even difficult cases. The claim is not that actual judges will agree on correct answers, or even that they will reach correct answers in most difficult cases; the claim is only that the law (in some sense) provides the resources for finding the answers and that for (almost) any issue, one answer will really be better than any other.

Is this denial of metaphysical indeterminacy plausible? We might think of the thesis as one about: (1) individual legal rules, standing alone; (2) all the legal materials in combination; (3) all the legal materials, plus (or including) morality; (4) all the legal materials, plus (or including) morality and consequentialist evaluation. No one of whom I am aware thinks that individual legal rules themselves always provide correct answers to borderline cases. Typically, as I have already suggested, judges need to refer to other legal rules, principles, and policies to resolve borderline instances about particular rules.

More appealing is the idea of approach (2) that all the legal materials in combination, as understood by the ideal judge, would yield correct answers. On this account, we need to suppose that a judge faced with what looks like a moral question, such as whether flogging is a "cruel" punishment within the meaning of the Eighth Amendment, can answer the question without making an independent moral judgment and without relying on prevailing social morality. A refined evaluation of legal history and presently authorized punishments will yield the answer.

Approach (3) introduces moral judgments that are not dictated by the legal materials.[152] It concedes that the legal materials alone will be indecisive on some significant questions, but supposes that morality figures *in the law* in at least two ways. Some particular legal standards, such as cruel punishment, authorize judges to make moral evaluations. More generally, a judge who interprets law must do so in light of moral premises, so some moral evaluations that are independent of the legal materials, in the sense of not being dictated by them, are inextricable from judgments about the legal materials. For the decision-maker, these evaluations are not separate from judgments about the law. Approach (3) has the advantage of introducing a somewhat broader range of judgments as being relevantly "within the law." It has the possible disadvantage of making the thesis of "one correct answer in law" depend on a further thesis that virtually all moral questions judges are called upon to make have correct answers. Someone who is a skeptic about moral judgments, believing them to be mere expressions of feeling, for example, cannot believe that approach (3) will provide correct answers.

A variation on approach (3) requires judges to resolve moral questions according to social morality. This variation turns moral questions into questions that are largely empirical. This variation would permit correct answers in law even in the absence of correct answers to questions of critical morality; but it is vulnerable to two crippling difficulties. Judges possess no single correct way to *construct* social morality for this purpose,[153] and judges are often called on to make moral judgments that are not fully dependent on legal materials or social morality, or the two together.[154]

Even when legal materials are supplemented with morality, gaps seem to remain. Many statutes are adopted to promote the collective welfare, and crucial borderline decisions do not involve morality in any ordinary, or narrow, sense. Perhaps difficult issues can be resolved in a correct way (within the law) only if a consequentialist evaluation of collective welfare is somehow part of the law and only if there are correct answers to questions of collective welfare. Approach (4) includes as part of the law standards of evaluation of collective welfare.

We see from this brief survey that what constitutes indeterminacy and what it means to have indeterminacy about legal decisions is far from straightforward. We need to understand these complexities to evaluate Schiffer's claim about the irrelevance for legal philosophy of positions taken by philosophers of language concerning vagueness.

For the purpose of testing Schiffer's claim about the irrelevance of philosophical theories of vagueness for jurisprudential concerns, we need to ask whether, under various accounts of how judges do and should answer legal questions, it will matter what one thinks about the status of borderline instances of vague concepts. At issue is both what a theorist will believe about answers to difficult cases and how a judge will behave if persuaded to one theory of vagueness or another. We need to ask three separate questions. Will a theorist's understanding of what judges do be affected by his theory of vagueness? Will a judge receive decisional guidance from the theory of vagueness she accepts? Will a judge be otherwise influenced by the theory of vagueness she accepts? Schiffer's important claims are about how decisions are reached, but, for the sake of clarity, I shall begin with the theorist's perspective.

If there is a connection between vagueness theories and jurisprudential concerns, the causal relations might go both ways. Someone with settled jurisprudential views might be led to accept one philosophical theory of vagueness or another. A person who is trying to develop views about both vagueness and jurisprudential topics might move toward positions about the two that are most compatible. Most students of the law are likely to have some idea about legal indeterminacy before they consider philosophical notions of vagueness, but for this analysis, I shall stick to Schiffer's own perspective, which starts with philosophical perspectives on vagueness. We will imagine that a person accepts a particular theory about vagueness, and then turns to examine its implications for judicial decision and legal theory.

A. A Theorist's Understanding of Decision in Difficult Cases

Our first, brief, inquiry is the relation between a theorist's view about the philosophical status of borderline applications of vague concepts and his view about the possibility of correct answers to difficult legal issues. A theorist who believes that the applications of vague concepts in borderline instances are either correct or incorrect is likely to incline toward believing there is a truth about how the more complicated assessments of borderline legal cases should come out.

The more interesting question concerns the theorist who thinks that over some middle range, it is neither true nor false that someone is bald. A person with this view would almost certainly have the same opinion about legal concepts, were each concept to be viewed in isolation. But the resources of the law are much richer. Perhaps these fuller resources of the law can yield correct answers, even if the individual vague concepts do not. As I have already suggested, a person might think that, at the borderlines, the statement that someone is bald is neither true nor false and also think that every moral question does have a correct answer—perhaps the answer that complies with God's will or serves average welfare. A person might similarly think that all legal questions, normative questions about what should be done, have a correct answer.[155]

B. A Judge's Practice

Schiffer's important claim is not about theoretical assumptions about whether answers to legal questions are true; it concerns the performance of judges and others within the legal system. A philosophical theory of vagueness, he asserts, does not guide practical decision. Further, once judges realize that they cannot know whether an answer to a legal question is true or false, they will behave in the same way whatever their views about whether some (unknowable) answer is really correct. Schiffer's view is well captured in the sentence, "No correct philosophical account of indeterminacy can be expected to affect the application of vague concepts, for those applications come first and the explication is tested against them."[156] Although I agree with Schiffer that a theory about whether vague concepts have correct applications at the borders does not *tell* one how to resolve practical problems, I think Schiffer's conclusion that theoretical belief will not *affect* applications is either wrong or misleading.

For a full assessment, we need to take a nuanced approach that considers which materials and perspectives count as part of the law, and we need to examine how judges resolve difficult questions, as well as how they justify their answers.

I will begin by assuming that a judge thinks that "the law" is composed of legal materials—that *independent* moral evaluation and assessment of collective welfare are not part of the law. The judge confronts an issue she thinks is very difficult; she is not sure how to resolve it. Suppose, first, our judge believes that for borderline applications of vague concepts, no answer is correct or incorrect, and, further, she thinks legal issues have a similar indeterminacy. Across some range, she thinks the law has gaps, and that in resolving cases in the gaps, judges must act like legislators. Such a judge is likely to assume that when she finds an issue to be very difficult, the law has probably "run out", that she may properly turn to nonlegal materials to resolve the case, taking account both of a desirable result and a sound legal rule for future cases.

Now, let us suppose that the judge embraces quite a different view of vagueness. She thinks that vague concepts have correct and incorrect applications even at the borders, *and* she thinks that legal issues similarly have correct and incorrect answers. What will she do with her very difficult legal issue? Schiffer speaks of theorists who suppose that applications of vague concepts are either true or false as conceiving indeterminacy as a kind of "irremediable ignorance,"[157] but it is just in this respect that a judge is crucially different from the person deciding whether someone at the border is bald. She has inexhaustible legal materials, and her judgment and written opinion for the case before her are important enough to warrant hard work. If she keeps studying all the materials, the judge may approach closer to what "the law requires." The person gauging baldness has no further inquiry to make.[158] If he says A is bald and his friend says A is not bald, each has reason to conclude that both are in a state of irremediable ignorance about the true answer (both believing that some answer is true). But a judge usually believes that further thought and research may advance matters. Moreover, the common experience of judges, legal scholars, and students who work with legal materials and are searching for correct answers is that individuals who reach contrary answers each develop some confidence that they have discovered the right answer.[159] Thus, a judge believing legal issues have correct answers within the law is likely to stick with the legal materials to arrive at an answer, not to reach outside, and she is likely to be rewarded with some psychological assurance that she has succeeded. The judge is *not* likely to throw up her hands, declare her irremediable ignorance about what the law requires, and proceed to decide on the same bases as the judge who is persuaded she must reach outside the law because the law has no correct answer. Of course, a judge *might* say to herself, "I think the law contains a correct answer but I am so unsure what it may be and so pessimistic about my prospects for discovering it that I will act like a legislator." But I am suggesting that this attitude is unusual among judges.

Thus, most judges who think vague concepts have correct and incorrect applications at the borders *and* have a similar view about borderline legal issues,[160] will be inclined to resolve cases somewhat differently from judges who believe that at the borders, applications of vague concepts and resolutions of legal questions are neither correct nor incorrect.[161] It is not that any particular view of vague concepts compels a view about how legal issues should be resolved; rather various positions about vague concepts are likely to correlate with styles of judging.

This difference among judges may not be evident from opinions, which tend to rely heavily on legal sources and to overstate the arguments in favor of the result that is reached. The judge who conceives of herself as legislating rarely says so in an opinion.

The difference in practical approach between a judge who conceives of herself as "filling gaps" and the judge who tries to discover right answers in legal materials erodes somewhat if the judge thinks "the law" includes independent judgments of morality and collective welfare. That is because the more that the law is conceived to include, the more a judge's bases for reaching a correct legal decision will resemble those a legislator might employ. Still, the judge as discoverer may eschew some lines of inquiry that the judge as legislator would employ. Subtle differences of approach may still exist depending on whether the judge believes she is trying to discover correct answers.

I have suggested that the starkest difference among philosophical theories of vagueness—that between belief that vague concepts have correct and incorrect applications even at the border and belief that such applications are neither correct nor incorrect—will probably correlate with competing views about whether difficult legal issues have correct answers. More importantly, I have suggested that judges who adhere to competing views about vague concepts (or would adhere to competing views if they thought about it) may behave somewhat differently from each other in difficult cases. The main reason why judges will be affected by their notion of whether the law (in some sense) provides correct answers is that they do not regard themselves as in a state of *irremediable* ignorance.

However, these conclusions must be understood to be very modest about the assistance philosophic theories of vagueness may provide judges, beyond the recognition that substantial vagueness is endemic in many of our concepts. Few lawyers and judges will begin with developed views about vagueness in ordinary discourse, which they then apply to law. Any causal relation is likely to be the reverse. Even more important, decisions concerning what sources to rely on should be determined by legal tradition and normative judgments about sound law, not by any notions about the exact status of applications of vague concepts or about the range of legal indeterminacy.

V. CONCLUSION

In this chapter we have looked at three broad subjects within the philosophy of language that have potential implications for legal interpretation. The last of these subjects, vagueness, is tied fairly closely to the question of whether the law is sometimes indeterminate. For more than a century, reflective judges and scholars have suggested that the law is fairly frequently indeterminate, that about certain legal issues that face judges, all one can say is that a decision either way would be acceptable and that the judges must make law one way or the other in the interstices. The assumption about indeterminacy has become the dominant jurisprudential view.[162] Most of those who accept that view have little or no acquaintance with philosophic writing about vagueness; but one can easily see a close resemblance between the notion that the application of vague concepts is indeterminate at the edges and a similar thesis about legal norms. Neither view, by itself, tells judges *how* to interpret. That is a separate issue; conceivably two judges who engage in identical practices of interpretation will have opposing beliefs about whether a correct answer is lurking somewhere, potentially to be discovered by the perfect judge. Yet, I have suggested that one's views about indeterminacy and vagueness may be tied to the interpretive techniques that one accepts. A judge who believes she is trying to discover a correct answer may rely on sources that are different (or are combined differently) than a judge who conceives herself as legislating in the indeterminate gaps of the law.

The general issue that vagueness and indeterminacy illustrates is how much interpreters discover and how much they create. As we shall see, this is a central issue for literary interpretation, dramatic and musical performance, religious interpretation, and general theories of interpretation, as well as for each discrete area of law.

The middle section of this chapter has much more straightforward implications for legal interpretation. General rules and presumptions about the use of language, including conventions about the implications one can draw in context from inclusions and omissions, apply to legal texts and are drawn upon by judges. It is, however, important to recognize that judges may attribute their conclusions in cases to considerations of this sort even when the real bases of decisions are their opinions about controversial issues of justice or social policy (such as the acceptability of the death penalty). Many cases we shall examine in this study turn on how much the textual language actually settles and how much must be resolved on some other basis.

In the first part of the chapter, we have explored approaches to meaning that emphasize speaker intent or linguistic conventions. For most kinds of legal texts, one interpretive question is how much to rest on what a reader would apprehend and how much to explore other evidence of what the writer(s) intended. This general question arises in other disciplines as well, and its precise contours look different in various domains of law. In some, it is controversial whether an inquiry into intent even makes sense. In the chapters and books to follow, I shall defend inquiries into intent as relevant, even when the "authors" are legislators or those who create constitutions, but I also stress that just when and how interpreters should investigate intent requires careful, complex analysis. Like the issue of creativity, the issue about intent is among the most pervasive problems about legal interpretation.

Notes

1 Anita Avramides, writing on Intention and Convention, in Bob Hale and Crispin Wright, *A Companion to the Philosophy of Language* 60 (Oxford, Blackwell Pub. 1997), writes that "use theories" and "formal theories" are the two basic approaches to understanding language. According to this division, speaker intent, and convention theories both fall on the "use" side and, by some accounts at least, may be fully reconciled. I do not devote attention to formal theories, which are "primarily concerned with the formal structure of language and the interrelations between sentences," id. at 61, because they do not seem to bear significantly on difficult questions about how legal texts should be interpreted.

2 Possibly someone who receives a communication will understand it in a way that is detached from what he takes to be the utterer's aims. Someone walking on a beach might find spelled out in shells: "Blue." Conceivably the "message" might affect the reader in a manner wholly independent from an idea of the specific purpose of the shells' arranger (or independent even of whether the reader assumes that a person or shifting ocean currents so arranged the shells).

3 See Paul Grice, "Meaning," 66 *Philosophical Review* 377 (1957); "Utterer's Meaning, Sentence-Meaning, and Word-Meaning," 3 *Foundations of Language, International Journal of Language and Philosophy* 225 (1968) "Utterer's Meaning and Intentions," 78 *Philosophical Review* 147 (1969); *Studies in the Way of Words* 290–97 (Cambridge, Mass., Harvard University Press 1989).

4 Stephen R. Schiffer, *Meaning* (Oxford, Oxford University Press 1972) in Introduction to paperback edition xi (1988). The approach to "expression-meaning is that each sentence of each language has some feature that (i) makes an utterance of the sentence prima-facie evidence that the speaker uttered the sentence with certain speaker-meaning intentions, (ii) is intrinsically specifiable in nonsemantic propositional-attitude terms, and (iii) is constitutive of the sentence's meaning." Schiffer's doubts that intention-based semantics can be successful are developed in his later *Remnants of Meaning* (Cambridge, Mass., MIT Press 1989).

5 One might think that in cases of natural meaning that if "x means p," x is always connected to p; but that would be a mistake. We can say that "dark clouds mean rain," even if dark clouds yield rain only 85 percent of the time. Grice also includes as a sense of natural meaning ideas such as "He means to go to the movie by driving his car." "Meaning" at 378. In his later work, Grice reflected on how one might move from natural meaning to nonnatural meaning. *Studies in the Way of Words* 290–97 (1989). To oversimplify, an involuntary grimace experienced because one is in pain could give rise to a statement about natural meaning: "His grimace means he is in pain." Over time, two people might come to understand that one who grimaces voluntarily conveys the nonnatural meaning that he is in a kind of pain that does not produce an involuntary grimace. From this, the persons might

move to a nonnatural use of language, such as "I'm in pain." Grice explains that the succession of stages is not "intended to be a historical or genetic account" but a myth "to exhibit the conceptual link between natural and nonnatural meaning . . . ." Id. at 296–97.

6 Grice here answers a proposal of C.L. Stevenson, developed in *Ethics and Language*, ch. iii (New Haven, Yale University Press 1944).

7 See Grice, "Meaning," at 379–80. The example Grice discusses is "Jones is an athlete." Athletes come in so many sizes, I doubt that this statement alone indicates much about Jones's height.

8 Another problem with the causal approach is that it furnishes only analysis of standard meaning, not what a particular writer or speaker means on a particular occasion. Id. at 381.

9 Id. Grice follows "meant" with the signal nn to indicate nonnatural meaning. Since I am concentrating on nonnatural meaning, I have omitted this signal here and elsewhere.

10 As Grice points out, had *A* drawn a picture of the friend's wife with her lover, and shown it to the friend, that would involve nonnatural meaning. Id. at 382–83.

11 "[W]e may say that '*A* meant something by x' is roughly equivalent to '*A* uttered x with the intention of inducing a belief by means of this intention.'" Id. at 384.

12 In his 1969 article, "Utterer's Meaning and Intentions," see note 3, supra, Grice faces yet more complex counter-examples and develops yet more complicated responses. In one of these, a subordinate smiles in a slightly phony way whenever he has a good bridge hand, so that his boss on the opposing team will respond accordingly and win. The subordinate wants the boss to know that he wants the boss to win, but he also wants the boss to assume that he is trying to make the smile appear spontaneous, not as an intended give-away. The smile fits Grice's earlier definition, but it does not communicate the nonnatural meaning that the subordinate has a good hand. (If the smile was intended to appear phony, I take Grice to believe that it would communicate nonnatural meaning.) To meet this and other illustrations, Grice adds further clauses narrowing the connection between the intentions of the utterer and what the utterer aims to have his audience perceive about his intentions. See id. at 156–77.

13 Id. at 166. A confession to a listener who, the speaker is aware, already knows what the speaker confesses is similar. Id. at 167.

14 Id.

15 Id. at 167–68.

16 Schiffer, *Meaning*, note 4 supra, at 42–43. I think the argument illustration is a little more complicated. If the speaker is an expert, he may be relying *partly* on the listener's recognition that he believes communism's fall shows markets are superior. Schiffer's discussion of reminding, answering exam questions, and confessions is at id. at 44–45, 72.

17 Grice, "Utterer's Meaning and Intentions," at 171. See also Grice, "Utterer's Meaning, Sentence-Meaning and Word-Meaning," supra note 3, at 230: the meaning-intended effect "common to indicative-type utterances [is] not that the hearer should believe something (though there will frequently be an ulterior intention to that effect), but that the hearer should think that the utterer believes something." To cover the situation in which I expect and hope that my listener will believe I am lying if I say "Pete is honest," one needs to qualify Grice's language to the

effect that the utterer intends to convey to the listener the impression that he, the utterer, is trying to indicate that he believes something (e.g., that Pete is honest), although the utterer's design is that the listener conclude that the utterer does not believe that.

18 Legal texts may be in descriptive form. "One commits murder in the first degree who intentionally and with premeditation kills another." "The sentence for murder in the first degree is twenty years to life in prison." But the significance of these sentences is to direct ordinary citizens, jurors, judges, and other officials how to act.

19 "Utterer's Meaning, Sentence-Meaning, and Word-Meaning," at 230.

20 Grice, "Meaning," at 383.

21 An illustration that fits such definitions but does not involve nonnatural meaning is the following. I throw a ten-dollar bill out the window, reasoning that my visitor will assume I want her to leave, believing that she will go after the bill, but she will actually leave because I want her to go, and she does not wish to stay where she is not wanted. I throw the bill intending my visitor to leave and intending that she do so because she recognizes my intention that she do so, yet my throwing of the bill does not have the nonnatural meaning that she should leave. "Utterer's Meaning and Intentions," at 155.

22 Id. at 155–56.

23 Id. at 173.

24 Stephen Schiffer, in *Meaning* at 69–70, has the Berkeley police announce that radicals may not hold a rally on campus, hoping and expecting that this will encourage the radicals to do just that. Schiffer is inclined to say that someone has not issued an order unless he intends it to be carried out, id. at 72, but his doubt is misplaced. A person may be punished for disobeying an order even if the superior issuing the order hopes and expects it will be disobeyed.

25 "Utterer's Meaning and Intentions," at 170–73.

26 Something similar occurs when the mainly responsible parent, the mother, is out of the house and says to her husband, "Tell Judy to go to bed at 9:00." The stepfather tells Judy to do just that, but both he and Judy realize that he is indifferent to whether she goes to bed then and he fully expects her to stay up later. He might act in this way because he has promised his wife he will or to get himself off the hook if she comes home and finds Judy up.

27 The sergeant example (like the stepfather example of note 26) depends partly on the presence of a third person concerned with whether the imperative has been issued and obeyed. Were the only two relevant people those who utter and receive the imperative, one might doubt that the "meaning" covers action that neither wants or expects to take place when both are fully aware of the actual intentions of the other.

28 In the law, it becomes a serious question what to do when someone does undertake to enforce such provisions.

29 "Meaning," at 387.

30 "Utterer's Meaning, Sentence-Meaning, and Word-Meaning," note 3 supra, at 225–42.

31 Id. at 227.

32 Id. at 233.

33 Id. at 231.

34 As Grice recognizes, this way of putting things does not quite cover the situation of someone who has a precise idea of what certain words would signify if

she uttered them or heard someone else utter them, but who would, in fact, never utter these words (as a prim person might never say "whore"). Id. at 234.

35 Id. at 233–34.

36 *Studies in the Way of Words*, at 298.

37 "Utterer's Meaning and Intentions," at 163–64.

38 *Studies in the Way of Words*, at 340. Asking why claims about meaning to recipients should be inferior to utterers' meaning, Grice acknowledges that the centrality of language for thought draws one in the direction of seeing language as "constitutive of thought rather than something the intelligibility of which derives from its relation to thought." Id. at 355. Nevertheless, he has yet to see a satisfactory alternative to his reductive analysis of meaning to psychology. Id. at 358.

39 David Lewis, *Convention* (Cambridge, Mass., Harvard University Press 1969).

40 David Lewis, "Languages and Language," from *Philosophical Papers*, Vol.1, 163–88 (Oxford, Oxford University Press 1983). (First published in English in Keith Gunderson, ed., *Language, Mind, and Knowledge, Minnesota Studies in the Philosophy of Science*, Vol. VII. 3 (Minneapolis, University of Minnesota Press 1975).)

41 *Convention* at 8.

42 Id.

43 Id. at 14.

44 Id. at 25.

45 Lewis points out that a practice established by agreement could evolve into one that is sustained by mutual expectations without agreement. Id. at 83–84. If people at one time agree that green will mean "go" and red will mean "stop," the practice may continue into a generation that has never discussed, or even thought about, options, but which continues to follow that practice.

46 Id. at 43.

47 Id. at 36. Precedent provides a unique equilibrium reached the last time.

48 In id. at 49, Lewis emphasizes use. In answer to his own question about whether people do not wish to use a language their neighbors will understand, he says that, given human nature, the neighbors will best understand the language they use. Lewis does not discuss the reality that the distinction between understanding and use can be sharp in bilingual households in which a parent and child may speak different languages to each other over a period of years, both aware that both understand both languages. In "Languages and Language," note 40 supra at 170, Lewis accepts a point made by Jonathan Bennett that *one person using* an idiolect and *several hearers who understand* it could comprise a population using the idiolect.

49 *Convention* at 51.

50 It is not a convention that people eat or sleep, though it may be partly a convention what time of day they do so.

51 Id. at 78. Convention differs from social contract, according to Lewis, in that the agent does not benefit from his own nonconformity if all others are conforming. Id. at 90. One who breaks a social contract can benefit.

52 "Languages and Language," at 165. The knowledge may be merely potential for many people, i.e., they would recognize the facts if they thought hard enough about it.

53 I have a minor quibble about this condition. In an area where virtually everyone speaks English, many people might think life would be most interesting if a few people spoke a different language, even *if*, or partly because, that made

communicating with these people more of a challenge. This should not affect a conclusion that use of English is conventional.

54 "Languages and Language," at 169. Of course, speakers sometimes lie, but communication would break down if most people lied most of the time.

55 In id. at 183, Lewis takes account of "irony, metaphor, hyperbole, and such" by treating such statements as truthful but not *literally truthful*.

56 Id. at 100. Other kinds of rules are "laws of nature," "mathematical truths," hypothetical imperatives (as for using insecticides), threats or warnings issued by those in authority, obligations of tacit consent and fair play, and rules "enforced with sanctions so that one would have a decisive reason to obey even if others did not." Id. at 103.

57 Id. at 106. Lewis disagrees with William Alston's suggestion that language is a matter of rules rather than convention.

58 In that paper, see "Meaning," note 3 supra, Grice found nonnatural meaning because a person intends to produce an effect in the audience by means of recognition of the intent to produce the effect.

59 *Convention* at 154. Herod's presenting John the Baptist's head to Salome does not involve a conventional signal; saying "He's dead" does.

60 Thus, when Lewis writes, "I am in no disagreement with Grice; for [nonnatural] meaning is a consequence of conventional signaling," id., we should not understand him to be covering every situation.

61 See note 10, supra. And when explorers communicated with "natives," it was not because they began with shared conventions of language and signaling.

62 Id. at 158. Responding to a comment of John Searle's that we must capture intentional and conventional aspects of communication, Lewis remarks that "once we capture the conventional aspects, we are done. We have captured the intentional aspects as well." Id. at 159. Since his own scarecrow example is at odds with the idea that communication can never take place without convention, he presumably means only that *when* convention is involved, to understand how the convention works is to understand the speaker's intentions.

63 See "Languages and Language," at 164.

64 See, e.g., Anita Avramides, *Meaning and Mind: An Examination of a Gricean Account of Language* 29, 67-75 (Cambridge, Mass, MIT Press 1989); Schiffer, note 4 supra, at 15-16, 128-38.

65 *Convention* at 106.

66 Id. at 165.

67 By an "aim to confuse" I have in mind something more subtle than a lie. With an outright lie, the speaker means what he says, not what he actually believes. One might aim to confuse by giving an instruction that a crucial recipient (say a judge) will discern correctly but will not be recognized for what it is by most readers.

68 From a collection by A.P. Martinich: *Philosophy of Language* 465-75 (3rd ed., New York, Oxford University Press, 1996), taken from *Philosophical Grounds of Rationality: Intentions, Categories, Ends*, ed. by Richard Grady and Richard Warner (Oxford, Oxford University Press 1986).

69 Id. at 466.

70 Id.

71 Id.

72 Id. at 467. On the last point, the idea is that the competence of the speaker or interpreter "is learned in advance of occasions of interpretation and is conventional in character." Id.

73 Id. at 469. In discussing Humpty Dumpty's "theory" that words mean what he chooses, Davidson writes, "A speaker cannot, therefore, intend to mean something by what he says unless he believes his audience will interpret his words as he intends . . . ." Davidson's use of "believes" here is too strong for some circumstances. When we try to communicate with someone with whom we have no shared language, we may say things *hoping* we will be understood, and doing the best we can to be understood, but believing we will probably not be understood. Our meaning then is in accord with how we hope to be understood.

74 Id. at 472. As Andrei Marmor points out in his discussion of Davidson's theory, *Interpretation and Legal Theory* 20 (Oxford, Clarendon Pr. 1992), speaking of a listener's "prior theory" is misleading; that might better be characterized as a combination of his "ability to use the language," id., and his sense of the speaker.

75 Davidson, note 68 supra, at 473.

76 The speaker's prior theory is what he believes the interpreter's prior theory to be, his passing theory is the theory he intends the interpreter to use.

77 Id. at 472.

78 Id. at 474.

79 Id. at 475. Suggesting that understanding communications in language is not fundamentally different from other things we understand, Davidson writes, "[W]e have erased the boundary between knowing a language and knowing our way around in the world generally."

80 Id.

81 Davidson's own theory relies on a principle of charity, according to which one interprets unclear statements generally to be true and coherent. In one formulation, Davidson writes of a method that, in part, "maximizes agreement in the sense of making Kurt (and others) right, as far as we can tell, as often as possible." *Inquiries into Truth and Interpretation* 136 (Oxford, Clarendon Press 1989). See also id. at 101, 153, 169, 196–97, 200.

82 Locke v. United States, 471 U.S. 84 (1985).

83 Collette v. St. Luke's Roosevelt Hospital (132 F. Supp.2d 256 S.D.N.Y. 2001).

84 E.g., Michael Moore, "A Natural Law Theory of Interpretation," 58 *Southern California Law Review* 277 (1985); David O. Brink, "Legal Theory, Legal Interpretation, and Judicial Review," 17 *Philosophy and Public Affairs* 105 (1988).

85 Brian Bix, "Can Theories of Meaning and Reference Solve the Problem of Legal Determinacy?," 16 *Ratio Juris* 281 (2003).

86 Glanville Williams, "Language and the Law, IV," 61 *The Law Quarterly Review* 384, 393 (1945), discusses a will in which a man who had lived with an unmarried woman for many years and had four children with her left her property "during her widowhood." Williams rightly criticizes the court for holding that the gift failed because she was not a widow.

87 Lawrence M. Solan, *The Language of Judges* 13 (Chicago, University of Chicago Pr. 1993).

88 Id. at 19. By contrast, if the remark is, "Fred thought he had convinced the jury," the sentence does not tell us whether the "he" refers to Fred or someone else.

89 Solan, note 87 supra, at 34.

90 Solan discusses the case at id., 34–36, and analyzes the "across the board rule" the court employed in preference to the "last antecedent" rule. Id. at 28–38.

91 This is a major, perhaps the major, theme of Solan, note 87 supra.

92 Id. at 56. Solan's discussion of the case is at 55–61.

93 That is, jurors could not rely on some prejudice that was not "mere."

94 Id. at 60–61. However, it might be argued that underlying views about the death penalty could justifiably underlie whether one indulged assumptions in favor of defendants or trial judges.

95 Id. at 6. Solan inclines to the view that judges are self-conscious about their unwarranted degree of reliance on linguistic principles. A degree of internal persuasion must sometimes be at work as well.

96 Id. at 1.

97 Stephen C. Levinson, *Pragmatics* 21 (Cambridge, Cambridge University Press 1983). As some indication of how complicated is the question of what Pragmatics covers, Levinson devotes pp. 5–35 to analyzing various definitions of the field.

98 Andrei Marmor, "The Pragmatics of Legal Language," 21 *Ratio Juris* 423, 443 (2008).

99 Id. at 442.

100 Id. at 445.

101 Not all conversations observe the Cooperative Principle. Participants are sometimes seeking to deceive and obscure.

102 *Studies in the Way of Words*, at 26.

103 Id.

104 Id. at 27. Geoffrey Miller, "Pragmatics and the Maxims of Interpretation," 1990 *Wisconsin Law Review* 1179, 1203, adds that one should not say anything he knows to be meaningless or self-contradictory.

105 *Studies in the Way of Words*, at 27.

106 Id. at 26. The manner in which the maxims are observed varies with culture, subject, and the nature of communications. Participants are looser in what they say during aimless chitchat than when they concentrate on a practical task. Cultures vary in respect to quality and relevance. In some, friendly conversation may be a succession of amusing stories bearing only a remote relation to each other, rather than a genuine dialogue on a specific topic, such as the fate of the stock market or a local sports team. Georgia M. Green, *Pragmatics and Natural Language Understanding*, at 92, note 6 (Mahwah, N.J., Lawrence Erlbaum Assocs., 1996), remarks that in some cultures narrative style may be more highly valued than accuracy, and M.B.W. Sinclair, in "Law and Language: The Role of Pragmatics in Statutory Interpretation," 46 *University of Pittsburgh Law Review* 373, 383 (1985), points out the social conventions governing different kinds of discourse are diverse. In "The Role of Linguistics in Legal Analysis," 47 *The Modern Law Review* 523, 530 (1984), Peter Goodrich, among others, has emphasized the "social and ideological determination of meaning," the extent to which institutional and ideological processes affect usage.

Conversation differs from writing; more needs to be said initially if the reader has no chance to respond with questions seeking clarification.

107 This insight, not novel with Grice, is central to the field of "Pragmatics" as a branch in linguistics for understanding the use of natural language. See Green, note 106 supra.

108 Id. at 106.

109 Id. at 110.

110 Id. at 101.

111 *Studies in the Way of Words*, at 33. Andrei Marmor, note 74 supra at 27, writes of "contextual assumptions" concerning "a particular state of affairs, knowledge of

which must be shared by the speaker and the hearer." When one is thinking of letters of recommendation, one might well discern conventions about what failures to address evidently relevant matters convey.

112 See Miller, note 104 supra, at 2111, 1224.

113 Andrei Marmor, note 98 supra, 434–38. Sinclair, note 106 supra, at 385–401, develops in considerable detail ways in which statutes differ from ordinary speech. Most of these differences would also characterize privately created legal documents such as wills and contracts.

114 See Marmor, note 98 supra, at 439.

115 This example is discussed in Levinson, note 97 supra at 97–98; Miller, note 104 supra, at 1191.

116 Marmor, note 98 supra, at 426. See Sinclair, note 106 supra, at 393–97.

117 See Grice, *Studies in the Way of Words*, at 32; Marmor, note 98 supra, at 431.

118 Miller, note 104 supra, at 1212.

119 Holy Trinity Church v. United States, 143 U.S. 457 (1892).

120 See Marmor, note 98 supra, at 437–38.

121 However, a drafter of a contract or statute might omit language intentionally, relying on a court's judgment of what that omission implies about the aims of language that is used. Such a strategy would be an instance of implicature of the kind Grice discusses.

122 However, one *might* regard an implicit conferral of discretion on courts or administrative agencies by language that is inconclusive as a failure of rational communication.

123 Miller, note 104 supra, at 1210–11.

124 See, e.g., Timothy Williamson, *Vagueness* (London, Routledge 1994); Dorothy Edgington, "The Philosophical Theory of Vagueness," 7 *Legal Theory* 371 (2001).

125 See, e.g., Timothy A.O. Endicott, *Vagueness in Law* (Oxford, Oxford University Pr. 2000); Jeremy Waldron, "Vagueness in Law and Legal Language: Some Philosophical Issues," 82 *California Law Review* 509 (1994); George C. Christie, "Vagueness and Legal Language," 48 *Minnesota Law Review* 885 (1964).

126 Vagueness is sometimes taken to include ambiguity (when a word means one of two specific things), and is sometimes distinguished from it.

127 Endicott, note 125 supra, at 1, 36–37.

128 Id. at 50.

129 Id. at 45–46.

130 See Waldron, note 125 supra, at 517–18, drawing on Ludwig Wittgenstein's famous analysis of games. In "Religion as a Concept in Constitutional Law," 72 *California Law Review* 753 (1984), and *Religion and the Constitution, Volume 1, Free Exercise and Fairness* 124–56 (Princeton, Princeton University Press 2006), I analyze such an approach to "religion" under the religion clauses of the First Amendment.

131 See Waldron, note 125 supra, at 536–34; W. B. Gallie, "Essentially Contested Concepts," 56 *Proceedings of the Aristotellian Society* 167 (n.s. 1955–56). As George C. Christie points out, note 125 supra, at 895–97, sometimes a combination of vague terms can achieve more precision than any of the terms standing alone.

132 Both Williamson, note 124 supra, and Endicott, note 125 supra, provide accounts of a range of theories about vagueness, directed at the puzzle of how vagueness does or does not fit the assumption of standard logic that statements are true or false. For the summary of one complex intermediate position, see Stephen Schiffer, "A Little Help from Your Friends?" 7 *Legal Theory* 421 (2001).

133 The reader should be aware that in a book providing a careful defense of the epistemic view, Timothy Williamson, note 124 supra at xi, remarks that he originally joined most philosophers in believing it to be "obviously false." This might give one some basis to distrust one's initial reaction.

134 Endicott, note 125 supra, at 155–57.

135 Schiffer, note 132 supra.

136 Id. at 421. As Christie notes, supra note 125, at 889–90, legislature and courts may choose vague language to postpone decisions about issues. Sometimes legislatures use vague or ambiguous language to make adoption of a statute possible in the face of sharply conflicting views about how an issue should be resolved. See Joseph A. Grundfest and A. C. Pritchard, "Statutes with Multiple Personality Disorders: The Value of Ambiguity in Statutory Design and Interpretation," 54 *Stanford Law Review* 627, 628 (2002).

137 Schiffer, note 132 supra, at 411.

138 Id. at 424.

139 Id. at 423. In other words, people do not base their practices on explanatory theories; the relation between these is the reverse.

140 I pass over the problem of the borderlines of *these* categories, since that problem does not matter for my point.

141 It is, of course, also true that in ordinary discourse coverage and borderlines may depend on the purposes for which someone offers a classification.

142 In the *Holy Trinity Church* case, note 119 supra, uncertainty was created not by semantic vagueness but by a severe tension between ordinary semantic meaning and the statute's underlying purpose.

143 See Chevron, U.S.A. v. Natural Resources Defense Council, Inc., 467 U.S. 837 (1984).

144 As far as citizens are concerned, the crucial worry about borderlines often concerns patterns of enforcement rather than authoritative constructions of a legal standard. A speed limit is set at 55 miles per hour. Drivers on major highways know police will not stop them if they are going under 65 miles per hour, but will stop them if they are timed at over 75 miles per hour. For drivers, the practical range of uncertainty about tickets for speeding is between 65 and 75.

145 Under this approach, the result is indeterminate if highly reasonable people have some combination of these attitudes.

146 A strict utilitarian might think otherwise, believing one flavor is capable of conferring more pleasure than any other.

147 Experts on that stage of the world's history might be able to provide a rough estimate in terms of probabilities.

148 A more restrictive account of epistemic indeterminacy is that a proposition is not indeterminate if an ideal observer could judge its correctness, even if we do not know whether it is correct and are incapable of judging its correctness. Under this approach, the rain question has a determinate answer, since an ideal observer would not be restricted by time.

149 A sense intermediate between the two I note here is that an ideally situated observer would not be able to determine the correct answer, if there is one. It is perhaps something like this that Schiffer has in mind since he assumes that theorists of vagueness who take an epistemic approach both believe in indeterminacy and in correct answers.

150 See, e.g., Ronald Dworkin, "The Model of Rules II", in *Taking Rights Seriously* (Cambridge, Mass., Harvard University Press 1977). Dworkin does not discuss the

possibility of correct answers that even an ideal judge (Hercules) would be unable to discern. Possibly he would acknowledge that an answer is indeterminate if it exists but cannot be discovered by an ideal judge.

151 On some occasions, what will otherwise be the best resolution may be undesirable because the supporting legal rule would be undesirable; on some occasions, the otherwise best legal rule might be undesirable because the resolution of the particular case that it dictates would be undesirable.

152 Approach (3) is a somewhat simplified version of what I take to be Ronald Dworkin's view. See Ronald Dworkin, *Law's Empire* (Cambridge, Mass., Harvard University Press 1986).

153 I mean there is no correct way that does not itself rely on some normative judgment that goes beyond social morality.

154 Responding to Melvin Eisenberg's suggestion that common law decisions rest ultimately on community opinions, *The Nature of the Common Law* (Cambridge, Mass., Harvard University Press 1988), I discuss these matters at greater length in *Law and Objectivity* 216–18 (New York, Oxford University Press 1992).

155 However, we have no guarantee that the addition of materials that a decision-maker considers will eliminate or even reduce the range in which no answer is correct. Additional materials could make judgment more difficult and actually increase the number of issues that will lack true answers.

156 Id. at 423.

157 Id. at 422.

158 Perhaps some further inquiry could be made, such as a precise evaluation of how every member of the society classes bald people; but it would be ridiculous to make the effort.

159 I omit practicing lawyers here, because they typically predict to clients what judges and other officials will do, and argue to judges and other officials for outcomes favorable to their clients.

160 As I have previously indicated, I think most judges and legal scholars are more likely to have a view about legal indeterminacy than about vagueness writ large. Their views about law might imply a position about vagueness they have not focused upon. The correlation with modes of resolution does not depend on a developed view about vagueness.

161 I am omitting an important complicating factor: the confidence of belief that a judge might have that she is in the range where an answer is neither correct nor incorrect or is epistemically indeterminate. Suppose a judge thinks that, for a small range, answers are neither correct nor incorrect. But she is never confident any particular question she must resolve is in that range. She may decide it is best to assume that any question she addresses has a correct answer, because she thinks that is much more likely about any particular question than the alternative that no answer is uniquely correct.

162 See, e.g., Benjamin Cardozo, *The Nature of the Judicial Process* (New Haven, Yale University Press 1921); H.L.A. Hart, *The Concept of Law* (second ed.) (Oxford, Clarendon Press 1994). The major modern advocate of the competing view is Ronald Dworkin, note 150 supra.

Chapter 3

Literary Interpretation, Performance Art, and Related Subjects

I. INTRODUCTION

The last chapter explored a disagreement between philosophers of language who emphasize the intentions of speakers and writers and those who focus on conventions of language shared by speakers and listeners. These themes extend to literary theories and theories about performances of music and plays, the main subjects of this chapter, but many theorists we will consider attribute a more active and creative role to readers (and performers) than the philosophers whose views Chapter 2 analyzes. This chapter also explores the perspectives of readers and interpreters in the course of two modest digressions that fit within the broad rubric of literature and law.[1] One examines the influence of literature on judges and other legal actors, the other explores a use of postmodern theory to interpret a famous work in social psychology that may have implications for the development of legal norms.

Why I begin with literary theory rather than general theories of interpretation, or the interpretation of sacred texts, requires a brief explanation. Since law is a subcategory of human endeavors involving interpretation, general theories might seem to have more obvious relevance than theories drawn from any other discrete discipline. But whether general theories will have much practical relevance for any particular exercises in interpretation is a major concern. Perhaps, as one author puts it, "it may be set down as a general rule of interpretation that there are no interpretive rules which are at once general and practical."[2] Moreover, understanding broad interpretive theories is easier if one begins with a sense of approaches and issues within particular disciplines. Thus, I have reserved the most general theories for Chapter 5.

Until the nineteenth century, hermeneutics was mainly thought to concern the interpretation of sacred writings; and many sacred texts include norms that societies have taken as laws. Thus, both in terms of historical lineage and likely relevance for modern law, one might well begin with theories focusing on the interpretation of religious texts, and then proceed to literary theories. However, within modern western academic communities, interest in literary theory exceeds attention to religious interpretation, and more has been written about relations between our (secular) law and literature than about relations between that law and religious texts. Therefore, we start with literary theory.

This book is primarily about how legal interpretation should proceed. Thus, our main interest in literary theory concerns how it bears on the interpretation of literature and (directly or indirectly) on the interpretation of legal texts. A recent introduction considers literary criticism as the practical application of literary theory: "Literary theory can be understood . . . in terms of principles and concepts, strategies and tactics needed to guide critical practice."[3] But we must be careful. Just as it would be a serious mistake to suppose that *all* legal theory (or all valuable legal theory) bears directly on interpretation, one should not assume that all literary theory is about how literary criticism should be practiced. Jonathan Culler has written that the persistence of the notion that interpretation is the goal of literary study leads to misconceptions about the point and value of "theoretical accounts of what is held to be most important in language, culture, and society . . ."[4] As we examine various theories, we need to be sensitive both to how (and to the extent to which) they recommend the ways that literary texts should be interpreted and to whether they yield broader insights about language, communication, and culture.

A. What Is "Literature"?

One question that literary theorists address is what constitutes "literature." Among some potential candidates are these: Literature is writing in the genres of poetry and fiction; literature involves the uses of special devices of language; literature is truly excellent writing; literature is what the community at a given time regards as literature; literature for any reader is what the reader regards as such; nothing distinguishes literature from (some or all) other pieces of writing except the contingent arbitrary classification of an individual "expert" or group of experts. Given that some essays and pieces of historical writing are usually included within the literary "canon" and that special devices of language are not found in all these writings and are found both in some writings that are not considered literary and in ordinary speech, it is hard, if not impossible, to come up with any objective division between literary and other writing.[5] One might give up the quest altogether or conclude that all that links writings that count as literature is what Ludwig Wittgenstein called "family resemblance." He pointed out that although we may have a relatively clear sense of what count as "games," we can identify no common feature characteristic of all games—different features may qualify something as a game.[6] That may be a helpful way to regard "literature."

I have no aim to solve this puzzle, but it leads to two pertinent observations. The first is that some legal texts may count as literature. An eloquent opinion by judges about an important legal and human issue could qualify. And whether or not one regards an opinion as literature, one can analyze its literary qualities. The same is true for legal briefs by lawyers that are designed to persuade. In short, at least some texts familiar within the law might be looked upon as literary exercises. It would be extremely unusual for an ordinary will, contract, or statute, to be regarded as a piece of literature, but the Declaration of Independence, which formalized the legal break with Great Britain, and some parts of our Federal Constitution, might be so conceived. And a broader range of documents drafted by lawyers could be examined in terms of literary qualities.

The second observation concerns the relevance of conclusions about how literature should be understood and interpreted. If a theory begins with the premise that literature is special in some way—distinctive among written uses of language—and forms of literary interpretation are proposed that are responsive to that special character, it would be highly surprising if the same forms were apt for all other uses of language, including the language of most legal texts. When we look at such theories, we might learn more about law by perceiving how it contrasts with literature. On the other hand, interpretive approaches built on theories that "literature" is not really different, or is not really different in crucial respects, from most other uses of language could promise more direct relevance for the interpreting of legal texts.

As Jane Baron has noted, writing about "law and literature" implies boundaries for each domain.[7] Although one might believe, along with James Boyd White, that engaging in law is essentially a literary exercise,[8] Baron believes that the more pervasive tendency is to categorize law as excluding features such as narrative, leaving it as an independent, bounded domain limited to the application of rules.[9] We should not suppose that the simple concept of "law and literature" itself implies exclusive categories; one might use that terminology for a general category and a subcategory or feature ("morality and generosity," "football and speed") or for somewhat overlapping categories ("wisdom and intelligence"). Nevertheless, we should be careful not to let the basic notion of "law and literature" lead us into assuming mutual exclusivity and a narrow scope for law itself.

It is possible that the interpretation of both literature and law share something that distinguishes them from other forms of interpretation of language. Thus, Ronald Dworkin has suggested that literary and legal interpretation are constructive or creative, different from conversational interpretation that characterizes ordinary attempts to understand what speakers are saying to us.[10]

Literary theory is not sharply marked off from other theoretical disciplines. Many literary theorists have drawn heavily from philosophers of language and from proponents of broad theories of interpretation, and a number of modern approaches to literary theory are built substantially on theories of social order and social change, including theories of domination.[11] In turn, literary theories are often extended into domains beyond literature. Gregory Castle places literary theory in the "avant garde" towards interdisplinarity, and claims that "[m]any literary theories can, with surprisingly little modification, be applied to a wide range of cultural forms, events, structures, and spaces."[12]

II. Influential Philosophies about Language

Among the most influential sources of literary theory in the twentieth century was the work of Ferdinand de Saussure, a philosopher of linguistics.[13] Saussure focused on the arbitrariness of linguistic signs. The vast majority of words in a language bear no relation to what they represent other than the conventional understanding that they have that meaning. Thus, the letters "t a b l e" could mean nearly anything; they happen to mean what we know as "table."[14] And, as Wittgenstein also emphasized, our categories of understanding depend significantly on how our language classifies, on what similarities and differences it picks out as relevant.[15] Thus, Terry Eagleton has said (with some exaggeration) "all experience involves language and language is ineradicably social."[16] According to Jonathan Culler, "The drive to demystify the natural . . ., to uncover the true conventionality of the allegedly natural, has been essential to the fortunes of literary and cultural studies in the past few decades."[17]

Another philosopher of language who has greatly influenced literary theory is J. L. Austin. In his *How to Do Things with Words*,[18] he began by positing certain uses of words as performatives. When couples take vows at marriage, when two people bet with each other, when a jury renders a verdict, the words are not employed mainly to describe, if they describe at all; according to linguistic and social conventions, they actually alter the status of those they directly affect.[19] Austin called this an "illocutionary" effect. As his thought developed, he realized that all utterances have both constative and illocutionary aspects.[20] Thus if I say, "The temperature is 93°F now," I am engaging in description but I am also performing the act of asserting my belief in what I describe—as would be very clear if I said, "I affirm my belief that the temperature is 93°." (According to Austin, an utterance also has a perlocutionary aspect, the effects a speaker hopes to achieve by it.)[21] Although Austin is not entirely clear about this, his generalizations about illocutionary effects do not actually detract from his original notion that some utterances change the social world in a special way.[22]

Austin's insights have affected literary theory in at least four different ways. He, along with Wittgenstein, has contributed to a modern understanding that meaning is a function of how language is used; it does not lie in words themselves or even in combinations of words. Said by one person to another, "It's 93° outside," could be a simple statement, an explanation for one's irritability, or a request that one's companion turn on the air conditioner.

A second kind of influence is seen in theories that literary works, at least poetry and fiction, are essentially performative. Their main significance lies in the author creating new patterns of words and new stories to have an effect on readers. Such literary works are not mainly descriptive. This use goes beyond the analysis of Austin himself, who indicated that he was focusing on ordinary speech to the exclusion of literature.[23]

Two other influences also extend Austin's expressed views. One possibility is to see expressions that one would not identify performatives as cumulatively functioning as a kind of performative over time. Suppose a family friend says in a daughter's presence, "She's a lovely girl," The remark is descriptive; it does not change anything in the way a promise commits one to action. But if enough friends keep repeating just this sentiment, their words may partly determine how the girl conceives of herself and of how she should behave.[24]

Finally, an extension of the idea of performatives is to regard nearly all forms of behavior as "performative." In this view, not only the "performing" of music and drama and the production of literature constitute performances but also our ordinary social activities, in which consciously or not we "perform" social roles, usually in a manner that is scripted by society. According to Irving Goffman, a status, position, or social place, "is something that must be enacted or portrayed," whether performed "with ease or clumsiness, awareness or not, guile or good faith."[25] Judith Butler has written similarly about gender as "a kind of persistent impersonation."[26]

III. THEORIES OF LITERARY INTERPRETATION

A. Author's Intent

Literary critics and scholars disagree about just how literary works should be interpreted. Many, if not most, of these theories have analogies within theories of legal interpretation. Reflecting on these analogies may help us to understand better what literary and legal interpretation are about. Whether grasping the arguments for and against a particular approach to literary interpretation will provide a basis for evaluating a similar approach to law is more doubtful, given striking differences in the ambitions of the two kinds of exercises.

A theory about the meaning of literature that has an enduring appeal but has fallen out of favor during much of modern times is that the meaning of a literary work depends on what the author intended. This is an approach that, at least in respect to the meaning of what has been written, interprets the text in a way similar (or identical) to the exercise one performs in conversational interpretation. Similar theories about the meaning of legal texts are familiar. They are the subject of sharp challenge for statutory and constitutional interpretation; but, as Chapters 7–9 reflect, they play an important part in respect to wills, contracts, and instructions to agents.

In order to be at all tenable in respect to literature, an "author's intent" approach must acknowledge the changing meaning of words and the difficulties of discerning an author's subjective intent, it must recognize levels of intent in respect to meaning, it must draw some distinction between meaning and application and between meaning and significance, and it must indicate the grounds on which one would choose author's intent over other approaches to discerning meaning.

Were words, and combinations of words, to retain constant meanings over time, discerning what any past author meant by using certain words would be much simpler than it actually is. In fact, standard meanings change in subtle and not so subtle ways. Sanford Levinson notes that according to the Oxford English Dictionary "sentimental" once meant "Of persons, their dispositions and actions; characterized by sentiment . . . in favorable sense," and has come to mean in a later use "addicted to indulgence in superficial emotion; apt to be swayed by sentiment."[27] Suppose a novelist, writing when the meaning of this word was in flux, portrayed Frances as saying, "George is sentimental. He'll make Mary a good husband." The novelist might have been using the old sense of sentimental, in which event Frances's remark makes straightforward sense. Or, the author might have meant the new sense, in which event perhaps Frances thought that Mary needed a husband who did not think too carefully. Or, the author might have been wishing to indicate that Frances is an old-fashioned person who doesn't keep up with contemporary uses of words and manages to confuse friends with whom she speaks. Any critic seeking to recapture an author's intent about meaning has his task significantly complicated by shifts in what words mean.

This is undoubtedly a genuine problem for legal interpretation that relies on the author's intent, but the problem's magnitude is usually much less. *Most* legal texts that officials interpret were written relatively recently; *most* of their language is more technical or simple than a fairly complex notion like sentimental; and most of them, unlike much poetry and fiction, are designed in the main to be clear. As a consequence, judges who are interpreting wills, contracts, and statutes, and are assuming that writers have probably intended standard meanings, will not very often face the serious difficulty of working back to a different era when standard meanings differed from those in the present.

One crucial move for anyone defending an author's intent approach to the meaning of literary texts is to draw distinctions between meaning and "significance" and between meaning and "application." When a speaker's expressed thought is simple and straightforward, the listener can grasp the basic message precisely, but significance is another question. Although everyone understands what it is to say a dog is male or female, the significance of having a male or female dog of a particular gender varies. A man may feel, for example, that having a male dog reinforces his own masculinity, an attitude he may or may not convey in his tone or facial expression as he responds to the simple question about his dog.[28]

In writings that constitute the fullest defense of an author's intent approach during the last half century, E.D. Hirsch has urged that the author's intent determines the meaning but not the significance of literature,[29] the latter encompassing the main concerns of literary critics.[30] The "significance" includes various attitudes and feelings that accompany communications, but do not touch the basic meaning of what is conveyed. Hirsch also assumes that the application of messages differs from "meaning;" insofar as an interpreter is involved in applying a prior communication to present circumstances, he properly does something more than discern the author's meaning.

Hirsch seems to regard application as one aspect of significance,[31] but, as I explain further in Chapter 5, someone called upon to apply a norm need not necessarily reach beyond the original meaning of a communication to discern what the norm requires (though, of course, he does need to decide whether to comply). A mother says, "Jack, brush your teeth every night." Jack applies this norm each evening. Special circumstances may raise questions about whether the mother's intent covers brushing on that particular evening, but for ordinary circumstances, her meaning, according to her intent (or, indeed, according to the standard sense of such an instruction given in typical family circumstances) is clear. Jack should brush his teeth. To know what action the communication directs, Jack need not consult attitudes or feelings, his mother's or his own.

In circumstances of this kind, there are three basic reasons why one might say that "meaning" is controlled by author's intent but actual application is not so controlled. Because of various practical concerns related to the nature of a discipline such as law, interpreters may eschew certain techniques for discovering the author's meaning. Thus, allowing evidence of relatives about what a testator said he meant to accomplish in his will might be regarded as too unreliable and too great an inducement to lying to be allowed. Were this so, a probate judge who was attracted to an author's intent approach when applying the will, might conclude that she was treating as the will's true meaning what *available* sources indicated was the author's intent, though she would be aware that that might vary from what she would have concluded had she consulted all possible sources about that intent.

A second reason why an author's intent might not control application would be because the problem to be resolved is simply not one about which the author of the crucial text had any relevant intent.

Third, even if the author had a discernible relevant intent, those in the present applying language that was communicated in the past may regard as relevant considerations that the author did not then take into account. They may conclude that the textual language should be treated in a way that does not track the author's probable meaning. (They might or might not think the actual human author does now (or would now) agree with this treatment that differs from his original intent.) Perhaps conditions have changed or the person doing the applying regards the author as having been unwise or unfair. This, according to Blaise Pascal in his Provincial Letters of 1656, was the attitude of Jesuits of his time to authoritative moral judgments of the Church Fathers. In order to avoid the force of those judgments, the Jesuits redefined terms (such as assassin) and treated many circumstances as special and therefore not covered.[32] In his biting account, Pascal makes clear his own view, in defense of a Jansenist perspective, that such evasions are deplorable. But, in general, if application is not controlled by author's intent, that leaves open the possibility that a person engaged in interpretation may *justifiably* and *self-consciously* deviate from the meaning of language (determined by author intent) when she applies that language to present circumstances.

The distinction between application and original communication is clear-cut, but can that be said about any broader distinction between meaning and significance? The possibility of maintaining that distinction has been challenged.[33] Hirsch acknowledges that subconscious intentions may be part of an author's meaning, but he says that in order to qualify, these must be coherent with the author's willed meanings.[34]

Among various remarks that people make, what some convey is less clear than an answer to the question about a dog's gender. Two examples from the previous chapter are a comment that someone has a good sense of humor and a request to be treated with respect. Recipients can immediately grasp the speaker's main idea in some messages without reflection; others require substantial input on their part. Sensible as the notion may be that basic meaning does not include all the attitudes and feelings accompanying that meaning, drawing the line between meaning and significance is often difficult enough to create doubt whether that distinction can serve as the main vehicle for dividing what author's intent controls from what it does not control.

If "meaning" is determined by an author's intent, then an interpreter's account of meaning in a literary work or elsewhere must be a probabilistic judgment, the kind of judgment a contemporary person must make about the occurrence of any historical event.[35] Conceding we lack perfect knowledge of the intentions of those who have written in the past, Hirsch points out that no one has certain knowledge of the intentions of any other human being in the present; and he strongly resists the idea that we are distinctively unable to discern the intentions of those who have lived in prior generations. He suggests, for example, that modern experts may better comprehend the meaning of William Blake's poetry than did his own contemporaries.[36] In an observation that I think is crucial for any defense of (or challenge to) an author's intent approach to interpreting meaning, Hirsch writes about "subtle matters of degree." A principle that "some degree of anachronism is necessarily present in any historical reconstruction" tells us nothing about "whether a particular reconstruction is severely or trivially compromised . . ."[37]

An idea familiar to students of constitutional interpretation is that an author may intend different levels of meaning. The author of a poem may conceive a certain meaning as he writes, but he may also conceive that he is writing in a manner to encourage later readers to supply meanings of their own. In this event, one aspect of the meaning of the poem would be that readers need not treat its meaning as controlled by the more specific original author's meaning. This complexity about levels of meaning need not totally undermine the theory that an author's intent controls meaning, but it does seriously complicate that theory.

Another troubling question is whether the "meaning" of literature or any other communication can critically be at odds with its apparent meaning. Hirsch writes that linguistic norms "impose limitations on verbal meaning."[38] "An author's verbal meaning is limited by linguistic possibilities but is determined by his actualizing and specifying some of those possibilities."[39] Hirsch sees the limit of "linguistic possibilities" as either/or—either a proposed meaning fits linguistic possibilities or it does not—but he apparently fails to attend to the influence of context and the reality that the degree of linguistic possibility might better be seen as a kind of scale than as all or nothing. This is evident with "slips" and likely slips. If I tell my students in any ordinary circumstances, "We'll meet at 3:00 A.M.," they know that I probably mean 3:00 P.M. Because it is so unlikely I would intend 3:00 A.M., the linguistic possibilities of this use of language in context includes 3:00 P.M. (This reminds us of Davidson's discussion of malapropisms in the last chapter.) If I say "6:00 A.M.," I probably mean 6:00 P.M., but that is somewhat less certain. If I say "7:30 A.M.," the students may be genuinely perplexed as to whether I am really proposing a very early meeting (but not so early as to be almost inconceivable) or have slipped in what I say.

No magic line separates possible meanings that are within linguistic possibilities from those that are not. The author's intent theorist must either accept that author's intent controls even when his words clearly convey a plausible meaning he definitely did not intend (he means "Shut the window" but says, "Shut the door," when shutting the door would make as much sense as shutting the window); or the theorist must work out a somewhat complicated account of when the probabilities based on the likelihood of a particular use in context override authorial intention.[40]

Why might one choose to rely on an author's intent for meaning? This is a question that obviously arises for any theory that an author's intent is *the* determinant of meaning, but it also arises for any theory that gives some weight to the author's intended meaning. Someone might claim that communication involves an intentional act of a speaker or writer, so it follows that the meaning of a communication depends on what the speaker or writer intended to convey. This simple view is too simple; it does not follow from the fact that communication is intentional that the person interpreting its meaning should take the author's intent as determining meaning.

Hirsch wisely recognizes that something more than aesthetic judgment is involved in deciding whether we should be guided by the author's intent.[41] In respect to literature, one might contend, as did various nineteenth-century critics, that the whole point is to allow readers to grasp the minds of authors insofar as possible, thus making the author's intentions an obvious guide to meaning. This claim is subject to various challenges that one cannot identify any overarching point of literature in such a manner. Hirsch relies, instead, on what he calls the ethics of language.[42]

We respect those who communicate with us by respecting their intentions, not merely using their words for our ends. If this is the basis for relying on author's intent, it represents a general theory that extends well beyond literature. But, on examination, the strength of this contention depends to a considerable degree on the kind of communication involved. It has powerful force for personal letters and emails, and for wills. It has less force for literary productions designed so that a reader cannot easily grasp what the writer had in mind. It also has less force for legal texts adopted by multiple authors and designed to be flexible enough to apply to changing circumstances.

Hirsch's treatment of the basic choice of interpretive method as ethical, not aesthetic, is worth remarking on. By adopting an aesthetic standard for the meaning of literature, a person is prejudging that the point of literature is mainly aesthetic. Although Hirsch's term "ethical" may suggest that the overall standard of judgment lies closer to ordinary judgments of morality than it does, he is right that we need to reach beyond aesthetic considerations.

A variation on intentionalism as a theory of interpretation is hypothetical intentionalism, which, according to some writers, looks to what a member of an appropriate (or ideal) audience would conclude best satisfies the author's intentions.[43] In this understanding, an interpreter is aiming to discern an author's intentions and is not restricted to the text alone.[44] She may employ available evidence about an author's life and his explanation of why he chose to write a book. But once the relevant evidence is assembled, the actual meaning is what the weight of that evidence suggests, rather than an undiscoverable subjective intention of the author as to which the evidence can yield only a probabilistic judgment.

I shall not pursue questions as to why, in the realm of literature, this hypothetical intentionalist approach might be preferable to one keyed to actual intentions; but we shall examine analogues in domains of law. One possible way to understand a binding instruction, will, or contract is to believe that its meaning depends on what a reader with all information that is legally usable and actually available would conclude about its author's (or authors') intentions. And a similar stance can provide one account of legislative intent for statutory interpretation, an account that is intermediate between one that makes meaning depend on the subjective intents of legislators and one that detaches reader understanding from the actual intent of those who enacted laws. As we shall see, within various areas of law, a concept of meaning based on some version of hypothetical intentionalism that includes information outside the text about intentions has considerable appeal.

B. Reader Response Theories

To say that an author's intent approaches have been out of favor in literary criticism for much of the last eight decades would be an understatement.

A bewildering succession of theories have followed one another. Many are difficult to understand, with their arcane terminologies, but the one thing they have in common is not placing the author's intentions at the center of interpretive meaning. Indeed the "death of the author" has been a frequent theme.

A theory that assigns at least a modest place to the aims of the author is reader-response. We shall take a brief look at the approach of one influential proponent, Wolfgang Iser, and ask how far it applies to communication in general, including legal texts, and how far it is limited to literature and other branches of art.

Iser writes that in considering literary works, "one must take into account not only the actual text itself but also and in equal measure, the actions involved in responding to that text."[45] Because a reader would be bored if everything were laid out cut and dried, a literary writer gives the reader less than the whole story, leaving something to the reader's imagination.[46] Although the written text sets limits on its "unwritten implications," the reader's imagination endows situations with greater significance than they might seem to have on their own.[47] Any one text may have several different realizations, with each individual reader filling in the gaps in his own way.[48] Modern texts exploit this process deliberately; with traditional texts it was more or less unconscious.

Each reader's experience of a text reflects his own disposition;[49] each reader strives to fit things together into a consistent pattern,[50] making decisions that exclude possibilities.[51] The "reader becomes the subject that does the thinking. Thus there disappears the subject-object division that otherwise is a prerequisite for all knowledge and all observation, and the removal of this division puts reading in an apparently unique position as regards the possible absorption of new experiences."[52]

Much of what Iser says does not apply to all communications, including most legal texts. Iser writes as if literary texts differ from most texts. Authors can, he thinks, write "boring" fiction in which everything is on the surface and nothing is left to the reader's imagination. Serious writers self-consciously seek to draw in their readers' imaginations. This alone gives pause about making an easy transposition from literary criticism to other domains, including judging.

No doubt, a reader brings his whole experience of life with him when he reads any text—including a "No Parking" sign, recipe, or railroad timetable. But many communications aim to provide the same basic message for readers of vastly different experiences and backgrounds, and "No Parking" signs succeed rather well. With statutes and contracts, one may think of some of those whose approval is necessary to give a text legal force as originally readers of texts that have been drafted by others who then become "writers" when their agreement makes the text legally authoritative. Typical legal texts, wills as well as statutes and contracts, are directed at a much narrower slice of the population than street signs; but many of them aim to achieve the same understanding among all of their intended audience. Thus, wills are written so that any judge will deal with expected contingencies in the same way; and many statutes and administrative regulations are drafted to give clear guidance.

When legal standards are open-ended or vague or difficult to apply to particular circumstances, a degree of judicial subjectivity is inevitable. But even then, the degree of subjectivity is less than it is as a self-conscious objective of literary work. Judges try to give reasons for their interpretations that will (or should) have similar force for other judges. They do not cite Iser and say, "Every reader has a unique response, and this is mine."

A critic might fairly respond that I have overstated the difference between reading literature and reading law. He might note, to begin, that it is misleading to compare understanding of subtle aspects of literary works with straightforward aspects of legal rules. Novels and short stories have their own indisputable features. Herman Melville's *Billy Budd* takes place aboard a British warship; its three main human characters are the sailor Billy, the Master-at-Arms, James Claggart, and the captain, Edward Fairfax Vere. Budd is condemned to death for striking Claggart after Claggart falsely accuses him. Vere expresses the sense that Budd is morally innocent, but nevertheless must die by hanging. Perhaps these points are analogous to simple applications of legal rules; asking about the "point" of *Billy Budd*, about which scholars disagree, is like asking about the "basic premises" of the American Constitution, about which scholars also disagree. When people interpret large aspects of the law to see what they reflect about society's values and aspirations, the answers may be no clearer than are fundamental themes of literary texts.

This observation is sound, as far as it goes. But it fails to recognize that the main point of reading literature is not getting the details right, it is grasping deeper meaning, having rich vicarious experience, increasing one's self-understanding, and, perhaps, enjoying oneself. The main point of legal interpretation is discerning what people may and may not do. For certain legal questions, the overall "point" of a large chunk of law will matter, but for most cases that point will not make a difference or will be uncontroversial.

C. A Best Answer Approach

It has been suggested that a literary scholar, like a judge, is looking for the best answer to a question he puts himself. Should one interpret Captain Vere as a benign well-intentioned figure or as obsessed with his own status? That depends, Ronald Dworkin has proposed, on what will make the story the best work of art it can be.[53] But a critic need not adopt a single standard of "best work of art." She may say one reading makes the novella artistically most successful, another presents the characters as the most realistic they can be, another conveys the most powerful moral message, another fits best with Melville's own ideas. She may or may not regard one of these inquiries as the most important. Indeed the same critic might

offer both an interpretation of the work as a clash between natural inno-
cence and the necessary demands of human law, in which event, treating Vere as concerned and dispassionate is sound, and an interpretation
that treats the work as a stinging indictment of an arbitrary perversion of
military justice, in which case Vere is best understood as consciously abus-
ing his office and unjustly compensating for his inadequacies at Billy's
expense.[54] Judges making legal decisions must decide what is best overall
in some sense, because practical, irreversible consequences depend on it.
Dworkin's conclusion that legal interpretation should make the law the
best it can be morally is actually more powerful than the analogy to literary interpretation that he uses to support it.

One possible constraint on reader response, a constraint that *might*
connect literary criticism and law, involves the community of readers.
Whatever limits an original text imposes on possible interpretations,
the interpretive community, through its practices and the premises
those reflect, also sets restraints. What interpreters have said in the past
about Shakespeare's *Hamlet* and the manner in which modern interpreters approach Shakespeare's plays render some interpretations "off the
wall" that might not be so in a different interpretive community. A single
modern interpreter may be unable to conceive interpretations that have
gone too far afield, and concerns about status will deter adventures of
that sort. All this has been suggested as closely analogous to how prior
interpretations and dominant present perspectives constrain judges and
lawyers.[55]

Similarity there is, but close analogy there is not. In common law systems, judges are "bound" to follow what prior judges have declared, a
constraint that is quite different from an inability to conceive an alternative or an unwillingness to jeopardize one's position by being far out
(though each of these factors can operate with judges as well). Within
any modern interpretive community broadly conceived, literary critics
may share certain basic premises about what they are doing. Nonetheless,
they adopt a wide variety of outlooks; and indeed it is often supposed that
originality, even exaggeration, is conducive to one's academic reputation,
something not common about judicial reputation. A tenured professor is
free to adopt whichever approach feels congenial to her without losing
her job; indeed nothing prevents her from reaching back in history to
adopt an outmoded theological approach or from looking toward a modern interpretive community radically different from the one in which she
is situated, though she may pay a price in professional respect. And if one
is thinking about readers in general, many of them read great works of
literature without any idea what critics have said about the works except
for what they learn from an introduction (if they choose to read it).[56] The
options are more limited for a judge; the community of past interpreters
exercises political authority for her, and she must advance interpretive
arguments she believes do or should have weight for her fellow judges.
For example, she may properly conclude that an explicitly theological

approach to interpreting legal texts is barred by a constitutional principle of "no establishment" of religion.

D. Focus on the Text

Among the wide range of literary theories, we can distinguish roughly between those that focus on the language of the text and those that connect literary texts to deep historical or psychological phenomena. Attention to the language of the text might or might not downgrade the specific substance of what the text conveys. The New Criticism, which dominated American literary theory in the mid-twentieth century, treated the text as autonomous, with a meaning that did not depend on an author's intentions.[57] Although individual words were taken to have the meanings they would have conveyed to original readers, poems and other literary works were otherwise to be treated as detached from their original historical and cultural context, calling not for rational cognition, but an aesthetic response linking the reader to the world.[58] Nevertheless, meaning was regarded as objective, and a "typical New Critical account of a poem offers a stringent investigation of its various 'tensions,' 'paradoxes,' and 'ambivalences,' showing how these are resolved and integrated by its solid structure."[59]

Whether or not most poems are well treated as substantially autonomous does not answer whether it makes sense to treat George Orwell's *Animal Farm* and *Nineteen Eighty-Four*, both written against a background of dismay over Communist governments,[60] in the same way. And whether poems should be regarded as autonomous tells us almost nothing about how most legal texts should be treated. It has virtually no bearing on whether an author's intentions should carry great weight in the interpretation of wills, or whether statutes adopted in a time past should be interpreted in light of the social problems to which they responded. In short, the reasons why one might accord weight to the understandings of authors and original readers are very different for legal texts than for poetry.

Some literary theories pay less attention to the surface messages of works than did the New Criticism. Drawing heavily from Saussure's linguistic theory, structuralists were interested in the general principles by which literature works. Images within a poem were not understood mainly in terms of what each might refer to externally. Rather, concentrating on language's signifying structures, and believing that the meaning of units of a system depends on their relations to each other, structuralists regarded the substantive content of a particular poem or story as relatively unimportant.[61]

Poststructuralists are much more skeptical about coherent structures. They emphasize the contradictory and incoherent aspects of texts. They "deconstruct." Meaning is found in absence as well as presence. In one summary by an outsider, "Meaning . . . is scattered or dispersed along the whole chain of signifiers: It cannot easily be nailed down, it is never fully present in any one sign alone, but is rather a kind of constant flickering of presence and absence together."[62]

What have theories such as structuralism and poststructuralism, or deconstructionism, to say to legal interpretation? Here, we must draw some basic distinctions. Insofar as these theories pay relatively little attention to the concrete, substantive message of the texts they analyze, they are not relevant for the kind of legal interpretation that seeks to discern whether a legal text does or does not cover particular circumstances, that is, for legal interpretation as it is normally conceived. The substance of what a will or contract or statute provides is of overarching importance; the structure or nuances of language by which it provides what it does are secondary. One cannot rest content with "deconstructing" a will to show that it lacks meaning or contains contradictory meanings; one needs to decide what the will does and does not do.

On the other hand, the insights into uses of language that these literary theories contain can usefully be employed to give content to legal texts in the ranges as to which their coverage is not obvious. One illuminating example of this is a piece by Jack Balkin in which he reviews a book that is highly critical of deconstruction.[63]

In understanding Balkin's approach, and other possibilities, it helps to have at least a fleeting sense of deconstructive theory more generally. This complex theory is grounded on the difficult-to-understand work of the French philosopher Jacques Derrida.[64] Derrida believed his approach applied to texts of all sorts, including philosophical writings, literature, political concepts, and law. He emphasized the centrality of language in human understanding, opposing both the belief that forms of thought are based on external points of reference (logocentrism) and a common inclination to treat oral speech as more fundamental than writing (phonocentrism).[65]

In opposition to logocentrism, Derrida coined the term "différance," which carries a sense of difference and delay or postponement.[66] The term suggests the claim that elements in language relate to each other and refer backward and forward, but that each is also distinct. Derrida focused on the implications of texts rather than on authors' intentions, and believed that these diverge significantly.[67] According to one who regards herself as a deconstructionist, the approach to reading literary texts involves "a careful teasing out of the conflicting forces of signification that are at work within the text itself. If anything is destroyed in a deconstructive reading, it is not meaning per se but the claim to unequivocal domination of one mode of signifying over another."[68] Jonathan Culler writes of "disrupting the hierarchical relations on which critical concepts and methods depend," thus preventing these "from being taken for granted and treated as simply reliable instruments."[69]

It is not difficult to see why this philosophical approach that has been applied to literature would prove attractive to those who want to challenge the comfortable assumptions of a dominant legal culture. In the United States, such challenges have come mainly from the left, including Critical Legal Studies. It is also not difficult to see why those who view the system as having considerable value will perceive challenges from such a perspective as threatening a desirable coherence, continuity, and stability.

In his version of deconstruction, Balkin eschews any claims of radical incoherence and indeterminacy in favor of "nested opposition, . . . a conceptual opposition each of whose terms contains the other or each of whose terms shares something with the other."[70] The metaphor that one term "contains" its opposite actually includes some "related concepts— similarity to the opposite, overlap with the opposite, being a special case of the opposite, conceptual or historical dependence upon the opposite, and reproduction of the opposite or transformation into the opposite over time."[71] The theory of deconstruction, in Balkin's view, is that conceptual opposition "can be reinterpreted as some form of nested opposition."[72] Insofar as this insight is valid, and any particular conceptual opposition not only *could* be interpreted as a nested opposition but is in fact best understood in that way, we can learn something about the nuances of all language, including legal language, and this might influence exactly how we would understand the coverage of an authoritative text.

These insights about linguistic possibilities hold out promise not only for interpreters but also for drafters of legal texts.[73] They may be able to employ subtle interrelations of concepts or, perhaps even more important, avoid pitfalls of confusion.

In considering the possible utility of deconstruction, and indeed other forms of analysis of literature, we need to distinguish ordinary legal texts, such as contracts and statutes, from judicial opinions (and lawyers' briefs) and from what we might call fundamental legal concepts. Judicial opinions are a kind of essay justifying a particular disposition of a dispute. In the way they present the narrative of the case and explain the grounds of judgment, their rhetoric can be extremely important. Justice Benjamin Nathan Cardozo compared judicial language to literature, both poetry and prose: "The search is for the just word, the happy phrase, that will give expression to the thought, but somehow the thought itself is transfigured by the phrase when found,";[74] and Richard Weisberg has written about Cardozo's own rhetorical choices in his opinions.[75] Robert A. Ferguson, using two notable flag salute cases, has argued persuasively that judicial opinions are typically in a Monologic Voice, in an Interrogative Mode (in which a fundamental decision is how to formulate the controlling question), and in a Declarative Tone (working toward certitude).[76]

The prospects for deconstructing judicial opinions are more promising than for deconstructing wills. Insofar as the critic can identify contradictions, and oppositions that do not quite rise to contradictions, her analysis may help to undercut the surface message of an opinion, perhaps even what that implies about the holding of a case, or the wisdom of the decision. Of course, if her theory is that all writing can be deconstructed in this way, she will have nothing more definite to put in its place, rather revealing the indeterminacy of all efforts at justification and explanation.

Deconstruction aimed at the basic concepts of a political order or legal system may seek to show that these concepts cannot be understood and applied in a coherent way because of internal tensions and contradictions.[77] If the critic's thesis is that all political and legal systems will be subject to a similar analysis, the critique cannot hold out hope for improvement in this respect, except in revealing the inherent inevitability of the dominant ideology and suggesting a similar fate for whatever might replace it.[78] If the critic's thesis is that the contradictions are inherent only in a particular kind of political order, she may believe we can move beyond that, as a Marxist may aspire to move beyond the contradictions of liberal democracy and capitalism to a more humane, more coherent socialism.

A pervasive issue about interpretation is whether a reader should start with the assumption that a text is coherent or is not coherent. As we have seen, deconstructionists emphasize the contradictions and incoherence of literary texts. Various deconstructionist approaches provide a similar perspective on law. To some outsiders, including myself, it often seems that theorists of this persuasion are reaching to find whatever incoherence they can find, rather than settling for incoherence only if coherent explanations are implausible.

Without getting deeply into the competing theories, we can understand that some legal texts are more coherent than others, some reflect a consistent point of view, others contain irreconcilable perspectives. Within law, the presuppositions with which judges and others begin may matter. Suppose it is not evident whether sections of a statute fit well together. A court must interpret Section A. If it assumes that Section A coheres well with Section B, then what B clearly provides will be one basis for construing A on a matter that is in doubt. If the court does not assume coherence, then B's coverage will seem to have little bearing on A's.

If one is asking about probable coherence in design or expression, it may be that a will written by (or for) a single individual at one time is likely to be more coherent than a statute that has gone through many amendments, responsive to the entreaties and pressures of diverse interest groups.[79] But within law, as within literature, there may be policy reasons to indulge or not indulge an assumption of coherence. For literature, one might think that readers best experience a work as a coherent whole or that exposing and emphasizing the variety of human attitudes and feelings, and the inevitable strains and limitations of language, is healthier. Either answer would hardly settle the question for law. Perhaps in the interpretation of legal texts, as well as in the interpretation of legal doctrine, there is social value in seeking or aiming for coherence, unless incoherence indisputably dominates. And it may matter greatly what kind of legal text is involved. For a constitution designed to last over time, it might be a virtue rather than a drawback that it does not displace or reconcile rival principles but becomes "their dialectal arena."[80] Whether legal interpreters should exercise a presumption of coherence is a decidedly different question from whether literary critics should do so.

E. The Pervasive Influence of Culture and Psychology

A number of modern literary theories tie literature to cultural patterns, typically patterns of domination by class, race, gender, and sexual preference, or to deep psychological truths. Thus, one could give a Marxist or feminist or Freudian reading to a piece of literature, claiming that the main point of a work of literature should be seen in these terms, that this is how the work should be understood, or, more modestly, that the work reflects deep background assumptions along one of these lines, although they need not embody what the work is "really about."[81] Without doubt, similar analyses are possible for legal texts. A legal text might carry out an author's self-conscious sexist attitudes; it might embody sexist attitudes of the author of which he is unaware; it might indirectly reflect sexist patterns of the entire culture. Without doubt, there is value for students of law in understanding the cultural presuppositions of various legal norms, especially when those presuppositions are now widely regarded as unjust, or should be regarded as unjust. But how this understanding appropriately affects textual interpretation is not simple.

If statutes are revealed as based on sexist premises, it is a basis for their revision and perhaps for judicial rulings that they violate the Equal Protection Clause of the Federal Constitution. But in what way should a sexist reading affect the interpretation of debatable language to determine its coverage? One might think that *as a matter of interpretation*, underlying premises should be effected, or one might conclude that *unjust* premises should not be accorded weight in the interpretation of meaning of texts whose import is unclear, or, to put this approach differently, that the meaning of unclear provisions should be considered to be in accord with what we now perceive as just premises, even when unjust premises lie behind the text as a whole and its clear provisions. The soundest answer to these queries may well depend on whether one is talking about a will, contract, statute, or constitution. The argument for carrying out unjust premises may be strongest for wills, given a testator's ability to draw arbitrary, unfair distinctions, and the relative weakness of public concern with a person's disposal of his property. For statutes designed to promote public welfare, reliance on premises whose unfairness is widely acknowledged is much more troubling. For hard-to-amend constitutions whose provisions need to last through time, the reasons against relying on once-held unjust premises are especially powerful. Subsequent volumes will discuss how judges should regard unjust premises when they interpret statutes and constitutional provisions, and when they decide issues of common law; but the crucial point here is one I have made in other contexts: The best relationship between identifying underlying sexist premises and interpreting what a novel means may be different from the best relationship between finding such premises and discerning the meaning of a legal text for purposes of determining what it allows and prohibits.

IV. A CRITIQUE OF ONE POSTMODERNIST, FEMINIST INTERPRETATION OF A WELL-KNOWN TEXT IN SOCIAL PSYCHOLOGY

This section of the chapter departs from the interpretation of literature and law as these areas are narrowly understood. But many texts may be regarded as literary, or having literary qualities, and many kinds of texts that are relevant for law may be subject to the varieties of analysis that characterize literary interpretation. A very important form of writing that matters for law is scholarship, both academic writing about law itself, including about judicial opinions, and writing in other disciplines that have consequences for desirable legal development. As we have seen, deconstruction and various other interpretive approaches may be thought to apply to a broad range of writing, including scholarship, whether that is descriptive or normative or both.

Here I have chosen to analyze an interpretation by a feminist legal scholar of a work in social psychology, because it presents clearly and in a striking manner an approach that differs from more traditional, standard approaches to the interpretation of scholarship. What interests me here is interpretive strategy, and my observations apply to the interpretation of more typical legal scholarship and to interpretation (from a scholarly perspective) of judicial opinions, as well as to writing in related disciplines. My example happens to be scholarship that involves a crucial issue in feminist thought, but the implications concern interpretive writing that comes from any perspective—radical, liberal, or conservative.

I focus specifically on an interpretation of Carol Gilligan's *In a Different Voice*—a widely read book in social psychology that has been greatly influential and highly controversial in feminist thought.[82] Mary Jo Frug, in her *Postmodern Legal Feminism*,[83] devotes a chapter to Professor Gilligan's famous suggestion that an ethics of care differs significantly from an ethics of rights and is not just a way station in the development toward an ethics of rights. Gilligan's conclusions were based substantially on studies over a period of years of the ways girls and women resolved hypothetical ethical dilemmas in comparison with how boys and men resolved those dilemmas. Gilligan writes of the ethics of care, an affiliative relational approach, as a typical approach of women in our culture—in contrast to an abstract, "objective," rights approach common to men.[84]

The interpretive question Frug sets is just how inextricably connected is the ethics of care to the female gender in Gilligan's book. Whatever answer Gilligan herself might have given, we can quickly see why the possible connection has profound importance for feminist theory. If women, as a consequence of their intrinsic nature or of social conditions not likely to be altered soon, will believe in and act upon an ethics of care that differs from the ethical approach of men, theorizing about the choices, the rights, and the expected social roles of women should take this stubborn fact into account. If, on the other hand, "masculine" and "feminine" are mainly just labels given to two styles of ethical thinking, and members of each gender are roughly equal in their capacity to be socialized into an ethics of care (or an ethics of rights), thinking about the relations between men and women and about the rights of women need not assume that women will act upon a distinctive ethics of care. *Nothing* I say about Frug's interpretation of Gilligan is intended to minimize the significance of this question or to propose a resolution.

Noting that Gilligan has been variously interpreted, Frug capsulizes a conservative and a progressive interpretation. Having provided a "brief and uncontroversial" summary of Gilligan's thesis,[85] she describes a conservative approach according to which the traits associated with the two ethical approaches are "universal characteristics of the sexes" and the ethical differences between women and men "*validate gender differences*" (italics from Frug's text).[86] According to a progressive reading, sex differences are "context-bound," more "associated with language . . . than individual identity"; changes in language can lead to transformations of gender identity.[87] Frug cites various passages from the book that could be used to support each interpretation. Proceeding from the ambiguity she thinks these passages establish in how Gilligan perceives the ethics of care, Frug remarks that "a reader's interpretation of the book can be a function of what she wants to find rather than what the book definitely says."[88] Frug concludes that a conservative reading can be used to justify socially conservative judicial results, by accepting a static interpretation of gender stereotypes that excludes alternatives.[89] The progressive reading, which sees sex-linked differences as "cautious, nondualistic, partial, contingent, and sensitive to many constituencies of women," is "a decided improvement over a conservative use of" the book.[90] Frug's entire book makes evident that this reading fits her belief that our understanding of the world is largely determined by our linguistic categories and that by deconstructing existing modes of thought and self-consciously altering our language, we can work profound transformations in human relations.

My response to Frug's approach is subject to three very important caveats. The first is that her entire book was a work in progress, published after she was murdered. Before she had herself reached closure on passages, she might have altered some of the ways in which she cast various ideas. My second caveat, related to the first, is that I am considering what she says, consistent with most of her own phraseology, as an *interpretation* of *In a Different Voice*, in the sense of the best understanding of Gilligan's book, not just as *use* or a *reading* of that book. I emphasize this, because "use" is crucially different from interpretation as best understanding. One might acknowledge that an essay asserts some large idea, say, the existence of God, and nevertheless *use* asserted facts or arguments within the essay, say, the misery of human beings, as helping to show the opposite, that God does not exist. To generalize the point, the *use* of a text need not imply that the text, taken as a whole, should be understood as conveying support of the use.

"Reading" is more ambiguous than "use;" it is sometimes a synonym for interpretation as best understanding; it also can mean something like "what I think is valuable to be drawn from this text", or it can suggest one among a number of plausible understandings. One variation of this third sense of "reading" is familiar to lawyers. Lawyers on each side of a dispute "read" prior cases in ways that are not too "far out" and are most advantageous to their clients. (Judges, as Chapter 2 and this chapter have briefly explored, very often perform a similar exercise in justifying results.) In this sense, "reading" is a form of interpretation but one governed by a predetermined objective, not by what the lawyer outside his litigating role would necessarily choose as the best interpretation. Yet a different sense of reading is a deconstructionist one that exposes inconsistencies and tensions without settling on one coherent understanding. Although Frug wants to deconstruct standard assumptions about gender, she does not in the final analysis treat Gilligan's book in this way.

My third caveat is closely tied to the second. If Frug meant only that her approach was a use or reading of Gilligan, one that best fits the actual social realities, her approach would *not* raise the problematic idea of interpretation to which I now turn.

In a Different Voice is a study in social psychology, intermixed with a basic judgment about normative ethics, namely that an ethics of care is as valuable, as appropriate, as an ethics of rights.[91]

As Frug discusses them, the differences between the conservative and progressive positions boil down to at least three: (1) how great are the correlations of the ethics of care to women and the ethics of rights to men?; (2) whatever the present correlations, how feasible would it be to alter them?; (3) how much of a causal factor in any present correlation is our linguistic usage and how feasible would it be to shift this usage to contribute to a significantly different correlation (or yet a new or revised conception of ethical responsibilities that does not fit either dominant pattern)? As to each of these questions, an interpreter might opt for the conservative or the progressive approach, for some amalgam or compromise of the two approaches, or for a conclusion that the book is indecisive or unrevealing on the particular subquestion. Frug, as we have seen, adopts the progressive branch for each answer.

How might an approach to interpretation that focuses on author's intent or on an overall sense of the text differ from Frug's postmodern approach? Let us begin with author's intent. Passages of the book do identify the ethics of care with actual women and other passages indicate that Gilligan is most interested in stressing the distinctively different ethical approaches, not the actual gender of the persons who happen to adopt each.[92] We can fairly surmise that Gilligan herself had more than a single attitude toward her work, with different aspects or variations reflected in the passages pointing one way or the other. But are the positions not reconcilable? Must we, should we, choose one branch *rather than* the other?

Suppose we came across a personal diary in which on many days the author wrote about a father who had died, "I hate my father"; on many days, "I love my father." We might conclude that he really hated (or loved) his father but for some reason could not fully accept those feelings; we might conclude he had both feelings in about equal measure. What we would not conclude is that he felt kind of medium or bland about his father. That "compromise" would not be available. Are Gilligan's two themes irreconcilable in anything like this way?

Frug's "conservative" interpretation is that the traits that go with the two ethical approaches are "universal characteristics of the sexes." Whatever Frug means exactly, no one could reasonably think that every woman exhibits an ethics of care and every man an ethics of rights. Although Gilligan characterizes one approach as that of women, the other as that of men, that division does not suggest universality any more than do statements that women are shorter, less heavy, or less strong physically than men.[93] What the division does suggest is significantly high correlations between the two ethical styles and the respective genders.[94] Thus, I take Gilligan as claiming that when she wrote, the two ethical stances were (at least in the United States) correlated fairly highly, but far from perfectly, with physical gender.

That claim is fully compatible with the view that the two ethical stances should be broadly recognized as alternative approaches that are not neatly ordered in any developmental or hierarchical fashion. In this view, "masculine" and "feminine" may be convenient labels for a difference that would exist even if the actual gender correlations changed radically.[95] Thus, if we ask about author's intent, we need not choose between the conservative and progressive approaches; we can accept what is plausible in each.

Turning to the question about how far language is the generating force of these differences in ethical approaches, I find little in *In a Different Voice* that focuses on that,[96] although one might conceivably think aspects of the underlying studies themselves could shed light on the importance of language. Indeed, Gilligan does not address the issue of whether "nurture" of various kinds or "nature" is mainly responsible.[97]

This leaves us with the second question: how locked in are the correlations between ethical approaches and gender? Gilligan certainly does not assert that the correlations are immutable, but her terminology and indeed her defense of an ethics of care suggests that she thinks the gender correlations of the two approaches are aspects of our culture that will not be swept away easily or quickly. Now, it might fairly be said that Frug is not assuming that change, with altered linguistic constructions as a crucial element, will be easy or quick, and that what distinguishes the progressive from the conservative approach is less a matter of empirical possibilities and probabilities, and more an issue of whether we should be trying to elaborate and defend an ethics of care or deconstruct the linguistic assumptions that lead to the two different ethical approaches and to their gender correlations. Gilligan's book is largely an exercise in elaboration and defense, and a plea that people, especially women, find their own voices. She does not address whether the progressive agenda, as outlined by Frug, might be feasible, as important as what she has done, and possibly compatible with that.

These two exercises are not by their very nature at odds with each other; people could conceivably explore and defend the ethics of care embraced by most women *and* seek to disestablish the correlation of ethical stances to gender. However, if one believed that the effort to give voice to an ethics of care would itself reinforce the linguistic categories that need to be deconstructed, one might conclude that those seeking a more just society for women would need to decide which course is more promising.

In sum, on the second question, Gilligan (1) would probably think that the gender correlation will not soon or easily be destroyed or greatly changed and (2), beyond encouraging women to find their own voice, would not claim to be prescribing the most desirable overall strategy to respond to the social reality she has revealed. Her probable opinions, taken together and as intended to be conveyed by her text, turn out to be far removed from both the simplified conservative and progressive interpretations.

My overall sense of Gilligan's text, somehow detached from the person of the author, is virtually identical to my attempt to discern her intent. I have, in fact, relied extremely little on anything I know about her that one would not discover from reading the text.[98] That the author is a committed, thoughtful scholar and a woman is revealed by the text's language. That she is engaging in scholarship rather than writing poetry or fiction, or expressing subjective personal reactions (though these are not entirely absent), helps us to fix the genre that we are interpreting. If we aim to understand as best we can the message that the text itself conveys, we will be led, I think, to conclusions close to those I drew about author's intent.[99]

We now reach my main point. Frug's exercise in interpretation varies radically from either of mine. She posits possibilities at two ends of the spectrum—admittedly ones that have been relied on by various advocates who have read *In a Different Voice*. She treats these as absolutely opposed to one another. She chooses as her interpretation the one that best reflects her perception of the social facts and will best serve the social and political objectives in which she believes. Although she seems to suggest that she has given us the best understanding of Gilligan's book, she never claims that hers is really the most plausible way to understand what Carol Gilligan was trying to convey or what one would gather from her text taken as a whole. If serious interpretations of academic work reduce to such an exercise, these interpretations really amount to something very like lawyers' briefs, with one's own sense of social reality, and of favored social objectives and the strategy to achieve them, replacing a client's interests as the engine to guide one's understanding of another's text.

One *might* defend such an approach as inevitable, a truth we can perceive once false consciousness is stripped away. Perhaps it is the best we can do because texts in ordinary language are so heavily indeterminate in meaning and because, relatedly, texts contain so many contradictory and oppositional aspects. Frug writes, "Thus, a reader's interpretation of the book can be a function of what she wants to find rather than what the book definitely says."[100] This passage suggests that if the text definitely (and consistently)[101] says something, one must so interpret it, but otherwise one can look for what one wants to find. This sentence is revealing, because we would not ordinarily assume that once we've exhausted all that a text "definitely says," we are free to plug in whatever suits us. Suppose that all a theater review says about the performance of actor A is, "A, unlike B, did not actually perform poorly." That sentence does not definitely tell us that A performed anything less than exceptionally well, but the implication is that A did not perform brilliantly, and we are confident that is part of what the reviewer meant to express (an intuition that fits Grice's theory of implicature). We typically infer many things from a text that it does not definitely say, and we exclude many possibilities that are not explicitly foreclosed. Once we have stepped over the edge of definite statement, we do not assume we fall into a chasm (or heaven) of indeterminacy.

An academic text is not a poem or a personal diary. When people (including editors) show me that written statements of mine in the same piece of writing seem contradictory or at odds, often I already possess a consistent view that one of the statements reflects poorly. If I have not yet identified and resolved the particular issue exposed by the contrasting statements, I may nonetheless see that one of the statements comports better with the overall positions I have expressed. Infrequently though it happens, I am initially stumped; I see the difficulty the reader has pointed out and find nothing in my text that helps me decide which of the two opposing positions to adopt. What I would hope from an interpreter—if the "at odds statements" remained to publication—is that if she could figure out which statement did fit my overall position best and which reflected a lapse in how I have expressed myself, she would say, "Greenawalt probably means X (or would think X) though one of his sentences points in a different direction."

That is one aspect of what we might understand to be "charity" in interpretation, an aspect that focuses on coherence of expressed thoughts rather than their likely correspondence with social reality.[102] For this purpose, I don't think it matters much whether one is referring to author's intent or the gist of the text taken by itself.[103] Such an approach to interpreting academic texts does assume that usually, not always, the authors have positions that are coherent in at least a minimal sense, that their writings are not just congeries of thoughts and feelings thrown together without any serious effort at consistency. Despite the text's shifts in emphasis, such an assumption is definitely warranted in respect to Professor Gilligan's book. I believe that scholars should entertain that assumption about other academic writing, including academic writing in law.

This belief may place me at odds with various postmodern approaches that emphasize inconsistencies and indeterminacy. My recommendation does not entail that critics should be hesitant to offer their own appraisal of a social reality that another author has exposed. Had Professor Frug clearly indicated that she was doing that, rather than offering a best understanding of *In a Different Voice*, I would have no disagreement with her method of interpretation.

IV. INTERPRETATION AND BEYOND: THE VALUE OF LITERATURE

The broad subject of law and literature includes much besides the relevance of theories of interpretation in the two domains. As I have briefly mentioned, there is reflection on legal writings as a form of literary exercise.[104] There are also claims about the value of reading literature for those concerned with law. A fair amount of fictional writing concerns itself with the law and with lawyers. Such accounts may bring to life aspects of legal institutions better than dry descriptions.[105] And some of this writing, such as that of Franz Kafka, may, with its exaggerated, bizarre settings, reveal people's attraction to the "authoritarian structure of law" or other deeply flawed premises of legal orders more forcefully than could more realistic portrayals.[106] Exactly what various authors have set out to do, and what the implications of their texts are, is frequently the subject of sharp controversy;[107] but that does not detract from the basic idea that one may learn about legal values and the law, past and present, from some great works of fiction.

I have chosen in this section to focus on one defense of a somewhat different (though not inconsistent) thesis: namely that those whose work is within the law can glean from fiction insights about human nature that will help them better perform their responsibilities.[108] That subject draws us, in a focused way, to inquiries about *the point* of literature for life.

In an illuminating treatment, Martha C. Nussbaum, a prominent philosopher, contends in her *Poetic Justice* that "the novel constructs a paradigm of a style of ethical reasoning that is context specific without being relativistic, in which we get potentially universalizable concrete prescriptions by bringing a general idea of human flourishing to bear on a concrete situation, which we are invited to enter through the imagination."[109]

Insofar as the author of a novel intends to construct the kind of paradigm Nussbaum discusses, or the text seems to reflect that, one might suppose that what one learns from the novel about ethical reasoning derives from one's interpretations of the (or a) message of the novel and from one's accepting that message (in some form).[110] Nussbaum's primary discussion is of novels whose authors are trying to convey ideas that she thinks should influence judges and legislators, but the possible benefits of reading novels need not depend on that.[111]

Professor Nussbaum asserts that the novel's focus on individual characters, on the richness and complexity of their lives, is a crucial element of thought about social policy and law. Decision-makers are insufficiently sensitive to the human condition if they address problems only from perspectives that see people in the mass, in the manner of crude forms of utilitarianism and economic maximization. The literary understanding, in Nussbaum's conception, should supplement, not supplant, reasoning based on approaches of social science. There may well be circumstances in which the government must treat people in a manner that does not respond directly to their individual characters and aspirations,[112] but officials should never forget the importance of the individual lives that are the subjects of the law's generalizations.

Nussbaum devotes much of her attention to the novel *Hard Times*, by Charles Dickens, which provides a scathing picture of Thomas Gradgrind's rigid utilitarian approach to life.[113] She stresses the need to guard against simplified models that begin "to look like the whole of reality," offering as a prime example George Stigler's comment that "all of man's deliberative, forward-looking behavior follows the principles of economics."[114] Nussbaum shows us how Dickens challenges the utilitarian philosophy by his development of characters and plot and by his literary style, leading the reader both to resist any idea that pains and pleasures can somehow be cumulated across individuals and to understand that freedom of choice is critical to a whole human life, that we are not mere receptacles of positive and negative utilities.

A central aspect of Nussbaum's theme, developed in a chapter entitled "Rational Emotions," is that emotions are built into the structure of novels and that many emotions are valuable. The value of experiencing emotions when one reaches decisions is tied to the profound importance of actual human vulnerabilities and needs; contrary to a detached Stoic perspective, external events in our lives are deeply significant.[115] The novel permits us to empathize with a great variety of persons who find themselves in vastly different circumstances. Nussbaum shows that emotions are typically related to beliefs—we are angry when we *believe* we have been unfairly treated—that they are not free-floating irrational sensations, or ill-formed sentiments that inevitably lead to misguided decisions.[116] The emotions that are appropriate are those that are reasonably related to circumstances. What those making legal decisions and other decisions of public import need is a certain kind of emotional perspective. Drawing from Adam Smith's idea of a judicious spectator, Nussbaum proposes that a judge or legislator should, from the standpoint of a spectator not a participant, experience emotions that are based on a true view of the facts as these facts affect all the actors in a case (or all the subjects of legislation).[117] "Among [the judicious spectator's] most important qualities is the power of imagining vividly what it is like to be each of the persons whose situations he imagines."[118] The reader of a novel is herself put artificially in the role of a judicious spectator,[119] and reading novels can help us develop the kinds of understanding of and empathy for others that will allow us to approximate the perspective of a judicious spectator when we play social roles.

In an essay written ten years after the publication of Professor Nussbaum's book, Amnon Reichman urged that the value of literature is not so much in encouraging empathetic judgments, but in teaching readers "to withhold judgment so that when judgment is ultimately rendered it is more profound and meaningful."[120] When we read great fiction we do not need to take stands, rather we enter "the rich, emotional world of sympathy, aversion, love, sorrow, pain, joy, enthusiasm, anger, and frustration that accompany our identification with literary characters."[121] This allows us to be more deliberate and thoughtful when we are called upon to reach judgments in the real, social world.

In a response, Nussbaum acknowledges that Reichman's argument about reading literature is "convincing," and that the suspension of judgment may be desirable to offset a tendency of judges to decide too hastily.[122] Still, she does not retract her original thesis about how literature can help decision-makers avoid judgments that fail to take people as individuals.

Always careful to caution that good judging in legal cases depends largely on various standards of judgment other than—in addition to—literary judging, Nussbaum gives us examples of cases in which she believes judges did or did not benefit from the literary perspective.[123] Among the cases she considers is the highly controversial *Bowers v. Hardwick*,[124] now overruled,[125] in which the Supreme Court rejected a due process "right of privacy" for people to engage in homosexual relationships. The Court's opinion, written by Chief Justice Burger, failed to see those engaged in such relationships in fully human terms, a defect he might have avoided by reading a novel such as E. M. Forster's *Maurice*.[126]

Another, less familiar, Supreme Court case was one in which the majority declared that prisoners had virtually no constitutional rights in their cells against searches and seizures; even if a guard destroyed an inmate's personal letters and photos purely out of a malicious desire to humiliate him, there was no unreasonable seizure in violation of the Fourth Amendment.[127] Justice Stevens, in dissent, argued eloquently for the importance for prisoners of preserving some minimal shred of personal space against arbitrary intrusions by the state. Although Nussbaum scrupulously refrains from asserting what result literary judging would (should) have yielded, the conclusion that adequate empathy for the prisoner's situation would have produced the opposite outcome is hard to resist.

Nussbaum's account, especially as amplified by Reichman's point about the suspension of judgment, is largely persuasive; but I have some reservations and a major doubt. Two of my reservations do not touch Nussbaum's claims about the importance and value of reading novels that realistically portray individuals and their lives.

First, I am skeptical that emotions are as tightly tied to belief as Nussbaum appears to assert. When things do not go my way, I may feel angry, even though my rational belief is that I have been treated fairly. During athletic contests, participants (and fans of professional teams) often feel anger at (even hatred of) opponents although fully aware that the opponents have done nothing to deserve that feeling. To take a different kind of illustration, I sometimes have emotions of happiness or sadness unconnected to any particular beliefs. Are the emotions generated by listening to great music intrinsically related to belief? I doubt it.[128] Nevertheless these illustrations do not deflect from Nussbaum's point that emotions very commonly *are* tied to belief.

A second reservation is about her assumption that novels have a power to create empathy that is greater than autobiographies, biographies, and history that focuses on individuals.[129] That assumption is tied to her claim, which draws from Aristotle, that because novels are about possibilities, inviting us to wonder about ourselves, and because empathy arises largely from our imagining that we might be in situations similar to those of the characters, novels have a distinctive effect.

In her response to Amnon Reichman, Nussbaum explains that she distinguishes empathy, which is ethically neutral,[130] from compassion, which may follow empathy but can exist without it—as in the instance of compassion for non-human animals, which people can have without imagining themselves in the circumstances of those animals.[131] Given the way she draws the distinction, I believe one is still speaking of empathy if one can imagine what a life would be like, even if one has no concern (even a deep subconscious one) that he may find himself in a similar position. Thus, a novel might create empathy in us for a Russian serf, even if we could not conceive of ourselves as actually being serfs.

The important point here is that I believe that one may develop the same kind of empathy from reading a biography as a novel (though I confess to reading more novels, because I find them more entertaining). Nussbaum discusses Richard Wright's *Native Son*,[132] which brings to life in fiction the experience of an African-American in a Chicago ghetto. But cannot a reader develop a similar degree of empathy from reading Wright's *Black Boy*,[133] Claude Brown's *Manchild in the Promised Land*,[134] or *The Autobiography of Malcolm X*?[135] Whatever the degree of imaginative sympathy that is needed, why would I, a relatively sheltered middle-class white person, attain a higher degree of empathy with the fictional character who is unlike me in many respects than the real person who is unlike me in somewhat similar respects? Indeed, since I realize many fictional characters are not realistic, I might be more likely to resist the idea that there could really be someone that is "so different" if I met him in a novel rather than in an apparently honest autobiography or an apparently perceptive biography.[136]

Having arrived at the generalities in the preceding paragraph, I decided to put them to a highly subjective personal test by reading in succession *Native Son* (which I had not read before) and *Black Boy* (which I read about fifty years ago). The main character in *Native Son*, Bigger Thomas, is truly frightening, and Nussbaum indicates that Wright deliberately impeded empathy with him in order to show whites that they could not understand an angry black man.[137] Having found himself with the drunken daughter of his rich white employer in her bedroom, and wishing to prevent her blind mother who entered the room from learning of his presence, Thomas suffocated the daughter, killing her by accident. He then burned her body in the furnace. "He did not feel sorry for Mary . . . . He felt that his murder of her was more than justified by the fear and shame she had made him feel [by making efforts to befriend him and treat him as an equal]."[138] Bigger subsequently killed his girlfriend Bessie to forestall her possibly providing information that could lead to his capture. He then felt that "[i]n all of his life these two murders were the most meaningful things that had ever happened to him. He was living, truly and deeply, no matter what others might think, with their blind eyes. Never . . . had his will been so free . . . ."[139] The novel effectively makes one feel how destructive a regime of systematic racial prejudice can be, but the reader wonders whether Wright is exaggerating, whether an author who has lived a life so different from Bigger's is in a position to know how a person who acted out his hostility in that way would think and feel.

Although most of *Black Boy* takes place in the South, as contrasted with *Native Son*'s Chicago setting,[140] the dire consequences of racial oppression across the entire spectrum of lives of oppressed Negroes is vividly conveyed, and Wright explicitly draws general conclusions from his own personal experience. We see the extent to which those, like Wright himself, who live lives that are generally law-abiding experience a hostility toward whites that resembles Bigger's. For me, *Black Boy* is at least as effective in generating empathy for the unjustly oppressed as is *Native Son*.[141] Both books are very effective.

Nussbaum herself writes that a biography written in an appealing narrative style may affect the imagination as does a good novel,[142] and *Black Boy* has a compelling narrative style. If one grants that a well-written autobiography, or biography, can generate an empathy similar to that of the good novel, the only effect on Nussbaum's main thesis would be to expand the relevant genre that could help someone attain judicious spectatorship.

The comparison between novels and purportedly factual accounts of actual lives suggests a further point that does not detract from Nussbaum's thesis. Perhaps part of the problem for judges and other leaders of government is they tend to lead lives too far removed from actual, significant personal contact with people whose social status is radically different.[143] Reading may be partly a way to fill a void in their lived experience.

We now reach more substantial concerns about Nussbaum's claims. She writes that realistic novels have a decidedly liberal bent, offering a vision that is particularistic without being relativistic,[144] and moving the reader toward a kind of democratic equality. I believe it is right that (most) novels draw us to care about and value individual characters, that they are implicitly opposed (if not explicitly so, as in the case of *Hard Times*) to social philosophies that are totalizing or maximizing, philosophies such as crude utilitarianism, totalitarian communism, and fascism. But we need to recognize that individualization does not necessarily mean increased sympathy for all kinds of characters. Some novels present certain characters as completely and irredeemably evil. (This is true of *some* characters in Dickens's novels.) The reader is led to hope they get their comeuppance in the worst possible way. A reader of such novels might begin to identify some real life individuals as similarly evil. The consequence might be a reduction of empathy, not an expansion of it, for these individuals.

My reading of *Native Son* suggests a more complex possibility. A reader might recognize that a character's undesirable features have been produced by social causes over which he has no control, causes that have frustrated his chances for a decent life. Yet she might also think that his antisocial inclinations are too powerful to be altered and are extremely dangerous to others. One might deeply regret what could make anyone like Bigger Thomas, yet believe that a real murderer with his outlook should be executed or put away for life. In that event, a judicial reader of Wright's novel persuaded that some actual people are like Bigger might be led to sentence certain offenders more harshly than she otherwise would.

My final doubt has to do with the connection of novels to a democratic outlook. Nussbaum emphasizes that novels typically deal with ordinary people, that readers develop a sense of the trials and triumphs of people in ordinary life. But we need to be careful here about which ordinary people are portrayed. Jane Austen and Anthony Trollope, for example, frequently write of ordinary people who read and write; they are not servants and manual laborers. In one of Trollope's novels, an important character is a desperately poor Anglican priest, but still he is a priest.[145] As a very rough guess, I'd think that the characters that form the overwhelming percentage of those portrayed in depth by Austen and Trollope were, by social standing, in the top ten to twenty percent of the English population at the times they wrote. Dickens, and Thomas Hardy, George Eliot, and D.H. Lawrence, do include members of the working class in their important characters. But writing about "ordinary people" doesn't *necessarily* lead educated middle-class readers to understand and value individuals who are in the working class or are unable even to function adequately in society.

Nussbaum offers two important qualifications that provide a kind of answer to this point, but they end up making her claim about democracy close to circular. She sensibly cautions that one must bring to bear one's ethical and political judgments in assessing novels.[146] From that standpoint, one might criticize Trollope for not paying more attention to the working class or at least note that his omission should definitely not be taken as showing that the poor and uneducated really don't count for much. Nussbaum also says that she is concentrating on Anglo-American novels that have "social and political themes."[147] These, of course, are the kinds of novels that more often than not have a democratic message and effect.[148] Thus, if we begin with a category of novels that are likely to have a liberal (individualistic) democratic message, and we apply an informed moral and political judgment to the novels in question (a judgment that for Nussbaum,[149] as well as for myself, would be liberal and democratic), the novels are likely to contribute to a democratic outlook. But it does not follow that novels in general, or even great realistic novels, will standardly promote liberal, democratic values and create empathy for individuals whose social plight in life is far worse than that of most of the novels' readers. The messages of novels—explicit, implicit, and unintended—are much more variegated.

V. MUSIC AND OTHER PERFORMING ARTS

A. What Is Special about the Performing Arts?

The performing arts differ from literature, painting, and sculpture. Although one can read a play or imagine how written music would sound, a play or piece of composed music is fully realized only if it is performed.[150] Two performances are never identical. As some writers have pointed out, performing arts have a similarity to law, which largely consists of rules to be applied by officials and by private persons. Just as a musical score tells musicians how to perform, legal norms instruct individuals and officials how to behave.

Is it true in law, as in performance, that no two applications will ever be the same? Yes and no. Every human situation is unique; in that sense, no two applications are precisely the same. But what officials do may not differ significantly. If the standard fine for parking next to a fire hydrant is $50, an officer writes a ticket to that effect, and the driver pays, it is a stretch to say that the officer's performance differs relevantly from that of another officer issuing a similar ticket.

But can it be correct that each "standard" performance of Mozart's *Jupiter Symphony* or Shakespeare's *Hamlet* is relevantly different but that standard applications of simple legal norms are not? With a performance of music, nuances in tempo and loudness matter, as do the actors' tones of voice and facial expressions in a play. When a police officer writes a ticket, the size of the letters and how he tucks the ticket under the windshield are legally irrelevant. We can say that many performances in law do not differ because the legal norm calls for a simple set of acts, and the details of how they are carried out are not significant.[151]

Lest it be said that examples of traffic offenses are misleading, because they are such an unimportant part of the law, we may note that for many "law-abiding" citizens, this is the only contact as offenders that they have with officials. More important, traffic tickets, including parking tickets, typify a large number of legal norms that apply straightforwardly.[152] When salaried workers pay income tax according to a standard scale, when tenants pay monthly rent, these also are applications of law.

As with other forms of interpretation, we need to ask how far reflection on performance can illuminate legal interpretation. Jerome Frank, a judge on the Second Circuit Court of Appeals and a leading legal realist, who was the best-known skeptic about legal "facts," compared a performer's interpretation of music with a judge's interpretation of legislation. Frank unambiguously drew one lesson about judicial performance and flirted with another.[153]

Frank relied heavily on the work on Ernst Krenek, a "brilliant modern musical composer," who "criticizes those musical 'purists' who insist on what they call 'work-fidelity.'"[154] According to Krenek, performers who try hard to do everything just as the composer intended fail to do justice to a work's spirit, producing "'an unbearable caricature of the composition,'" as erroneous as the disregard by some romantic interpreters of the composer's aims.[155] Instead, a performer should aim to capture the spirit of a work as filtered through "'the medium of [his] personal life.'"[156] Performers will perform scores somewhat differently, but variant interpretations may be "'equally good . . . and satisfactory.'"[157]

We can reduce Frank's account of Krenek's analysis to the following propositions: (1) Composers cannot completely control musical interpretation; the characteristics of performers *will* influence performance; (2) attempts by performers to stick too doggedly to every aspect of a composer's design produce inferior performances; (3) performers are constrained to a considerable degree by what the composer has written, but they are well advised to reflect a composer's essential objectives rather than replicate each detail of how the composer conceived of his work being played;[158] and (4) the most wholesome outcome is different interpreters playing the same piece of music differently, importing something of their own feelings into their performances.

How do these propositions relate to law? Proposition (1) concerning the inevitable effect of interpreters' personal characteristics is indisputably applicable in some circumstances. When meaning is straightforward in context, vastly different readers arrive at the same understanding of what a legal text requires, although even then judges, as well as juries, may self-consciously or unconsciously determine facts in a way to evade the application of a rule that strikes them as unjust in the circumstances.[159] When meaning becomes debatable, an interpreter's special character may influence judgment.[160] According to Proposition (2), about the undesirability of dogged reproduction of detail, and Proposition (3), about interpretation that aims at essential objectives, judges should not stick slavishly to every literal aspect of statutory language; they should be guided by the spirit of a text. Proposition (4) suggests that wise interpreters of law would not "fight" the subjectivity of their own inclinations but would give them relatively free play.

In Frank's view, differences in legal interpretation are no more avoidable than differences in musical performance.[161] Interpretation is "inescapably a kind of legislation."[162] Sometimes judges should interpret legislation literally, but often that "will yield a grotesque caricature of the legislature's purpose."[163] Judges should cooperate with a legislature by using "their imagination in trying to get at and apply what a legislature really meant, but imperfectly said,"[164] discovering meaning in all parts of a statute, not a single provision.[165] Judicial creativity should be limited, "but, within proper limits, it is a boon, not an evil."[166] Were courts to acknowledge their creative power, they might be more restrained in exercising it.[167]

Frank is much more specific about the restraints on judges than about those on musical performers. If the legislators make plain that they want literal interpretation, judges should follow them.[168] More generally, when the legislature employs relatively precise terms, judges have much less room for creativity than when a statute contains a vague and flexible standard.[169] Judges should adhere to the legislature's polices,[170] eliminating their personal views of policy as far as possible.[171] When they do make value assessments, they should rely on the community's sense of values.

Frank does not quite endorse the desirability of a judge rendering different interpretations of a legal "score," and it is not hard to guess why he hesitated. It is fine if Sir Thomas Beecham plays Mozart symphonies slowly and Arturo Toscanini plays them quickly, if the New York Philharmonic plays them on modern instruments and The English Concert plays them on period instruments. No one suffers (much), and when people become aware of various styles of playing, they can choose the performances they wish to hear. In law, someone is coerced to behave in a particular manner because of the way a judge construes a rule, and the doctrines courts announce serve as precedents for future cases. Although judges can no more run away from their essences than can musical performers, they may need to bring a different attitude to their task. The performer can reflect: "The composition leaves room for individuating interpretation. I will give the best performance of which I am capable if I give voice to my own personal sentiments within the bounds the composer has set." The performer need not ask: "Exactly how would most other competent performers choose to perform this piece?"; or "What reasoned arguments can

I make that my interpretation is more faithful to the original composition than any other interpretation?"[172]

The traditional aspiration for judges has been to decide on the basis of reasons that have persuasive force for other judges. According to this aspiration, a judge should not rest content with deciding according to her deeply held intuitive feelings, as might the performer; the judge must test a tentative answer against the perspectives of other judges and against the power of competing arguments. One who looks at Frank's judicial opinions sees that he did not accept the most radical subjectivist implications of the musical analogy; rather he tried to adopt alternatives called for by the legal materials and he presented reasons that would have persuasive force for other judges. His article presents no argument that this aspiration in law is misguided, however hard it may be to fulfill.

In a striking essay, Sanford Levinson and Jack Balkin concentrate on the passage of time as it affects performance and interpretation.[173] Reviewing essays called *Authenticity and Early Music*,[174] which discuss whether playing music with instruments of the kind used when it was composed is more authentic than using modern instruments, the authors side with essayists who claim that playing on period instruments is not *more* authentic; indeed, they argue, or at least strongly imply, that playing on period instruments is less authentic. It is easy here to see the legal analogy. Interpreting ancient standards in light of modern conditions is more desirable (or more authentic) than trying to preserve their ancient meaning in all its detail.

The authors initially raise two specific questions about modern concert performance that concern following what the composer wrote. Given the inability of pianos of Beethoven's time to reach F-sharp, should a modern pianist play that note in the first piano concerto, because it fits the melody better than the F-natural Beethoven actually wrote? Given the capacity of modern audiences to hear pieces of music many times, should performers decline to play "repeat signs" that Schubert wrote for his late piano sonatas?

Moving to a general thesis, the authors claim that musical performance may be a particularly promising analogy for legal interpretation, because a composer's notations "appear to be law-like commands."[175] "[W]hat is a musical score but a series of *directions* concerning tempo, meter, pitch, rhythm, attack, and orchestration that are to be carried out over time by a group of performers?"[176] They go on, "Just as the music of the *Eroica* is not identical with its score, but needs a performer to realize it, so too the social practice of law is not fully identical with its written texts, but needs the activity of those entrusted with its performance to be realized."[177]

The authors review a range of questions about performance of early music, including the number of instruments and pitch as well as type of instruments. "Woodwinds and horns often sound out of tune, despite the best of intentions and the most skilled players."[178] If a modern instrument can play notes much more accurately than the instrument used at the composer's time, could this possibly be a reason to prefer the old instrument?

More broadly, the aura of the original cannot be re-created. Modern performers cannot replicate early performances.[179] Technical difficulties are only part of the problem. As Morgan writes, "Perhaps even more crucial . . . than original performance inflections is the deeper context in which the works were originally experienced—their status as integral components of a larger cultural environment that has disappeared and is fundamentally irrecoverable."[180] The authors remark on the irony of playing an "authentic" recording of Bach while driving down an interstate highway. They compare the search for old "authenticity" unfavorably with a living tradition, strongly exemplified in jazz, in which a "classic" serves as the basis for new creations by other musicians.[181] Paraphrasing one of the essayists, Levinson and Balkin write, "Authentic performance . . . is a creation of our times, satisfying modern aesthetic preferences which are nonetheless justified and even sanctified by claims of historical accuracy."[182]

Shifting to a wider cultural perspective, the authors assert that the early music movement, in its claim of authenticity, is an "invention of tradition," a "pseudo-traditionalism."[183] They suggest, to oversimplify a rich discussion, that the anxiety of modernity, the sense of isolation and estrangement, leads people to seek a past that has been irrevocably lost.[184] Genuine authenticity involves an organic relation to tradition, but the "more one self-consciously tries to be authentic to a tradition, the less authentic one's practice becomes . . . ."[185] Turning to law, the authors see insistence on original intention as analogous to the "authentic performance" movement; no less than the highly skeptical claims of the critical legal studies movement, it is a response to the anxiety of modernism.

The Levinson-Balkin essay is illuminating both in suggesting an analogy to legal performance in musical performance and in proposing a broad cultural explanation for the attractions of originalism. But we would do well to be cautious both about the debate over "authentic performance" and its relevance for law. At one point, the authors cite an essayist who remarks that performance on original instruments is like putting art into a museum. But what are we to make of this analogy? With plastic arts, as well as music, we can never perceive them as did the audiences for whom they were originally produced. But we can see paintings and sculptures as they were originally done. One genuine reason to restore the painting on the ceiling of the Sistine Chapel to its original colors was that those were the colors Michelangelo had painted. Few would have found persuasive the argument that the painting should not be touched because an organic tradition had developed with the colors becoming darker and darker.[186] We can never perceive what those in Rome of 1512 perceived, but we reasonably would like to see a painting that is as close to what the master painted as possible. Looking at paintings in a museum is not the same as viewing them in an expensive drawing room, but more of us can see a painting in a museum; and, when we do, we prefer the original colors to a discolored version.

Unless these preferences in the plastic arts are misguided, it is a reasonable aspiration to wish to hear musical works more or less as they sounded at the time they were written. It is fanaticism to think that this aspiration should displace hearing the works on modern instruments. But, whatever may be the historical causes of the early instrument movement, one cannot write it off as the false pursuit of an authenticity we cannot have.[187] The issue of whether a performance that self-consciously seeks to produce original sounds is more or less authentic than performance on modern instruments seems idle. Both kinds of performance can be pleasing and valuable.

When we turn to law, matters are different. Judges and other officials choosing how to apply a law cannot say, "Let's do old instruments today and new ones tomorrow," or "You, Judge R, do old instruments and I, Judge S, will do new ones, and we'll have a nice combination."

If we ask whether the law as a total package should be applied as it was understood in the past, or brought up to date in light of modern conditions, the answer is indisputably the latter. Law cannot remain static. But by itself this answer does not assign roles. The interpretive originalist may say: "As far as statutes and constitutions are concerned, let those who adopt and amend them worry about updating. That is not the job of judges." This position may be seriously mistaken (I think it is), and the idea that modern anxiety leads people to wish to recapture the past in various areas of human endeavor, including classical music and law, *may* help to explain why that view is both misguided and attractive. But neither conclusions about the comparative authenticity of performing old music on old and on modern instruments nor cultural explanations for desires to recapture the past can show that originalism in law is a misconceived approach.

The law's aspects of power and coercion distinguish it from musical performances. Levinson's and Balkin's efforts to minimize this difference achieve only modest success. They say that substantial economic consequences, including people's jobs, depend on the popularity of the authentic performance movement.[188] It "has become increasingly clear that many acts of interpretation are performative utterances which simultaneously constitute acts of power."[189]

A narrow way to take this point is that a conductor who decides upon a particular interpretation compels members of his orchestra to play it that way, and he forces those in attendance to listen. We can imagine an unhappy patron complaining, "He forced me to listen to that drivel," but it is hard to think of the patron—free to leave and alerted to avoid similar performances in the future—as being coerced in any serious sense.

Levinson and Balkin seem mainly to have in mind a broader notion of coercion. If a particular type of performance becomes very popular, those who perform differently will lose business. A critic, who may also be a conductor, can generate this effect by successfully arguing that a particular kind of performance is authentic and condemning its opposite. But these analogies to law's coercive character are more remote than close. Within the boundaries of a market economy, performers are free to play as they wish; the audience they attract will depend on the appeal of their performance, which will partly depend on people's sense of how music should be played, which will be influenced by critics. All this is true. But if two performers adopt nearly identical styles, one may be more proficient that the other, or seem more proficient to a critic, and the critic may say so. The performer who is judged inferior loses opportunities, but that does not make coercion a central element of performances or of what critics write. The same is true when performances differ in style rather than competence. The pervasive connection between performance and criticism and economic power hardly establishes that coercion is central to music in the way that it is for law, which informs people that if they keep refusing to act as they are directed, they will have money forcibly taken from them or will be physically confined.

VI. CONCLUSION

The two primary subjects of this chapter have been literary interpretation, in the sense of an account of what a work of literature means, and interpretation involved in performance, whether of musical or dramatic works. Both forms of interpretation involve efforts to attribute meaning and significance to underlying texts, but performers, unlike critics, actually replicate the texts for audiences. Within the law, judges may seem to resemble performers more than critics, although their applications of texts to concrete circumstances are not repetitions of the words of the texts but decisions about what consequences they entail. Legal scholars often aim at recommendations about desirable interpretations, but not all legal scholarship takes that form. Some scholarly explanations and critiques do not focus on how judges might best interpret legal texts.

Our review of theories of interpretation for literature and musical performance highlights two of the basic themes that apply to law: how much is interpretation discovery of something already created, how much does it involve creative input by the interpreter; how far is meaning or desirable performance determined by the intentions of the writer of the text. In respect to these questions, literary, dramatic, and musical interpretation can enrich our breadth of vision and suggest interesting analogies for thought about law, but they do not yield definitive conclusions that carry over in some straightforward way to legal interpretation. Decisions about how to interpret legal texts depend heavily on the nature of law itself and on the best roles for particular actors within any legal system.

Additional sections of this chapter have focused on how methods of interpretation like those proposed for literature relate to the interpretation of scholarship, and how judges (and legislators) may benefit from reading literature. Both subjects have an evident bearing on how legal interpretation may best proceed; although what judges may learn well from literature is only one element of what they need to appreciate, and how legal texts should be interpreted is different from and more complex than desirable approaches to interpreting scholarly work.

In the chapter to follow, we will look at texts that in many respects lie closer to those of the law but have their own very special aspects.

Notes

1 Other domains within the general field of law and literature are: 1) the law that relates particularly to literature (such as copyright and freedom of speech); 2) literature about legal institutions that illuminates their nature and may provide a basis for criticism; 3) the relevance of stories within the law as a basis for understanding the scope of legal rules; 4) the use of rhetoric in legal writing and law read as literature. This chapter has nothing to say about the law that relates to literature and mentions the other three subjects only fleetingly. The relevance of stories within law is treated as one issue about Jewish law in the next chapter.

2 E.D. Hirsch, Jr., *Validity in Interpretation* 202 (New Haven, Yale University Pr. 1967). See also Sanford Levinson and J.M. Balkin, "Law, Music, and Other Performing Arts," 139 *University of Pennsylvania Law Review* 1597, 1604 (1991), suggesting that according to a tradition identified with Wittgenstein and his successors, there are only diverse "practices" of interpretation.

3 Gregory Castle, *The Blackwell Guide to Literary Theory* 2 (Oxford, Blackwell Publishers, 2007).

4 Jonathan Culler, *The Literary in Theory* 231–232 (Stanford, Cal., Stanford University Pr., 2007). For a similar comment that distinguishes anthropology from legitimation and includes legal theory, see Levinson and Balkin, note 2 supra, at 1655, n.232.

5 That such an effort is futile is strongly advocated by Terry Eagleton, *Literary Theory: An Introduction* 1–16 (2d ed. Minneapolis, University of Minnesota Pr., 1996). Richard A. Posner, *Law and Literature* 11 (Rev. ed., Cambridge, Mass., Harvard University Press 1998), suggests that survival in the literary "marketplace" is our only basis for classifying literature as great.

6 Ludwig Wittgenstein, *Philosophical Investigations*, §§ 66–67 (G.E.M. Anscombe trans., 3rd ed., New York, Macmillan, 1958).

7 Jane B. Baron, "Law, Literature, and the Problems of Interdisciplinarity," 108 *Yale Law Journal* 1059 (1999).

8 In *Heracles' Bow* xi (Madison, University of Wisconsin Press, 1985), he writes that "the activity of law is at heart a literary one . . . ."

9 Baron, note 6 supra, at 1078–79, 1084.

10 Ronald Dworkin, *Law's Empire* 49–53 and passim (Cambridge, Mass., Harvard University Press 1986).

11 Prominently these include theories of domination according to class, race, and gender.

12 Castle, note 3 supra, at 11.

13 See Ferdinand de Saussure, *Course in General Linguistics* (London, Peter Owen 1979).

14 My example oversimplifies by disregarding the degree to which English gets its words from other languages in which the meaning of particular words is already established.

15 See Wittgenstein, note 6 supra.

16 Eagleton, note 5 supra at 60. The exaggeration, as I see it, is in failing to recognize that some experiences need not involve language (although an account of them would necessarily do so). I have in mind particularly, experiences of acute physical pain and some pleasurable sensations from physical exercise. Drawing from the work of Suzanne Langer, Jerome Frank claimed that language is a poor medium to express the complexities of emotions. Jerome Frank, "Say It with Music," 61 *Harvard Law Review* 921, 932 (1948).

17 Culler, note 4 supra, at 120.

18 J. L. Austin, *How to Do Things with Words* (2nd ed., J.O. Urmson and M. Sbisà, eds., Cambridge, Mass., Harvard University Press, 1975).

19 Id. at 4–7.

20 Id. at 91–108.

21 Id. at 101–04.

22 See G. Warnock, "Some Types of Performative Utterance," in Isaiah Berlin et al., eds., *Essays on J.L. Austin* 69 (London, Oxford University Press, Clarendon Press, 1973). Elsewhere I have claimed that recognition of this reality helps clarify what language is properly regarded as speech under the First Amendment. Kent Greenawalt, *Speech, Crime, and the Uses of Language* 57–76 (New York, Oxford University Press, 1989).

23 Austin, note 18 supra, at 22.

24 See Judith Butler, *Bodies That Matter: On The Discursive Limits of "Sex"* 225–35 (New York, Routledge, 1993).

25 Irving Goffman, *The Presentation of the Self in Everyday Life* xi (1956; repr., New York, Doubleday, 1959).

26 Judith Butler, *Gender Trouble: Feminism and the Subversion of Identity* x, xxviii (New York, Routledge, 1990). See Culler, note 4 supra, at 137–40, 156–59.

27 Sanford Levinson, "Law as Literature," 60 *Texas Law Review* 373, 376 (1982).

28 One of my sons asked me recently if I felt less masculine when walking a friend's female miniature poodle.

29 E.D. Hirsch, Jr., *The Aims of Interpretation* 1–12 (Chicago, University of Chicago Pr. 1976). Thus, in answer to the assertion of I. A. Richards, *Principles of Literary Criticism* 226 (4th ed., San Diego, Harvest/Harcourt Brace Jovanovich Pub., 1930), that a poem cannot be defined as the artist's experience, since only the artist has that experience, Hirsch would respond that most elements of the artist's experience involve significance, not meaning. For more recent defenses of an intentionalist position, see Noël Carroll, "The Intentional Fallacy: Defending Myself," 55 *Journal of Aesthetics and Art Criticism* 245 (1997); Noël Carroll, "Interpretation and Intention: The Debate Between Hypothetical and Actual Intentionalism," 31 *Metaphilosophy* 75 (2000); Gary Iseminger, "Actual Intentionalism vs. Hypothetical Intentionalism," 54 *Journal of Aesthetics and Art Criticism* 319 (1996).

30 E.D. Hirsch Jr., note 2 supra, at 9.

31 Hirsch, note 29 supra, at 3.

32 Letter VI, Pensées and The Provincial Letters 388–90 (New York, Modern Library, 1941).

33 E.g., Eagleton, note 5 supra, at 69–70.

34 Hirsch, note 2 supra, at 54.

35 See Hirsch, note 2 supra, at 14, 174; Hirsch, note 29 supra, at 71.

36 Hirsch, note 2 supra, at 43.

37 Hirsch, note 29 supra, at 82.

38 Hirsch, note 2 supra, at 29. See Carroll, "Interpretation and Intention," note 29 supra, at 76–77.

39 Hirsch, note 2 supra, at 47.

40 That intention might be discoverable by independent means—as when the speaker later says, "I slipped," or "I now realize I completely misunderstood the meaning of that word."

41 Hirsch, note 29 supra, at 83–92.

42 Id. at 90–92. For a modern view emphasizing respect for the intentions of writers and artists, see Carroll, note 38 supra, at 75.

43 William Tolhurst, "On What a Text Is and How It Means," 19 *British Journal of Aesthetics* 3, 13 (1979); Jerold Levinson, "Intention and Interpretation in Literature," in *Aesthetics and the Philosophy of Art* 200–22 (1996, reprinted in Peter Lamarque and Stein Olsen, eds., Blackwell 2004) (1996); see Alexander Nehamas, "Writer, Text, Work, Author," in *Literature and the Question of Philosophy* (Anthony Cascardi, ed., Baltimore, Johns Hopkins University Press, 1987).

44 A different conception of a hypothetical or implied author is one that builds from the text alone.

45 Wolfgang Iser, *The Implied Reader: Patterns of Communication in Prose Fiction from Bunyan to Beckett* 274 (Baltimore, Johns Hopkins University Press, 1974).

46 Id. at 275.

47 Id. at 276.

48 Id. at 280. When we read books a second time, the time sequence of the first reading is unrepeatable, and this modifies the reading experience for any individual.

49 Id. at 281.

50 Id. at 283.

51 Id. at 287.

52 Id. at 292. That is why readers' relations with literary texts have so often been misconceived as identification.

53 See Ronald Dworkin, "Law as Interpretation," 60 *Texas Law Review* 527, 531 (1982).

54 See Richard H. Weisberg, "How Judges Speak: Some Lessons on Adjudication in *Billy Budd, Sailor* with an Application to Justice Rehnquist," 57 *New York University Law Review* 1 (1982). Weisberg defends his account in *Poethics, And Other Strategies of Law and Literature* 104–16 (New York, Columbia University Press 1992) against the challenge, among others, of Richard Posner, note 5 supra, at 165–73. I believe critics rarely do adopt conflicting positions, unless they have changed their minds. Perhaps this shows that any actual reader is drawn to an interpretation that seems best overall in some sense, but, in contrast with the legal analogue, I see no reason why a critic is constrained to adopt this attitude. And I disagree with Dworkin's assumption that the standard of "best" is what makes something the "best work of art" according to aesthetic criteria. See text following note 41, supra.

55 Stanley Fish, *Is There a Text in This Class? The Authority of Interpretive Communities* (Cambridge, Mass., Harvard University Press, 1980); Fish, *Doing What Comes Naturally* (Durham, North Carolina, Duke University Press, 1989).

For one legal theorist's account, which puts an emphasis on disciplinary rules that Fish regards as misconceived (*Doing What Comes Naturally* at 120–40), see Owen M. Fiss, "Objectivity and Interpretation," 34 *Stanford Law Review* 739 (1982). In the volume on constitutional law, we will look at Fish's theory in more detail.

56 Their readings may be influenced to a degree by progressively vague recollections of what they were taught in high school or college courses in literature.

57 See Monroe Beardsley and William K. Winsatt, "The Intentional Fallacy" (1946), reprinted in *Philosophy Looks at the Arts* (Joseph Margolis ed., Philadelphia, Temple University Press, 1987) (1946); Monroe Beardsley, "Intentions and Interpretations: A Fallacy Revisited," in *Aesthetics and the Philosophy of Art* 193 (Peter Lamarque and Stein Olsen, eds., Oxford, Blackwell, 2004) (1982). Beardsley distinguished literature from ordinary acts of speaking and writing.

58 John Crowe Ranson, *The New Criticism* 128 (Norfolk, New Directions, 1941).

59 Eagleton, note 5 supra, at 46, 48, 49.

60 Mark Schorer, "An Indignant and Prophetic Novel," *The New York Times Book Review*, June 12, 1949, in *Nineteen Eighty-Four to 1984*, p. 146 (New York, Carroll and Graf Press, 1984).

61 Ann Jefferson, in Ann Jefferson and David Robey, eds., *Modern Literary Theory* 92, 95 (London, B.T. Batsford Ltd., 1986), says that "the structuralist approach sets aside all questions of content." See Eagleton, note 5 supra, at 94.

62 Id. at 128. See Jonathan Culler, *On Deconstruction: Theory and Criticism after Structuralism* 22 (Ithaca, Cornell University Press, 1982).

63 J.M. Balkin, "Nested Oppositions" (Reviewing John M. Ellis, *Against Deconstruction*), 99 *Yale Law Journal* 1669 (1990).

64 For a brief explanation by him, see his Letter to a Japanese Friend, reprinted in Jonathan Culler, ed., *Deconstruction*, Vol. 1, 23–27 (London, Routledge, 2003). A much more extensive development is in Jacques Derrida, *Of Grammatology* (Baltimore, Md., Johns Hopkins University Press, 1976).

65 Jefferson, note 61 supra, at 113.

66 Id. at 114.

67 See Jonathan Culler, "Critical Consequences," in Culler, note 64 supra, Vol. II at 38, 63, on Derrida's reading of Rousseau and Paul de Man's critique of that reading.

68 Barbara Johnson, "Teaching Deconstructively," reprinted in Culler, note 64 supra, Vol. II, at 204. Jefferson, note 61 supra, at 118, writes in a similar vein, "A deconstructive reading tries to bring out the logic of the text's language as opposed to the logic of its author's claims. It will tease out the text's implied presuppositions and point out the (inevitable) contradictions in them."

69 Culler, note 67 supra, at 35.

70 Balkin, note 63, supra, at 1676.

71 Id.

72 Id.

73 While crediting Balkin with a "cute phrase," Richard Posner, note 5 supra, at 215–16, suggests that the main aspects of Balkin's claim "were commonplaces of tort scholarship when Balkin was in high school." Of course, insofar as that critique is accurate, the insights are already grasped by those working in the law.

74 Cardozo, *The Growth of the Law*, (New Haven, Yale University Press 1924), reprinted in *Selected Writings of Benjamin Nathan Cardozo* 225 (New York, Fallon Publications 1947).

75 Weisberg, *Poethics*, note 54 supra, at 6–34.

76 Ferguson, "The Judicial Opinion as Literary Genre," 2 *Yale Journal of Law and Humanities* 201 (1990).

77 One notable illustration is Roberto Mangabeira Ungar, *Knowledge and Politics* (New York, Free Press, 1975).

78 One might, of course, still believe a different political order could be preferable to the present one. Concern about challenges that undermine the idea that texts have meaning and stress persuasive indeterminacy are not limited to critics from the right. Robin West has warned that the "indeterminacy thesis" "undercuts the possibility of cultural or social criticism of any sort." *Narrative, Authority, and Law* 16 (Ann Arbor, University of Michigan Press, 1993).

Just how far the thesis of legal indeterminacy represents a challenge to the value of Critical Legal Studies is discussed in Guyora Binder, "Beyond Criticism," 55 *University of Chicago Law Review* 888 (1988), and in Robert Weisberg, "Reading Poethics," 15 *Cardozo Law Review* 1103, 1120–23 (1994).

79 Posner, note 5 supra, at 239, emphasizes that, given statutes written in haste by busy people with diverse objectives, one should not pay attention to every detail and should expect repetitions and inconsistencies.

80 Bray Hammond, *Banks and Politics in America: From the Revolution to the Civil War* 120 (Princeton, N.J., Princeton University Press, 1957), quoted in Levinson, note 27 supra, at 399.

81 Jonathan Culler, note 4 supra, at 174–76, makes this illuminating distinction in commenting on Toni Morrison's interpretation of Ernest Hemingway's *The Garden of Eden* as shaped by Africanism.

82 Carol Gilligan, *In a Different Voice: Psychological Theory and Women's Development* (Cambridge, Mass., Harvard University Press 1982, 1993).

83 Mary Joe Frug, *Postmodern Legal Feminism* (New York, Routledge, 1992).

84 Gilligan, note 82 supra, at 2, specifically eschews any claims "about the origins of the differences described or their distribution in a wider population, across cultures, or through time."

85 Frug, note 83 supra, at 38–39.

86 Id. at 39.

87 Id. at 40.

88 Id. at 43.

89 Id. at 45–48. She reaches her conclusion after analyzing a conservative reading by Susannah Sherry. Sherry herself does not believe such a reading justifies socially conservative results.

90 Id. at 48.

91 In a Letter to Readers in her reissued book, at xiii (published after Frug's book), Professor Gilligan says that "whether women and men are essentially different or who is better than whom . . . are not my questions." Nevertheless, one aspect of the original book is to counter arguments that an ethics of care is on some scale inferior, a sign of less maturity, than an ethics of rights, and in some passages, Gilligan seems to incline toward an ethics of care as more humane.

92 In her third paragraph, id. at 2, Gilligan writes, "The different voice I describe is characterized not by gender but theme. Its association with women is an empirical observation, and it is primarily through women's voices that I trace its development. But this association is not absolute, and the contrasts between male and female voices are presented here to highlight a distinction between two modes of thought and to focus on a problem of interpretation rather than to represent a generalization about either sex."

93 In the passage quoted in note 92, she specifically states that "the association is not absolute."

94 This claim that would be satisfied if, say, 80% of women and 20% of men exhibited the ethics of care and 80% of men and 20% of women exhibited an ethics of rights. One aspect of some of her studies, which she acknowledges, is that they involved girls and young women who were mainly from relatively affluent families; but she does not suggest she thinks it likely that an ethics of care would be much less common among other groups of women. My own guess would be that the ethics of rights might be more common among men of the same social class than among all American men, since I think advanced education tends to develop such ethics.

95 Not having done academic research on the topic, but having been married during my life's most important years to a woman from a different cultural background (a mix of Serbian and Croatian, which we then considered Yugoslav), I believe there are significant cultural differences in ethical approaches that could be fitted along Gilligan's categories.

96 In Gilligan, note 87 supra, at 6, she does mention that language is not neutral, "that the categories of knowledge are human constructions."

97 In her 1993 letter, id. at xix, Gilligan is "deeply disturbed" by the posing of the question of biology versus social construction, because the question itself implies that all of us are "without voice," without opportunity for resistance and change.

98 She was a classmate of mine at Swarthmore with whom I have had limited contact since our graduation, including hearing her talk about her work at a 2008 reunion.

99 With judicial opinions, especially those written for a majority, I would suppose that significant divergences between an author's intent and the implications of the text are much more common.

100 Frug, note 83 supra, at 43.

101 A text may definitely say two things that are directly and obviously at odds with each other. In that circumstance, the text as a whole may not assert either thing.

102 It is often thought that charity in interpretation involves taking what someone says, when the matter is in doubt, in the way that coheres best with what is true or sound. That is fine if otherwise it is a real toss-up between two possibilities. But what is the interpreter to do if he thinks that the author probably (85% probability) had in mind the less sound idea, though he might have meant (15% probability) the more sound idea. I would want an interpreter of my work to concentrate first on what seems more likely in relation to my expressed ideas.

103 But, see note 99 supra in respect to judicial opinions. For majority opinions at least, the text typically matters much more than the individual writer's intentions.

104 See, e.g., White, *Heracles' Bow*, note 8 supra; Ferguson, note 76 supra. Robin West, note 78 supra, at 434–35, has suggested how the use or neglect of narrative by the opinions' authors can affect one's reaction to the results of cases affirming imposition of the death penalty.

105 Among the many examples are Melville's *Billy Budd*, Dostoevski's *Brothers Karamozov*, Mark Twain's *Pudd'nhead Wilson*, and more recently, Tom Wolfe's *Bonfire of the Vanities*.

106 Robin West, note 78 supra, at 27–87, reads Kafka as showing the poverty of Richard Posner's economic approach, according to which consensual transactions

are crucial to human satisfaction. Posner's response is in Posner, note 5 supra, at 182–205.

107 As note 54, supra, indicates, there is sharp disagreement over how to understand *Billy Budd*. Barbara Johnson provides a deconstructivist account emphasizing internal tensions, in "Melville's Fist," in Culler, note 64 supra, at 213–43. Richard Weisberg and Richard Posner have sharply contrasting views about how to understand the legal proceedings in *The Brothers Karamazov*, Weisberg, *The Failure of the Word* 45–81 (New Haven, Yale University Press, 1984); Weisberg, *Poethics*, note 54 supra, at 198–200, Posner, note 5 supra, at 173–78.

108 The influential work of James Boyd White has focused on a somewhat different aspect: the complexities and ambiguities of language and of life that help participants understand law as a form of discourse of possibilities from which community may emerge. See, e.g., *Justice as Translation* (Chicago, University of Chicago Press, 1990); *Heracles' Bow*, note 8 supra.

109 Martha C. Nussbaum, *Poetic Justice* 8 (Boston, Beacon Press, 1995).

110 The interpretation would not need to be self-conscious and the acceptance could be more emotional than intellectual.

111 A novel might have a valuable significance for a reader that goes beyond a meaning residing in the text itself or in the writer's intentions. Nussbaum's treatment is one illustration of how blurry the line can be that distinguishes interpretation of meaning from significance that goes beyond interpretation. That distinction does not figure in Nussbaum's claims, and I pay slight attention to it in this section of the chapter.

112 The income tax code, for example, although it does contain some acknowledgment of variations in circumstances, necessarily falls far short of individualization.

113 Id. at 1–52.

114 Id. at 47. One would need to know more about what Stigler means here by "the principles of economics" to evaluate how far he is oversimplifying and flattening reality. Richard Posner, perhaps the leading proponent over the years of an economic approach to legal problems, has written, note 5 supra, at 319, that "as a tract against economic thinking" *Hard Times* "is shallow and easily refuted," because no economist falls into Gradgrind's approach to life.

115 Nussbaum, note 109 supra, at 65–67.

116 Id. at 53–70.

117 Id. at 72–74.

118 Id. at 73. A judge should feel the kind of anger that one feels when others are badly treated, not the anger engendered by oneself being the victim of bad treatment.

119 Id. at 75. A somewhat similar theme is developed in West, note 78 supra, at 7, 258, who writes of the value of metaphor and narrative in creating an empathetic bridge to the lives of others.

120 Amnon Reichman, "Law, Literature, and Empathy: Between Withholding and Reserving Judgment," 56 *Journal of Legal Education* 296, 297 (2006).

121 Id. at 305.

122 Martha Nussbaum, "Reply to Amnon Reichman," 56 *American Journal of Legal Education* 320 (2006).

123 Nussbaum, note 109 supra, at 99–118. We need to recognize here a distinction between bases for judgment and qualities of opinions. An individual judge might be fully responsive to literary aspects and yet write (or join) a bland opinion

that did not reflect that, something one would guess is fairly frequent when opinions are written for a court's majority (and even more frequent in the style of opinion writing found in the civil law tradition). Conversely, a judge might be woodenly blind to the appeal of literature as it affects law and yet marshal literary language in support of her conclusion. Nussbaum's main concern in the book is how judges (and others) reach decisions, not the style by which they defend them; but she reasonably assumes in her three case studies that a judge whose opinion reflects a literary approach to a case has also decided in that light.

124 478 U.S. 186 (1986), considered in Nussbaum, note 109 supra, at 111–17.

125 Lawrence v. Texas, 539 U.S. 558, 578 (2003).

126 Discussed in Nussbaum, note 109 supra, at 97–98.

127 Hudson v. Palmer, 468 U.S. 517 (1984).

128 Martha Nussbaum, *Upheavals of Thought: A Theory of the Emotions* (Cambridge, Cambridge University Press, 1997), has a more extensive treatment of the subject, including consideration of situations in which we initially feel anger at people who are not to blame, at 28–29, and experience emotional responses to music, at 249 ff. Despite her analysis of these complexities, I am left with the sense that she thinks emotions are more closely linked to beliefs than I do.

129 Nussbaum, supra note 109, at 5.

130 The empathy that a male reader of pornography might feel for a violent male character who is beating up a woman lacks all value, she writes. Nussbaum, note 122 supra, at 327.

131 Id. at 325. She rejects Aristotle's notion that perceived similarity is necessary for compassion. Id. at 326. I am doubtful that the distinction between the conditions necessary, respectively, for empathy and compassion is as sharp as Nussbaum suggests. We assume that the animals for whom we feel compassion do have experiences of pain and loss not wholly unlike ours. I am not sure whether people can experience compassion for plants, cars, and dolls without investing those objects with feelings somewhat like our own.

132 Richard Wright, *Native Son* (The Restored Text Established by the Library of America) (New York, HarperCollins, 1993).

133 Richard Wright, *Black Boy* (The Restored Text Established by the Library of America) (New York, HarperCollins, 1993). The original published version of *Black Boy* omitted Wright's account of his time in the North, entitled *The Horror and the Glory*.

134 Claude Brown, *Manchild in the Promised* Land (New York, Touchstone, 1993).

135 Alex Haley and Malcolm X, *The Autobiography of Malcolm X* (New York, Grove Press, 1965).

136 A friend has recently said that were she to have read in fiction the life biographer Janet Wallach described in *Desert Queen* (New York, Doubleday 1996), she would have strongly doubted that any real woman could have done what Gertrude Bell did.

137 Nussbaum, note 122 supra, at 328.

138 *Native Son*, note 132 supra, at 114.

139 Id. at 239.

140 Although racial oppression is never absent from Wright's northern experience, much of that part of his autobiography focuses on the difficulties for writers inclined to independent thought who were members of the Communist Party.

141 When in the summer of 1965 I spent some time doing civil rights legal work in Jackson, Mississippi, I was struck by how friendly blacks were to whites. *Black*

Boy would have made me realize that some of that (perhaps a great deal) was protective cover.

142 Nussbaum, note 109 supra. It may be relevant here that various critics have believed that Wright's construction of *Black Boy* may have strayed from a representation of the actual events of his life. See, e.g., Yoshinobu Hakutani, "Creation of the Self in Richard Wright's *Black Boy*," in William L. Andrews and Douglas Taylor, *Richard Wright's Black Boy (A Casebook)* 131 (New York, Oxford University Press, 2003).

143 One might, of course, make the same comment about the lives of many business leaders and professors.

144 Nussbaum, note 109 supra, at 45, 70 (referring to Lionel Trilling's claim that the novel's vision of community is liberal).

145 Trollope, *Barchester Towers* (New York, Oxford University Press, 1953).

146 Nussbaum, note 109 supra, at 10. Robert Weisberg, note 78 supra, at 1110, writes that "highly poetic descriptions [may] distort the moral realities in insidious ways."

147 Id.

148 However, one would need to count *Atlas Shrugged*, which has an explicitly libertarian message, and various novels that supported racial segregation, including Thomas Dixon's *The Clansman*, the novel from which the movie *Birth of a Nation* was drawn.

149 Nussbaum draws significantly on Walt Whitman's generous and tolerant democratic vision. Note 109 supra, at 80–82, 118–21.

150 Jerome Frank, in "Words and Music: Some Remarks on Statutory Interpretation," 47 *Columbia Law Review* 1259, 1264 (1947), quotes a musical scholar who says that "music does not exist until it is performed."

151 One might resist this conclusion by regarding the subject of a law as an audience for official performance (or as another performer). (On the notion that all legal actors, including ordinary citizens, are engaged in performances, see Levinson and Balkin, note 2 supra, at 1657–58.) The total experience of a motorist personally receiving a ticket for a moving violation will depend on how the officer behaves, and on the age, gender, and ethnic background of the two. But these differences, unlike analogous ones in music and plays, have nothing to do with how the law is interpreted.

152 That speed limits confer on officers extreme discretion about whom to stop is a serious problem, but it is not one about interpreting the limit the legislature has set.

153 Frank, note 150 supra.

154 Id., at 1260, quoting Krenek without specific citation. In footnote 9, id., Frank refers to Krenek's *Music Here and Now* (New York, W.V. Norton 1939) and his "Composer and the Interpreter," 3 *Black Mountain College Bulletin* (1944).

155 Id. at 1261, quoting Krenek. Wagner was so disappointed with interpreters who tried to follow his metronomic markings too faithfully that he decided to dispense with such markings.

156 Id., quoting Krenek.

157 Id., quoting Krenek.

158 Frank does not concern himself, nor need we, with how much study performers should devote to the background of works or with exactly what aspects of musical interpretation are left free and what aspects are best resolved for all performers by the composer. Many classical composers leave space for cadenzas

that performers develop; but should performers regard themselves as free to alter rhythms the composer has noted or to deviate from the actual notes the composer has written, if the spirit moves them or if they think that some other notes are obviously superior? (Sanford Levinson and Jack Balkin discuss the propriety of playing a note that Beethoven probably would have written had pianos of his time been capable of playing it. Note 2 supra, at 1598–99.)

159 See Frank, note 16 supra, at 927–29.

160 A performer's personal character may always influence musical performance to some degree; that may not be true of all "either-or" interpretive judgments in law, though the quality of any written opinion reflects its author.

161 Frank, note 150 supra, at 1267.

162 Id. at 1269. Frank quotes Bishop Hoadly's famous utterance, "[W]hoever hath absolute authority to interpret any . . . laws, it is he who is truly the Law Giver."

163 See id. at 1262.

164 Id. at 1263.

165 See id. at 1267 (referring to Gestalt psychology).

166 Id. at 1264.

167 Id. at 1271.

168 See id. at 1267. Interestingly, Frank says that composers can give similar directions, and describes Stravinsky as asking his interpreters "to be wholly unimaginative." Id. Stravinsky's approach is more fully explained in Levinson and Balkin, note 2 supra, at 1641–43.

169 See Frank, supra note 150, at 1259, 1263, 1266.

170 See id. at 1263–64.

171 See id. at 1267.

172 Of course, some interpretations may be "off the wall," and reasoned argument may explain why these are not good. Musical performers who devote substantial study to the origin of a work and its evolution in prior performances may consider interpretations unacceptable that would not seem to be so for someone who reads a score for the first time. The critical point is not the breadth of the range of performances that are "equally good," but that some significant range of this sort exists.

173 Note 2, supra.

174 N. Kenyon, ed., *Authenticity and Early Music* (Oxford, Oxford University Press, 1988).

175 Id. at 1608. The authors characterize their interest as in the theory of interpreting commands, id. at 1602, and note that both Richard Posner and Robin West conceive interpretation of authoritative legal texts as discerning the meaning of commands. Id. at 1607.

176 Id.

177 Id. at 1609.

178 I once heard one of Mozart's horn concertos played on a valveless horn. As unmusical as I am, it struck me that soloist missed an astonishing number of the correct notes.

179 Id. at 1621.

180 Id.

181 Id. at 1623.

182 Id. at 1626.

183 Id. at 1627.

184 Id. at 1630–31, relying on the work of Eric Hobsbawn.

185 Id. at 1633.

186 However, restoration was opposed on the ground that it would eliminate layers of paint that were important to the painting's quality.

187 Some passages suggest that Levinson and Balkin are criticizing the playing of music on old instruments, as well as challenging exaggerated claims that such performances represent the one true way to perform ancient works.

188 Id. at 1610–14.

189 Id. at 1613.

Chapter 4

Religious Interpretation

I. INTRODUCTION

In this chapter we turn to a form of interpretation that has received less attention from modern legal scholars than literary interpretation but is in crucial aspects more closely analogous to legal interpretation. A significant amount of religious interpretation concerns texts that, unlike literary works, explicitly address how people should behave, carrying direct normative authority as do ordinary legal texts.

Those within religious communities interpret both authoritative texts and broader traditions. Although they often aspire to receive deeper guidance or insight, they also aim to determine the acceptability of various actions. As with other kinds of interpretation, by examining methods of religious interpretation, we can perceive interesting analogies to nonreligious interpretation; and comparisons between the two can enahnce our understanding of both. In contrast to literary interpretation, some forms of interpretation of religious texts replicate closely standard techniques used in secular legal systems.

When a religious tradition treats as sacred ancient texts whose most straightforward meaning is in tension with modern beliefs and practices, interpreters face a problem similar to that facing judges who interpret enduring constitutions: how to create continuity over time when patterns of life and informal social norms shift but basic authoritative textual sources remain constant. Like those interpreting secular law, interpreters within a religious tradition seek consistency among texts that point in different directions. And they may look for standards for behavior that are sufficiently clear both to guide individuals and be administered by those who review what individuals have done.

Certain aspects of much religious interpretation—including the status typically assigned to authoritative texts—distinguish it from nonreligious interpretation and limit the assistance it can give in choosing an exact set of strategies for interpreters of secular law. Still, examination of religious interpretation can reveal strengths and weaknesses of certain approaches, and it powerfully suggests the inevitability of some evolution over time.

Because authoritative religious texts are themselves so varied and are understood in such radically different ways, it helps at the outset to sketch some crucial differences and explain how these matter in relation to the ordinary law with which we are familiar.

The Hebrew Bible and the Quran both contain significant amounts of law-like material, setting out specific standards for behavior. In earlier eras, standards drawn from these and related sources formed much of the legal rules that governed actual societies. Even now, in some Muslim countries, the Quran and other sources of Islamic law are accepted as guides for what the enforceable law of the governments should be; and the relevance of traditional Jewish law continues to a degree within the state of Israel. Interpretation of concrete standards in religious texts, designed to discern what behavior is prohibited, required, or permissible, can be an exercise similar to secular legal interpretation, and we should not be surprised to find common interpretive techniques. What differs from ordinary law is the ancientness of many texts, their perceived religious authority, the common search for multiple levels of meaning, and the possibility that some of the interpretations of the texts may themselves carry religious authority.

The New Testament of Christians has very little specification of behavior of the sort one would expect in a legal system. Of course, Christians accept what they call the Old Testament as authoritative in a sense, but from the time of Paul,[1] the standard view has been that in Jesus, God freed people from the constraints of Judaic law, insofar as that law reaches beyond basic moral requirements of the kind contained in the Ten Commandments, such as the prohibitions of murder and theft. Thus, most of the specific behavioral requirements in the Torah, the early books of the Hebrew Bible, and in the oral part of Jewish law, are now regarded as irrelevant for Christian life. Although certain passages in the New Testament, such as the suggestion by Jesus that divorce is wrongful,[2] have been taken as guides for actual legal prohibitions, most of the normative material, including injunctions that one turn the other cheek, love one's enemies, and not judge others,[3] does not translate into specific legal requirements, although these biblical ideals of conduct can indirectly affect legislative decisions.

In various ways the New Testament is taken as a fundamental guide to how we should understand human existence and lead our lives. Much of the Hebrew Bible and Quran, in addition to what they prescribe about specific behavior, have a similar import. Insofar as the interpretation of religious texts focuses on these broader themes, the objectives bear little resemblance to the reasons to discern the meaning of ordinary legal texts; but such interpretation may shed light on the understanding of broad constitutional norms that mirror attitudes about a just society, and it may tell us something about how interpreters try to preserve continuity during historical change.

As with literary criticism and performance art, appropriate techniques of interpretation are a central issue for religious texts. For religious interpretation, questions also arise about authoritative texts and interpreters that bear some resemblance to problems about secular law. As we proceed in more detail in this chapter, we need to keep in mind the range of ways in which religious interpretation might be instructive about interpretation within our legal order.

This chapter is limited in its ambitions. In Judaism, Christianity, and Islam, the interpretation of sacred texts has played a major role. In other leading world religions, that is less important. Even within these three religions, textual interpretation is only one source of insight. Many believers think responses to prayer and other forms of direct inspiration yield insights from God. Within the Christian natural law tradition—particularly prominent among Roman Catholics—rational reflection on human experience is taken as a crucial ground for understanding. An inclusive notion of interpretation could encompass both how people understand what they take as direct personal inspiration and their reasoned reflection on the human condition.

This chapter restricts itself here to the interpretation of texts and to other ideas formulated in language. My discussion of Jewish and Muslim interpretation concentrates on how sources that deal with legal issues are treated. This is partly because the relevant texts are much more legalistic than the texts that are peculiarly Christian. It is also because their law is a crucial component of the identity of Jewish and Islamic cultures. When I treat Christian interpretation, I cover much broader aspects of religious interpretation, ones that reach well beyond law-like texts.

Because the whole of religious interpretation concerns itself with the character of God, the origin of the universe, the nature of physical reality, the possibility of life after death, how human beings should conduct themselves in relation to God, and many other subjects, concentrating as heavily as I do on the moral and political dimensions of religious interpretation involves a degree of distortion. Even in respect to those dimensions, most religious outlooks include a significant transcendent element thought to pervade authoritative texts. I assume that within most modern legal systems, judges should not rely directly on particular religious premises, such as the truth of Scripture.[4] It is a critical question how far any interpretation that puts God at the center of beliefs and practices can illuminate understanding of secular (nonreligious) systems and inform interpretive choices within these systems.

The main topic of this chapter is how religious texts are interpreted. I preface that discussion by briefly exploring two related topics that are also relevant for ordinary law: (1) What count as authoritative or canonical texts to be interpreted?, (2) Who can render authoritative or reliable interpretations? The subject of this chapter is vast, covering interpretation of religious sources that has gone on for over 2000 years. My selective comments cover much that is illuminating for a comparison with modern secular law, but they leave untouched other important topics and omit many nuances and controversies.

II. WHAT IS TO BE INTERPRETED?

Within major religious traditions, as well as within secular law, certain texts are treated as especially authoritative. Other materials have interpretive relevance. Because the status of various sources is closely related to methods of interpretation, the discussion here is partly a preliminary to the inquiry about methods. It is also a reflection about possible analogies between particular religious perspectives and the status of the materials that underlie secular legal interpretation.

For Jews, the religious texts with special authority are the Hebrew Bible and representations of the Oral Law and Tradition contained in the Talmud. For Christians, the New Testament is added to the Hebrew Bible. For Muslims, the Quran, complemented by the Sunna, reports of the prophet's activities, has overarching authority. In all three instances, this authority goes beyond a recognition that the texts are particularly reliable or insightful, they are regarded as binding on the people to whom they apply.[5]

What is the significance of a text being part of the "canon" and how is it determined what is within the canon? The simplest division is between what lies within and what is rejected. At the time of the early Christian church, a number of accounts of the life of Jesus and his spiritual message circulated. The emerging church leaders declared some of these to be authoritative, mainly the four gospels of Matthew, Mark, Luke, and John, and the letters of Paul. Others, including the "Gospel of Thomas" and other "Gnostic" writings, were declared heretical and suppressed. The church fathers purportedly relied on "neutral" criteria, such as whether a gospel reported an eyewitness account of the life of Jesus, but in retrospect, it seems clear that the content of writings mattered greatly.[6]

Most practicing Christians take for granted the spiritual authority of the books of the Bible. Unaware of the process of selection, they may, if they reflect, believe that the early church authorities were to be trusted, that Divine inspiration guaranteed proper choices, that acceptance over two millennia shows that the choices were sound, or that *our* tradition rests on those choices, whatever their original merit.[7]

The basic problem of inside or outside the canon is fairly simple for most secular law. Within a legal system, most of what counts as law is widely agreed upon.[8] Laws are issued by legislative bodies;[9] and private instruments, such as contracts and wills, have authority because they are made in the manner the law prescribes. Within Anglo-American systems, judges' rulings in common law cases also count as part of the law.

The pervasive problems of canonical status in religious interpretation are not "in" or "entirely out," but what are the levels of priority within the canon, how far the "canon" fails to include other things with interpretive relevance, and how weighty that relevance is. On the first point, Luther, with his fundamental principle of "justification by faith," not only privileged Paul's letters over the legalistic sections of the Hebrew Bible but also implicitly privileged those letters and the Gospel of John over the three synoptic gospels, which were mainly devoted to reports of the life of Jesus.[10] As within other secular legal systems, American law has clear hierarchies of legal sources; federal law is superior to state law, and constitutional law, statutory law, and common law are aligned in that order.

In respect to the status of materials with interpretive relevance, Catholic and Protestant traditions divide. Many Protestants, in accord with Luther's principle of *sola scriptura* (Scripture alone), have believed that the Bible has ultimate authority as a Christian text; the Catholic Church has maintained that church tradition, largely reflected in important church documents, has equal authority.[11] Thus, the Church's interpretations of Scripture have themselves become part of the canon for subsequent interpreters. Suzanne Last Stone has written of a reverence for the collective wisdom of sages who rendered legal decisions reported in the Talmud as contributing to a view that these decisions cannot be reopened, and notes that some authorities take a similar view about some post-Talmudic material, together suggesting "an ongoing process of canonization of authoritative rabbinic legal literature."[12] For much of the history of Islamic law, it was believed that a consensus of the experts about the lessons of the Quran and Sunna was itself certain to be correct.[13] These consensus judgments thus carried great authority.

The idea of interpretations that themselves became authoritative objects of interpretation is familiar in common law systems, with their doctrine of precedent; as with religious traditions, this approach promotes continuity. The authoritative status of precedents is most apparent within the development of the common law itself, but it also extends to constitutional and statutory adjudication. Of course, secular assessment of just how much authority should be accorded earlier interpretations cannot rest on any assumption that the earlier interpreters have enjoyed divine assurance or inspiration, although one might conceive an earlier generation as being particularly wise or imagine a kind of Burkean cumulative wisdom built over time.

Two prominent scholars have drawn from Protestant and Catholic approaches to illuminate divisions over constitutional interpretation. Sanford Levinson has compared Protestant and Catholic views to competing constitutional theories.[14] Some Justices—Levinson uses Justice Black but Justice Scalia might serve as well—say that interpretation should be limited to the federal Constitution, the document. Other Justices, such as Justice Harlan, have believed that a tradition of liberty, a living thing, matters for constitutional interpretation.[15]

Ronald Garet's more elaborate account distinguishes between a simple and complex object of interpretation.[16] In developing his general theme that forms of normative hermeneutics rest on different worldviews that affect the sense both of what an authoritative text is and of how one interprets it, Garet writes that Protestant reliance on the Bible is an example of a simple object constituting a focal text, whereas Catholic reference to a "deposit of faith" represents a complex object, which "includes traditions both written (the writings of the Church Fathers, which reflect the views and practices of the early church) and nonwritten (liturgical and sacramental rituals)."[17] Having suggested that much of the struggle over church traditions centered on the Protestant effort to demote these from a canonical or quasi-canonical status to a mediating role,[18] Garet asks whether constitutional case law is strictly canonical, or quasi-canonical, or something less, and what makes particular case law canonical. He concludes that constitutional law resembles the Catholic model more than the Protestant one.[19]

The analogy of Catholic versus Protestant conceptions is not helpful for most ordinary legal texts. We know that wills, contracts, and statutes are interpreted substantially according to the meaning of the words they contain, and we also know that all interpretation of communications takes place against general assumptions about human behavior and aims. In all branches of law, experts disagree to some extent about how far ordinary language or accepted general principles should control if the two seem to conflict. For these matters, reference to Catholic and Protestant views would confuse more than clarify.

In respect to constitutional law, the comparison between competing Christian views about the place of Scripture and tradition has greater relevance, but even here we need to distinguish between constitutional law *as law* and the Constitution as a symbol of our polity. *Brown v. Board of Education*, which Garet regards as canonized,[20] is extremely unlikely to be overruled, and courts take its ruling that racial segregation in state schools is unconstitutional as a fixed point for reasoning about other cases. But this much can be said about certain other cases about which the public is totally ignorant, for example, bedrock decisions about jurisdiction. As law narrowly conceived, all these cases may have achieved a status comparable to that of the constitutional text itself, but *Brown* differs from the obscure precedents in representing what has become a fundamental constitutional principle.

How clarifying is the divide between Catholic and Protestant perspectives when we ask about the influence of general principles and values on constitutional adjudication? No justice or scholar asserts that constitutional adjudication can proceed wholly on the basis of construction of the ordinary meaning of the Constitution's language. When interpreting broad provisions like the Free Speech Clause, the Supreme Court, uncontroversially, elaborates general principles and rules, such as the rule against viewpoint discrimination, that are consonant with the clause's ambitions. For some constitutional clauses, the natural language (for example, about "reasonable searches") is at least partly an implicit reference to a set of principles drawn from the common law. Here, justices who would rely on settled practices when the clause was enacted diverge from those who would interpret more flexibly in light of basic values. Another disagreement is between those who would limit references to broad cultural values to provisions that are highly open-ended in scope and those who would extend such flexible interpretation to many other constitutional clauses. Unable to assume that God has ensured that particular constitutional interpreters or all sincere readers will get things right, one thinking about how far secular judicial interpreters should draw from sources outside the text must ask about the competence of judges and about how political authority has been allocated. Indeed, part of Garet's thesis is that certain religious convictions which could underlie a Lutheran idea of Scripture cannot be entertained about secular law.[21]

Perhaps what is most important in all this is that although disputes between Luther and the Catholic Church over what is "canonical" can highlight possible attitudes toward interpretive sources, disagreements within our constitutional order over the status of texts and traditions are more subtle than those disputes, or at least they are subtle in different ways.

III. WHO INTERPRETS, AND WITH WHAT AUTHORITY AND CONSEQUENCE?

Any legal system needs interpretation. Someone must decide what the significance is of undoubted legal norms. For modern legal orders, and for this study, the main focus of interpretation is resolving issues of application: How should a legal standard be understood in relation to disputes that have arisen and are likely to arise in the future? But another kind or aspect of interpretation may also be involved, an illumination of the deeper significance of the law and what it reveals about a community and its aspirations.

With regard to these various aspects of interpretation, the participants in different legal systems may embrace different assumptions about who has the responsibility and privilege of interpreting, and about the respective importance of various interpretations. As we shall see, disagreements about those matters can also arise within single systems. Within religious communities, the manner in which these questions are resolved, or not resolved, can tell us a great deal about the religion itself, and it is closely connected to the methods of textual interpretation that prevail. The ordinary assumption about secular legal orders is that a hierarchy of interpreters is an essential part of the system. Within common law jurisdictions, the most important interpreters of legal norms are judges whose rulings determine the outcome of cases and guide future interpretations. Administrative agencies and executive officials are also important interpreters of law.[22] In the United States, certain nongovernmental organizations, such as the American Law Institute, convey systematic views about the standards in various domains of law, and have achieved a kind of quasi-official status. Occasionally individuals may achieve such prominence in a field that their views are similarly regarded.[23] Civil law systems differ significantly. Judges and administrative agencies resolve cases, but their expressions about the law are not taken as binding precedents. Treatises written by noted scholars typically exert a powerful influence on how public officials understand the law. In both civil and common law systems, private lawyers engage in two forms of interpretation— predicting what others will decide and advocating for their clients—roles conferred by a license to practice law.

Understanding variations among different religions, and within particular religions over time, can enrich our sense of possibilities for interpretation within systems of secular law. But we need to be sharply attuned to differences between religious and secular legal systems that may limit the usefulness of these comparisons for imagining desirable allocations of responsibilities.

In approaching religious traditions, we can conceive a spectrum ranging from equal authority of all persons within the faith to interpretation exclusively by a holy or expert body.[24] Of course, ordinary individuals cannot avoid *all* interpretation; even if the interpretation of sacred texts is done exclusively by a supreme authority, individuals will need to interpret what that authority has told them. And an ideal of equal authority is realizable only in a qualified sense in practical human relations. When people in a group are assigned equal responsibility—a jury is an apt example— some, by dint of intellect or personality, will be particularly respected and disproportionately influential. Within a Quaker meeting, in which no one has clerical authority, some members, who gain particular respect for their insights, will come to "speak with authority."[25]

Another phenomenon common among some religions is at odds with a conception of equality that allows each person to make up his own mind, without fear of any negative consequences. When a close acquaintance who is a minister in the United Church of Christ told me that members of her confirmation class wrote their own statements of belief, I inquired whether any statements of belief—such as outright atheism—could disqualify someone; she responded, "No," although such a statement might lead her to ask whether the person genuinely wished to be confirmed. Historically, most Protestant churches have eschewed such a thoroughly tolerant model. Leading Reformers assumed that interpretations can be true or false, sound or unsound. An individual who erred, expressing views that deviated too far from the collective understanding was criticized and, finally, severed from the church body. Equality did not protect against excommunication.

Nevertheless, within the general range of real possibilities, religious traditions have extraordinarily wide differences in their notions of authority to interpret. Authority within the Catholic Church is hierarchical, with great power placed in the Pope and Councils, the most extreme aspect of which is captured by the rarely invoked doctrine of papal infallibility. The power of the Catholic hierarchy is conceived not only as an authority to interpret, but also as an authority to legislate in order to adapt to changing conditions.[26] On many matters, individual Catholics are free to dissent from judgments of the hierarchy; but Catholics are told to give these judgments great respect, and on some important issues, such as the moral permissibility of abortion, they are supposed to conform their behavior to the church's position. Ordinary members of most Protestant churches may conceive their pastors as having some special competence to interpret Scripture, but they are largely free to disagree with their ministers and with higher church officials about the messages that Scripture conveys.

Within Jewish communities, rabbis have typically been recognized as having special authority to interpret the law and its applications. And even when those communities have existed within gentile political orders, local Jewish judges have had the power to render authoritative decisions on some matters of Jewish law. But during most of Jewish history and at present there has been no broad hierarchy of authority, no highest official interpreters of Jewish law. (However, the state of Israel, whose legal order is in limited respects influenced by Jewish law, has a hierarchy of legislative and judicial authority like that of other modern systems of law.)

The development of Jewish law has been complex, and we find disagreement over its central themes. As one aspect of an approach that emphasized how law embodies a community's aspirations, that embraced multiple and conflicting interpretations, and that detached healthy interpretation from a hierarchy of state officialdom, Robert Cover stressed the freedom of those deciding issues of Jewish law to render different, even conflicting, interpretations,[27] a freedom evidenced by the Talmud's inclusion of dissenting positions. In responding to the use by Cover and others of Jewish law as a countermodel to the state-centered concepts of law of liberal democracies, Suzanne Last Stone suggests both how complicated the aspects of Jewish law are and why the religious character of that law inhibits any easy transposition from it to secular legal systems.[28] She acknowledges that accounts of Jewish law contain competing interpretations, but notes that the publication of opposing positions in the Talmud is typically to indicate the grounds of dissent, perhaps for use by those making decisions in later periods, not to endorse the dissenting views as having equal validity to prevailing ones.[29]

She remarks on other features of Jewish law which, together, have led to well-settled standards for the community's life. These include the idea that law is divinely revealed, veneration by later generations for decisions made by early masters of the tradition, common techniques of interpretation, and the assumption that what the majority decides governs.[30] This last assumption is perhaps most strongly illustrated by the Talmudic story of the Oven of Akhnai, according to which Rabbi Eliezer demonstrated by a series of miracles culminating in a voice from heaven, that his interpretation was correct, but was told that the competing majority interpretation would control, because interpretation was not "in Heaven."[31]

Although this much-analyzed story does suggest a freedom of interpreters to depart from some notion of original intent or understanding,[32] it also reflects the settled nature of a process of decision and the perceived need to arrive at definitive judgments.[33]

In his account of the history of (Sunni) Islamic legal theories, Wael B. Hallaq writes of periods in which interpretations of the Quran and Sunna, needed to deal with novel cases, were rendered by expert creative jurists, called mujtahids, a group often equated by theorists with jurisconsults (or mufti) who had a special obligation to provide opinions and legal education.[34] Laymen were required to follow the opinions of the mujtahids, and if the opinions did not diverge, courts treated them as proof of the correct interpretation.[35] In contrast to common law systems, the development of legal interpretation of the divinely inspired Quran and Sunna was in the hands of non-state jurists, but a range of authority to legislate on other matters was left to governments; and in modern times, some theorists have proposed a broader role for democratic legislatures in developing Islamic law.[36] Not surprisingly, such a shift in understanding about authoritative interpreters coincides with a shift in view about how much the details of the rules in the ancient texts should be used to govern contemporary social orders.

For many subjects for which religious texts may be interpreted, individuals with variant views and practices may, if willing, coexist together. Were members of a Protestant church to disagree over the truth or significance of the doctrine of the Trinity or whether Christ is present more than symbolically in communion, no impasse need be created. And this latitude extends to many matters of behavior. Various members may engage in sexual acts that others regard as immoral. On the other hand, certain matters demand settlement. Members must decide when services will be held, what church structure to build, whether those who openly engage in sexual practices that have traditionally been condemned can become ministers, and whether to use wine or grape juice (or offer a choice) during communion. And, insofar as religious law extends into what we tend to think of as ordinary civil controversies, such as grounds for divorce or liability for the infliction of harm, these subjects also need settlement. The decision of some individual or group, based on whatever interpretation is needed, must resolve a dispute[37] (although the grounds for decision may or may not be regarded as controlling for future disputes).

Views about authority to interpret religious texts are typically connected to an encompassing perspective on how God acts in the world and the nature of the texts themselves. In the Roman Catholic understanding, the Church, staffed by priests in apostolic succession, has a special divine mission envisioned by Jesus when he told Peter that he was "the rock" upon which he would build his church;[38] and the text of the Bible is complex with multiple meanings that will escape an ordinary reader. Believing that the Church has special authority to interpret fits naturally with these conceptions.

Professor Stone has shown a variety of ways in which concepts of interpretation and authority to interpret are connected to theological presuppositions. What might otherwise seem to be great flexibility for interpreters, who are not bound to discern an original intent, is constrained by belief in the revealed status of rules that govern interpretation and decision-making, by deference to past generations, and by the sense that each word in Scripture is significant and that the whole is a unifed expression of God's will.[39] The conviction that opposing positions may both reflect God's will is supported by a religious sense of a partnership between man and God.[40]

How far do varying religious approaches to authoritative interpreters have relevance for secular law? In secular systems there is neither a text provided by God nor a divinely ordained process of interpretation.[41] We may accept special authority based on consent, the wisdom of the founders, or presumed competence to interpret, but we do not assume a divine designation. And whether to seek final determinative resolutions or not requires premises other than theological ones.

Within multicultural modern societies, questions of interpretive authority arise in relation to the practical need to settle disputes. A family planning to be away for the year agrees to rent its house; an unexpected crisis arises and it cannot go away. What options does it then have? Even if few people will want to invoke the formal machinery of law, it helps to have rules for what people should do, and to have someone who can make a decisive judgment if that should become necessary. Within modern systems of law, officials reach decisions by interpreting the law (or following the decisions of other officials), not by simply following the views of nongovernmental experts.[42]

To say that within secular legal systems, officials who must resolve controversies have a status that other people do not possess does not resolve every question about interpretive authority. Robert Cover raises the intriguing, though somewhat confusing, question whether nonofficial groups have authority equal to officials in interpreting the United States Constitution. Cover urges that various subcommunities within the political order have different narratives and different visions of the Constitution and that these possess intrinsic merit as great as that of official interpretations.[43] Various interpretations are jurisgenerative; official interpretations, by contrast, are jurispathic because they cut down other interpretations.

When we consider Cover's thesis about official and nonofficial interpretations having equal merit and about the jurispathic import of official interpretations, we need to distinguish practical legal resolution from "correct resolution" and from broad vision. Officials may have a kind of monopoly for binding practical resolutions, but a citizen making a judgment about how courts should really resolve an issue may say, "The law now for practical purposes is 'x' but what the law is (or would be) under a correct (or better)[44] interpretation is 'y.'" As far as a broad vision of the Constitution is concerned, officials definitely have no monopoly. Religious minorities can continue to think of the Constitution as protecting religious exercise to a far greater degree than the Supreme Court acknowledges.[45]

Cover deems court interpretations jurispathic because they kill various interpretations held by groups within society. But, as he himself urges, groups can maintain their own interpretations against those provided by the courts. Further, if official constitutional interpretations are jurispathic, so also are enacted constitutional provisions.[46] What constitution-makers, and legislatures, do can be as "jurispathic" in respect to broad visions as can interpretations by judges.[47] Without doubt, interpretations over time can achieve the kind of solidity of the original text, making nearly unimaginable that what has been established will be altered in any foreseeable future. Someone whose vision is of a country with sharp legal distinctions based on race and gender will find it hard to say that his vision fits with our Constitution; the misfit is created by formal additions to the original constitutional text, by statutes, and by judicial interpretations. *All* these kinds of legal materials restrict what visions are plausible accounts of the nature of our society.

Cover is on solid ground in suggesting that, as with his conception of interpretation of Jewish law, what has become an established interpretation of our Constitution need not control what non-officials conceive as the correct understanding of constitutional values and norms; but within secular legal systems, officials do have a distinctive, indispensable role. More broadly, notions of authority to interpret, and with what consequences, within any religious system of law may offer suggestive analogies, but we can make no simple transition to what is desirable for the law of diverse civil societies.

IV. HOW TO INTERPRET AND THE FRUITS OF INTERPRETATION

I now address the crucial question of how texts are to be interpreted, alongside a related question about the purposes of interpretation. We have already touched upon one aspect of the central question. If what is to be interpreted includes church tradition as well as Scripture, it follows that Scripture will be interpreted in light of that tradition. Of course, it is logically possible for someone to rely on two different sources without assuming any basic compatibility—as a child of divorced parents who do not speak to each other might try to interpret the guidance of both—but those within a religious tradition assume that the tradition corresponds, at least usually, with Scripture.

One reason is that earlier interpreters within the tradition have aimed to act consistently with Scripture, as they have understood it. Given a common view of the church, a second reason to assume compatibility comes into play. Adherents of a religion may believe that the church (or analogous organization) is, like Scripture, inspired by God. This cannot mean that ignorance, misjudgment, and corruption are absent altogether—history contradicts this fantasy too obviously. But a person may think that the church will make few mistakes on matters of great importance. Respect for tradition extends to Protestants, who often suppose that in some manner the Holy Spirit moves participants within the church, and that long established basic understandings are probably correct—though very important mistakes may have occurred, say about the place of women (including their eligibility for the clergy) or the morality of homosexual relationships.[48]

People who live within a secular legal system must abandon any assumption that God's spirit specially ensures correct interpretations of basic legal texts.[49] They may believe that if interpreters over a period of time have tried conscientiously to reach sound judgments, they have probably succeeded. But whether such confidence is warranted is controversial, given claims that class, gender, and self-interest have influenced many interpretive efforts.

Another way in which a text, religious or secular, might fit with tradition is if sound interpretation depends more directly on tradition. Perhaps basic texts should be interpreted flexibly over time, so what they (best) mean at one time is different from what they (best) mean at a subsequent time. Serious interpreters might be thought to have a special sensitivity to the needs of their time. On this view, recent interpretations within a tradition could provide evidence for the best present interpretation.[50] Whereas a religious interpreter might believe that an inspired religious community is particularly likely to interpret well, one would need some other basis to trust the work of recent interpreters of secular law. Alternatively, or in addition, one might attach great value to maintaining continuity, independent of the wisdom of prior judgments.

With this sketch of views of how interpretation within a religious tradition might be regarded, we turn to methods of interpretation within three major religious traditions, all of which accept a basic text that has a divine imprint. Jews have historically believed that the Torah was given by God to Moses. Christians have thought that their Bible, including the New Testament, was inspired by the Holy Spirit. And Muslims have regarded the Quran as based on God's communications to the prophet Muhammad.[51] Among the critical questions that must be resolved in interpretation of these sacred texts are: (1) whether they form a unity; (2) what kind of message they are meant to convey; (3) how far they settle basic questions permanently, as contrasted with responding to the context of a time and place; (4) what techniques or methods of interpretation are called for to discern their messages; and (5) what latitude subsequent interpreters are left to fill in gaps. For each of these questions, we are particularly concerned with the degree to which answers within religious legal systems bear on possible answers to analogous questions within a secular legal order.

Although the concepts governing interpretation in each of the three religions have been influenced historically by theorists of one of the other religions, it is essential at the outset to draw a fundamental distinction that places Judaism and Islam on one side and Christianity on the other. As I have noted, the Hebrew Bible and the Quran contain many passages that set law-like rules of behavior, rules intended to govern community life. Both Judaism and Islam have been rightly regarded as legalistic cultures.[52] Of course, their sacred texts contain much more than norms of behavior, but interpretation of passages that contain these norms has aimed to discern what actions they treat as appropriate, to determine what measures may be needed to assure conformance, and to reveal deeper truths about the religious culture.

Over the centuries Christians have also interpreted passages in both the New and Old Testaments as establishing norms of behavior, such as the general impermissibility of divorce or the sinfulness of homosexual relations, but most Christian interpretation has followed another pattern. With the Pauline understanding that in Jesus Christ, God has freed believers from the need to follow the specific strictures of Jewish law, and given the generality of the basic moral norms set out in the Ten Commandments, most intriguing and important questions of biblical interpretation have not been about specific rules of behavior, and have been more remotely related to typical interpretations of secular legal texts than the focus of much Jewish and Muslim interpretation.

The difference between Jewish and (some) Christian understandings is forcefully illustrated in an account that Chaim Saiman, a Jewish scholar, gives of his encounter with a group at a Presbyterian church. Having initially surprised the group by noting that the first commandment in the Bible (as "every Talmudically-trained Jew would have understood") is to "'[b]e fruitful and multiply,'" and having asked the group what is the content of that duty, Professor Saiman explained the exquisite detail with which the Talmud addresses how the basic requirement of having two children applies in variant circumstances.[53] When asked by Saiman how they took the verse, the Presbyterians' "answers clustered into a few categories," but none perceived the passage as directing "individuals to undertake specific acts"; and the rabbinic approach of considering just how many children were called for in what circumstances was "deeply foreign" to them.[54]

Despite differences in what they seek to draw out of authoritative texts, religious interpreters, like interpreters within secular legal systems, must rely on some combination of "text, tradition, and reason."[55] Each of the three major religions we are considering has enjoyed a rich and diverse history of interpretation. The most I can do in a chapter of this sort is to mark some distinctive elements and controversies and draw a few unrefined comparisons. I begin with Jewish law and then turn to Islamic law. I save Christian interpretation for last because it focuses much less on rules of behavior. Even when religious interpretation does not concentrate on

rules of behavior, it may shed light on more general problems of interpretation and provide a partial basis for general theories, the topic of the
next chapter.

According to an article in the *Jewish Encyclopedia*, during the thousand
years after the collection of the books of the Hebrew Bible, intellectual
effort "was directed almost exclusively to the exegetic treatment of the
Bible and the systematic development of the law derived from it."[56]

In addition to the writings found in the Bible, Jewish law was taken to
include an oral law, also believed to be conveyed to Moses on Mt. Sinai.[57]
By roughly 200 C.E. the oral law, or Mishnah, was compiled. The Mishnah
was based on the rulings of scholars during the prior centuries. During
much of those centuries, the Sanhedrin, or High Court, apparently func-
tioned both as a judicial body interpreting the law and as a legislature,
building new law from the basic guide of the Torah. Its work is one part of
what the Mishnah contains. During the next three centuries, scholars discussed and analyzed these earlier rulings. The records of these discussions
(the Gemarah), along with the Mishnah, constitute the Talmud, which
exists in a Palestinian version and a fuller, later, Babylonian version. Other
material of this period consists of rabbinic study of biblical passages and
is called *midrash*.

In its codification, as an authoritative legal code, the Talmud successfully "subsumed the pre-existing differences between different rabbinical schools."[58] The Talmud itself came to have great authority, first being
accepted as "law" in a broad sense, and later being treated as law to be
applied to particular controversies.[59]

In accord with the idea, reflected in the story of the Oven of Akhnai
and elsewhere, that interpretation of the divinely conveyed law was a
human enterprise, interpreters did not seek the intentions of an author.[60]
Rather, they parsed the significance of the language of the text, believing
that the text as a whole is a unity reflecting God's will and that every
word of Scripture is significant and intentionally included.[61] In one striking example, a passage in Deuteronomy states that parents shall not be
put to death on account of their children and children shall not be put to
death on account of their parents, followed by a rule that a person can be
put to death only for his own crime. The passage was interpreted to mean
that a person could not be put to death on the basis of the testimony of
his child or parent, because, were the passage limited to prohibiting death
for a crime that one's parent or child committed, all the language about
parents and children would be redundant (given the stated rule that one
can only be put to death for his own crime).[62] The common consequence
of minute examination of texts was a legalism, but one that in various
domains went far beyond the text itself.

Chaim Saiman suggests that "The rabbis view the corpus juris of the
Torah as having a dense and intricate legal architecture, whereby each
area of the law has its unique rules and principles."[63] Saiman provides an
example of the incredible detail with which the prohibition of writing, as

a form of labor on the Sabbath, is to be understood. One can write with fruit juices in the dirt but not with ink on two angles of a corner; whether one can scratch on his own body is disputed.[64]

One of the most striking examples of legal proscription that goes beyond the biblical text concerns kosher requirements. Based on passages in the Torah that prohibit cooking a kid in its mother's milk, the Talmud forbids any eating of any meat together with any milk, including meat of animals, such as poultry, that are not similar to goats.[65]

Just what role purpose plays in detailed interpretations and expansive prohibitions, and how purpose is discerned, are contested. One claim is that although many explanations in the Talmud fit the wording and context of the Torah, a large number "of expositions [are] far removed from the actual meaning of the text," because rather than genuinely seeking original meaning, expounders sought Biblical authority for rules of conduct they believed sound.[66] Yet, at least sometimes, ideas of soundness can be drawn from the underlying text.

The Torah forbids engaging in *melakha*, work, on the Sabbath. The rules regarding the Sabbath in the Talmud include detailed prohibitions of activities that count as work as well as certain other activities. Maimonides, the great medieval theorist, categorized these other activities as similar to those the Torah prohibits, as ones that, if allowed, might lead to violations of the Torah's prohibitions, and as ones not conducive to the day's spiritual quality.[67] Even if these rules do not involve textual interpretation as narrowly conceived, we can understand them as implementing prohibitions in the Bible and the values those prohibitions reflect.

Within Jewish law, an important division for interpretive efforts is between matters of ritual and "monetary" subjects. Instructions about the latter are designed to govern interactions of members of the community concerning what count as injuries and what constitutes appropriate compensation. The monetary or civil rules tend to be stated in general form and to have a discernible basis related to the welfare of the community.

The instructions about ritual tend to be more precise and narrower, and often their rationale is regarded as beyond human understanding.[68] Needless to say, the more difficult it is to figure out why particular rules have been laid down, the harder it is to interpret them flexibly in light of their evident objectives. As we shall examine in subsequent volumes, skepticism about judges discerning purposes raises important issues in statutory and constitutional interpretation, but that skepticism is quite different from a notion that God may have established rules of behavior whose purpose is beyond human understanding.

The proper places of narrative and reason have been, and are, significant issues within Jewish law. In his influential article on Nomos and Narrative, to which I have already referred, Robert Cover drew upon his sense of Jewish law. He urged that people understand norms of behavior in light of a broader story or narrative in which they place themselves; he claimed that we should understand constitutional interpretation in accord with the narratives that different groups in society construct.[69]

One could take Cover's thesis in an analytic, or trivial, way that would deflect its significance. Whenever we are faced with a norm of behavior, we understand it in light of some broader story and our place within it. Thus, if we do precise calculations of our tax liability, we have a sense of a society that imposes taxes like this on people like us and we acknowledge that we are willing (or not) to bear that burden. Different people in the same economic situation will have different narratives, but it hardly follows that people with different narratives will usually reach different conclusions about their tax liabilities.[70]

A crucial part of Cover's argument is that narratives will make a difference not only to the overall social visions people have, but also to what they perceive as the content of their constitutional rights and obligations. Thus, a minority religious group like the Amish will have an idea of the free exercise of religion that ties to its own history and to its conception of American history. For Cover, it is important that the Supreme Court frame its own fundamental constitutional decisions within a persuasive narrative, and he criticizes the Supreme Court for not rooting a decision unfavorable to a religious university that was engaging in racial discrimination, strongly enough in a narrative of racial equality.[71]

An important contrast to Cover's approach has been a long-standing assumption within Jewish law that "fluid or ambiguous narratives" in the Mishnah and Talmuds enjoy no legal status.[72] Under this view, stories classed as aggadot[73] are not relevant for determining Jewish law, or halakhah, which has been seen mainly as a formal and positivist law. By an interesting twist, scholars affected by the movement toward using principles and narrative for understanding American law—a movement in which Cover's work has played an important role—have reexamined the proper place of stories in Jewish law.[74]

Moshe Simon-Shoshan claims that "most of the Talmudic texts about rabbinic sages which we might define as 'stories' . . . are brief, stereotypical [and] decidedly halakhic." They report "an individual rabbinic teaching, ruling, or practice in the context in which it originated."[75]

Suzanne Last Stone compares the use of some aggadot in the rabbinic legal corpus to common law cases, narratives that inform one of the boundaries of the relevant legal rule.[76] She provides a rich illustration with three different versions of the story of Honi the Circle-Drawer, a story connected to the Mishnah's "puzzling rule" that although the people may, indeed must, cry out when other calamities occur, one must not pray for rain to stop.[77] She suggests that one way to read the story as it is in the Mishnah itself is to cast doubt on whether the rule against praying for rain to stop should be understood in absolute terms.[78] In the Palestinian Talmud, Honi's successfully praying for rain to cease even after recognizing that doing so was wrong is an example of breaking the applicable rule.[79] Stone writes that in the Babylonian Talmud the prayer is treated as reflecting "the true import of the mishnaic rule,"[80] one that includes a qualification of the apparently absolute prohibition.

Stone powerfully shows how the coloring details of a story that is connected to a rule can shed light on how the content of the rule is and should be conceived.[81] Indeed, because the stories to be drawn from here are themselves part of the authoritative materials, this exercise in a sense is more evidently appropriate than Cover's suggestion that various subcommunities properly develop and rely on their own competing narratives.[82]

If the use of narrative in religious interpretation seems natural, it does not follow that it is equally so in a secular legal system if the use is to resolve disputes, is self-conscious, and goes beyond a reliance on authoritative sources. The Hebrew Bible, the New Testament, and the Quran are largely in narrative form. Explicitly normative material is often connected closely to the narration of events and spiritual reflection. Further, the narration is believed to reflect an inspired history of a people (the Jews) or individual (Jesus or Muhammad). Interpreters approaching such texts may perceive normative obligations as closely related to narrative truth. Certain broad constitutional provisions may be best understood in terms of the country's history, and Cover is on solid ground in thinking that our understanding of free exercise and equal protection should be rooted in narrative. But the text of a constitution is overwhelmingly normative, not narrative. A conclusion that narrative should figure less prominently in secular determinations of legal rights and duties than in religious interpretation holds even more strongly for ordinary legal texts, such as statutes and contracts.[83]

A broader question about interpretation of Jewish law is how much freedom interpreters should conceive themselves as having and how far they should rely on reason—a reason that may include going beyond the logical implications of particular passages. Related to these questions is the degree of tolerance for pluralist interpretation. Cover strongly emphasizes multiple accounts of meaning within the Jewish tradition, and Stone writes of the Jewish "tendency to think in oppositional and paradoxical interdependencies."[84] She notes that modern studies indicate that the Babylonian Talmud is more open to legal pluralism than the Palestinian Talmud.[85]

Sometimes the reason for an interpretation that does not fit easily the literal sense of the text can be drawn from the logic of the text itself. Deuteronomy distinguishes between punishment of a betrothed girl who is sexually taken by force in the open country and one who is in the city, indicating that the girl is innocent only in the former circumstance. The passage was interpreted not to distinguish per se between the open country and the city, but to make critical whether anyone would be available to save her if the girl cried out.[86]

In respect to a biblical passage that forbids taking a widow's garment as a pledge for a debt, some authorities interpreted the passage literally as applying to all widows; others reasoned that the rationale was to protect poor widows and did not apply to rich ones.[87] A threefold division over how narrow were the grounds for a husband to divorce his wife does not seem resolvable on the basis of any clear reason to be discerned from the relevant passage; various interpreters may have been influenced by their own sense of a husband's desirable latitude.[88]

On occasion, the use of reason may effectively eliminate the force of a passage being interpreted. The passage in Deuteronomy setting out the circumstances in which parents may have a wayward and rebellious child stoned to death was interpreted so narrowly as to completely, or virtually, eliminate the possibility that this could ever happen.[89]

According to Christine Hayes, who attempts to refine the assumption that rabbis of the Talmudic period engaged in "unrestrained and convoluted exegesis by which almost anything was read out of, or perhaps into, the biblical text,"[90] anxiety over radical techniques is already reflected in the Talmuds, especially the later Babylonian Talmud. In interpreting an incident from the Mishnah in which the calendar is established on the basis of clearly erroneous testimony about the moon's phases, both Talmuds treat the rabbinical decision not as an action in the face of known facts but as based on an assumption about what facts were true.[91] The Palestinian Talmud, dealing with the situation of a woman who has remarried—after her husband has gone away, failed to return, and been believed dead—and is subsequently surprised by the return of the first husband, indulges the fiction that the first husband is not legally recognized.[92] The Babylonian Talmud, averse to fictions of this sort, treats the teaching as covering only the circumstance in which the wife really does not recognize her first husband.[93]

As these various examples illustrate, part of what is at issue is how far interpreters may depart from the apparent implications of authoritative texts to reach reasonable resolutions of practical problems. Some later interpreters, including Maimonides, who was influenced by Greek philosophy, emphasized reason in understanding biblical stories.[94] The place of reason in understanding Jewish law is a substantial modern issue. Of course, one possible response to "higher criticism" about biblical sources[95] and to any sense that the demands of Jewish law ill fit the outlooks and conditions of modern life is to conclude that that law is not binding. Rather than abandoning participation in a religious community altogether, many Reform and Conservative Jews no longer adhere to the laws that still govern the life of the Orthodox.[96]

A more perplexing question is the potentiality of reason as a basis to reinterpret or explicitly reform Jewish law. Professor Stone reflects on these options in relation to tensions between traditional Jewish law and egalitarian ideals—conflicts involving unequal treatment for women, unequal treatment of non-Jews which helps foster "an unfortunate attitude of disdain toward and even denigration of them," and negative attitudes toward forms of conduct such as homosexual activity and abortions.[97] Referring to Ronald Dworkin's theory that legal decisions are made on the basis of principles that constitute part of the law, Stone inquires whether equality and reciprocity are deep-seated principles of Jewish law. She suggests that the religious element of that law creates a special anxiety about explicit rewriting[98] but also provides more leeway to effectuate the spirit of the Torah.[99] She regards it as important that the values for reinterpretation be internal, not simply drawn from outside, but recognizes that interpretation is needed to determine if values are internal or foreign.[100] Showing that Jewish notions of creation do not support modern ideas of equality,[101] Stone cautiously concludes that halakhic values can support amelioriations of inequality, but that given the complexity of the social phenomenon, we should perhaps settle now for "muddling through" rather than expect broad coherent principles.[102]

Although the place of reason—in the sense of belief about a sound conclusion arrived at apart from what the text itself says—continues to be a substantial issue for interpreters of Jewish law, the system has undeniably proved capable of evolution over time.[103] This is partly the product of a range of legislative authority to settle matters that are not themselves covered by authoritative texts,[104] but also playing roles have been the acceptance of a multiplicity of perspectives, shifts in interpretations over time in response to changing social conditions and attitudes, and the significant place accorded custom[105] in the interpretation of Jewish law.[106]

Muslim culture is often characterized as a "legal culture."[107] The traditional theory of Sunni Muslims has rested on a literal interpretation of the roughly 500 passages in the Quran with legal content and on the Sunna, reports of the prophet Muhammad's example, from which a large amount of material for the law is derived.[108] Like Jewish law, Muslim law, which includes both understanding of God's law and *siyasa* rules for "administration, policy, management," formulated by rulers,[109] was from the outset developed to govern entire societies. Most specific legislative rules are not dictated by religious sources, but legislators are supposed to be guided by the basic principles those sources reflect.[110] Because some modern countries aspire to be governed by Muslim law, issues of interpretation for contemporary times remain pressing for some actual political orders.[111]

From fairly early in the history of Islam, various schools of interpretation have flourished, ones with competing ideas of proper methods. Islamic law did not experience the kind of consolidation achieved by the Talmud. In response to those who have suggested that the differences among schools are minor, Imran Ahsan Khan Nyazee has urged that the separate and independent theories of the schools influenced the legal doctrines they accepted.[112]

Muslims have understood the will of God as articulated in the Quran.[113] Within the first century after Muhammad, interpreters developed a textual attitude toward the Quran.[114] After a beginning period when judicial officials drew from various sources that included all preexisting law and custom and the sunna (or exemplary modes of conduct) of various

individuals, the Quran and the Sunna of Muhammad became the dominant sources of law.[115] During the second century following Muhammad,
one authority claimed that the Quran and Sunna were the "sole material
sources of law,"[116] from which one could reason by analogy and *a fortiori*.
One issue that interpreters faced and resolved was what to do about contradictory passages. In general, later passages were treated as abrogating
previous directions.[117]

In contrast to those who believed all conduct should be regulated by
authoritative texts were scholars who relied heavily on their own reasoning.[118] Muhammad Ibn Idrīs al-Shafi'ī developed a middle position,
one that subsequently gained wide acceptance and became more fully
articulated.[119] He said that law must be derived from the Quran and the
Sunna; reasoning based on them had to be by stricter and more systematic
methods than the rationalists had employed.[120]

Influential theorists developed followings, but only four of these survived over time as schools. By the middle of the fourth century (roughly
the tenth century C.E.), the main components of legal development were
in place.[121]

All Sunni schools accepted four sources of Islamic law, the Quran and
the Sunna (the two primary sources), consensus of opinion, and *qiyās* (a
variety of legal arguments including analogy).[122] What the schools disagreed about was the status of other possible sources, such as opinions
of Companions to Muhammad and customs during his time, and how
exactly to understand consensus and relevant forms of legal argument.[123]
Although jurists in each school agreed about their methods, they might
disagree about particular doctrines.[124] In contrast to matters of faith,
which were regarded as certain, particular legal conclusions were thought
to be only probable, and sometimes opposing "opinions" were considered
equally valid.[125] Laymen were supposed to adhere to the conclusions of
jurists, but jurists, not bound to conclusions of prior jurists, were free to
reach the best understandings they could on the basis of appropriate legal
reasoning.[126]

A typical example of reasoning by analogy is the conclusion that given
the Prophet's prohibition of the drinking of wine made from grapes it
should also be against the law to drink wine made from dates.[127] Both
present the same danger of causing irresponsible behavior. In drawing
analogies, interpreters relied on the ratio legis of the original text and
applied it to the novel case. In some instances, the ratio legis was explicit,
in others not; and there were some texts for which it was not possible to
discern the rationale.

Two examples of *a fortiori* reasoning are (1) that if the Quran forbids
possession of a small amount of material, possession of a large amount
of the same material is also prohibited; and (2) that if the Quran tells
children not to say "Fie" to their parents, they should not strike their parents.[128] Variations on these forms of reasoning encompassed in the term
qiyās were developed with considerable subtlety.

Law was understood as derived from theology.[129] Jurists believed "that revelation is intended to lay down a system of obligation, and the imperative and prohibitive forms (whose prototypes, respectively, are 'Do' and 'Do not do') constitute the backbone and nerve of that system's deontology."[130] It was widely assumed that God's purposes would not be understood by human beings, apart from revelation. Although juristic reasoning from the texts was believed to yield propositions that were merely probable, a consensus among experts was conceived to be certain.[131]

In developing a comparison with forms of American constitutional interpretation, Asifa Quraishi discusses some important differences among schools of interpretation. The Zāhirī school, which was important in the third century after Muhammad but subsequently disappeared, "advocated adherence to the literal or apparent meaning of divine words."[132] Its founder, Dāwūd Ibn Khalaf al-Zahiri, rejected even analogical reasoning, instead confining "all interpretation to the apparent (zahir) meaning of the textual evidences."[133] Not surprisingly members of other schools objected that such an approach was insufficient to deal with the complexities of many actual cases that required resolution.[134]

In referring to the Mālikī school, which placed great weight on understandings in Medina during and after Muhammad's life there, Quraishi explains that this was not a matter of inferring some ordinary authorial intent of the Quran, believed to be given to Muhammad by God. Rather, since Muhummad was regarded as the initial and best interpreter of the Quran, and the Quran commands the following of his example, the practices in his own locality were thought to provide the best evidence of how to understand his life.[135] Critics responded that the divinely inspired life of the Prophet could not be inferred from the ordinary practices of descendents of members of his community, which were not divinely inspired. Instead, primary reliance should be placed on the text of the Quran and authentic records of Muhammad's life.[136]

The place of reason and of purpose for interpreting Islamic law have been a pervasive concern throughout most of its history. By the ninth century C.E., influential theorists accepted a method of juristic preference according to which one conclusion arrived at by analogy could be abandoned in favor of another;[137] thereafter, still broader evaluation in terms of public interest appeared in legal reasoning.[138] As one might expect, these shifts in forms of reasoning reflected changing ideas of desirable rules of law. By the eleventh century, Greek notions of logic (particularly induction) influenced Islamic legal theory, and the precise relation between logical induction and analogy was a matter of dispute.[139] A summary of the position of an influential theorist of that century, Abu-Hamid al-Ghazālī, bears a striking similarity to one side of the modern dispute over the relation between analogy and syllogism, which will occupy us in the next volume: the difference "lies in the epistemic quality of the premises, for the form and structure of analogy do not differ from those of the syllogism in that both types of premises require the subsumption of a particular under a general."[140]

Ghazālī identified five divine purposes—religion, life, mind, family, and property—and claimed that each divine rule contributed to at least one of these.[141] Analogical reasoning was appropriate from a general principle even if not based on a specific text.[142] Later jurists conceived all particular divine purposes as fulfilling an overall purpose of the public good (maslaha) of society. This approach, as Quraishi suggests, introduces a powerful element of reasoned purpose into interpretation, although scholars continued to disagree about how closely a legal rule had to be connected to a divine text,[143] and most jurists denied that reason alone could be an independent source of moral value,[144] thus rejecting natural law as it is typically conceived.[145] One influential jurist with this view was Abu Ishaq al-Shātibī, an expert who opposed the use of foreign sources and abstract reason about the good, argued that revelation was for the unlettered, as well as the educated, and claimed that interpreters should always consider how Arabs at the time of the Prophet would have understood the text.[146]

In certain respects, the content of traditional Islamic law fits uncomfortably with modern Western notions. To some extent, the tensions concern compatibility with modern technologies and economic relations such as lending money at interest. It is hard to square some specific prohibitions of traditional law with modern business practices. If the economy is to function in a modern world, and Islamic principles are not to be altogether disregarded, two alternatives are ingenious formalistic reasoning and frank recognition that the acceptability of specific practices needs to be evaluated in light of changing conditions.[147]

Perhaps still more intractable issues involve the status of women, religious freedom (including equality for persons of various religious persuasions), and democratic political structures. One example of the first issue is the Quran's allotment to daughters of one half of the inheritance of sons, originally a practice to enhance the financial security of women.[148] Universal human equality has been considered a core idea in Islamic beliefs and law,[149] but the rule about inheritance does not comport with modern ideas of gender equality.

Given a severe tension between traditional rules and assumptions underlying most modern societies, a particular society may choose to retain traditional rules, despite their incompatibility with premises widely accepted elsewhere. Alternatively, it can abandon many of those rules as bases for general governance, a course that still leaves a place for religious individuals to regulate their personal lives by Islamic law (as Orthodox Jews in secular democracies follow Jewish law).[150] Two general approaches that have been developed in an attempt to connect basic Islamic ideas to modern societies are religious utilitarianism and religious liberalism.

Religious utilitarianism posits a broad theory of public interest. It sets aside specific doctrines of the old jurists, whether or not achieved by consensus, in favor of the broad spirit of Quranic verses and prophetic reports.[151] One theorist, Turābi, rejects conventional legal theory as connected to traditional society.[152]

The second, less influential, approach, religious liberalism, sees the text of revelation as related to the social order of its time. Muslim law, Shari'a, must be brought to reflect modern reality, with wide discretion accorded to democratic governments.[153] An example of this kind of shift in specific rules might be regarding polygamy. Understood in its background, the Quran accepts polygamy as a way to protect the children of widows who need support and protection. From this perspective, a modern society should not endorse polygamy as a general principle.[154] Marion Holmes Katz makes the point that shifts from specific practices prescribed in the Quran or accepted by Muhammad have not been limited to liberals and to moderns; centuries ago conservatives determined that women should be kept from mosques although Muhammad did not conceive such a general restriction.[155]

Forms of modernization have been criticized as lacking a cohesive methodology, thus allowing "a variety of lines of reasoning that are not necessarily compatible" and creating "problems of inconsistency in legal reasoning and hence in the legal system."[156] One can regret the possible absence of a coherent methodology, something that may seem especially disquieting for a system that claims an origin in divine revelation; but we need to recall that Muslim law has survived, flourished, and evolved without authoritative settlement of either different methods used by different schools or different specific doctrines within the schools.[157] When one thinks of American constitutional law, and of a Supreme Court where justices disagree about interpretive methods, and some individual justices might be hard put to formulate a coherent approach for themselves (perhaps using the interpretive methods that lead to what they think are sound results without having a clear sense of how those devices might fit into a comprehensive theory), one realizes that a legal system can function fairly well without an overarching coherent methodology.[158]

When we turn to Christian biblical interpretation, we, for the most part, move away from efforts to discern the meaning of law-like rules as they apply to a variety of actual or imagined situations. In one striking modern formulation, Sandra M. Schneiders writes that Scripture is normative for the Church and individual Christians but "this normativity must be conceived in a much more holistic way than is possible when the scriptures are considered a kind of source book of dogmas, commandments and prohibitions."[159] Even if religious texts are so understood, their interpretation raises important general questions about hermeneutics that apply to law as well as other human endeavors.

Before the Renaissance, virtually all serious reflection on interpretation of texts concerned religious interpretation; only in 1629 did Johann Dannhauer coin the word "hermeneutica" and project a philosophically based general theory of hermeneutics that would embrace how various disciplines determine the meaning of texts.[160] Thus, the division between much of this part of this chapter and the following chapter on general interpretive theory is somewhat arbitrary. The history I shall briefly summarize is relevant for general theories; and certain modern theorists of biblical interpretation develop ideas that are highly important for general theories as well.

Among the major questions Christian writers on biblical interpretation have faced are these: (1) How far is the text to be understood in a literal or nonliteral way?; (2) How far are the phenomena the text describes now to be understood in a literal way?; (3) Who should be conceived as the author of the biblical canon?; (4) Is interpretation of Scripture essentially similar to interpretation of other texts or not?; (5) What capacities are needed for someone to interpret Scripture? (6) How far should Scripture determine theological understanding; how far should theological understanding determine Scriptural meaning; and (7) How does one understand or respond to Scripture—is one's response mainly understanding in the ordinary sense or something else, and does this depend on the kind of endeavor in which one is engaged? Some of these questions, as we have seen, are also central for Jewish and Islamic legal interpretation.

Christian thinkers early faced questions about how biblical texts should be conceived—questions raised in part by the use of allegory by Greek thinkers to interpret passages of Homer in which gods acted in ways at odds with a rational logos,[161] and generated more directly by Paul's powerful allegorical construction of parts of the Hebrew Bible. In urging that those with faith in Christ are not bound by Jewish law, Paul refers to Abraham's two children, one born naturally of Hagar, a slave, in the ordinary way according to the flesh, and one born to Sarah as the consequence of a promise. Paul explicitly says, "This can be regarded as an allegory," indicating that believers in Christ are free children of the promise, like Isaac (Sarah's son), not constrained by the old law.[162]

The early Church was divided between exegetical schools of Antioch, "noted for its literal and grammatical interpretation of the Bible," and Alexandria, which emphasized allegory and sought to avoid literal understandings of anthropomorphisms of the Old Testament.[163] Origen, one of the most important Alexandrians, viewed the Holy Ghost as the author of Scripture. As Paul had, he perceived the Old Testament as full of passages that prefigured the coming of Jesus. He also, in the words of one modern commentator, thought that the Holy Ghost "scattered purposeful discords and contradictions in his narrative to alert the spirit of worthy and attentive readers to the need for surpassing the literal."[164]

In his writing, Augustine suggested that it was unproductive to quibble over the meaning of passages so long as the claims about meaning do not depart from what in fact is true. He wrote in his Confessions, "[S]ince every person tries to understand in the Holy Scriptures what the writer understood, what harm is done if a man understands what thou, the Light of all truth-speaking minds, showest him to be true, although the author he reads did not understand this aspect of the truth even though he did understand the truth in a different meaning."[165]

Although Augustine relies on a more objective notion of truth than many modern literary critics, this passage resembles the idea that different readers may attach different meanings to literary works without one necessarily being "more correct" than another. As the last chapter and the discussions of Jewish and Islamic law suggest, the notions that one interpretation could really be as good as a proposed alternative, and that "correct" interpretation may reach beyond what the authors of texts intended certainly *may* apply to secular legal standards. Nevertheless, if variant interpretations would yield different outcomes for a dispute that requires resolution, the legal order must resolve on one answer or the other, and there is some value in having resolutions that are consistent for similar disputes.

With some conceptual variations, all the Church Fathers believed scriptural interpretation needed to go beyond the literal. During the medieval period, the standard approach was in terms of a fourfold sense of Scripture: literal, allegorical (most notably typological premonition of the life of Jesus), moral or tropological, and analogical (indicating what we are striving for).[166]

During the millennium and a half prior to the Reformation, the Catholic Church developed a detailed canon law, which governed not only spiritual subjects but such matters as marriage and divorce, wills, libel, usury, and just price.[167] This law applied alongside a civil law, with not infrequent contestation between civil and church officials over domains of authority. According to one summary, canon law "was a slow accretion of old religious customs, scriptural passages, opinions of the Fathers, laws of Rome or the barbarians, the decrees of church councils, and the decisions and opinions of the popes."[168] Although the precepts of canon law were based partly on principles reflected in the Bible, such as Jesus' rejection of divorce, the law's development did not depend on the kind of refined textual analysis and use of analogy we have found in Jewish and Islamic law.

Without abandoning the basic assumption that much in the Old Testament prefigured the life of Jesus, Luther, and Protestant leaders more generally, rejected the complex medieval approach in favor of literal meaning, literal in the sense of how the words in context would ordinarily be understood.[169] (As William Tyndale noted, in this sense of literal "Look ere thou leap" means "Do nothing suddenly or without advisement.")[170] Luther, in contrast to the Catholic scholastics, emphasized the accessibility of Scripture to ordinary people;[171] his rejection of the complexities of the medieval approach fit well with his rejection of the special authority of the Catholic Church in biblical interpretation. Luther believed that faith in Christ, not good works, was the source of salvation. This theology affected how he interpreted scripture, what he thought sound interpretation would yield, and whom he regarded as competent interpreters.

It is helpful in these respects to contrast Luther with Erasmus, a Roman Catholic translator of the Bible deeply influenced by classical learning. For Erasmus, interpretation and translation of the Bible was not fundamentally different from interpretation (and translation) of other texts.[172] It required, above all, erudition, a knowledge of Hebrew, Greek, and Latin, and of the historical context in which texts were written.[173] He wrote, "One comes nearer to perceiving the sense of Scripture if he considers not only the situation and what is said, but also by whom it is said, to whom it is said, the words that are said, what time, what occasion, what precedes and what follows."[174]

Luther, though not denying the usefulness of the kinds of knowledge Erasmus emphasized, thought that biblical interpretation and translation had to be inspirational.[175] The Bible was not like other texts; a nonbeliever was not in a position to interpret it. Considering faith the most important fruit of interpretation, Luther constantly had in mind the kind of interpretation preachers offer to parishioners. This focus suggests the difference between how an interpreter tries to reach understanding and how he conveys that understanding to others—a difference bearing some resemblance to that between how judges determine how to understand a legal text and what they convey in their written opinions.

Flacius Illyricus, a collaborator of Luther's, developed a more comprehensive approach to scriptural interpretation, stressing the importance of knowledge of grammar and the juxtaposition of related passages.[176]

Building on the Augustinian notion of two kingdoms, a civil kingdom to keep the peace and a spiritual kingdom for true believers, Luther rejected the wide claims of authority made by the Catholic Church for its canon law.[177] Governance of ordinary affairs was to be left to civil magistrates. That did not mean religious premises should be wholly absent from the law; regulation of subjects such as marriage and divorce should respect Christian principles. Theorists who followed Luther, such as Philip Melanchthon, were more respectful of the importance of legal regulation and of the contribution of canon law, and they stressed the need to use the Bible as a source of earthly law;[178] but they, like Luther, understood the heart of the Christian message in other terms.

Higher criticism of the last two centuries, along with modern scientific understanding, has yielded skepticism concerning a number of traditional assumptions about the Bible. Careful study of history as well as close comparisons of the language and styles of various biblical texts have dispelled confident belief that Moses actually wrote the first five books of the Bible, that apostles wrote any of the four gospels themselves, that all letters attributed to Paul were actually written by him, that the synoptic gospels give an account of the life of Jesus that is in accurate temporal order, and that Jesus said all that he is reported to have said in those gospels. Human understanding of why writers were inclined to make particular claims at particular places and times have made it harder or more complicated to suppose that the Holy Ghost is the author of the Bible, though one may retain that belief, in the sense of a faith that divine inspiration does somehow shine through the human aspirations and foibles of individual writers.[179] The general assumption that physical events in the world are generated by natural causes subject to universal physical laws has led to doubt about the literal truth of miracles that both the Hebrew Bible and New Testament report, about the supposition that Mary conceived Jesus without ordinary sexual intercourse, and about an event often believed central to the Christian faith, the bodily resurrection of Jesus after his crucifixion.[180]

These developments have generated various responses. Large parts of the Western world have experienced a precipitous decline in religious faith. In the United States, by contrast, a significant percentage of Christians has refused to credit the most corrosive forms of skepticism, maintaining belief in what the Bible says over what the historical critics and scientists assert. (The adherence to creationism or intelligent design over evolution is one notable manifestation of this stance.) Early in the twentieth century, liberal Christians regarded Jesus as primarily a moral reformer, and they believed in a social gospel that would progressively improve the world. This sensibility has largely foundered on strong evidence that Jesus' attitude toward his own mission was quite different, and on the deeply disturbing course of world events during much of the last century.

An influential view most completely represented in the work of Rudolf Bultmann has been to try to preserve a fundamental Christian understanding in a way that demythologizes the Bible. Bultmann was heavily influenced by Martin Heidegger, and his existential approach shares a great deal with that of Hans-Georg Gadamer, who I examine in the next chapter. In brief, Bultmann claims that we bring a pre-understanding to every text, in that we must have some relation to the subject matter if the text is to have meaning for us.[181] It does not necessarily follow that that pre-understanding will determine the meaning we find in the text, but, given Bultmann's view, one's prior understanding is bound to affect one's exegesis.[182] Bultmann distinguishes between the kinds of texts that provide objective information about the world and those, such as the Bible, with deeper existential meaning that may promote self-understanding.[183] In most respects, Bultmann, himself an expert interpreter of the Bible, assumes that biblical interpretation should proceed like the interpretation of many other texts with complex meanings. Both since our modern understanding suggests that many narratives purporting to describe physical events in the Bible are probably not literally true *and* because that mythical way of presenting deeper truths is not congenial for modern audiences (although they may have been effective in times past), the Bible should be interpreted in a demythologized way.[184] Thus an interpreter should seek the deeper meaning revealed by claimed miraculous occurrences, and present them in a way that does not rest on the miracles themselves.

Bultmann understands the basic Christian message as a proclamation (or *kerygma*) of God's love as revealed in the life and death of Jesus.[185] Here, his essential Lutheranism shines through. Interpretation, as it was for Luther, is guided by faith and its most important consequence is not to reveal propositional truths but to give people a sense of God's effect in their lives—an existential response in which they achieve a self-understanding of their existence.[186] Although Bultmann wants to demythologize much else in the New Testament, including the reported miracles and the bodily resurrection of Jesus, he does not treat the life and death of Jesus in this way. They form the solid historical core that reveals God's saving love.[187] Only through faith in God's proclamation can people lead authentic lives,[188] one of Bultmann's outlooks that sharply distinguishes Christian interpretation of the Bible from other forms of interpretation.

Christian interpretation, like the interpretation of Jewish law, is touched by ways in which the Bible (in many passages) strongly diverges from modern notions of justice, perhaps most strikingly in the roles of women. One response is to reject the Biblical version in whole or in part on this ground. Another, along the lines of Ronald Dworkin's "best reading" approach to legal interpretation, is to interpret in "the best light," emphasizing biblical passages that conform with our sense of just relations.[189] In her feminist interpretation of the story in John in which an exchange between Jesus and a Samaritan woman leads to the acceptance by Samaritans of Jesus and his mission, Sandra Schneiders combats traditional interpretations that treat the woman as a whore and minimize her role.[190] She argues that the reference to the woman's five marriages are not about sexual sin but are symbolic of the Samaritans falling away from God. Nevertheless, Schneiders is very clear that not all problems inhere in sexist interpretations; much of the biblical text itself is male-centered, marginalizes women, and justifies their oppression. In her view, one cannot avoid the reality that this aspect of the Bible is the product of fallible male authors with a patriarchal perspective.

This cursory survey of forms of religious interpretation provides suggestive analogies for understanding law and interpretation within secular legal systems. It certainly shows that various questions that plague legal theorists are not unique to the domain of ordinary law. But our survey at many points also reveals important differences between ordinary legal interpretation and religious interpretation. Much religious interpretation, like literary interpretation, does not concentrate on how law-like standards should be applied, the staple of most ordinary legal interpretation. And even when the interpretation is of that sort, a person's religious perspective affects whether he assumes that the crucial text is divinely inspired and what he believes about the status and role of interpreters.

One aspect in which belief in divine inspiration can matter for interpretation concerns possible "unity" of the text. For people who believe that Scripture mixes inspired and highly fallible human accounts, a religious text need not be consistent or unified. But many believers have supposed that God's hand assures that Scripture is unified, that it presents a consistent set of messages, a general approach that includes the typical Christian conviction that much of the Hebrew Bible prefigures the life of Jesus. If Scripture is unified, interpretation of one part must fit with the interpretation of other parts; how one understands one part will bear on one's sense of other parts. This relation of parts to one another has been a staple of Jewish, Muslim, and Christian interpretation.

Even if one had no confidence in the consistency or soundness of particular Scriptural messages, one might take the following attitude. The *significance* of interpreting Scripture is to guide our understanding of God and God's will. Whatever flaws Scripture may possess, God's will is consistent; therefore Scripture should be interpreted in a consistent way, even when to do so strains the apparent meaning of particular passages.[191]

Those who interpret a secular constitution or a large body of statutory law have no good reason to assume it is consistent in principle. People enacting a single set of provisions may make compromises with basic principles, as with the treatment of slavery in our original Constitution. Ununified features become even more likely as new provisions are adopted over time. Attitudes of legislators change. Interpreters of one enactment, or a few closely related enactments, should begin with a rebuttable presumption that provisions fit with each other. But if we ask what the lawmakers were really about, we have no reason to indulge any grander assumption about a unified corpus of law.

A different question about "unity" is whether interpreters desirably treat the corpus of law as if it were consistent. The answer to this question may be "yes." This position resembles the idea that finding unity in an ununified Scripture corresponds with God's will, but the rationale remains quite different. For religious interpretation, someone may start with the likely wishes of a benevolent God; for secular interpretation, the inquiry is about what will work well for the law (or how a government should best conceive itself), overall, in practical terms. Unless one focuses on ordinary human reasons to keep a religious community together and functioning well,[192] whether religious interpreters should assume a unity of scriptural text based on God's will is of little assistance in deciding whether secular judges should assume a unified set of constitutional or statutory provisions.

When we turn to more specific questions about how to interpret, we again find analogies between religious and secular legal interpretation, but we also find factors in religious interpretation that constrain its usefulness as a guide for secular law.

The issue of "literal interpretation," as we have seen, arises in both domains. A crucial question is how literally the Bible should be interpreted. Many passages obviously call for something other than literal interpretation in the narrow sense; the parables of Jesus are notable examples. Interpreters disagree about whether some passages were intended to be taken literally. Does the story of the loaves and the fishes tell us that Jesus miraculously created food, or that he encouraged followers to be generous with what they had? Yet more difficult questions arise with passages that definitely appear to be meant literally, making a claim to historical accuracy. Of course, acceptance of literal truth need not, and did not historically, preclude additional meanings. Thus, one may believe both that Jonah survived three days inside a whale (or fish) and that this event prefigured the death and resurrection of Jesus. But what is the interpreter to do if she concludes that the human writer probably understood the story of Jonah literally, but she doubts that God performed such a miracle? If she thinks all of Scripture is inspired, she cannot say the story is false and without value; she must find a nonliteral understanding that exemplifies God's truth in spite of her inability to accept the writer's literal truth.

More comprehensively, we have seen that people differ substantially about the significance of Scripture. How far does it develop doctrinal truths and establish norms of behavior?; how far does it tell the story of God's relationship with the Jewish people and of the life of Jesus or Muhammad?; how far is the fundamental point of Scripture to inspire readers, as contrasted with teaching them what is true? In terms of fruitful inspiration, two very different interpretations of a parable may be equally "true," if they lead readers to react to the living God.

If one thinks the Bible's specific moral norms, such as those within the Ten Commandments, have independent significance, calling for adherence, he needs to interpret their meaning and application. "Adultery" is forbidden, but when the commandment was issued, a married man's intercourse with a single woman was regarded as a form of polygamy (then permitted), not adultery. Should we understand the biblical bar on adultery to cover this behavior now?[193] A crucial issue about New Testament interpretation is whether to take many recommendations of Jesus, such as turning the other cheek, as admonishments about how we should now behave, or only as ideals of good behavior that show us how far from the ideals all human beings live.

How much relevance do these various possibilities have for secular law? Law, including constitutional law, is mainly a set of standards for behavior. Narratives may be implicit but they are not the primary focus. Most legal norms are intended to be taken literally, though occasionally the stated norm ("55 miles per hour") is meant to encourage behavior that is not too far off (not going more than 70 miles per hour). Legal norms are not mainly metaphorical, symbolic, or inspirational. In contrast with Scripture, as it is understood by many believers, an official interpreter may suppose that the point of a legal norm is misconceived; but, unless the norm is unconstitutional or the interpreter can discern some other reason to disregard it, she must give it some effect. It is a crucial question how far interpreters are warranted in interpreting norms so that they conform with sound purposes, even if this involves straining their apparent meaning; but interpreters do not say they will forego literal or intended meaning in favor of a metaphorical sense.

When one surveys this terrain, one must conclude that some premises of religious interpretation (at least under relatively orthodox approaches) and of secular legal interpretation are sufficiently different so that resolutions in respect to the former are not a confident basis to resolve troublesome issues with the latter.

This chapter's sketch of religious interpretation does strongly suggest that as social conditions and attitudes evolve, interpretations of norms inevitably do and should change. Only with such change can religious traditions flourish over time. But even this insight does not help much in resolving crucial questions about interpreting secular law. The reason is that, although everyone agrees that secular law, as a whole, must change, that does not establish that judges, as contrasted with legislators and constitutional enactors, should be self-conscious organs for statutory and constitutional evolution.[194]

Notes

1 See Paul, "Letter to the Galatians." According to Thomas Aquinas, among others, the moral precepts of the Old Testament that conform with natural law do apply to Christians. See Edward A. Synan, "Some Medieval Perceptions of the Controversy on Jewish Law," in Clemens Thoma and Michal Wyschogrod, eds., *Understanding Scripture: Explorations of Jewish and Christian Traditions of Interpretation* 102, 120 (New York, Paulist Press, 1987).

2 Mark 10:2–10; Luke 16:18; Matthew 5:31–32, 19:1–9 (divorce impermissible except for fornication).

3 Matthew 5:39–40, 43–44; 7:1–5.

4 I have developed this contention with respect to the United States—and its principle of nonestablishment—in *Private Consciences and Public Reasons* (New York, Oxford University Press, 1995), and *Religion and the Constitution, vol. 2, Establishment and Fairness* (Princeton, N.J., Princeton University Press, 2008).

5 Gerald L. Bruns, *Hermeneutics Ancient and Modern* 76 (New Haven, Yale Univ. Press, 1992); Paul Ricouer, "The Canon Between the Text and the Community," in Petr Pokorný and Jan Roskovec, eds., *Philosophical Hermeneutics and Biblical Exegesis* 7, 17, 19 (Tübingen, Mohr Siebeck, 2002). Moshe Halbertal, *People of the Book* (Cambridge, Mass., Harvard University Press, 1997), explores various kinds of "canons" and the text-centeredness of Jewish tradition.

6 Those chosen corresponded with the religious convictions of church leaders. Elaine Pagels, *The Gnostic Gospels* (New York, Random House, 1979), and see *Beyond Belief* (New York, Random House, 2003), has suggested that institutional reasons led leaders to emphasize acceptance of a specific Christian revelation, as John does, in contrast with the inner reflection favored by Thomas. To say the leaders had institutional reasons is not to say the leaders self-consciously chose gospels specifically because they would best support the church; any influence of institutional interest on conviction was almost certainly more subtle than that.

7 An individual Christian perusing the Gnostic writings *might* conclude that the Gospel of Thomas has as good a claim to authority as the Gospel of John, although Reformers who stressed that all individuals can interpret the canon did not assert that individuals could determine what constitutes the canon. Luther (and other Protestants) did reach a conclusion at variance with that of the Roman Catholic

Church on whether a few texts whose status was controversial within the early church should be included in the New Testament. John William Aldridge, *The Hermeneutic of Erasmus* 81-86 (Richmond, Va., John Knox Press, 1966).

8 An issue of "in" or "out" can arise in revolutionary situations in which the status of "legal" pronouncements of two competing groups, such as Tzarists and Communists, is in question. An individual might take the attitude that he should count as "legal" the rules set by those with a right to govern, rather than the rules set by the group with greater control of the territory.

9 Constitutional criteria for valid law that include a moral principle do raise a problem of "in" or "out." For example, if a state legislature adopts a criminal penalty that is so cruel it may violate the federal constitution's ban on cruel and unusual punishment, people may, at least prior to judicial resolution, disagree about whether the debated penalty is part of the "canon" of law. At least four relevant questions are raised. One issue is the probable fate of the penalty. Another is how to characterize a law that is likely to be held invalid. A third issue focuses on which officials or citizens need to make a determination. (An executive official, prior to a judicial determination, may properly treat as valid a law that a court properly declares invalid.) A final issue is whether the relevant officials should treat the debated penalty as valid or not.

10 W. Schwarz, *Principles and Problems of Biblical Translation* 169 (Cambridge, Cambridge University Press, 1955), writes that on Luther's inspirational view of the point of interpretation, "justification by faith" was the basis to interpret all of the Bible.

11 Thomas C. Grey, "The Constitution as Scripture," 37 *Stanford Law Review* 1, 3 (1984), suggests that this standard distinction between Protestant and Catholic approaches is rejected by many modern theologians. Sandra M. Schneiders, in *The Revelatory Text* 81, 83 (New York, HarperCollins, 1991), writes that Catholics and Protestants have divided over whether scripture and tradition are equal in authority (with tradition enjoying superiority in practice), or scripture is superior to tradition; but that recently both sides have recognized, and tried to minimize, the dangers of their positions.

12 Suzanne Last Stone, "In Pursuit of the Counter-Text: The Turn to the Jewish Legal Model in Contemporary American Legal Theory," 106 *Harvard Law Review* 813, 853 (1993). Menachem Elon devotes a volume of 555 pages to what he calls "literary sources" of Jewish law, discussing different stages and the place of commentaries and novellae, codificatory literature, such as the main work of Maimonides, and responsa, recorded decisions by authorities in Jewish law in response to questions put to them. *Jewish Law: History Sources, Principles, Vol. III* (Philadelphia, Jewish Publication Society, 1994).

13 Wael B. Hallaq, *A History of Islamic Legal Theories* 75–77 (Cambridge, Cambridge Univ. Press, 1997).

14 Sanford Levinson, "The Constitution in American Civil Religion," 1979 *Supreme Court Review* 123.

15 One might quibble that as far as Justice Harlan was concerned, a flexible idea of due process produced this conclusion; on some other matters, such as reapportionment, he accepted historical understanding as dispositive.

16 "Comparative Normative Hermeneutics: Scripture, Literature, Constitution," 58 *Southern California Law Review* 35, 48–49, 54–55 (1985) Drawing from David Kelsey, Garet takes the meaning of the term "Scripture" as implicating ideas of "tradition, community, identity, and authority." Id. at 63.

17 Id. at 55.

18 Id. at 61. Thus, Luther accepted the writings of the Church Fathers as traditional interpretive aids but not as having a higher status.

19 Id. at 75. From within the Roman Catholic tradition, Sandra Schneiders, note 11 supra, at 66, 78, 82, 84–85, draws on the analogy to American constitutional interpretation to explain the role of the church in a hierarchical system of biblical interpretation.

20 Garet, note 16 supra, at 58. Michael J. Perry has written of norms that have "achieved a virtual constitutional status." "What Is 'the Constitution'? (and Other Fundamental Questions)," in Larry Alexander, ed., *Constitutionalism: Philosophical Foundations* 105 (New York, Cambridge University Press, 2001).

21 Id. at 74–76. Schneiders, note 11 supra, at 81–82, asserts that it is "presumptuous" to suppose that God has miraculously enlightened ordinary readers so they can understand complex biblical Scripture emanating from a culture vastly different from our own.

22 For one perspective on how to conceptualize the relations of different interpreters, see Kent Greenawalt, "How to Understand the Rule of Recognition and the American Constitution," in *The Rule of Recognition and the U.S. Constitution* 145, edited by Matthew Adler and Kenneth Himma (New York, Oxford University Press, 2009).

23 One thinks of Corbin and Williston on contracts and Prosser on torts.

24 I put aside the possible competence of those outside the faith to interpret. They can, of course, render the kind of interpretation that does not involve commitment, involvement in the community, or spiritual insight—as a modern scholar can interpret the law of an ancient, unappealing society; but insiders, and an outsider himself, may think he cannot do the kind of interpretation that would guide those who are within the religious community.

25 One might reasonably argue, contrary to the drift of this paragraph, that genuine equality is not diminished if some people accept as true the views of others they perceive as better informed or more insightful.

26 Silvio Ferrari, "Adapting Divine Law to Change: The Experience of the Roman Catholic Church (with Some Reference to Jewish and Islamic Law)," 28 *Cardozo Law Review* 53 (2006). The authority to legislate has been complemented by an authority by the same bodies to interpret what they have legislated. Id. at 61, 63.

27 See Robert M. Cover, "The Supreme Court 1982 Term—Foreword: Nomos and Narrative," 97 *Harvard Law Review* 4 (1983); Robert M. Cover, "Obligation: A Jewish Jurisprudence of the Social Order," 5 *Journal of Law and Religion* 65 (1987). Nahun M. Sarna, "The Authority and Interpretation of Scripture in Jewish Tradition," in Thoma and Wyschogrod, supra note 1, at 9, 10, has written, "Rabbinic exegesis is firmly grounded in the cardinal principle that embedded in the sacred text is a multiplicity of meanings, the full richness of which cannot be expressed through a single body of doctrine or by any monolithic system that is logically self-consistent." See also José Faur, "Law and Hermeneutics in Rabbinic Jurisprudence: A Maimonidean Perspective," 14 *Cardozo Law Review* 1657 (1993).

28 Stone, note 12 supra.

29 Id. at 836–37. She writes, id. at 839, that only rarely does the Talmud explicitly regard "two contradictory behavior-regulating norms as equally valid, final resolutions of a legal problem."

30 Id. at 849, 852, 860.

31 Id. at 841. As Menachen Elon, note 21 supra, Vol. I, at 242, captures the point in a section heading, there is "no suprahuman authority in halakhic determinations."

32 See, e.g., Robert Burt, "Precedent and Authority in Antonin Scalia's Jurisprudence," 12 *Cardozo Law Review* 1685, 1691–94 (1991).

33 Stone, note 12 supra, at 855–60; Samuel Levine, "Jewish Legal Theory and American Constitutional Theory: Some Comparisons and Contrasts," 24 *Hastings Constitutional Law Quarterly* 441, 4742–74 (1997). Although it is generally assumed that human interpreters are not divinely inspired, some accounts of the Greek translation of the Hebrew Bible include a miraculous coalescence of views. See W. Schwarz, note 10 supra, at 23–24.

34 Wael B. Hallaq, note 13 supra, at 121–24. Some theorists claimed that jurisconsults had to take religious matters seriously, as well as be just and trustworthy. By the thirteenth century (C.E.), it was no longer assumed that in order to qualify as a jurisconsult one needed to be a *mujtahid*. Id. at 144–46. For a summary of how the fundamentals of Shi'i interpretation differ from the Sunni tradition, see Haider Ala Hamoudi, "You Say You Want a Revolution: Interpretive Communities and the Origins of Islamic Finance," 48 *Virginia Journal of International Law* 249, 264–73 (2008).

35 Hallaq, note 13 supra, at 124, 153–54.

36 Imran Ahsan Khan Nyazee, *Theories of Islamic Law* 55, 111 (Islamabad, International Institute of Islamic Thought 1994), claims that the law in the texts of the Quran and Sunna is "more or less fixed," but these cover only a small percentage of the activity of a modern state. Other matters are left to legislative choice guided by Islamic values but responsive to changing social conditions. For an account of views that legislatures should develop Islamic law broadly, see Hallaq, note 13 supra, at 233–35.

37 A small, very close-knit community may be able to manage without coercion in respect to such issues, everyone voluntarily acquiescing in the judgments of those with the power to decide.

38 Matthew 16:18.

39 Stone, note 12 supra, at 852, 855, 862, 864.

40 Id. at 863.

41 Schneiders, note 11 supra, at 27–61, provides one account of the spectrum of Christian perspectives on how the Bible may be regarded as the "Word of God," and the extent to which it is colored by fallible human assumptions.

42 Often individuals must interpret the law for themselves (or rely on lawyers to interpret for them). They will wish to know how courts will resolve various situations, and conscientious ones want a sense of their legal responsibilities, even when they know that any official resolution is unlikely.

43 Cover, "Nomos and Narrative," note 27 supra, at 25–44.

44 If one thinks that over a wide range, courts have "discretion" to decide either way and establish the law, one will hesitate to say that the Constitution requires something different from what the Supreme Court has said, but one may still say a different interpretation would be preferable.

45 Racists may believe that the Constitution does not guarantee racial equality to nearly the same extent as present interpretations suggest.

46 After the American Revolution, an Episcopalian might have believed that his faith, cut off from the Church of England, should become the national church; that interpretation of the significance of Episcopalianism for the new nation was

foreclosed (barring future amendment) by the no establishment clause, which made it clear that the national government could not establish any particular faith.

47 Cover does suggest that the Constitution is not a "universally accepted basis for interpretation" in our society, but it is typically treated as foundational. Id. at 25. He does not discuss whether its supplanting of other foundations was jurispathic.

48 One also thinks of the use of Scripture by the Dutch Reformed Church in South Africa to defend apartheid.

49 One could conceivably believe that God's spirit aids all interpretation, religious or not.

50 An extreme view of this sort is portrayed and deplored in Blaise Pascal's Provincial Letters. Pascal, Pensées and The Provincial Letters, Letters V and VI, pp. 372–401 (New York, The Modern Library 1941) (originally published in France in 1656 as a defense of Jansenist positions and a critique of the Jesuits).

51 Bruns, note 5 supra, at 125–26, explains the belief that Muhammad received the contents of the book orally from the Angel Gabriel over more than twenty years, and that the text in writing leaves open some questions about how it should be vocalized.

52 Justice Elon, note 12 supra, Vol. I, at xlvii, suggests that Jewish life and Jewish law are two sides of the same coin . . . ." Nahum M. Sarna, "The Authority and Interpretation of Scripture in Jewish Tradition," in *Understanding Scripture*, note 1 supra, at 9, writes that the interpretation of Hebrew Scriptures "was the major source for the national language, the well-spring of the peculiar life-style of the Jew, the font of Jewish values, ideals, and hopes." José Faur, note 27 supra, at 1660, 1672, claims that "Law" in the Jewish tradition is the "ultimate," "absolute authority," and that "Judaism owes its very existence to exegesis." See also Moshe Halbertal, note 5 supra. Wael B. Hallaq, *The Origins and Evolution of Islamic Law* 1 (Cambridge, Cambridge University Press, 2005) says that "Islamic law is today a significant cornerstone in the reaffirmation of Islamic identity."

53 Chaim Saiman, "Jesus' Legal Theory—A Rabbinic Reading," 23 *Journal of Law and Religion* 97, 102–05 (2008). José Faur, note 27 supra, at 1658–59, 1674, emphasizes that rabbinic interpretation is not Platonic and does not appeal to an unwritten law, but relies on drawing out implications of authoritative texts.

54 Saiman, note 53 supra, at 104, 102. With their acceptance of natural law and their reliance on church tradition, Roman Catholics have an approach to forms of behavior that is more legalistic than that of many Protestants, but they would not be likely to parse biblical passages in the manner Saiman describes.

55 The title of a 2006 Symposium in the *Cardozo Law Review*, Vol. 28, pp. 1–332, is "Text, Tradition, and Reason in Comparative Perspective."

56 Wilhelm Bacher et al., "Biblical Exegesis" in Jewish Encyclopedia, http://www.jewishencyclopedia.com/view.jsp?artid=1029+letter=B (last visited June 5, 2010), taken from Isidore Singer and Cyrus Adler, eds., *The Jewish Encyclopedia: A Descriptive Record of the History, Religion, Literature, and Customs of the Jewish People from the Earliest Times to the Present* (New York and London, Funk and Wagnalls, 1901–05).

57 A brief account of the references of central terms and their places within the history of Jewish law, a helpful guide to those not familiar with that law, is found in Stone, note 12, supra, at 816–17, n.13.

58 Adam Seligman and Suzanne Last Stone, "Preface to Symposium," note 54 supra, at 10.

59 See Hanina Ben-Menahem, "The Second Canonization of the Talmud," in Symposium, note 54 supra, at 37. Justice Elon, note 12 supra, Vol. I., at 39–40, writes that the Jewish world received the Talmud "as the accepted elucidation of the Oral Law, beyond contest or reconsideration," and subsequently Halakhic authorities and judges decided on the basis of that literature rather than consulting the Torah independently.

60 See Christine Hayes, "Rabbinic Contestations of Authority," in Symposium, note 54 supra, 123, 124; Stone, note 12 supra, at 855.

61 Id. at 864.

62 Elon, note 12 supra, Vol. I, at 303–05.

63 Saiman, note 53 supra, at 109.

64 Id. at 111–12. (By contrast, Jesus was concerned that the Pharisees got entangled in mental gymnastics that lost sight of ultimate goals. In the words attributed to Jesus in the Gospels, he does not clearly present Paul's position that believers in his ministry are freed from the law altogether, as contrasted with urging a much more flexible understanding of the law to serve the values of human life. See id. at 107–14.) According to one author, authorities can look to the "intertext" because "they treat the Bible as a perfectly harmonious unit written by one source: God." Note, "Looking to Statutory Intertext: Toward the Use of the Rabbinic Biblical Interpretive Stance in American Statutory Interpretation," 115 *Harvard Law Review* 1456 (2002). Interpreters may disagree with each other but each will assume the Torah is internally consistent. Id. at 1466.

65 Samuel Levine discusses this example in "An Introduction to Legislation in Jewish Law, with Reference to the American Legal System," 29 *Seton Hall Law Review* 916, 922 (1999).

66 "Biblical Exegesis," note 56 supra, at 12.

67 Levine, note 65 supra, 922–23.

68 Levine, note 33 supra, at 462–66. Elon, note 12 supra, Vol. I., at 4, 111, emphasizes the inseparability of "religious" and legal law, the common sources and methods of interpretation of both.

69 Cover, note 27 supra. James Boyd White, *Heracles' Bow: Essays on the Rhetoric and Poetics of the Law* xi–xiii, 36 (Madison, University of Wisconsin Press, 1985), has similarly emphasized the ways in which people construct a social universe of character, community, and culture through the language of law.

70 No doubt, different narratives could make a difference in borderline cases about what taxes one thought he owed, and they could certainly make a difference to whether he willingly paid what he owed. Contrary to what I assume in this study, Cover writes, "The transformation of interpretation into legal meaning begins when someone accepts the demands of interpretation, and through the personal act of commitment, affirms the position taken." Note 27 supra, at 45. See id., at 37, n.104 ("no two people can be said to agree on what the text requires if they disagree on the circumstances in which it will warrant their actions").

71 Bob Jones University v. United States, 461 U.S. 574 (1983).

72 Suzanne Last Stone, "On the Interplay of Rules, 'Cases,' and Concepts in Rabbinic Legal Literature: Another Look at the Aggadot on Honi the Circle-Drawer," *Diné Israel*, vol. 24, 125, 128 (2007).

73 Exactly how to define aggadot turns out to be highly complicated, See Berachyahu Lifshitz, "Aggadah Versus Haggadah: Toward a More Precise Understanding of the Distinction," *Diné Israel*, vol. 24, 11 (2007). Stone says the most common definition is everything that is not halakhah, "Preface," *Diné Israel*, vol. 24, 1 (2007).

74 See Stone, n. 72 supra; Moshe Simon-Shoshan, "Halakhic Mimesis: Rhetorical and Redactional Strategies in Tannaitic Narrative," *Diné Israel*, vol. 24, 101, 102 (2007). See also Elon, note 12 supra, Vol. I, at 93–94, emphasizing the "persistent reciprocal relationship between Halakhah and Aggadoh." Elon also analyzes disagreements over the significance of the midrash, whether, as most authorities believe, it created law as well as integrated preexisting law with Scripture. Id. at 285–86.

75 Simon-Shosha, note 74 supra, at 102.

76 Stone, note 72 supra, at 129.

77 Id. at 135–36.

78 Id. at 135, 140–42.

79 Id. at 145–46. There are further questions about what exceptional people of piety, such as Honi, may do if others would definitely be prohibited. Id. at 146–48.

80 Id. at 149–50.

81 One *might* counter that the import of these different stories is ambiguous enough so that drawing reliable conclusions about how the rule itself was perceived is difficult.

82 Stone does not say how one should now respond to the fact that the two Talmuds have very different implications. She is focusing on whether in each account the story sheds light on how the rule is conceived.

83 As we did with respect to the comparison between legal and literary interpretation, we need to distinguish strictly legal interpretation from the popular sense of the significance of the Constitution. Narrative is bound to loom larger in anyone's overall sense of the Constitution, and of one's perceptions of why we have the rights and duties the legal system provides (or should provide), than in determinations of the vast majority of particular rights and obligations. Cover's own approach focuses significantly on broader visions, but he declines to privilege state interpretations even when they concern actual legal standards.

84 Stone, note 12 supra, at 887.

85 Id. at 848.

86 Elon, note 12 supra, Vol. I, at 339–40.

87 Id. at 295–96.

88 Id. at 292–95. The passage reads in part, "She fails to please him, because he has found something obnoxious about her, and he writes her a bill of divorcement . . . ." One school took "obnoxious" as requiring sexual impropriety. A second school gave that term a broader reading. R. Akiva said it was enough that the husband find someone more beautiful, on the ground that "She fails to please him" would be superfluous if obnoxious behavior was required. One supposes that he may have adopted this approach, one contrary to the drift of the passage itself, because he favored maximum liberty for the husband.

89 See id. at 365–66.

90 Hayes , note 60 supra, at 130.

91 Id. at 132–33.

92 Id. at 135–36.

93 Id. at 136–37.

94 "Biblical Exegesis," note 56 supra, at 30.

95 Experts have concluded that Moses was not the author of the first five books of the Bible, and that the order of the writing of the various biblical texts was much more complicated than a reading of them would suggest. Bruns, note

5 supra, at 64–65, writes that "all we know is that the texts we now call the Hebrew Bible are rooted in centuries of scribal activity that originated, borrowed, compiled, revised, amplified, and redacted various sorts of biblical material in ways no longer possible to describe."

96 For them, the overall nature of Scripture (though not its dominant message) may resemble the way many Christians view their Bible.

97 Suzanne Last Stone, "Formulating Responses in an Egalitarian Age: An Overview," in Marc D. Stern, ed., *Formulating Responses in an Egalitarian Age* 53 (The Orthodox Forum) (Lanham, Md., Rowman & Littlefield Pub., 2005).

98 She rejects the idea that showing past historical adjustment is a legitimate argument for present change. Id. at 66. I'm inclined to think that a substantial number of past changes carries some weight in a judgment about the acceptability of present change.

99 Id. at 60.

100 Id. at 65.

101 Id. at 70–73.

102 Id. at 76–77.

103 Elon, note 12 supra, Vol. I, at 46, writes of the "continuous and ongoing nature of the development of Jewish law . . . ."

104 See Elon, note 12 supra, Vol. II, at 477–879.

105 The custom meant here goes beyond what have been taken to be the implications of the text.

106 Id., Vol. II, at 880–944.

107 Hallaq, note 13 supra at 209. Wael Q. Hallaq writes, *The Origins and Evolution of Islamic Law* 1 (Cambridge, Cambridge University Press, 2005), "Islamic law is today a significant cornerstone in the reaffirmation of Islamic identity . . . as the foundation of a cultural uniqueness."

108 Id. at 1–4, 207. The amount of legal material in the Quran has been said to be as much as that in the Torah. Hallaq, note 107 supra, at 21. For some differences in approaches between Shi'i and Sunni interpreters, see Hamoudi, note 34 supra.

109 Asifa Quraishi, "Interpreting the Qur'an and the Constitution: Similarities in the Use of Text, Tradition, and Reason in Islamic and American Jurisprudence," Symposium, note 55 supra, at 67, 72–73.

110 Nyazee, note 36 supra, at 110.

111 However, the flexibility legislators have outside the specific standards drawn from the Quran and Sunna, see note 36 supra, ameliorates somewhat the problem of interpreting those standards in modern times. By comparison with countries that seek to be guided by Islamic law, the law of Israel is primarily secular— not resting on particular religious premises—although the only Jewish marriages within Israel are Orthodox marriages (the state does accept other marriages of Jews made outside Israel) and those immigrants who must convert to become citizens must convert to Orthodox Judaism. Israel's "law of return" for Jews relates powerfully to a religious vision of the past.

112 Nyazee, note 36 supra, at 8–10. See also Hallaq, note 107 supra, at 151. For an influential work that propounded the thesis of a "common legal theory," see Joseph Schacht, *Introduction to Islamic Law* 60 (Oxford, Oxford University Press, 1964). Hamoudi, note 34 supra, at 254, 289–90, remarks on the modern dissolution of the schools, and the confusion and uncertainty that has caused.

113 Hallaq, note 13 supra, at 9, 4–5. Muhammad suggested that Christians and Jews also had divine laws, which they should follow.

114 Id. at 8.

115 See Hallaq, note 107 supra, at 29–78.

116 Hallaq, note 13 supra, at 18.

117 Hallaq, note 107 supra, at 66–67, 136–38.

118 Hallaq, note 13, at 18.

119 Id. at 17–18, 30–35.

120 Id. at 19, 30–31.

121 Id. at 2, 129.

122 Nyazee, note 36 supra, at 131–33.

123 Id.

124 Wael B. Hallaq, *Authority, Continuity and Change in Islamic Law* 121–25 (Cambridge, Cambridge University Press, 2001).

125 Hallaq, note 107 supra, at 129–30.

126 Nyazee, note 36 supra, at 133.

127 Hallaq, note 13. supra at 83–84, 101–02.

128 Id. at 96–97. Nyazee, note 36 supra, at 140–41. With such examples, it was disputed whether any inference was needed or whether the conclusion was implicit in the textual language.

129 Hallaq, note 13 supra, at 38, 39.

130 Id. at 47.

131 Hallaq, note 107 supra, at 110–11.

132 Quraishi, note 109 supra, at 78. See Hallaq, note 13 supra, at 32.

133 Nyazee, note 36 supra, at 185.

134 Quarishi, note 100 supra, at 83.

135 Id. at 85–86, 90–92.

136 Id. at 93–94.

137 Hallaq, note 13 supra, at 131.

138 Id. at 132.

139 Id. at 133–41.

140 Id. at 139.

141 Quraishi, note 109 supra, at 101–02.

142 Id. at 103. See Nyazee, note 36 supra, at 208–09, 222.

143 Quarishi, note 100 supra, at 105.

144 Id. at 109.

145 Nyazee, note 36 supra, at 44–47, describes the controversy among Muslim jurists over this issue and the majority's conclusion that reason cannot be used as source of law for subjects on which the religious sources are silent.

146 Quraishi, note 109 supra at 107–09. Hallaq, note 13 supra, at 162–206. He regarded the text of the Quran as an integrated whole and treated the Sunna as having secondary status. Id. at 195–96.

147 See Hamoudi, note 34 supra, who criticizes formalist Langdellian reasoning and analyzes the more radical approach of Shi'i jurist Muhammad Baquir al-Sadr. The aim would be to develop principles in which economic relations are not dominantly self-seeking on the capitalist model but reflect a sense of cooperation faithful to Islamic principles.

148 Hallaq, note 109 supra, at 23.

149 Bernard K. Freeman, "Some Reflections on Post-Enlightenment Qur'anic Hermeneutics," 2006 *Michigan State Law Review* 1403, 1423–40.

150 In putting the choice this starkly, I am omitting the wide range of legislative authority any government is granted under Muslim law to deal with contemporary

social conditions. See note 36 supra. Within that domain, Nyazee urges that all laws be reviewed for their consistency with principles of the religious law. Nyazee, note 36 supra, at 293–94.

151 Hallaq, note 13 supra, at 215–16.

152 Id. at 226–28. In Hallaq's opinion, versions of religious utilitarianism, which has been fairly influential, are only "nominally Islamic." Nyazee, note 36 supra, at 266, ridicules "the ludicrous attempt by some to associate this principle ['maṣlahah' or public interest] with Bentham's principle of utility."

153 Hallaq, note 13 supra, at 231–35.

154 Id. at 241–42. See Marion Holmes Katz, The "Corruption of the Times" and the Mutability of the Shariʾa, Symposium note 55 supra, at 171.

155 Id. at 172–85.

156 Hallaq, note 13 supra, at 211. Freeman, note 149 supra, is critical of the failure of Islamic jurists to develop a post-enlightenment hermeneutics.

157 The precise dimensions of the problem of a lack of authoritative settlement would, of course, depend on how far differences survived within the same geographic area.

158 One is reminded of Suzanne Stone's suggestion that "muddling through" may now be the best one can hope for as Jewish law accommodates egalitarian ideals. See text accompanying note 102 supra.

159 Schneiders, note 11 supra, at 57.

160 Jean Grondin, *Introduction to Philosophical Hermeneutics* 47–48 (New Haven, Yale University Press, 1994).

161 Id. at 22–24. Living at the time of Jesus, Philo, a Jew from Alexandria, developed allegorical interpretations of much of the Hebrew Bible.

162 Letter of Paul to the Church in Galatia 4:21–31 (The Jerusalem Bible).

163 Robert M. Grant, *History of Interpretation of the Bible: I Ancient Period*, in *The Interpreter's Bible, Vol. I* 106, 109–10 (New York, Abingdon-Cokerbury Press, 1952).

164 Grondin, supra note 160, at 30. He noted, for example, that it did not make sense to speak of days in the creation story before God had created the sun and the night.

165 Augustine, *Confessions*, Ch. 18, as reprinted in Barrie A. Wilson, *About Interpretation* 69, 71 (New York, Peter Lang, 1988).

166 Grondin, note 160 supra, at 31–32; Wilson, note 165 supra, at 97–90, 100–11 (passages from Cassian and Thomas Aquinas). However, Bruns, note 5 supra, at 140–41, understands scholastic writers in the Middle Ages as cutting back on allegory and moving toward coherent literalism.

167 Will Durant, *The Age of Faith* 755 (New York, Simon and Schuster, 1950).

168 Id. at 756.

169 On the continuation of interpretive pluralism in the Reformation, See R. Grant, *The Bible in the Church: A Short History of Interpretation of the Bible* 129 (Philadelphia, Fortress Press, 1984).

170 Wilson, note 165 supra, at 107 (excerpting William Tyndale, *The Interpretation of Scripture*).

171 Id. at 116–17 (excerpting Martin Luther, *The Clarity of Scripture*).

172 John William Aldridge, *The Hermeneutic of Erasmus* 111 (Richmond, Va., John Knox Press, 1966).

173 Id. at 19, 27–29, 62.

174 Id. at 62.

175 W. Schwarz, note 10 supra, at 167–21.

176 Grondin, note 160 supra, at 40–41.

177 John Witte, Jr., *Law and Protestantism* 1–117 (Cambridge, U.K., Cambridge University Press, 2002).

178 Id. at 10–11, 119–40.

179 For one expression of the idea that the New Testament is both the Word of God (understood metaphorically) and a text produced by fallible human authors, see Schneiders, note 11 supra, at 27–61.

180 Freeman, note 149 supra, at 1416–20, compares developments in Islam to those in the West.

181 See Schubert M. Ogden, *Christ Without Myth* 50 (New York, Harper & Bros. 1961). Schneiders, note 11 supra, at 17–18, 66–68, 82–86, 126–27, 140–42, 159–60, 175–76, offers a more recent Roman Catholic account that draws from the general interpretive theory of Gadamer, and emphasizes the central place of the community.

182 Barrie A. Wilson, "Bultmann's Hermeneutics: A Critical Examination," 8 *International Journal for Philosophy of Religion* 169, 171–74 (1977).

183 Ogden, note 181 supra, at 48–50. He does not here mention simple imperatives about ordinary matters, such as "Please pass the salt," but we may assume that in this context these should be classed with simple information.

184 Id. at 34–39, 43; Norman Perrin, *The Promise of Bultmann* 76, 80 (Philadelphia, J. P. Lippincott Co. 1969).

185 Id. at 70, 102.

186 Id. at 32, 40. From a Catholic perspective, Schneiders, note 11 supra, at 31, 157, also emphasizes God's gift of personal disclosure, and the reader's entering into the text's world of meaning and thereby being changed.

187 Ogden, note 181 supra, at 77, 80–81.

188 Perrin, note 184 supra, at 30, 36, 45–46, 60.

189 See Linell E. Cady, "Hermeneutics and Tradition: The Role of the Past in Jurisprudence and Theology," *Harvard Theological Review* 79:4 (1986) 439, 443–60. As we have seen, text accompanying notes 97–100, Suzanne Last Stone suggests a similar approach to Jewish law.

190 Schneiders, note 11 supra, at 180–97. In contrast to the interpretation given by Mary Jo Frug to *In a Different Voice*, discussed in the last chapter, Schneiders does seem to aim at a best understanding that would fit the author's understanding and be grasped by sophisticated readers.

191 An alternative approach to a partially flawed Scripture would be to acknowledge that a passage in Scripture means one thing—say that homosexual acts are immoral—but that this passage does not reflect the will of God.

192 From outside a religious tradition, one may think that interpreters within the tradition are moved substantially by ordinary reasons for coherence that could apply to all organizations, religious and secular. And interpreters within a tradition may self-consciously take such reasons into account.

193 We could say no, but still conclude that it is wrongful in God's eyes.

194 The closest analogy to evolving interpretation of a set religious text is a constitution that is very difficult to amend. If amendment is impractical, the argument for evolutionary judicial interpretation is strong.

Chapter 5

General Theories of Interpretation

I. INTRODUCTION

In this chapter we turn from theories of interpretation developed in particular disciplines to general theories. Everyone agrees that legal analysis involves one form (or a number of related forms) of interpretation. Thus, any truly general theory will apply to law. But that does not tell us just how a theory will apply to various branches of law and how helpful it may be for those whose overarching interest concerns law. In the bulk of this chapter, I examine the approach of Hans-Georg Gadamer, the most influential modern hermeneutical theorist, and consider the relevance of his approach for understanding interpretation in law and for addressing issues about how that interpretation may best proceed.

My concentration on Gadamer needs a brief explanation. Other theorists may develop his basic insights in ways that are clearer and more consistently persuasive,[1] and without some of Gadamer's assumptions about law that one may criticize. But part of what stands out in Gadamer's major work are his references to applications of law as illustrations. Also important, two prominent legal theorists with broad theories of interpretation, Ronald Dworkin and Aharon Barak, have drawn significantly from Gadamer's basic conception of interpretation,[2] and a number of other writers have undertaken to examine the implications of his theory for legal thought.[3] Focusing on his writing can help us to grasp what plausibly can be said, and what cannot plausibly be said, about the force of such a theory for exercises in legal interpretation. In subsequent volumes, we will examine Dworkin's interpretive theory as it applies to American constitutional, statutory, and common law. These volumes will also comment on matters covered by Barak's "purposive" theory, crucial aspects of which I discuss in the concluding chapter of this book.

My treatment of Gadamer's theory is preceded by a brief historical account of general hermeneutical theories. In the introductory section, I highlight some major questions and distinctions. Awareness of these is necessary to avoid misunderstanding and to discern just what aspects of efforts to determine the meaning and coverage of legal norms are within the coverage of a general theory of interpretation. The book's initial chapter has already noted a number of these questions and distinctions, but they have special relevance to the content of this chapter.

A. Theories about How to Interpret Contrasted with Theories about the Nature of Interpretation

Modern theories about interpretation reach well beyond texts to understanding a wide variety of events and social practices. Whatever the object of interpretation, theories may focus on actual and desirable methods, or on the basic quality or nature of interpretation. One kind of theory need not displace the other, and whether it is explicitly recognized, each kind of theory will have implications for the other kind. Most obviously, someone building a general theory must pay attention to what people actually do when they engage in interpretation in various domains. And it is hard to develop a general theory that has *no* implications for desirable methods. If the theory indicates that all understanding of texts and practices is of a particular kind, then a purported method within a discipline that differs radically from that must either misdescribe what actually occurs, be seriously misguided in what it attempts, or stand in need of some complex explanation why those in the discipline are justified in attempting what they are. These are crucial inquiries about Gadamer's theory, among others, as it may relate to law.

B. What Texts, Communications, and Practices are Subjects of Interpretation?

Within this broad study of legal interpretation, I have adopted an inclusive notion of interpretation, one that embraces all attempts to determine the meaning of what has been written or said. We have seen that, both in respect to literary theory and religious interpretation, a distinction is often drawn between ordinary uses of language and literature, or Scripture. Those who offer general theoretical approaches to interpretation often distinguish between what is clear and straightforward, on the one hand, and what demands thought on the other. Charles Taylor treats interpretation as making clear; its "object must, therefore, be a text or a text-analogue, which in some way is confused, incomplete, cloudy, seemingly contradictory—in one way or another unclear."[4] As Gadamer puts it, "We speak of interpretation when the meaning of a text is not understood at first sight; then an interpretation is necessary. In other words an explicit reflection is required on the conditions that enable the text to have one or another meaning."[5]

As our last two chapters make evident, a text may be clear in one respect and not clear in another, a truth strikingly borne out by the understanding that certain events described in the Hebrew Bible have been interpreted to prefigure the life of Jesus. Another important caution is that some of what is claimed in leading general theories does seem to apply whether or not meaning is immediately clear. And at times the reader is puzzled whether assertions apply to all efforts to determine meaning or only those in which "interpretation" is needed to deal with meaning that is unclear. We face difficulties of this sort when we look at what Gadamer says about law.

Everyone agrees that people interpret both oral and written communications, but scholars disagree about how different these exercises are.

C. The Relation of Text to Interpreter

A range of crucial connected issues fall within this broad topic. Is the text (or text-analogue) an external object to be examined by the subject who interprets, or is there a kind of interaction or dialogue between the interpreter and the text? (Needless to say, the idea of dialogue is simplest when communication is oral and two people actually speak to each other.) Is the interpreter searching for something about the author (her meaning, or some deeper truth about her), about the text, about how the text bears on his life or on some more general concern, or some combination of these? Is the important fruit of interpretation something one can state in propositions, or does it involve experience of a certain kind (as Luther and Bultmann believed about the interpretation of Scripture), or does it produce an opening up to new dimensions of life? One frequent claim is that the interpreter is involved in a hermeneutical circle with the text, and we need to do our best to understand that conception.

D. The Interpreter's Viewpoint and Historicism

A central aspect of modern theories is that interpreters do not come at a text as a blank slate. They begin with a viewpoint or pre-understanding. Interpretation takes place in a historical and social context. We cannot expect those who interpret a text today to have the same perception of it that someone would have had one hundred years ago. If we are influenced by our position in history, it is also evident that we are influenced by our position within the society at the present time. If I am incapable of replicating the original understanding of a text written by a trained lawyer of 1908, I am incapable of replicating the original understanding of a text written by a Japanese artist or a female African-American factory worker of 2010.[6] Just what influences bear most heavily on us as we try to interpret is a crucial, debated question. Gadamer emphasizes the inevitability of tradition, and we need to be very careful about what that entails for him—whether it is, as critics have argued, an essentially conservative stance.

E. Objectivity, Relativism, or Something in Between?

A central issue, for law as for other disciplines, is whether interpretations may be right or wrong, objectively correct or incorrect. If all of us begin with pre-understandings and these vary from age to age, how could interpretations of one age be correct or better than those of another age?

One *might* believe in some sort of historical progression, so that interpretations improve from one era to the next, or that at least at some
pinnacle of history true understanding will be achieved. Or one might
think history is a setting for progressive degradation, with interpretations
worsening as time goes by. A third possibility is that some interpretations
may be objectively misguided and mistaken, although among a range
of other interpretations one could not be said to be more correct than
another. It is also possible that for a given time and place (and perhaps
perspective delimited in other ways) an interpretation could be the best
possible, although not necessarily better than a different interpretation at
a different time and place. To illustrate with one element of Bultmann's
approach to biblical interpretation, perhaps a literal understanding of biblical miracles was the best possible for 300 C.E., but in the twentieth
century, a demythologized, non-literal understanding was more sound. As
readers of Anglo-American jurisprudence are aware, and as we shall see in
subsequent volumes, Ronald Dworkin holds out the idea of time-related
correct answers to legal issues.

Finally, it is crucial to distinguish whether an approach is objectively
better than another from whether we are in a position to perceive that.
The precise significance of this distinction is closely related to what an
interpreter should be looking for and take away from her efforts. If the aim
is to understand as well as possible what the author subjectively meant
by a text, we might agree with Hirsch that one's conclusions can only be
based on probabilities. One's interpretation can be more or less accurate,
even if one cannot know for certain whether one has "got it right," and
even if one lacks compelling arguments why one's estimates of the probabilities are better than those of someone in a preceding or succeeding
generation, or of a colleague in one's own department who disagrees right
now. On the other hand, if a good interpretation is what "speaks to one's
condition," it is hard to see how a present interpretation that speaks to
my condition can be better or worse than different interpretations that
spoke or will speak much better to the conditions of others in ages past or
future. These troubling questions about objectivity and possible correctness will occupy us in this chapter and in our intensive engagement with
approaches to legal interpretation throughout this study.

II. A SKETCH OF THE HISTORY OF GENERAL THEORIES
OF INTERPRETATION BEFORE GADAMER

In this section, I offer an extremely brief sketch of general interpretive
theories before Gadamer. The modest ambition is to provide a sense of
where Gadamer and other modern theorists stand and of the kinds of
questions that were important for Gadamer and remain so.

As we have seen, the early history of interpretive theories involved
analysis of how particular kinds of texts, in particular canonical religious

texts, should be understood. The first theorist to propose a universal hermeneutics, reaching across disciplines, was Johan Conrad Dannhauer, who in 1629 created the neologism hermeneutica.[7] That word points back to the Greek god Hermes, who brought messages from the gods to human beings.[8] For Dannhauer, the task of hermeneutics was to determine the intended meaning of a text, to clarify what the author were attempting to say, whether or not that was true.[9] In the eighteenth century, Johann Martin Chladenius wrote that the task of hermeneutics was not to assure textually correct passages (e.g., correcting mistranslations of ancient texts), or to deal with insufficient insight into a text's language, or with passages that are ambiguous in themselves, but rather to counter insufficient background knowledge of facts that are needed to render an author's meaning comprehensible.[10] In order to attain a "complete understanding of a passage," the interpreter must grasp the viewpoint of the author.[11] Georg Freidrich Meier subsequently proposed a universalist hermeneutics embracing not only communication in language but all "signs," both nonlinguistic signs of human beings and natural signs.[12] One commentator has called Meir's "the last instance of a rationalist hermeneutics."[13]

Perhaps the two most of influential theorists of interpretation during the nineteenth century were Friedrich Schleiermacher and Wilhelm Dilthey. With Schleiermacher, regarded as the "father of a modern hermeneutics as a general study,"[14] we move from the Enlightenment to Romantic Thought.[15] For him, hermeneutics was "related to the concrete, existing, acting human being in the process of understanding dialogue."[16] The aim of the interpreter was to re-experience the author's mental processes, not his emotional feelings or his motives, but his actual thoughts.[17] This can only be achieved by a hermeneutical circle.[18] Just as the parts of a text can only be understood in terms of the whole and the whole can only be understood by the meaning of the parts, an interpreter can discern the meaning of a text only by means of what she already knows and by the ways in which her grasp of the text affects what she knows. In both these aspects, one can think of circles of understanding, and should recognize, as did Schleiermacher, that a degree of intuition is unavoidable.[19] The interpreter enters into a dialogical relation with the text, a kind of conversation.[20] As Schleiermacher's thought developed, he shifted from a hermeneutics centered on language to one oriented toward psychology.[21]

Dilthey emphasized the autonomy of the human sciences, and saw hermeneutics as the foundation for all the humanities and social sciences.[22] The understanding necessary for interpretation differed, he claimed, from the kind of explanation appropriate in natural sciences.[23] It was based on lived experience, and was not purely cognitive.[24] Our experience is not isolated and individual; Dilthey agreed with Hegel that life is a historical reality, that we understand ourselves through history.[25] The interpreter orients herself to the inner conversation that a text bears within it.[26] Despite his emphasis on the historical situatedness of the self,

Dilthey defended "the certainty of understanding against historical skepticism and subjective arbitrariness."[27]

Martin Heidegger, writing in the first part of the twentieth century, had a decisive influence on both Rudolf Bultmann and on Gadamer. He stressed the historicity of human beings, and the temporal, intentional, and historical nature of understanding.[28] All understanding has a forestructure,[29] and understanding itself is less a matter of knowledge than of knowing one's way around,[30] of grasping possibilities for one's being in the world.[31] This emphasis differs sharply from that of both Schleiermacher and Dilthey. In his later writings, Heidegger emphasized the linguisticality of being; words and language are not merely reflections of an external reality, things come into being in words and language.[32] We have seen in Chapter 4 how Bultmann built an approach to biblical interpretation from Heidegger's basic theory; Gadamer's general hermeneutical theory is similar in this respect.

III. THE THEORY OF HANS-GEORG GADAMER

By far the most influential general theory of interpretation is that of Hans-Georg Gadamer, developed most fully in his *Truth and Method*.[33] Crucial elements of his theory warrant a careful examination to see how they may apply to law and whether, in various applications, they are convincing. Gadamer does not leave us with conjecture about relevance for law, because important passages take up that subject, though it is less than clear just how much law he intends to cover. I shall trace major aspects of his theory and fundamental challenges to it and then investigate two reflections on its application to American constitutional law, the second of which suggests serious dangers if legal interpretation is conceived as fitting neatly into Gadamer's vision.

Gadamer argues that truth and understanding are not limited to what can be discovered by the methods of natural science. Most human understanding is hermeneutical, involving an interpretation by a person who acts at a particular moment in history. Interpretation is critical not only for law, theology, and literature, but for all art, including performance art, for history, for other human sciences, for conversation, and for all reading of language. Further, interpretation is also involved in natural science, most prominently in the choice of problems scientists set for themselves.

Although Gadamer comments on some differences in interpretive approaches, his main emphasis is on common features and close similarities, which he presents at a high level of abstraction, with a dearth of examples. Because Gadamer's concern is not exactly with hermeneutical methods of various disciplines, we need to be cautious when we come across passages that seem to have a direct bearing for legal interpretation.[34]

Among Gadamer's central theses are that interpretation is motivated by present interests and involves a "historically effected consciousness,"[35] that "application is an element of understanding,"[36] and that each application involves interpretation.

Part I of *Truth and Method* focuses on truth in the experience of art. That involves judgment—something other than rational proof[37]—which cannot be taught in the abstract but "only practiced from case to case . . . because no demonstration from concepts can guide the application of rules."[38] The function of judgment is familiar from jurisprudence. "At issue is always something more than the correct application of general principles. Our knowledge of law, and morality too, is always supplemented by the individual case, even productively determined by it. The judge not only applies the law in concreto but contributes through his very judgment to developing the law ('judge-made law')."[39] Aesthetic judgment, Gadamer says, is similar.[40]

For Gadamer, aesthetic appreciation is not "a pure aesthetic consciousness, but the act of a mind and spirit that has collected and gathered itself historically."[41] Like other human sciences, aesthetics seeks to find truth in experience.

The contemporaneity or "being present" that is true of religious rituals is also true when we experience art.[42] It is obvious that different performances of dramatic or musical works will be different; with plastic arts, a work "displays itself under various conditions," and the "viewer of today not only sees things in a different way, he sees different things."[43] Gadamer subsequently extends his conclusions to literary works of art and written texts of all kinds. In the fundamental aspects of interpretation, all these texts are similar; "understanding them transforms the dead trace of meaning back into living meaning."[44]

Turning more broadly to understanding in the human sciences in Part II, Gadamer rejects the view that the main point of hermeneutics is the avoidance of misunderstanding of an original production.[45] Hermeneutics is the foundation for the study of history; not only are the sources texts, "but historical reality itself is a text that has to be understood."[46]

Echoing Heidegger, Gadamer draws on a concept of our "life-world," which is not an object for us, but "the pregiven basis of all experience."[47] It generates fore-meanings that determine understanding. A person who is trying to understand a text reads the text with expectations that he projects onto the text as a whole.[48] Tradition is always a part of us. Tradition and custom have a nameless authority "that lies beyond rational grounding and in large measure determines our intuitions and attitudes."[49]

In the human sciences, the present and its interests motivate the theme and object of research.[50] When we understand, we participate in "a process of transmission in which past and present are constantly mediated."[51] When we try to understand a text, we aim to see how what the author is saying could be right, transposing ourselves into the perspective within which he formed his views.[52]

A hermeneutical circle involves not merely the relation of the whole to its parts, but also "the interplay of the movement of tradition and the movement of the interpreter."[53] "Understanding involves a fusion of present and historical horizons."[54]

It is worth pausing over these basic concepts, so central to the theory of Gadamer and so elusive to grasp. The relation of text to reader that he conceives is by no means simple. The reader comes to a text with a pre-understanding, and this is something well beyond the points that someone will not read a text unless he has a reason to do so and has at least a minimal grasp of the subject matter. One's pre-understanding will influence how one perceives a text initially and that influence will never disappear completely, but it does not follow that one will always read a text in a way that best fits the pre-understanding. Gadamer conceives the text as in dialogue with the interpreter. Of course, the "dialogue" with a written text does not involve an actual conversation,[55] but nonetheless understanding involves questions the interpreter puts to the text and which the text answers.[56] Charles Taylor suggests that understanding a text or event in history, and other inquiries in human sciences, should be conceived on a "conversation" model in which the interpreter listens to his "partner," and may "redefine what [he is] aiming at."[57]

Perhaps my response to one element of Clifford Geertz's famous essay on Balinese cockfighting[58] will provide an illustration of Gadamer's notion of dialogue. The essay shows how important cockfighting is within Balinese culture, and undertakes an illuminating explanation of its multifaceted significance. One question Geertz discusses is why people bet more money on some fights than, on surface utilitarian analysis, makes rational sense. Geertz explains what is at stake with "deep play." In his account, the betting of large amounts of money (with wins and losses likely to balance out over the long run) involves critical matters of esteem, honor, dignity, and respect.[59] Geertz writes, "The Balinese attempt to create an interesting, if you will, 'deep' match by making the center bid as large as possible so that the cocks matched will be as equal and as fine as possible, and the outcome, thus, as unpredictable as possible."[60]

My question (or initial skepticism) concerned the relation of the betting to the fighting ability of the cocks and to the emotional investment of their owners and their kin in the outcomes. Aware of the rooting interest of Americans in teams of their schools, colleges, and cities, and having played sports in high school and college (and been extremely disappointed and ashamed when our archrival Haverford beat us in my final college basketball game), I reflected that in the United States for most people the amount of money they bet might well symbolize their attachments to teams and their performances; it would not itself be the main source of their pride and joy or shame and despair at an outcome. I wondered whether for the Balinese their main identification and some of what made a match important might not be their emotional investment in birds they have bought and trained, with the bets of secondary importance. I did not find in Geertz's essay an obvious answer to the question, but I recognized that his conclusions were based largely on interviews. Those might well have revealed that the bets figure much more importantly than, say, bets by most fans of the two competing teams in the Super Bowl or World Series. And when I reread the sentence I have quoted, I realized that it was not very clear about the comparative significance of the large bet and the basic desire that one's bird triumph. Perhaps that is itself a distinction that the Balinese would not make, perhaps it would not be evident to an outsider, perhaps it was a topic that Geertz did not think worth pursing in depth.

Gadamer's fusion of horizons is clearly connected with his assumption that present interest drives interpretation. He does not suppose that the present horizon will simply determine the understanding of an older text, or that the interpreter will be able to accept the past horizon in some pure form. The "fusion" implies a mixing, blending, or meeting, an interpretation that is the product of both horizons together.[61] Thus, my initial pre-understanding definitely affected how I read this part of the Geertz essay; the essay undermined any easy assumption of mine that the relation between pride in a team or in an individual competitor to betting on a contest is always as I conceived it; and one consequence was a question in my mind that I did not find fully answered by the essay. The hermeneutical circle, or circles, involved both my sense of the parts and the whole of the Geertz essay and my mediating my own cultural experience with my perception of the text. Comparing my own experience with what Geertz describes also had another effect that is central to Gadamer and other existential theorists—interpretation led to some modest advance in my own self-understanding, in my coming to see that what I previously regarded as "natural" may be more personal or connected to a particular culture.

The concept of "tradition" is both central, and controversial, in Gadamer's thought. To put "tradition" in the most unattractive light, from a theoretical point of view,[62] Gadamer is asserting some kind of uniform or overarching perspective that inevitably and dominantly dictates interpretation and desirably does so. One literary critic has sharply suggested that Gadamer's idea of tradition resembles a "club of the like-minded."[63] Critics have worried that Gadamer's idea of tradition favors conservative interpretation, but this is not Gadamer's aim.[64] An interpreter may read a text against her tradition, and her exposure to the text may lead her to do so. Defenders of Gadamer have resisted the notion that traditions are unified rather than multifaceted.[65]

We can easily understand that some interpreters may begin with a pre-understanding that is contrary to what may be the dominant tradition, if one can be indentified. Thus, a Karl Marx or an early feminist might conceive himself or herself as in sharp reaction to crucial features of the dominant outlooks. Each of them would approach texts from their distinctive approach. That might draw from aspects of a dominant outlook (as Marx drew his dialectical approach from Hegel and feminists relied on broad notions of equality and justice), but even in reading *against* a dominant view, an interpreter is inevitably influenced by it. If we are to give Gadamer's notion of tradition its most plausible and sympathetic reading, we must conceive a wide diversity of influences on people's "life-worlds." What is impossible is that they can address texts and social practices in a way that is genuinely detached from those influences.

In response to the claim that he has legitimated a prejudice in favor of existing social relations,[66] Gadamer reiterates that we cannot free ourselves from tradition, but that does not mean that social reform is impossible or unwise. Gadamer continues, "I find it frighteningly unreal when people like Habermas ascribe to rhetoric a compulsory quality that one must reject in favor of unconstrained, rational dialogue."[67] For Gadamer, clarifying the effect of tradition is not a recommendation of blind adherence; indeed, the more acute our awareness of the basis for our pre-understandings, the better the chance that we will be able to be self-critical about their influence.[68]

Gadamer's notion that an interpreter begins the task of understanding by trying to see how what the author is saying could be right may well describe much reading of literature and work in the social sciences, including history, but it is not a universal feature. I shall subsequently comment about this idea in connection with law; suffice it to say here that some reading is motivated by a desire to discern flaws and errors. If one begins with an assumption that the text is fundamentally misguided, as might a Roman Catholic who sets out to read Luther, one may be looking for what may be wrong more than one is looking for what may be right.

In contrast to older distinctions between understanding, interpretation, and application, Gadamer says that all are encompassed within interpretation. Recognition that application is an integral aspect of understanding helps to explain why philosophical, legal, and theological hermeneutics are closely related.[69] For law, understanding is always application. "A law does not exist in order to be understood historically, but to be concretized in its legal validity by being interpreted . . . . This implies that the text . . . if it is to be understood properly—i.e., according to the claim it makes— must be understood at every moment, in every concrete situation, in a new and different way."[70] Gadamer denies that there is any unequivocal distinction between dogmatic and historical interest in law. The jurist must understand historical change, and the historian needs to mediate between original and present applications of the law.[71]

Turning to orders, Gadamer notes that not every failure to carry out an order is disobedience. An order's recipient may realize that obeying an order would be inappropriate in a concrete situation. Undertaking creatively to understand its meaning, he must look not to the order's words nor the mind of the person giving the order, but must understand the situation and what would be responsible action on his part. "Thus, there is no doubt that the recipient of an order must perform a definite creative act in understanding its meaning."[72]

In his third part, Gadamer pursues the idea "that the fusion of horizons that takes place in understanding is actually the achievement of language."[73] Tradition is essentially verbal in character, something most clear in the case of written tradition.[74] An ideal for a historian of leaving his own concepts behind is not only unattainable, but misguided.[75] "To try to escape from one's own concepts in interpretation is not only impossible but manifestly absurd."[76] It follows that there can be no single correct interpretation of a text. Human experience of the world is verbal.[77] Gadamer says, "Every word causes the whole of the language to which it belongs to resonate and the world-view that underlies it to appear."[78] If this is accurate, one would expect any message to convey something subtly different to each reader, since each will have a subtly different world-view and sense of some words.

Among the major challenges to Gadamer's theory, and others like it, are: (1) it emphasizes language too greatly in comparison with factors like material welfare and power relations of class, race, and gender; (2) it mistakenly denies the possibility of objectively correct answers to interpretive questions; (3) it posits a coherence of texts, and an interaction between texts and interpreters that does not exist.

In Chapter 3, in our discussion of Frug's interpretation of *In a Different Voice*, we have already seen how our ways of speaking could or could not be central to our conceptions of ourselves, of social relations, and of ethical responsibilities. It is difficult here to generalize without failing to advance beyond the obvious. A great many of our experiences are embedded in language; even in respect to other experiences, such as acute physical pain, our understanding and explanation of them will be in language. It does not *necessarily* follow that our experiences would be much different if the words and concepts of our language were themselves very different, but often that will be the case. In one striking example, Charles Taylor suggests that the whole concept of negotiation, which affects how we think about many aspects of our lives, was absent in the life of traditional Japanese villagers.[79] One might also believe that this difference in perception about negotiation reflects the influence of relations of class or power in the development of such concepts. If, typically, it is virtually impossible to single out the influence of language, as compared with other factors, in how people perceive social relations, the best we can do is to be very attentive to how our language does affect our thinking and to be sensitive to how changes in language might affect our understanding.

Some thinkers have refused to accept Gadamer's skeptical conclusions about uniquely correct answers. Gadamer does not fall into complete relativism, assuming as he does that some interpretations can be better than others, but does reject the notion of any transhistorical correct answer. [80] Every interpretation is for a particular time and place, and interpretations of our generation would not be apt for those of preceding and succeeding generations. This approach rejects any Hegelian or Marxist notion that at the end of history there will come a time when the Spirit is fully realized or false consciousness is swept away. Without asserting that kind of historical development, some modern thinkers have supposed that the best answer is one that would be reached in ideal conditions, and that our efforts should be directed to imagining what people in such a position would understand and decide. Most famously, Jürgen Habermas has looked to what people would agree upon in ideal conditions of free, undistorted dialogue.[81] Karl-Otto Apel has sought a regulative principle in "the idea of the realization of an unlimited community of interpretation which everyone who argues presupposes implicitly as an ideal instance of control."[82] Michael Riffaterre conceives of a "superreader" of literary texts.[83] Without trying to resolve whether one can speak of correct or best interpretations for a wide range of disciplines, we shall, in our study of various forms of legal interpretation, refer to claims about correct answers in these domains. Prior chapters have already suggested that given the coercive effect of law and the desirability of uniform interpretations, there are much stronger reasons for seeking an interpretation that will (or should) be widely regarded as correct (or sound, or desirable) than may be true for works of poetry and abstract art. Of course, reasons for seeking a correct interpretation do not show that one is available, a proposition already apparent from Chapter 2's treatment of vagueness and law.

A radically different challenge to hermeneutics as presented by Gadamer is that it assumes a cohesiveness of texts and a relation between text and interpreter that does not exist. One may take this as the message of "deconstruction," which emphasizes the elusiveness of texts, their internal contradictions and gaps. A fruitful interaction with a text may consist not in aiming to discern a unified message but in "play," focusing on the rich variety of signifiers. We might regard this kind of approach, represented by Jacques Derrida among others,[84] as a species of highly negative hermeneutics or as rejecting interpretation altogether.[85] Whatever the value of this outlook for literary criticism, it seems inapt for many ordinary messages people convey to each other. And unless one thinks it would be desirable to undercut the basic premise of legal systems,[86] it is unhelpful in its most negative form for law. Nevertheless, insights into contradictions and into surprising relationships between concepts, of the sort Jack Balkin has written about and which Chapter 3 discusses briefly, can be valuable contributions to legal interpretation.

In what he says, as well as the space he devotes to various subjects, Gadamer is mainly interested in artistic interpretation, how that relates to historical interpretation, and how both of these differ from the methods of natural science. He has a substantial interest in biblical interpretation. He uses legal interpretation mainly to help him make points about other forms of interpretation and to build his vision of a universal theory of hermeneutics. This may help explain why he does not more directly confront some of the more questionable aspects of his generalizations as they apply to law, aspects that those interested in legal interpretation need to review carefully.

A relatively minor point concerns Gadamer's assertion that no sharp distinction exists between the jurist's dogmatic interest and the historian's interest in law. A legal historian may have a number of interests, each of which relates in some way to present concerns, but what would be the most appropriate present application of legal concepts, the main concern of most jurists, need not be a major one. The historian may be primarily interested in a description of how the facts of the legal system have come about; the typical jurist's reflections, while taking account of history, are heavily normative.

Of far greater importance is what Gadamer says about applications of legal norms, suggesting that they inevitably involve judgment and create new legal meaning. Given what he says about understanding language in general, and about complying with orders, it is hard to know just how to take his comments. More particularly, it is not clear whether his remarks are intended to reach all instances in which the applications of orders and legal norms are involved, or only those for which the reach of the orders and norms is debatable. Since our main aim is to clarify what can reasonably be said on this subject, rather than resolve exactly what Gadamer or his text is suggesting, we need to examine the possibility one of his passages appears to suggest, that every decision to follow an order or apply a law involves a creative act of understanding.

In approaching this topic, I undertake a modest digression about categories of communication that has broader relevance for claims about definiteness and indefiniteness of applications of imperative language. I show that in certain crucial respects, imperatives do not differ from descriptive statements, and rules of behavior do not differ from individual imperatives. If the applications in all of the examples within these four categories were thought to involve judgment and to create new meaning, the sense of "judgment" and "new meaning" would be very watered down indeed, and useless. Once we see that any more robust sense of "judgment" and "new meaning" is obviously inapt for other forms of language, we can easily grasp its implausibility for many applications of legal rules. Whatever Gadamer means exactly about the application of law, it is, without some qualification or clarification, substantially misleading. I shall treat in turn individual descriptive statements, individual imperatives, general descriptions, and general imperatives.

Four members of a family are sitting at breakfast as the sun rises. The mother, who is watching the television, comments, "The weather report says it is 20° out." (The others understand that the scale is Fahrenheit.) The life significance of this report of cold weather will differ among the family members, and the report itself may affect their lived experiences differently, but the other three understand the meaning of the mother's statement in the same way. It would be odd to say that the reception of the information by each involves judgment or creates new meaning.

Are imperatives different? The father addresses his daughter and says, "Please pass the sugar." If the sugar is on the table, and the father typically puts sugar in his coffee, the request is perfectly straightforward. Here, it is true, more is involved than the pure receipt of information; the child must decide whether to pass the sugar. She might refuse because her father's doctor said sugar is dangerous for him or because Dad made her do her homework last night, but these deliberations whether to comply do not go to the meaning of what he has said.[87] They do not, despite what Gadamer says about following orders, involve a kind of interpretation of her father's request that involves judgment or creates new meaning. (The next two chapters, on informal instructions and the law of agency, explore the distinction between interpreting an order in unexpected circumstances and not following an order.)

Does the analysis change if one is speaking of more general descriptive remarks or normative rules? Suppose a friend tells me, "Water put into trays will freeze if placed in a working freezer." I need not exercise judgment to conclude that I can make ice in my well-functioning freezer if he is right. Similarly, if a parent tells a child, "You should brush your teeth every night before going to bed," the child is aware that if he is not ill or unusually exhausted, or off on a camping trip, he has been told, in effect, that he should brush his teeth on a particular evening. That guides to behavior are not so different in this respect from descriptive statements may be confirmed by thinking about timetables, which operate as norms of behavior for those running trains or buses and as predictions for passengers (based on their understanding that the people responsible will attempt to comply).

Two kinds of judgments are involved when people construe rules of behavior. The subject of a rule, or a judge of that person's behavior, must determine whether the situation is one that is obviously covered, or obviously not covered, by the rule, or whether, for some reason, it is on the edge of possible coverage. (For this purpose, we may regard the edges of coverage as including both situations that are borderline given the rule's language and its evident aims, and situations that seem covered but involve extraordinary circumstances that may lift them out of the rule's application.) It is conceivable, but very rare, that *no* situation will seem obviously covered. A person considering the import of a rule will have to determine whether the circumstances are within the rule's coverage. In many, many instances there is really no room for argument; the rule applies (or does not apply) and there is no extraordinary circumstance. Most assessments of parking violations and determinations of tax liability fall clearly within straightforward rules, and no exception is remotely plausible. Whatever "judgment" is needed is minimal, and the application hardly creates new law, except in the obvious sense that the rule has been followed by, or applied to, a particular individual. If someone chooses not to obey a rule that definitely covers a situation, that ordinarily does not affect the rule's content. If it is taken as a general claim, the idea that each law, to be properly understood, "must be understood at every moment, in every concrete situation, in a new and different way,"[88] is mistaken.

Gadamer's reliance on Aristotle's idea of equity as a necessary correction of the law does not save his thesis. Aristotle claimed that "the law" requires equitable correction in highly unusual circumstances. According to Gadamer, a law "cannot contain practical reality in its full concreteness . . . . The law is always deficient, . . . because human reality is necessarily imperfect in comparison to the ordered world of law, and hence allows no simple application of the law."[89] It is a huge, unwarranted leap from the proposition that "the law" *sometimes* needs correction to the conclusion that it is "always deficient" and "allows of no simple application."

It may be relevant that Gadamer draws heavily from Aristotle's notion of practical reason developed in his writing on ethics.[90] For Gadamer, hermeneutical understanding is like practical thinking about ethics. At least one plausible view about ethical choice is that it must be made in terms of understanding each situation in its full concreteness.[91] But what legal rules do, as Joseph Raz has emphasized,[92] is in a sense supplant ethical choice. They dictate what should be done in a broad range of situations identified in advance.

IV. APPLICATIONS OF GADAMER'S THEORY TO AMERICAN CONSTITUTIONAL LAW

In this section, I discuss two interesting, quite different, articles about how Gadamer's theory might apply to, and affect our understanding of, American constitutional law. The first aims to show how that theory applies and illuminates that understanding. The second cautions against serious risks created by thinking about constitutional interpretation in Gadamerian terms, risks generated mainly by important factors for decision that may then be disregarded or seriously undervalued.

In an article entitled "Law, Hermeneutics, and Public Debate,"[93] Georgia Warnke examines the relevance of Gadamer's theory for law and offers a general theory about interpreting texts and social meanings that she applies to constitutional interpretation.[94] She employs the movie *Sense and Sensibility* as her major nonlegal illustration, not because she claims it is distinctive but because it shows clearly the task of a modern interpreter dealing with a text from a different era.

Two preliminary observations and a brief exploration of aspects of constitutional interpretation may assist in understanding and evaluating Warnke's account. The first observation is that what Gadamer has to say seems much more promising in relation to many issues of constitutional law than for simple applications of No Parking rules and the assessment of tax liabilities. The second is that the fundamental soundness of Gadamer's theory of interpretation might bear on the wisdom of a form of legal interpretation without itself yielding a decisive answer to whether the form is feasible or desirable. The possibilities of significance are more complex than "not relevant" or "determinative."

Much constitutional interpretation differs from the application of modern, standard legal rules in three related dimensions. The basic text to be interpreted derives from an earlier historical era. Many provisions are cast in highly general and open-ended language: "Congress shall make no law . . . abridging the freedom of speech, or of the press"; "cruel and unusual punishments [shall not be] inflicted"; no state shall "deprive any person of life, liberty, or property without due process of law; nor deny to any persons . . . the equal protection of the laws."[95] Such provisions typically reflect deep cultural and historical assumptions, and their interpretation in difficult cases depends on sensitivity to such assumptions. These features combine to make relevant sources and understandings more complex than what one needs to construe parking rules.[96] (However, within our system, earlier authoritative judicial decisions will often simplify the task of a court dealing with a novel constitutional case.)

To take one example of a constitutional issue that is now highly controversial, should partners of the same gender have a constitutional right to marry? Charles Taylor has urged that our notion of "value" implies a range of choice that would not have been conceived in other ages, in which people might choose to do good or evil but would not have been understood as having the freedom to decide for themselves what is good or bad.[97] If Taylor is right, the choice to engage in "deviant" sexual behavior may once have been viewed as a yielding to temptation to do what is unnatural and wrong. The notion that those carrying on such relations would have a right of liberty to marry or to constitute a relevant group that is being denied equal protection of the laws if they are not allowed to marry, would have struck most citizens as odd, perhaps inconceivable. Our modern notions of government are far less connected to religious and moralistic conceptions of right and wrong.[98] Many now perceive the choice of sexual partners to be a basic liberty and consider gays as a group that should be protected from unjust discrimination regarding the privilege to marry. Of course, this view is far from universal among our citizens, and it may not yet be held by a majority. But whether we agree or not with the conclusion, we can now understand a view that the norms of due process and equal protection should extend to a constitutional right to marry a partner of the same gender. Such a view represents one interpretation of a historical text in light of modern concerns, an exemplar of the manner in which Gadamer conceives historical interpretation. One author has proposed that a constitutional right to die could be similarly conceived.[99]

As these examples also illustrate, one *might* take the soundness of Gadamer's basic theory as supporting constitutional interpretations that are responsive to modern appraisals of fundamental rights and social desirability; but, in responding to Professor Warnke, I shall argue that much else needs to be considered.

People understand things, Warnke says, in light of historically contingent expectations and presumptions. Legal texts, like other texts, set limits on what are legitimate interpretations, but they must be concretized at various moments of history in new ways. Interpretation and application inevitably reflect the perspectives and needs of those who do the interpreting. For constitutional interpretation, Warnke urges that we must understand provisions like the First Amendment and Equal Protection Clause in the light of history, including our history since these parts of the Constitution were adopted.[100] The force of the "must" is epistemological rather than moral; that is, we are incapable of understanding constitutional texts in any other way, because of our own cultural and historical context.[101] Warnke adds to Gadamer that, because of significant differences among groups and individuals within a single broad culture at any time in history, we should also expect differences of interpretation among contemporaries.

According to Professor Warnke, Emma Thompson's version of Jane Austen's *Sense and Sensibility* interprets the book's text from a contemporary perspective.[102] The movie emphasizes Elinor Dashwood's consciousness of her ethical duties toward others and treats her effort to maintain self-restraint as heroic, an understanding different from what would have attached to her behavior when Austen wrote her book.

Warnke leaves us with the distinct impression that a modern interpretation must speak to the sensitivities and concerns of a modern audience. She writes that "the way we understand [Austen's depiction of English] propriety necessarily differs from the way in which Austen understood it."[103]

Moving from literary to constitutional interpretation, Warnke suggests that we cannot understand the Constitution according to the "original intent"; rather, "we must understand the principles themselves in terms of the perspectives the new situation sheds on them."[104] Warnke then considers the debate over abortion. In an interpretive discussion, people should learn from, and accommodate, different ways of understanding.[105] Warnke suggests that interpreters should seek to achieve a unity of part and whole and try to understand a text so that it has something to teach, so that what "it claims or expresses might be illuminating."[106]

Although Warnke may be right that interpretation is necessarily in light of present concerns, we must distinguish what is inevitable from what is conscious choice or resistible inclination. More particularly, hermeneutic theory, standing alone, cannot demonstrate that a jurisprudence that concentrates on the original meaning of a text is misguided.

As we can see in respect to different kinds of endeavors, whether descriptions of nature or of human society, or performances based on classic literature, interpreters have a choice as to how much to focus on specific contemporary concerns. Studies recount how bees live. Our tendency to anthropomorphize may lead us to fantasize what being a queen bee or a drone is like, but scientific presentations do not tell us how bees see life. Such studies, of course, do speak to our concerns in some senses. They help satisfy curiosity about how fellow creatures live. An imaginative reader may transfer practice in a beehive to corporate organizations; others may discover how to exterminate bees in their attics. But scientists are not mainly trying to teach such lessons, and many readers will not draw any. Studies of higher animals often use mental concepts like "want," "intend," "care," "pain"; but writers usually do not attempt to relate their studies to a particular cultural consciousness or contemporary set of social problems.[107]

For history and anthropology, the question of our contemporary concerns is sharper. Anthropologists and historians can never shed the skin of their own cultures and stages in history. They will never see another culture as "it really is" or exactly as people within that culture see it, but they have a range of choice. They may begin with categories of their own societies and investigate "how those people do (or did) it." Thus, Llewellyn and Hoebel identified Cheyenne institutions of law and adjudication,[108] hoping, in part, for lessons that might aid our law and adjudication. Alternatively, an anthropologist may attempt to understand a culture from the inside, as its participants see (or saw) it, trying to be as faithful as possible to their own vision.[109] The author's aim is not to teach particular lessons to readers, although his study presents forms of social life that readers may not previously have understood. Only sometimes will readers consider unfamiliar forms as potentially relevant in their own lives.[110] Although any anthropological or historical account will be responsive to some modern interest (and perhaps any account of different ways of being increases to a degree our sense of our own way of being), writers have a distinct choice whether or not to focus on what may aid our comprehension of problems and choices in our own social life.

This brings us to Jane Austen and *Sense and Sensibility*. Professor Warnke refers to Austen's own understanding with some confidence, remarking that "Austen had no basis for contextualizing English self-restraint . . .. We cannot understand Austen the way she understood herself because history has proceeded . . . ."[111] Of course, no one can replicate Austen's understanding with precision. Beyond the general impossibility of fully knowing another's mind stand substantial barriers of history and culture. Yet, if Warnke realizes how Austen's vision differed from Emma Thompson's more contemporary focus, we see that Thompson had a choice of presenting the novel to reflect Austen's own perspective as closely as possible or (putting it crudely) responding to modern concerns.[112]

But can anyone present Austen's own vision if we "cannot understand Austen the way she understood herself"? Part of our incapacity is that we are aware of a vast number of social possibilities that did not occur to Austen; she took for granted many things that we cannot take for granted. Passages about the chasm between ourselves and Austen reminded me of how we view our own childhoods. As children, we take for granted many things that we no longer take for granted as adults. I cannot now understand myself as a six-year-old the way I understood myself when I was six, but I can (through memory) grasp to some degree how I then understood myself and the world around me. With help from others explaining Austen's time and place, and with imaginative recollection of how we as children inhabited a narrower world of settled values,[113] we might be able to roughly approximate how Austen saw things, even though we could never adopt her perspectives, because we know too much. A conceivable choice to display Austen's own vision as fully as possible differs from viewing the novel self-consciously from the perspective of contemporary concerns.[114]

Attempted reconstruction of the author's vision, as completely as possible, is *one* appropriate technique of interpretation. For performances of literary works, one may conclude that various approaches are valuable, including attempted reconstruction; one need not choose any approach over all others as the best.[115]

That this conclusion is not limited to the understanding and performance of literary works can be seen in relation to a recent disagreement over the status of Roger Williams's writing in the first half of the seventeenth century about religious liberty and separation of church and state. In her *Liberty of Conscience*, Martha Nussbaum urges that certain crucial claims of Williams stand independent of his theological premises.[116] Influenced partly by scholars who regard Williams's perspective as thoroughly influenced by his religious understanding,[117] and taking account of the pervasiveness of religious references and his clear position that a small segment of true Christians should separate from the unregenerate mass, I have been disinclined to take these passages as unconnected to his underlying religious vision. On reflection, I have seen that one might ask what Williams himself believed about whether the claims in the passages depended on theological premises, what most knowledgeable readers of the time would have understood as the degree of connection, what most careful readers now would perceive, and finally, how we might best understand the passages in our own consideration of desirable relations of government and religion. A historian trying to understand how persons of Williams's time and place understood the relation of theological beliefs to conclusions about the role of government and law might be mainly interested in one or both of the first two questions. A theorist engaged in normative political philosophy right now would find the last question the most important.[118] Given the legitimacy of these different inquiries, it may well be misguided to think there is one simple answer to what these passages "really mean."

As Chapter 3 develops, legal interpretation differs significantly from literary interpretation. The ultimate question a judge typically faces is how a legal norm should be applied to present conditions. The nature of this question, combined with basic principles of legal interpretation, reveal two ways in which a particular legal standard is less self-contained than a literary or philosophical work.

One aspect of individual legal rules that makes them less self-contained than literary works is that when social values and practices change, so also does the overall corpus of legal norms. There is good reason to interpret particular legal rules of long standing so they fit reasonably well with other legal rules, many of which will be relatively contemporary.

On occasion, older legal norms must be applied to circumstances that the norm-makers did not conceive at all. A striking example is electronic communication. If we ask how the Free Speech and Free Press Clauses apply to electronic media, we know that people in 1791 did not have a specific view about that. If judges want to use the specific intentions of authors as a guide, they can rely only on hypothetical judgments—judgments about what the authors of an earlier era would have thought. Their answers to such questions are likely to be much less confident than expert evaluations of what Jane Austen actually understood.[119] And a judge may wonder how to frame the critical question. Should he imagine a social world of 1791 in which radio, television, computers, and the Internet are suddenly introduced; or should he consider how these forms of electronic communication function in modern society? The latter approach seems obviously more apt. If modern social conditions are introduced for novel technology, should not all constitutional problems be assessed against modern conditions? But, critics answer, judges who ask themselves what people of 1791 would have desired for unforeseen conditions may find it hard to distinguish that judgment from their own personal sense of how the constitutional language would best apply. A further complexity is that some of the most important unforeseen conditions are how people view themselves and their fellows, a point illustrated by Charles Taylor's account of the development of beliefs about autonomy and choice in respect to values. To ask how a citizen of 1791 would have responded if he were a different kind of person hardly seems a historical exercise at all.

Unlike literary interpreters, judges making practical decisions about laws challenged as unconstitutional must decide (implicitly at least) on a best approach. Perhaps Warnke is right that there may be "different, equally legitimate interpretations of common constitutional principles,"[120] but judges cannot throw up their hands and declare that legal cases are ties.

What I have said thus far about legal interpretation actually supports most of Professor Warnke's own ideas on that subject. Attempts to reconstruct and present authors' understandings may not always be doomed as interpretive projects, but applications of old law to new circumstances and the extensive need for hypothetical judgments render the reconstructive endeavor even more difficult for old constitutional norms than it is for old literary works. Yet a further problem for law that does not exist for the authorial understanding of Jane Austen is the presence of multiple authors.

How might a critic resist a conclusion that judicial interpretation should be responsive to modern concerns in more or less the manner of Emma Thompson's interpretation of *Sense and Sensibility*? She might insist on an allocation of responsibilities that does not assign this function to judges. She might argue that the business of judges is to try to figure out what the lawmakers intended (or readers then understood) in some narrow sense, however difficult this endeavor may be. Bringing controlling constitutional and legislative norms in line with modern concerns would not be within the proper sphere of judges; it would be the business of those who make statutes and amend constitutions. Even if she conceded that answering hypothetical questions about what the lawmakers would have wanted for altered conditions involves highly uncertain interpretive efforts, the critic might nevertheless believe that an original intent standard desirably affords modern judges less latitude to act upon their own notions of right and good than do other approaches to judicial interpretation. General observations about hermeneutics cannot demonstrate that this position is mistaken, though they may make us skeptical about its feasibility and promise.

Given the vagaries of appraisals of hypothetical judgments and the open-ended quality of many constitutional provisions, an original intent jurisprudence actually restrains judges relatively little in much of constitutional interpretation. When one adds the difficulties of formal amendment of the federal Constitution, interpretation that attends to modern perspectives is, as I shall argue in a later volume, substantially more attractive than interpretation whose dominant guiding principle is original understanding. Some form of original intent is a more serious alternative for the application of relatively recent statutes; but original understanding should not be the exclusive mode of interpretation even then. The crucial judgments by which I arrive at these conclusions are mainly ones of moral and political evaluation, although hermeneutic theory can tell us that no one can reconstruct original understanding precisely, and it can warn us of the great difficulties in any such enterprise.

Concentrating on the problem of abortion, Professor Warnke devotes the latter part of her paper to public debate over constitutional principles. Her treatment of conflicting views about abortion might lead a reader to suppose that public debate and narrower legal debate of problems should be in nearly identical terms and should eventuate in the same resolutions. That is not necessarily so.

Discussion of the legal status of abortion takes place on at least three levels. Are abortions (or most abortions) morally acceptable or a moral wrong? Should the government prohibit (most) abortions or leave women free to decide on their own? Should a woman's ability to choose whether to have an abortion be considered a constitutional right? Perceiving these three questions as discrete reminds us forcefully that allocating responsibilities is a crucial aspect of law. Legal discourse will contain elements, such as the importance of following precedents, that will be at most a very minor theme in public dialogue. Many law professors who believed states should not have prohibited abortions also thought *Roe v. Wade*[121] was wrongly decided, and that a state legislature's decision to protect incipient human life was an acceptable legal choice under the Constitution. Many of these same professors believe that the constitutional rule of *Roe v. Wade* is now firmly enough established so that it should not be overruled.

Her focus on learning from public debate leads Professor Warnke to standards of legitimate, or valid, interpretation that are vulnerable when one concentrates on legal interpretation. Her claim that an interpretation of a text is "presumptively illegitimate if it does not admit of a unity between part and whole"[122] rings true for moral judgments and may ring true for literary interpretation but does not do so for much constitutional and statutory law. Rules adopted over time by different lawmakers may not admit of much unity, and even simultaneously adopted rules may lack any coherent justification, except the need for political compromise. When legal standards are interpreted, seeking unity of part and whole is definitely one appropriate guide. But it is far from the only guide, and not every legal interpretation that fails on this dimension is "presumptively illegitimate."[123]

Warnke's proposal that a text should be interpreted to "be illuminating" is more perplexing.[124] I have reservations about this as a standard of legitimate interpretation for many nonlegal contexts. If two people are inclined to interpret a text in exactly the same way, could that interpretation be legitimate for one who finds illumination and not legitimate for one who fails to find that?[125]

My problems with this standard as it relates to law, including constitutional law, go deeper. Legal interpretations end up asserting that some legal norm applies, or does not apply, to particular social circumstances. Many legal norms are highly technical, not meant to be illuminating. Straightforward applications teach us little, if anything. A debatable interpretation may teach us something about the rule involved, but that need not illuminate our lives in any broader sense. Great constitutional decisions, like *Brown v. Board of Education*,[126] do that, but many constitutional adjudications are fairly mundane applications of settled principles to concrete facts—e.g., the police did (or did not) have sufficient basis to believe in guilt to make an arrest and search consistent with the Search and Seizure Clause of the Fourth Amendment. An opinion may say something educative about the Fourth Amendment, but broad educative value is neither a standard of a legitimate legal opinion nor of a legitimate legal decision.

In responding to Warnke's presentation of a Gadamerian approach, I have concentrated on the interpretation of legal texts. Although no one can recapture the past with precision, attention to the specific intentions of lawmakers is one possible method of interpretation. It is a method that might be given overarching importance, treated as irrelevant, or used in combination with other approaches. In suggesting the extent to which we are limited by history and culture, hermeneutic theory reveals grave difficulties with a jurisprudence of original intent for fundamental constitutional norms; but that theory alone cannot settle what role that intent should play in judicial decisions. In particular, the notion that in some senses interpretation must be responsive to present concerns does not tell us whether judges should undertake attempted reconstruction of original intent, and, if so, what weight they should assign it. Political and moral judgments are needed to draw conclusions about that.

Not every interpretation of every text or social practice is "legitimate"; but each of the two standards Professor Warnke emphasizes is questionable in relation to law. We should not expect each legitimate interpretation of law to teach us something significant. And, although unity of whole and part definitely is *a* standard of legal interpretation, courts frequently need to accept particular rules made by legislatures (and constitution makers) that do not fit easily with other aspects of the law.

In an article responsive to pieces from a symposium on how well Gadamer's theory fits with critical legal thought (a term that includes critical legal studies, critical feminism, and critical race theory), Robin West has an objective quite different from Warnke's.[127] Concerned with the pervasive influence of Gadamer's interpretive approach on critical thought, Professor West warns about valid perspectives that may be lost as a consequence. Her primary focus is on how scholars of a more or less radical persuasion view constitutional law, but what she says also has implications for the ways in which judges decide constitutional cases, and she raises many cautionary flags that those of moderate and conservative persuasions need to consider.

West's general theme is the "interpretive turn" in thought about constitutional law. She identifies seven different, though related, ways in which the turn toward interpretive theory is a turn away from something. In many respects, the "turns away" are less a necessary logical implication of interpretative theory than the natural consequence of disregarding one thing because you are concentrating on something else.

The first turn is one that West, in a sense, welcomes: a turn from constitutional intentionalism, a reliance on framers' intent as the standard for constitutional adjudications and evaluation.[128] Her misgivings here are, first, that historical understanding should often count to a degree in the development of constitutional law, and, second (more important), that we should not (blandly assuming that no interpretation can be truly intentionalist) lose sight of significant, independent reasons not to rely heavily on the intentions of those who made our Constitution. One passage that reflects this second reservation is this: "Contrary to myth, the framers were not saints, but were, arguably, a notably self-interested, class-conscious and amoral bunch, as anxious to secure the institutions of slavery and property against democratic redistribution as they were to secure the rights of individuals against overly zealous states."[129] As I have already stressed, when we come to consider forms of constitutional interpretation, we need to consider the various major arguments for and against each of them. West rightly stresses that there are reasons to reject an intentionalist version of constitutional originalism that go beyond the general interpretive difficulty of recapturing intentions of an earlier time.

West's second turn is the concession by scholars who once considered themselves proponents of noninterpretivism that they are really interpretivists after all.[130] Although this shift may desirably eliminate a kind of rhetorical advantage previously held by those of a more conservative persuasion, West is concerned that it may draw critical scholars away from the recognition that what goes on in constitutional decision should include assessment of much that is outside the document, much that is not easily captured as an interpretation of the text itself.

The third turn is the sense of the commonality of interpretation, the idea that all kinds of interpretation share the same fundamental character. Professor West is concerned that this approach tends to detract from the important understanding that constitutional interpretation is unique, that it differs from mundane, ordinary interpretation of legal documents.[131]

The next three turns are away from criticism of law in terms of the desirability of the consequences that it produces,[132] from nontextual social criticism,[133] and from sympathy as a source of moral judgment.[134] West's reservations about all those are that a primary focus on interpretation in Gadamer's sense will exclude or diminish other legitimate sources of evaluation and criticism. We should not, West urges, turn away from attention to the social world as it exists, an attention that underlies consequentialist thinking and is an essential element of social criticism. Whether or not a Gadamerian approach may yield radical legal criticism, West believes that Gadamer's emphasis on an intrepreter's tradition as the basis for her approach to a text is at odds with radical social critique.[135] In her treatment of sympathy, West expresses doubt about the extent to which the capacity for moral judgment and action is linguistically constructed. An interpretive understanding of moral judgment involves a turn away not only from a Kantian conception of right but also from what she calls a "sentimental" conception of human good, one that posits the "moral emotions."[136] An overarching attention to language is bound to understate the degree to which social and legal judgments should depend on other factors.

The final turn West notes and criticizes is the perception that all of life involves interpretation.[137] As she contends, one can see all human activity as interpretive only if one extends the notion of interpretation so broadly that it becomes unhelpful.

Gadamer's basic ideas have a good deal to teach us about the endeavors of those who interpret texts and the practices of other cultures. But when we come to consider particular interpretive efforts in various domains of ordinary life and law, we need to be careful not to disregard significant variations in exactly how people do interpret and how they should interpret. We also need to be careful not to disregard possibly legitimate bases for legislative and judicial decisions that can be obscured by the themes of general interpretive theories. Whatever one's political proclivities and inclinations about how far judges should be social critics, Robin West's observations are a very helpful caution on this latter score.

As I noted at the outset of this chapter, the interpretive theories of Ronald Dworkin and Aharon Barak contain Gadamerian conceptions of the interpretive process, with Barak's more pervasively influenced by Gadamer's own writing.[138] In subsequent chapters in this volume and succeeding ones, we shall examine how far these two theorists manage to avoid the misleading aspects of Gadamer's own account of the law and whatever tendencies that account may produce of downplaying what should be important considerations for legal decisions of the kind West emphasizes. We shall also see how far they make use of Gadamer's fundamental insights about interpretation in developing their own theories. Both are very clear about a point I have emphasized—that desirable interpretive strategies in law, as well as in any other discipline, cannot simply be drawn out of basic concepts of interpretation; they depend on judgments about the point of interpretation in the discipline, or within a subdivision of the discipline. Because Justice Barak relies more explicitly on Gadamer, because his theory includes interpretation of texts that are privately created for legal enforcement, and because the degree of congruence between his theory and my claims in this volume is both complex and somewhat greater than might initially appear, I treat aspects of his theory in some detail in my concluding chapter, saving extended comment on Professor Dworkin's approach for volumes to follow.

Notes

1 Compare Hans-Georg Gadamer, *Truth and Method* (2nd Revised ed.) (New York, Crossroad Publishing Company, 1989) (the ironical title suggesting that truth is discovered outside method), with, e.g., Charles Taylor, "Understanding the Other: A Gadamerian View on Conceptual Schemes," in Jeff Malpas, Ulrich Arnswald, and Jens Kertscher, eds., *Gadamer's Century*, 279–97 (Cambridge, Mass., M.I.T. Press, 2002) (a virtually identical essay is Taylor's "Gadamer and the Human Sciences," in Robert J. Dostal, ed., *The Cambridge Companion to Gadamer* 126–42 (Cambridge, Cambridge University Press, 2002)); Charles Taylor, *Human Agency and Language* 215–91 (Cambridge, Cambridge University Press, 1985).

2 See Ronald Dworkin, *Law's Empire* (Cambridge, Mass., Harvard University Press, 1986) (his fullest account of his interpretive theory); Aharon Barak, *Purposive Interpretation in Law* (Princeton, N.J., Princeton University Press, 2005). Although both theorists refer to Gadamer's work, Justice Barak does so more frequently, and appears to have been much more heavily influenced by it.

3 Francis J. Mootz III has written a number of articles on this subject, including "Law in Flux: Philosophical Hermeneutics, Legal Argumentation, and the Natural Law Tradition," 11 *Yale Journal of Law & the Humanities* 311 (1999); "The Ontological Basis of Legal Hermeneutics: A Proposed Model of Inquiry Based on the Work of Gadamer, Habermas and Ricoeur," 68 *Boston University Law Review* 523 (1988); "Rhetorical Knowledge in Legal Practice and Theory," 6 *Southern California Interdisciplinary Law Journal* 491 (1998). Among other writings on this theme are William N. Eskridge, Jr., "Gadamer/Statutory Interpretation," 90 *Columbia Law Review* 609 (1990); Robin West, "Are There Nothing but Texts in This Class? Interpreting the Interpretative Turns in Legal Thought," 76

Chicago-Kent Law Review 1125 (2000), and other articles from a Symposium devoted to the relation between critical theory and hermeneutical approaches, 76 *Chicago-Kent Law Review* 719–1124 (2000); R. George Wright, "On a General Theory of Interpretation: The Betti-Gadamer Dispute in Legal Hermeneutics," 1987 *American Journal of Jurisprudence* 191.

4 Charles Taylor, "Interpretation and the Sciences of Man," as reprinted in Paul Rabinow and William M. Sullivan, eds., *Interpretation and Social Science: A Second Look* 33 (Berkeley, University of California Press, 1987).

5 Hans-Georg Gadamer, "The Problem of Historical Consciousness," in Rabinow and Sullivan, note 4 supra 82–140, at 90. See also Jean Grondin, *Introduction to Philosophical Hermeneutics* 18 ("apparently unfamiliar meaning is made intelligible"), 46 (New Haven, Yale University Press, 1994); Andrei Marmor, *Interpretation and Legal Theory* 20–21 (Oxford, Clarendon Press, 1992) (interpretation occurs when meaning is not determined by rules or conventions).

6 Charles Taylor, in *Understanding the Other*, note 1 supra, emphasizes the relevance of Gadamer's theory for our understanding of different cultures. Reem Badhi develops an interesting application for domestic applications of international law. If the domestic courts of different countries approach texts in light of their own historical and social context, we should not expect their agreement on the meaning of binding norms of international law. "Truth and Method in the Domestic Application of International Law," XV *Canadian Journal of Law and Jurisprudence* 255 (2002).

7 Jean Grondin, note 5 supra, at 48.

8 Richard Palmer, *Hermeneutics* 13 (Evanston, Northwestern University Press, 1969); Gerald L. Bruns, *Hermeneutics Ancient and Modern* 215 (New Haven, Yale University Press, 1992).

9 Grondin, note 5 supra, at 49.

10 Id. at 50–54.

11 Id. at 54–55.

12 Id. at 56–59.

13 Id. at 56.

14 Palmer, note 8 supra, at 97.

15 See Grondin, note 5 supra, at 63–65, on the sharp break between Enlightenment theorists and Schleiermacher, which Grondin attributes to the influence of Kant's thought.

16 Palmer, note 8 supra, at 85.

17 Id. at 86, 89; Grondin, note 5 supra, at 68.

18 Palmer, note 8 supra, at 87.

19 Id.; Grondin, note 5 supra, at 71.

20 Id. at 74.

21 Palmer, note 8 supra, at 92.

22 Id. at 98.

23 Id. at 102–05.

24 Id. at 98–99, 114–15; Grondin, note 5 supra, at 85.

25 Palmer, note 8 supra, at 103, 114–17.

26 Grondin, note 5 supra, at 88.

27 Id. at 90.

28 Palmer, note 8 supra, at 140.

29 Grondin, note 5 supra, at 92–93.

30 Id. at 93–94.

31 Palmer, note 8 supra, at 131.

32 Id. at 135, 152.

33 Gadamer, note 1 supra.

34 In a Foreword to the Second Edition, Gadamer says explicitly that he did not mean to describe or direct "the methodological procedure of the human sciences" or to put his "findings to practical ends." Id. at xxviii.

35 Id. at xxxiv.

36 Id. at xxxii.

37 Id. at 23.

38 Id. at 31.

39 Id. at 38.

40 Id. at 39.

41 Id. at 97.

42 Id. at 128. Jean Grondin, note 5 supra, at 110, writes of Gadamer's path through aesthetics as a "detour," offering "less an aesthetic than an anti-aesthetic" and showing that the idea of an autonomous aesthetics needs to be attacked so that we can understand better what knowing is in the human sciences.

43 Gadamer, note 1 supra at 148.

44 Id. at 164.

45 Id. at 185, 192–93.

46 Id. at 198, 199.

47 Id. at 246–47.

48 Id. at 267.

49 Id. at 281.

50 Id.

51 Id. at 284.

52 Id. at 290.

53 Id. at 293.

54 Id. at 306.

55 Paul Ricouer, among others, has challenged the idea of a dialogue with an absent writer; David Couzens Hoy, in response, defends the notion of a dialogue with the text. David Couzens Hoy, *The Critical Circle* 85–86 (Berkeley, University of California Press, 1978).

56 Id. at 52–53; Grondin, note 5 supra, at 11.

57 Taylor, "Understanding the Other," note 1 supra at 279–81.

58 Clifford Geertz, "Deep Play: Notes on the Balinese Cockfight" in Rabinow and Sullivan, note 4 supra, at 195–240. For an illustration that involves interpretation of various legal texts that bear on a case, see Eskridge, note 3 supra, at 651–59.

59 Geertz, note 58 supra, at 218–19.

60 Id. at 216.

61 An illuminating account of the sense of horizons is in Taylor, "Understanding the Other," note 1 supra.

62 I put it this way not because this understanding would be conservative in its implications but because it would be highly implausible.

63 In *Literary Theory*, Chapter 3, note 5 supra, Terry Eagleton writes, "History for Gadamer is not a place for struggle, discontinuity and exclusion, but a continuing 'chain,' an ever-flowing river, almost, one might say, a club of the like-minded." (Quoted in Bruns, Chapter 4, note 5 supra, at 195.)

64 See Hoy, note 55 supra, at 115. For an account of Gadamer that perceives his work as highly authoritarian, see Richard Wolin, "Untruth and Method: Nazism

and the Complicities of Hans-Georg Gadamer," *New Republic*, May 15, 2000, pp. 36–45.

65 Bruns, note 8 supra, at 205–06.

66 Gadamer, note 1 supra, at 566.

67 Id. at 568. Rejecting the idea of reason that Habermas offers, Gadamer asserts that consistency is important for every kind of rationality, but the consistency of practical experience is not rationally choosing means, but the "consistency of desire itself." Id. at 570.

68 Hoy, note 55 supra, at 45. Eskridge, note 3 supra, at 630–32, recognizes that Gadamer's approach need not be uniformly conservative, but that its emphasis on tradition inclines in that direction.

69 Gadamer, note 1 supra, at 308.

70 Id. at 309.

71 Id. at 325–28.

72 Id. at 334.

73 Id. at 328.

74 Id. at 390.

75 Id. at 396.

76 Id. at 397.

77 Id. at 450.

78 Id. at 458.

79 Taylor, note 4 supra, at 52–55. By contrast, Robin West, note 3 supra, at 1136–37, 1162–63, suggests that many significant experiences in life are not heavily dependent on culture, and many do not involve interpretation (unless that term is understood very broadly).

80 Taylor, "Understanding the Other," note 1 supra at 288, indicates that truth values will remain in respect to historical interpretation, even if the central questions, issues, and features will seem different. Within any particular vantage point, there can be better or worse historiography. Among interpretive theorists who have concentrated on law and maintained the possibility of correct answers are Ronald Dworkin, see *Law's Empire* (Cambridge, Mass., Harvard University Press, 1986), and Emilio Betti, an Italian scholar. On Betti, see Richard Palmer, note 8 supra, at 56–59, George Wright, "On a General Theory of Interpretation: The Betti-Gadamer Dispute in Legal Hermeneutics," 1987 *The American Journal of Jurisprudence* 191. Eskridge, note 3 supra, at 624–27, treats Betti among theorists who find the meaning of texts in authorial intent, and, at 648–51, criticizes Dworkin's chain novel theory of statutory interpretation. Kenneth Henley, "Protestant Hermaneutics and the Rule of Law: Gadamer and Dworkin," 3 *Ratio Juris* 14 (1990), suggests that both theorists rely heavily on individualized judgment and that neither theory can underpin the kind of reassurance about settled law that is a premise of the traditional ideal of rule of law. In subsequent volumes, we will have occasion to consider aspects of Dworkin's theory at some length.

81 Grondin, note 5 supra, at 129–34; Hoy, note 55 supra 117–26. See generally Fred R. Dallmayr, "Borders or Horizons? Gadamer and Habermas Revisited," 76 *Chicago-Kent Law Review* 825 (2000).

82 Grondin, note 5 supra, at 108.

83 Id. at 153.

84 Id. at 78–84; Patrick Chatelion Counet, "Paroimiai (John 16:25): A Post-Hermeneutical Model," in Petr Pokorný and Jan Roskovec, eds., *Philosophical Hermeneutics and Biblical Exegesis* 252, 255–61(Tübingen, Mahr Siebeck, 2002).

85 See Bruns, note 8 supra, at 214 (a hermeneutical "exercise in disruption"); Counet, note 84 supra ("post–hermeneutic").

86 See, e.g., Eskridge, note 3 supra, at 627–30, treating Gadamer's emphasis on constructive inquiry as a normative choice. If one were a true anarchist or one thought that a present legal system should be dismantled in favor of a radically alternative structure of government, one might favor forms of interpretation that would undermine law as it stands. I might add that, even if this approach would be unwise for a judge, scholars might believe that a sharp challenge to interpretive practices could desirably reduce the oppressiveness of a legal system without compromising it altogether.

87 However, if the daughter surmises that her father has forgotten what the doctor said, and might on reflection not want sugar in his coffee, she may ask whether his request in these circumstances really covers her passing the sugar.

88 Gadamer, note 1 supra, at 309.

89 Id. at 318.

90 Aristotle, *Nicomachean Ethics*; see Hoy, note 51 supra at 56–58. P. Christopher Smith has emphasized the degree to which Gadamer's concept of dialogical reasoning draws from Aristotle. "The Uses of Aristotle in Gadamer's Recovery of Consultative Reasoning: Sunesis, Sungnômê, Epieikeia, and Sumbouleuesthai," 76 *Chicago-Kent Law Review* 731 (2000).

91 Gadamer, note 5 supra at 122–23, suggests that the idea of an equitable solution is valid for all concepts in which people determine what ought to be.

92 Joseph Raz, *Practical Reason and Norms* 65–71 (London, Hutchinson & Co., 1975); The Morality of Freedom 44, 60 (Oxford, Clarendon Press, 1986). My own view is that those who adopt legal norms (or the norms themselves if one chooses to personalize them) do not necessarily aim to preclude either ethical choice about compliance or ethical evaluation to determine borders of coverage.

93 9 *Yale Journal of Law & the Humanities* 395 (1997). For a discussion that arrives at more skeptical conclusions about how much Gadamer's theory can tell us about desirable constitutional interpretation, see John T. Valauri, "Interpretation, Critique, and Adjudication: The Search for Constitutional Hermeneutics," 76 *Chicago-Kent Law Review* 1083 (2000).

94 She talks of text-analogues such as actions, social practices, and norms. Georgia Warnke, *Justice and Interpretation* 2 (Cambridge, Polity Press, 1992).

95 U.S. Constitution, Amendments 1, 8, and 14, §1. For a discussion of one issue of freedom of speech, see R. George Wright, "Traces of Violence: Gadamer, Habermas, and the Hate Speech Problem," 76 *Chicago-Kent Law Review* 191 (2000).

96 Robin West, note 3 supra, at 1144–47, suggests that the Constitution has distinctive features, one of which is that it functions as a kind of memorial. She fears that a danger of acceptance of Gadamer's theory is that it can blur understanding of what makes constitutional interpretation special.

97 Taylor, "Understanding the Other," note 1 supra, at 284–85.

98 Charles Taylor, *Varieties of Religion Today* 80–111 (Cambridge, Mass., Harvard University Press, 2002).

99 Allan C. Hutchinson, "Work-in-Progress: Gadamer, Tradition, and the Common Law," 76 *Chicago-Kent Law Review* 1015 (2000), analyzing Washington v. Glucksberg, 521 U.S. 702 (1997), from the perspective of his reading of Gadamer. Hutchinson resists the conclusion, supported by Francis J. Mootz III, in "Law in Flux: Philosophical Hermeneutics, Legal Argumentation, and the Natural Law

Tradition," 11 *Yale Journal of Law & the Humanities* 311, 326 (1999), that Justice Souter's concurring opinion upholding a state's authority to refuse to recognize a right to die represents a sound application of Gadamer's theory, urging instead "a more critical and radical reading of Gadamer" that could have yielded a contrary conclusion, one less respectful of prevailing moral assumptions. 76 *Chicago-Kent Law Review* at 1063–80, 1071.

100 Warnke, note 93 supra, at 401.

101 Id.

102 Id. at 396.

103 Id. at 398.

104 Id.

105 Id. at 408.

106 Id. at 411, 410.

107 There are many exceptions. A study of territoriality in animals may be partly intended to help human beings understand and cope with their own "instincts" to dominate particular spaces.

108 K. N. Llewellyn & E. Adamson Hoebel, *The Cheyenne Way: Conflict and Case Law in Primitive Jurisprudence* (Norman, OK, University of Oklahoma Press, 1941).

109 I assume that in relevant respects, studies of one's own culture at some earlier period are similar. For an interesting example of the portrayal of the social life of an earlier period, see Emmanuel LeRoy Ladurie, *Montaillou: The Promised Land of Error* (Barbara Bray, trans., London, Scolar Press, 1978) (depicting the life of a heretical community based on detailed accounts of the Inquisition).

110 The life of the other culture may seem reprehensible or unacceptably "primitive"; if some features are attractive, these may seem too bizarre, or too closely linked to unattractive features, to become practical options. Or, the culture and practices may seem attractive, but too different to affect our lives.

111 Warnke, note 93 supra, at 398.

112 I assume for this purpose that a moviemaker has a choice, even if an option is unlikely to be a commercial success.

113 For many reasons, values may seem much less settled now than when I was a child.

114 How does Professor Warnke regard this possibility? She thinks, and I agree, that our "horizontal horizon" will affect our understanding of a text; but that does not settle whether attempted reconstruction of a previous historical understanding is one legitimate mode of interpretation. Although passages in her original article leave some doubt about Warnke's view, she subsequently indicated that reconstructing original intent, so far as one can, may be appropriate. See "Reply to Greenawalt," 9 *Yale Journal of Law & the Humanities* 437, 438 (1997).

115 Warnke takes a similar position about the multiplicity of valid aesthetic interpretations. See Warnke, note 94 supra, at 31, as well as related passages in Warnke, note 93 supra.

116 Martha Nussbaum, *Liberty of Conscience* 34–71 (New York, Basic Books, 2008).

117 Especially Timothy Hall, *Separating Church and State: Roger Williams and Religious Liberty* (Urbana, IL, University of Illinois Press, 1998).

118 That is their primary relevance for Nussbaum's book.

119 This depends, I should add, on exactly what question is put about the electronic media. If the question is whether a system of governmental approval of all

program content is appropriate, the answer is that the adopters would not have wanted that.

120 Id. at 406.

121 410 U.S. 113 (1973).

122 See Warnke, supra note 93, at 409.

123 One might say that the "unity" lies in the ability of lawmakers to adopt requirements (the parts), even if the parts do not fit well substantively with each other.

124 Even for texts from which one hopes to find illumination, one may discover none is to be found.

125 Warnke subsequently emphasizes that what is crucial is that the interpreter be open to the possibility that the text will teach him something he does not know. Warnke, supra note 114, at 439.

126 347 U.S. 483 (1954).

127 West, note 3, supra.

128 Id. at 1130–37.

129 Id. at 1130.

130 Id. at 1138–44, Among prominent noninterpretivists were Paul Brest, "The Misconceived Quest for the Original Understanding," 60 *Boston University Law Review* 204 (1980), and Thomas C. Grey, "Do We Have an Unwritten Constitution?," 27 *Stanford Law Review* 703 (1975). Compare Thomas C. Grey, "The Constitution as Scripture," 37 *Stanford Law Review* 1 (1984) ("We are all interpretivists").

131 West, note 3 supra, at 1144–47.

132 Id. at 1147–52.

133 Id. at 1152–55.

134 Id. at 1156–61.

135 Other expressions of similar worries are in Stephen Feldman, "How to Be Critical," 76 *Chicago-Kent Law Review* 893 (2000) (suggesting how the truth of Gadamer's theory makes critical evaluation difficult); Gary Wickham, "Foucault and Gadamer: Like Apples and Oranges Passing in the Night," 76 *Chicago-Kent Law Review* 913 (2000). Ingrid Scheibler, "Gadamer, Heidegger, and the Social Dimensions of Language: Reflections on the Critical Potential of Hermeneutical Philosophy," 76 *Chicago-Kent Law Review* 853, 881 (2000), emphasizes the essential negativity of the openness of an interpreter and Gadamer's basic notion of dialogue as providing a basis for critical thought.

136 West, note 3 supra, at 1158. Here, West refers to Martha Nussbaum's *Poetic Justice*, which we considered at some length in Chapter Three.

137 West, note 3 supra, at 1161–64.

138 See note 2 supra.

Chapter 6

Starting from the Bottom

Informal Instructions

I. INTRODUCTION

This chapter is a bridge between broader themes of interpretation and specific forms of legal interpretation. It concentrates on informal instructions given by people in authority. Although many scholars have written about how legal interpretation resembles interpretation in fields such as literature and religion, few have compared informal instructions and legal rules.[1] Yet, a focus on informal situations illumines the standards that people use in performing instructions and the kinds of meaning they attribute to instructions. By reflecting on what constitutes faithful or desirable performance of informal directives and on the more conceptual question of what these prescriptive standards "mean," we gain insight into how to understand ordinary language in law and into the possible legal relevance of the intent of those who issue directions.

Since legislation, executive orders, and wills, as well as instructions from principals to agents, may be conceived as directives about what people should do, informal illustrations may help us to grasp what is central in these parts of the law. Of course, no easy move takes us from simple personal examples to most legal ones. One critical obstacle involves the complexities of multi-member bodies. Another concerns the characteristics of legal systems, including what Robert Summers calls its formal aspects,[2] and the tripartite relations between people who formulate legal norms, those directly subject to the norms, and the agencies responsible for enforcing the norms.

In subsequent chapters about legal texts, I draw cautiously from the conclusions of this one. Examination of simple instructions can help us to distinguish between problems about interpretation of language that are generic to authoritative prescriptions and problems that are particular to legal systems. That examination also allows us to identify possible relationships between the meaning of a directive and the best, or desirable, carrying out of the directive. One benefit of studying informal instructions is that we can attain a degree of detachment from our preexisting opinions about contested issues in legal philosophy and politics and about the merits and demerits of particular judges.

Once we perceive the difficulties in choosing any single standard for the desirable performance of instructions, in adopting a single standpoint to determine meaning, and in fitting meaning to desirable performance, we will hardly suppose that matters will be more straightforward when we turn to law.[3]

This chapter inquires about the performance and meaning of instructions in various kinds of circumstances. Rather than beginning with any overarching theory about performance and meaning, and their relationship, I ask how people involved would see things, after some reflection. This inquiry leads to skepticism about any simple, systematic theory about how performance relates to meaning.

Discussing in turn (1) instructions whose import is clear in context, (2) instructions that are unclear in context because of incompleteness, vagueness, ambiguity, or a possible slip, and (3) instructions whose application is affected by changing conditions, I conclude that one cannot reduce the best carrying out of informal instructions to any single criterion. Rather, a number of standards affect desirable performance. In this chapter, although not the following chapter on agency, I assume that both the giver of instructions and their recipient assume that the recipient should act without seeking a clarification or further instructions.

In respect to what an instruction might mean, Chapter 2 has discussed common distinctions, as between speaker's meaning and sentence meaning. The idea that the *meaning*, that is the crucial meaning, can be summed up in some straightforward formula, such as literal meaning, or ordinary meaning, or speaker's intent, does have more plausibility than a parallel approach to performance. According to such proposals, whatever other variables may figure in decisions about how to perform involve something other than determining meaning. We saw a comparable approach in distinctions between meaning and "significance" and between meaning and "application" in Chapter 3. Along the same lines, one might distinguish "interpretation" of instructions (perhaps limiting that to discerning meaning) from other elements that might affect a recipient's desirable performance.

Although this sort of approach is not demonstrably mistaken, it runs up against intuitions about the heterodoxy of meaning, including the inclination to tie meaning more closely to speaker's intent when that intent is crucial for performance than when it matters much less.

One option is to tie the meaning of instructions very closely to desirable performance—to say that what instructions mean in context depends on how they should best be carried out. That, indeed, is the usual tendency in law; judges often say that texts really mean what is determined to be their best application. Yet, tying meaning too closely to performance is awkward. As we shall see, proper performance often turns on issues of authority that are not well captured as debates about meaning. With informal instructions, we do best not to settle on any single sense of meaning, whether that sense is stated as a standard separate from performance or links tightly to proper performance.

II. NONLEGAL INSTRUCTIONS – THE BASIC SETTINGS, AND POSSIBILITIES CONCERNING COMPLIANCE, FAITHFUL PERFORMANCE, AND MEANING

The examples in this chapter have the following general characteristics. A person issues instructions to a definite person or class of persons. The person issuing the instructions has authority to prescribe what the person following the instructions should do.[4] Correlatively, the person who receives the instructions has a duty or obligation to follow them. Usually the recipient is subordinate to the person giving the instructions, but I include (as recipients) professionals with duties to carry out the instructions of clients. The recipient understands the instructions, perceives their objectives, and can exercise judgment about them.[5] Among situations fitting this pattern are most instructions of parents to "nannies," employers to employees, officers to soldiers, directors to musicians, dancers and actors, coaches to athletes, and clients to lawyers. A typical (though not universal) feature of these instructions is that the instructor directly oversees the recipient's response, as with directors of plays, or reviews her performance after the fact.

A recipient can follow instructions or disobey them, or she may depart from instructions without disobeying them. Suppose a coach tells her basketball players: "You are three points ahead, and there are twenty-four seconds left. Don't shoot; run out the clock." If the players pass and dribble the ball without shooting, they have obeyed the instructions. If a player takes a shot of ordinary difficulty, she has disobeyed the coach. What if Cheryl takes an extremely easy shot that she nearly always makes? If she reasonably and correctly perceives that the coach was not considering shots that easy, we may say Cheryl has departed from the instructions (in the sense of no longer carrying them out) without disobeying them.[6]

Beyond the question of whether a recipient has complied with an instruction lies the further question whether compliance, or noncompliance, is justified. Answering that question calls for evaluation that reaches outside the import of the instruction. An attempt to justify disobedience may rest on the very objective that underlay the instruction,[7] or on some external objective or value.[8]

What constitutes "faithful" performance of instructions—that is, a performance faithful to the recipient's role?[9] Even for simple instructions, common and desirable strategies of performance do not reduce to a single consideration. The specificity of the instruction's language, the extent to which conditions may have changed, and relations between the issuer and recipient can all matter. The term "faithful performance" need not imply that only one particular action complies with instructions; instructions may leave a range of possibilities available. Even when they do not, the standard that a recipient of instructions should use to guide his actions may vary from the standard that someone evaluating those actions should use.

Inquiries about performance help reveal perplexing questions about "meaning." We might best recognize that the effort to discern one crucial "meaning" is essentially a practical endeavor, that meaning may vary depending on the kind of activity that is involved, and according to the stage at which an instruction is considered. Even for one instruction at a single point in time, whether we can speak usefully about *the meaning*, as contrasted with various senses of meaning, is doubtful. One can decide what the speaker meant, how most people would understand the instruction, and how the instruction would best be understood. The doubt is whether any of these, or something else, may comfortably be called "the meaning."

In my consideration of meaning, I try to depict how an ordinary speaker of the language might talk when he or she is being very careful (and perhaps after being presented with various alternatives). One reason why reaching conclusions is difficult is that English (and other natural languages) lack precise forms to mark many subtle distinctions,[10] ones revealed in efforts to decide between conceptual possibilities.

My choice to begin with performance and then turn to meaning reflects the emphasis on practical choices within the law and this study.[11] Lawyers, at least, are inclined to suppose that legal norms usually should be observed and applied according to their meaning. They typically see the significance of "meaning" as bearing on a practical decision. What I do, in this less than systematic account,[12] is to test the sense that "meaning" should accord with "faithful performance" in respect to informal instructions.[13]

III. HOW TO INTERPRET INSTRUCTIONS

At a conference of linguists and legal scholars, William Eskridge embellished an old illustration that raised fascinating issues of interpretation. We can learn a good deal by teasing out its implications. Professor Eskridge said:

> Here's the hypothetical I want to set forth. It's based upon Francis Lieber's book…. Georgia is the head of a household. Kent is her housekeeper, basically. Georgia… has several children. Among the many directives, she says…: "Kent, I'm going away for a while. Here is a laundry list of things you have to do. First and foremost, I want you to fetch soupmeat every Monday from Store X."
>
> The directive to Kent might require some degree of interpretation. But perhaps very little, because there might have been much fetching of soupmeat before Georgia's departure. Kent knows from earlier interactions with Georgia that this soupmeat has a fairly narrow range of connotations. Store X is a store that's about five or six blocks down the street…. So for the first several Mondays,… what Kent does is precisely what Georgia expect[s] him to do. Kent trots on down…. into Store X, and there is a counter that says "Soupmeat." It's where he's always bought it, and he buys the soupmeat. Some kind of beef, let's say…. The longer Georgia is gone away, the more

likely it is that the directive's interpretation will change. Several weeks later, Kent trots down to the area, and Store X has burned down. So, he goes to Store Y. Now he in some ways has violated the literal terms of the directive, because he is fetching soupmeat from Store Y. But he cannot get a hold of Georgia right in the middle of his errand, and it's not cost beneficial for him to do so. He almost reflexively goes to Store Y....

Several months later, Kent... received another directive from Georgia in a letter saying Georgia has read that children with high cholesterol rates have health difficulties later in life. She says, "I'm very worried about this. From now on I want you to buy lots of apples, bran and oranges, things that this article says are low in cholesterol because I think this will be good for the children."

Kent goes to Store Y. In casual conversation with Judith, the butcher of Store Y, he learns... that soupmeat is extremely high in cholesterol. "Indeed," Judith says, "my Lord, this is the highest cholesterol rate in the entire store. You might just as well be mainlining cholesterol into these children by feeding them soupmeat!" Kent decides that he will now buy chicken for soup rather than cholesterol-filled soupmeat.

Some months later, Kent trots down to Store Y intending to buy chicken. Posted on the door of Store Y is a new rationing system that the city has adopted because of exigent circumstances entailed by war or famine or something like that. Under the rationing system, each family (and Kent is now the surrogate head of Georgia's family), gets only so many rationing tickets, only so many economic units to buy food. Based upon this rationing system, Kent decides to forego buying meat at all, because he believes that meat is an extravagance under this system and decides to buy other things that will fill up the children's little stomachs.[14]

In this example, Kent is the housekeeper of Georgia, who definitely has the authority to tell him what to do. Crucial aspects of her instructions are clear and precise, so long as ordinary conditions prevail.[15]

A. Instructions That Are Specific in Context

When the language of instructions is straightforward in context and no unexpected obstacles to performance present themselves, the instructor's intentions will coincide with a recipient's reasonable understanding of the instructions' force. Their "meaning" will correspond with the behavior of a faithful recipient, leaving little doubt about proper performance or meaning. However, even clear, specific instructions can generate complexities about a recipient's controlling guide, sowing seeds of uncertainty about equating "meaning" with faithful performance.

1. Faithful Performance

Should Kent be guided by what a reasonable listener might conclude about Georgia's instructions or by her subjective (mental state) intentions? One point is obvious. Kent's faithfully carrying out the instructions does not depend on what a reasonable listener who was unaware of past dealings between Georgia and Kent would understand.[16] The concept of a "reasonable listener" is relevant for faithful performance only if the hypothetical listener is aware of relations between Georgia and Kent that bear on her instructions. These past relations form the context for understanding the instructions.

One can hardly distinguish between performance that adopts the perspective of such a fully informed listener and performance that aims to fulfill Georgia's intentions. A reasonable listener will assume Georgia has framed her instructions to express her wishes. She has given her instructions to achieve the objective of Kent buying soupmeat on Monday at Store X. She intends her instructions to communicate to Kent that she is directing him to behave in this way. A reasonable listener will conclude that Kent's carrying out the instructions will involve doing what Georgia wants (in a mental state sense).[17]

Analysis becomes more complicated if Georgia has made a mistake, and her explicit applicable language differs from her intentions. Her mistake may be signaled by other specific aspects of her instructions or their objectives, or by conditions of performance. For example, unless the household has an odd schedule, Kent will assume that when Georgia writes "Shop at 3:00 A.M.," she intends 3:00 P.M. (or conceivably a later morning hour). In that event, faithful performance and reasonable understanding deviate from the literal import of a term.

When the instructions themselves do not signal that the writer has slipped, more serious difficulties arise. Suppose Georgia's written instructions tell Kent to shop on Monday, but Kent has usually shopped on Tuesday and is aware that Georgia frequently slips when she names days of the week. If Kent, unable to reach Georgia, is confident that she has slipped, he will probably try to fulfill her subjective intentions by shopping on Tuesday.[18]

Uncertainty about probable intentions raises a more interesting conundrum. Suppose that Kent reasonably concludes that Georgia, having written Monday, probably (55% likelihood) meant Tuesday but may (45% likelihood) have meant Monday. If Kent takes Georgia's immediate subjective intentions as his exclusive guide, he will shop on Tuesday. Is that what he should do? Two related factors, what we might call the responsibility to communicate effectively and the psychology of review, raise doubt.

Georgia bears the basic responsibility to state the day correctly. A reader uncertain what she wanted should perhaps take her words at face value.

The prospect of review could suggest a similar course. If Kent guesses right about what Georgia wanted, he should be safe, but what if his action does not fit Georgia's actual purpose? Suppose, first, Georgia wanted Monday, as she wrote, and Kent must explain why he shopped on Tuesday. People commonly underestimate their propensity to err, and are not fond of being told they make many mistakes. Georgia may not appreciate Kent's second-guessing her when she has expressed her wishes in clear language. She may say, "Please do what I say unless you're sure I've slipped." If, instead, Kent shops on Monday, although Georgia as he guessed, wanted Tuesday, his explanation that he thought it best to stick with what she wrote, may lead Georgia to respond: "The mistake was mine." Given this second order of evaluation, a reasonable recipient might decide that when the probabilities are close, he should do what is written, even if that fails to correspond with his best estimate of the instructor's mental state intention.[19]

Reference to a speaker's intent that reaches more broadly than the immediate circumstances can partly account for the complexities possible slips introduce. Recognizing the principle of speaker's responsibility and her own likely annoyance if a servant guesses wrongly that she has slipped, Georgia may want Kent to follow her expressed literal meaning unless she has clearly made a mistake. In that event, Georgia's overarching intent would be that recipients of her instructions not always follow her probable narrower specific intent. Kent then would comply with her dominant general intention by deviating from his best estimate of the day she wanted.

Regrettably, such an approach to intentions cannot fully resolve the problem. Georgia's broader intentions need not reflect everything that Kent legitimately takes into account.[20] Georgia may not realize that she underestimates her slips or is so disturbed at having possible slips "corrected." Kent may perceive that Georgia's idea of a good approach to possible slips may differ from the responses that will actually lead to the best relations between him and her.

The subordinate's job is not to fulfill the superior's intentions, no matter what. Subordinates retain some independent judgment of what will work best, if they think that differs from what a superior attempting to state broad principles might say (but has not said).[21] More generally, the aspiration to follow instructions well is not always reducible either to what the language signifies or to one's best estimate of the speaker's intentions about the instruction. The sensitive subordinate will be guided by a subtle combination of these (and perhaps by other factors), in which estimates of probabilities will figure.

My discussion of slips has introduced continuing relations between Georgia and Kent as a significant factor. Not only do past relations between a superior and subordinate affect how a directive is understood, the prospect of future relations can influence what is its best performance. Thus, two recipients might conceivably reach exactly the same estimate whether a writer has "slipped" in otherwise identical instructions. A recipient in a continuing relationship with the writer might best choose to follow *expressed* language, even if the other recipient, in a one-time encounter, might best choose likely *intended* language.

2. Meaning

What do instructions mean? Does meaning always coincide with best performance, with a speaker's intentions, with a reasonable listener's understanding, with literal language, with some combination of these, or with something else?

Addressing these questions is both easy and hard when we consider straightforward, specific instructions, with no slips, that unambiguously require particular behavior in the circumstances. Speaker's intent, reasonable listener appraisal, and literal expressed language fit comfortably together, and the "meaning" of an instruction coheres with the behavior that fulfills it. Thus, we need not choose between alternative accounts of meaning.

The alternatives surface, however, when an obvious slip, such as "3:00 A.M.," appears. Faithful performance follows the intended, sensible time; that is both what the writer meant and what a reasonable reader would assume. But the literal language is different.[22] We might say, "The instruction means 3:00 P.M., because that is what Georgia wanted and what every reader would conclude." We might say, "The instruction means 3:00 A.M., but Georgia meant 3:00 P.M." Or, uncomfortable with this stark choice, we might equivocate, "The language of the instruction means 3:00 A.M., but the writer obviously meant 3:00 P.M. and that is how a reader should understand the instruction." When a slip is obvious, an equivocation that distinguishes semantic meaning from speaker meaning seems best, since any bare statement that the instruction means 3:00 P.M. or 3:00 A.M. is misleading.

Analysis is further complicated when a slip is possible but not certain, as with the possible mistake of "Monday" for "Tuesday." Here we are tempted to say, "The instruction means that Kent is to shop on Monday."[23] That is certainly what the literal expressed language indicates, and nothing in the language or standard circumstances (like ordinary shopping hours) suggests a slip.

If one concludes that meaning depends wholly on speaker intent or wholly on the semantic sense of the language of an instruction, one will sometimes see a wedge between the best performance of an instruction and its meaning. The best performance might be on Tuesday, although the instruction's meaning according to its language would designate Monday. And, if one says that the meaning follows Georgia's specific intent, and she happened to intend Tuesday, a recipient's correct estimate of meaning might not fit with his best performance (according to the analysis that might give priority to the literal language when the probability of a different intent is slightly higher).

Were "meaning" to follow best performance exactly, "meaning" would encompass all the subtle calculations that would resolve what action by the recipient is best. Yet, it seems counterintuitive to think that the "meaning" of an instruction shifts, depending on whether the instructor will be upset by a wrong guess that her intent differs from her expressed language, or on whether her relationship to the recipient is a continuing one. In light of these various alternatives, an option that does not try to attribute any single, simple approach to the meaning of instructions is appealing.

B. Instructions That Are Vague or Ambiguous or Incomplete in Context

More complex problems about performance and meaning are generated when (despite the absence of any "slip") the way instructions apply is uncertain in context. Because Eskridge's "soupmeat" story involves clear application or new knowledge or changed external circumstances, we return here to the basketball illustration.

The coach says, "Don't shoot," believing that no player is likely to have the opportunity to take an extremely easy shot. The coach might want to convey that her players should take no shots, however easy, or that they should take no shots, except extremely easy ones.[24] Or the coach may not have resolved whether a player should take an easy shot.[25] No player asked about easy shots and Cheryl has the chance to take an unguarded lay-up she nearly always makes.

1. Faithful Performance

Cheryl must quickly choose. She might believe her coach's wishes should guide her or that, since the coach's comment does not decisively resolve what she should do, she should exercise her own judgment, or that she should act according to some mix of the coach's wishes and her own best judgment. What most coaches who say "Don't shoot" in similar circumstances would want could be *evidence* of what her coach wants or of the best strategy, but it would not be directly determinative. Cheryl is interested in her coach and the best judgment she, herself, can make.

In what follows I make the simplifying assumptions that Cheryl adopts her coach's wishes as her exclusive guide and is sure the coach had a definite opinion about easy shots. Within a half-second or so, Cheryl must bring to bear her knowledge about the coach's likely wishes.

Cheryl's best effort to fulfill the instruction would involve a simple estimate of probable intentions were it not for the complications introduced by choice when probabilities seem close.[26] Although knowledgeable basketball players would understand that the coach's instruction does not *clearly* cover easy lay-ups, the coach's literal language fits better with Cheryl's declining such a shot than taking it. If Cheryl doesn't shoot, she can explain that she was following what the coach said. This may placate a coach who actually wished players to take easy shots. The coach may be angrier if Cheryl shoots, despite her wish that she not.[27] If Cheryl values smooth relations with her coach, she may decide not to shoot, even though she thinks the coach is slightly more likely than not to want her to shoot.

2. Meaning

If Cheryl's practical task reduces to carrying out her coach's wishes, how should we conceive the instruction's meaning? Its meaning might be: (1) according to its literal language, (2) according to general usage, (3) according to the coach's intentions, (4) according to the coach's understanding of what she has said, (5) according to a reasonable person's understanding, (6) according to the most perceptive person's understanding, (7) not dispositive for the choice Cheryl faces.

A quick examination reveals that alternatives (1), (2), and (7) leave a large gap between Cheryl's efforts to perform faithfully and what one would conclude about meaning. It is tempting to associate "meaning" with literal meaning. Doesn't "Don't shoot" *mean* "Don't shoot, period," covering all possible shots?[28] However, in ordinary discourse, people very often prescribe without qualification. A mother who tells her son, "Go to your room and stay there for fifteen minutes," does not want the child to remain if a bear pushes through the window. Saying that the mother's instructions *mean* that her son should not behave as anyone would want and expect (leaving the room when the bear enters) is awkward. If "literal meaning" requires taking words and phrases without implicit qualifications, or ellipsis, it frequently deviates from ordinary meaning or generally understood meaning.[29]

A defender of the approach that meaning is literal meaning might retreat to this position: "Literal meaning is not the meaning when that would obviously be inapt; but in cases of doubt we should understand meaning as literal meaning." A basic problem with this position is its equation of "meaning" with the literal meaning of expressed language when that is one possible construction, even though the speaker did not so intend his instruction and no listener would understand it in that way. We have no neat place to draw the line at which the most likely understanding (if it is nonliteral) should yield to literal meaning. That is, if literal meaning is not the meaning when it would be patently inapt, we lack a guide to just how implausible literal meaning must seem before we rule it out as *the meaning*.

The second possibility is that the directive's meaning would follow general use and understanding of this sort of utterance. Although this position allows a more natural rendering of what remarks mean than any view that "meaning" covers circumstances in which no one would expect or want an instruction to be followed, it faces what we can call the pressure towards specific context.

If one asks about general use and understanding, one needs to describe what count as similar situations. We might limit the focus to "Don't shoot," spoken by coaches at the final stages of basketball games when the coaches' teams are ahead. Two variables now become critical: skill and score. A coach of fifth graders would probably aim to convey that no shots at all be taken, whereas a professional coach, realizing that her players nearly always identify and make "easy shots," would *probably* not mean to forbid easy lay-ups.

Score would also matter. If a team is five points ahead with 24 seconds to go, another two points could help a lot, and would not leave the team vulnerable to a quick tie. But if the coach's team is only one point ahead, she might worry that an easy two-point shot would allow her opponents to tie the game with a three-point basket. She might be more likely to want no shots taken.

We will find ourselves unable to provide a *general* answer to what a coach's "Don't shoot" communicates about very easy shots. And if we narrow the question to teams of similar abilities involved in games with comparable differentials in score, why not go further and focus on the particular coach and her team? As with any plausible reliance on literal meaning, we come up against an arbitrary line. How does one delimit those matters of context that do figure in a general inquiry from whatever matters of particular context are excluded?[30]

The seventh possibility for meaning is that the instruction simply does not resolve whether Cheryl should regard herself as free to shoot. That approach would not help Cheryl, insofar as she seeks to be guided by the coach's intent. Although we might reach this conclusion if we find the considerations for competing interpretations to be in exact equipoise—if the instruction seems, on balance, to forbid easy shots or allow them—we would hesitate to conclude that the instruction's meaning doesn't bear on Cheryl's choice.

Each of the other possibilities appears more promising. At the very least, each connects much more closely to Cheryl's practical choice. The simplest approach, number (3), would be to say that meaning depends on the speaker's actual intent.[31] Under this approach, as we saw in our examination of literary interpretation, all anyone can do is to estimate or guess about the meaning of instructions. People often infer the intentions of others with a high degree of reliability, but they do not have direct access to someone else's mind; they must rely on the person's speech and other behavior.[32]

Contrary to what some people have asserted, Wittgenstein's comments about the impossibility of private language do not undercut the idea that meaning may depend on (ultimately) undiscoverable mental states.[33] In our simple case, the coach had one of two mental states, each of which is comprehensible and fits her language moderately well. The intent was publicly discoverable, even if it has not been confidently discovered and cannot be discovered with absolute certainty. The only difficulty is assessing which of the two mental states the coach had. There is no incoherence in making meaning depend on that; just as there is no incoherence in asserting that something may be a matter of historical fact, even though we lack a solid basis for determining it.

What *is* troubling about relying exclusively on the coach's intent is that the real meaning of her instruction might then deviate from a reasonable, or the best possible, assessment of what it conveys.

The fourth approach to meaning is a variation on the third. According to it, the meaning of the instruction depends on the speaker's sense of what he has actually said. It is as if we replayed for the speaker what he communicated and asked him what his expression meant. On reflection, he might decide that he made a mistake about a crucial word or, in the heat of the moment, implied something he did not want to imply. In either event, his sense of what he expressed could differ from what he intended to say. Recipients who sought to determine meaning would need to estimate what the speaker's mental state would have been if he had reflected on his words. A player seeking to be guided by the coach's wishes will care about the coach's underlying intent, rather than the coach's reflective sense of her expression, if the two diverge; but a student of meaning might contend that if the coach's intent on a point does not make it into her instruction, as she reflectively understands the instruction, the meaning of the instruction fails to correspond to that aspect of her intent.

Each of the two remaining alternatives focuses on a listener's assessment of what the coach meant to convey. We might say that the meaning of the instruction tracks what a reasonable listener (approach 5) or the most perceptive listener (approach 6) would decide about the coach's intent. Insofar as meaning depends on the use of language in context, a highly perceptive listener may better grasp relevant facts than an ordinary reasonable listener, and thus gauge the speaker's wishes more accurately.[34] If he is making a practical choice, the more perceptive listener should typically respond in accord with his superior insight. If faithful performance depends on assessment of the speaker's intent, then, subject to a qualification I will mention, it makes sense to tie meaning to the best possible human assessment of that intent.[35]

Three questions emerge about what we should understand about the listener assessing the coach's intent: from whose perspective is the assessment to be made, at what time, and with what available information? Although one might adopt the perspective of a knowledgeable outsider, asking what a recipient of the instruction might understand is preferable.[36] The needed assessment should be one a player could conceivably make.[37] This has consequences for both the content of relevant information and the time of assessment.

An assessment may employ the speaker's own explanations. An explanation at the time probably counts as part of the instruction.[38] An explanation after the initial instruction but before the player's decision how to act would count similarly.[39] From a perspective that emphasizes a listener's judgment, information that some outsider (say, the coach's husband) has that is not accessible to players should not count for what the instruction *means*.

If one limits relevant information about an instruction to what the recipients might know, any information that counts must be available prior to the time of choice. A corollary is that if two recipients receive the instruction and one has background information not available to the other, it is possible that the meaning will differ for the two recipients. It also follows that an instruction that extends through time could mean one thing for one recipient and another for a recipient who later follows the instruction (with additional available information, but without change in surrounding circumstances).[40] Thus, the best assessment approach incorporates the possibility of differences in meaning according to information available to different recipients, and of changes of meaning with the availability of new information, most particularly reliable explanations by the speaker of what she meant.[41]

If we focus *exclusively* on circumstances in which the recipient's practical task is following the instructor's intent, conceiving meaning directly as based on speaker's intent is simpler than conceiving meaning in terms of the recipient's assessment.[42] Each of these approaches ties probable meaning fairly closely to what would be the best performance of an instruction, though meaning can diverge from best performance under both approaches when intent is uncertain and the wisest performance is to act upon the less probable of two possible intentions because that represents a safer course of action.[43]

C. Instructions That Require Immediate Coordination; and Reviews of Performance

Questions about performance and meaning look different in two other situations: when an instruction requires recipients to *coordinate* immediately (without discussion); and when someone is *reviewing* an initial performance. For these circumstances, the grasp of a person with ordinary abilities, not the most perceptive listener, may be critical. The very perceptive listener realizes that others will not see all that he does; coordination will have to take place on the basis of what others understand. And when someone reviews an ordinary person's actions under instructions, conceiving meaning according to what that person could understand may make sense. These variations suggest further that the meaning that counts may depend on practical considerations and can be variable even for the same instructions.

In respect to coordination, suppose instructions are issued to a group, and its members must act together without seeking further clarification or engaging in discussion. Imagine that at a vital point in our basketball game, one play would be very likely to succeed. The new coach shouts a number for a less promising play, a number close to that for the ideal play. Only Cheryl, who is especially perceptive, has become aware that the coach makes "play number" mistakes under stress. Cheryl is sure her coach wants the "better" play. But knowing that other players will perform the announced play,[44] Cheryl should do the same.

This problem affects whether we want to conceive meaning as tracking what the most astute recipient or an ordinary recipient would understand. If meaning relates to how one best carries out instructions, meaning for coordinated group instructions may follow the understanding of most members of the group.[45] *If* meaning is so understood, the meaning of otherwise similar instructions could depend on the number of listeners and their interrelationships, on the task they must perform, and on the overall institutional system in which they act.[46]

Coordination, of course, is crucial for legal systems, but usually in ways that differ from my example. The legal instructions contained in statutes, for example, lie someplace between a directive to an individual and one to a group that must instantly coordinate its actions. The instructions do affect many people, *and* they have no realistic opportunity to seek quick clarification from the legislature. But someone who is confident words are not meant literally usually has an opportunity to explain why to others; and, *ordinarily*, different responses to a statute are not self-defeating in the manner of players carrying out different plays.

The stage of review, also of vast importance for the law, introduces similar complexities. Even if a recipient should be guided by an instructor's actual intent (or the most perceptive estimation of that), someone who assesses how satisfactory a recipient's performance has been will give overarching significance to how a reasonable person would have taken the instructions (unless the reviewer thinks the recipient *deliberately* chose to act against the instructor's intent). If we conceive meaning as connecting closely to faithful performance, we may think that the meaning for the recipient determining how to comply with an instruction differs from the meaning for someone reviewing his choice. Or, as we shall see in respect to the law of agency in the following chapter, the stage of review may not even attempt to discern one decisive meaning or one best performance.

A different approach to these complexities would be to seek one steady account of "meaning," and to say that the differences in how best to carry out instructions, and differences between performance and review, introduce elements other than meaning. *Neither* general usage nor philosophical clarity dictates any of these approaches as *the* correct one. Different forms of conceptualization may "work," so long as we realize that the best understanding of instructions depends on variable factors related to situations. We need to recognize that "the meaning of an instruction" is vague and may be answered in different ways.[47] Anyone who talks about such meaning in a theoretical way should make clear just how he is using the term.

D. Changed Conditions

I turn now to situations in which the circumstances the instructor has in mind have changed. In our main example, the first of these is that Store X has burned down.

1. Faithful Performance

Kent must now go to a different store. If the absence of Store X is the only changed condition, *and* Store Y is similar in all important respects, Kent is as faithful as he can be to Georgia's instructions when he buys the soupmeat at Store Y. One may be faithful to instructions without adhering to every detail, if adhering to every detail is impossible.

How should we describe Kent's performance? Does he continue to perform Georgia's instructions, or carry out their spirit, or perform what her instructions would be given the change?

Many terms carry their own flexibility and invite minor deviations. If Georgia said, "Shop at 5:30," she would not ordinarily mean that shopping at 5:29 is too early or 5:31 is too late. Even if Kent shops later than would count as 5:30 because a household crisis precludes his leaving the house earlier, I would say he is still performing the instruction.[48]

How should we regard Kent's choice to go to Store Y? Georgia has specified three major elements for performance, and one has become impossible. If Georgia had *previously* suggested going to Store Y when Store X was closed for a holiday, we might say that her instructions *implicitly* told Kent to use Store Y if Store X was unavailable. If Georgia had never thought about Store Y, we might say something like, "By choosing Y, Kent best fulfilled Georgia's instructions."

If Store Z is a reasonable alternative to Store Y, where should Kent shop if he is fairly sure that Georgia prefers Store Y, but he believes Store Z is better. His assessment is this: "Store Y is a much more pleasant place to shop, and that gives Georgia confidence in the quality of its meat; but the meat is actually better at Store Z." In deciding whether to rely on his judgment, Kent must consider at least four variables: the specificity of Georgia's expressions; his confidence in his judgment as compared with hers; their understandings about comparative competence; and his belief about the degree of difference in light of Georgia's fundamental aims.

Kent is clear that Georgia has the authority to pick whatever store she wants. Georgia has chosen Store X. Suppose on past occasions, Georgia has always told Kent to go to Store Y rather than Store Z when Store X was closed. Kent might decide that "Shop at Store X" is a kind of short-hand for the ordering Georgia prefers, that she has her preference for Store Y *in mind*, that she *means* him to adhere to that, and that she formulated her communication so that it will be understood by him in this way. In that event, the force of the instruction itself is strongly in favor of Store Y over Store Z.

Kent might decide, instead, that Georgia has not thought about any stores other than Store X when she gives the instructions, but he knows that nothing has altered her past expressed preference for Store Y over Store Z. Since Georgia has authority over him, her past expressions carry great weight, although, should Kent go to Store Z, he will be able to say, "I didn't disobey you because you didn't tell me which store to use if Store X was closed."

Suppose Georgia has never indicated a preference between Stores Y and Store Z? Ordinarily, Kent would then be much less sure what Georgia *would want*; but he may understand her reasons for liking Store X well enough to be virtually certain she *would* prefer Y to Z, and perhaps *has silently* preferred Y. Still, she has never said so to him. By going to Store Z, he is not disobeying her, he is only failing to carry out her *unexpressed* or *hypothetical* wishes.[49] As this example suggests, previously expressed wishes that an instructor has implicitly included in her directive usually carry more weight than her previously expressed wishes not implicitly included; and her expressed wishes of any sort (assuming their continuance) usually carry more weight than similar unexpressed or hypothetical wishes.

Why would Kent do anything *other* than follow Georgia's actual or hypothetical wish? Georgia's primary concern is the quality of meat. Kent may disagree with Georgia about which store better satisfies her own objectives. The more confident Kent is that he is right, the greater the degree of difference he perceives, the more inclined he will be to do what he thinks best. One critical factor does not depend on either person's opinion alone. In some relations, a person *with authority* and a *subordinate* recognize that the former not only has a right to dictate action but also greater competence (though she lacks the time or inclination to perform the action herself).[50] In other contexts, both parties realize that the subordinate is more expert. In the old days, wealthy parents may have regarded tutors and governesses like this; many modern suburbanites so regard people who care for their yards. Yet another possibility is that subordinates and those in authority regard themselves as about equally expert.[51]

These various understandings affect expectations about instructions. The more the subordinate is recognized as "the expert," the freer he is to exercise his own judgment, absent specific instructions that control. In our example, Georgia's past expression of a preference for Store Y would not be determinative if both she and Kent understand that he has discretion to choose a store *unless* she directs otherwise.

The relevance of particular relations of authority extends beyond fundamentally changed conditions to situations in which the speaker has used language that is vague, ambiguous, or incomplete for the choice the subordinate must make.[52]

So long as instructor and recipient share a common view of their relations, they are likely to agree on how much latitude instructions leave to the latter's judgment. If they disagree radically and obviously about the recipient's precise role, conflict will ensue and the relations are likely to be severed. But subtle and modest disagreements about role, ones that can affect what each person regards as the best performance of instructions, can survive for a long time.

Among human beings, disagreements about role do not necessarily reduce to misunderstanding by a subordinate of the superior's conception of proper relations.[53] With doctors, lawyers, professional childcare persons ("nannies"), actors, star dancers, soloists, and others, part of the subordinate's idea of role may include a sense that he may use his own judgment in the absence of a specific directive that clearly applies.[54]

A further complexity about some relations of authority concerns what we may call "independent objectives." The instructor or the recipient may have objectives that are not shared by the other and are outside the range of purposes for which the relations of authority exist. Store Z, unknown to Georgia, is owned by Kent's cousin. Kent wants to help his cousin, but he realizes that Georgia would not count that as a reason to spend money at Store Z. In a more complex example,[55] Cheryl realizes that if she scores two more points in her final college game, she will break a scoring record. She has a reason to shoot a lay-up that is not related to efforts to win the game. Conversely, as Stephen Garvey points out, an instructor may be motivated by objectives outside the range of those he could expect subordinates to accept.[56] To take a stark illustration, a coach may be aware that a very close friend has bet on the opposing team with a "point spread" of five points. The optimal outcome for the coach may be to win by less than five points.

When a subordinate's objective is wholly inappropriate, it should not affect how he understands instructions. If the authority's objective is similarly inappropriate, a subordinate may disobey instructions, or interpret them as if that objective did not exist. The complexities arise when the unshared objectives fall within an acceptable range. Georgia may not mind if Kent directs some business to relatives if the household does not suffer. Then the presence of his accepted independent objective might tip the balance in how Kent performed the instructions,[57] allowing him to shop at Store Z. We notice here a point obliquely illustrated by the example of a possible slip. The best performance of instructions from the point of view of *shared* objectives of a speaker and recipient may not necessarily be best if the recipient also takes into account other (acceptable) objectives of his own that the speaker does not share.

One might ask what is best overall, as well as what is best for Georgia or best for Kent.[58] In some circumstances, one may conceive of the general welfare as including acceptable objectives that either the speaker or listener may not share. Perhaps Kent wants to use Store Z to help the poor, to whom the owner gives a share of his profits, but Georgia (as Kent knows) is indifferent to the poverty of others.

A final point remains to be made about relations of authority. One can easily conceive of an authority's expressed or probable opinion as lying at either of two poles: either the opinion is "advisory," not binding the subordinate who is free to use his own judgment, or it is what Joseph Raz has called "exclusionary,"[59] purporting to supplant the subordinate's own judgment. We need to recognize that between the poles is an entire spectrum.[60] Both parties may understand that the superior's opinion carries weight, having independent force on its own, but leaves some room for the subordinate's judgment. The subordinate may disregard the opinion if, in his judgment, the countervailing reasons are extremely strong, but he should follow it if he thinks the balance of reasons is only moderately against the authority's opinion. This reduces to: "Give *some weight* to her opinions just because they are her opinions."

2. Meaning

What does an instruction "mean" when circumstances change? If Georgia had previously told Kent to go to Store Y when Store X was closed, we might understand the original instructions implicitly to include Store Y as the alternative if X is unavailable.[61]

If Georgia had not ever told Kent to shop at Store Y, her original instructions do not implicitly include Store Y as an alternative. Can we say that most instructions implicitly include a direction to carry out the project as well as possible, should compliance with the original terms no longer be feasible?[62] Perhaps, but we might better say that the meaning of Georgia's instructions, instructions which continue in force, has changed in the sense that an addition (or substitution) is made. We *now* take the instructions to include the possibility of going to Store Y if Store X is unavailable. This conceptualization requires us to understand Kent as having the power or authority to treat the instructions as having a changed meaning, in order to carry them out as best he can when performance of their original terms has become impossible.[63]

Variations in which Store Z is a reasonable alternative to Store Y and in which role conceptions are crucial present much greater difficulty for "meaning". Suppose that Georgia has previously expressed to Kent her preference for Store Y, but both Georgia and Kent understand that he can choose a store unless she has explicitly directed otherwise. In that event, her instructions do not implicitly direct him to use Store Y if Store X is unavailable. Nor do they implicitly direct him to use Store Z. Perhaps they implicitly direct him to use his best judgment, but even that is doubtful. Very likely, Georgia would not *mind* if he went to Store Y (her preference), and Kent is aware of that. Perhaps we should say that the meaning of the instructions has changed to allow shopping at another store, leaving Kent free to adhere to Georgia's preferences or use his own judgment about the best store.

Problems about meaning are sharpest when two people disagree about their respective roles. A crucial question Kent must ask himself is whether Georgia has successfully circumscribed his latitude of choice. Georgia cannot do so merely by *wishing* Kent to do something—even if Kent happens to guess her wishes; she must express a direction that he do something. As to whether Georgia has limited his choice, Kent will not concede that she has done so simply because she wished and intended to do so by her utterance.[64] He may conclude that if her utterance did not adequately convey a limitation to him, he is not circumscribed. Kent will not take Georgia's probable intentions as his exclusive guide for understanding her instructions, especially if he thinks he is more competent or has acceptable independent objectives. What she *successfully* communicated to him will be independently important.

If the idea that speaker's intent might determine meaning seemed initially attractive, that was largely because we assumed that the listener should try to act upon that intent. Once we drop that assumption, speaker's intent seems less crucial. The recipient's apprehension of what is conveyed seems equally important. But this creates yet another barrier to talking about "the meaning" of an instruction. Suppose Georgia and Kent take opposing views as to whether she has constrained Kent's choice of store. No basis may exist to privilege Georgia's intent over Kent's understanding, and no "averaging" the idiosyncrasies of the two, to arrive at a "real" meaning, may be possible. Rather, *if* we are going to talk about "the meaning", as something different from what either Georgia or Kent may conclude, we are pushed toward some idea of how most people, or a reasonable or perceptive person, situated as was Kent, would understand what Georgia said. Once speaker and listener perspectives are given equal significance, the move toward some sort of *objective meaning* is natural.

A related complication about meaning is how to describe disagreements about role that yield different understandings of how far instructions constrain recipients. If two players share exactly the same view about what their coach intended when she said, "Don't shoot," and the players further agree on what the phrase means generally, they still may disagree about what to do because they differ about the coach's authority. Similarly, a player and coach (like Georgia and Kent) might disagree about the player's exact role vis-à-vis a coach. If *meaning* were conceived as following a full assessment of how a recipient should take an instruction, these disagreements among players and between coach and player would be about meaning. Although this is one possible conceptualization,[65] we might instead say, "Since Kent understands Georgia's state of mind and the general meaning of her terms, he and Georgia do not disagree about the 'meaning' of the instruction, rather they disagree only about how far he should carry out her previously expressed wishes or probable desires."[66]

Our discussion of possible "independent objectives" has revealed yet another difficulty with tying meaning closely to faithful performance. If we can imagine that the performance that is "best" may vary depending on whether we focus on all the (acceptable) objectives of the instructor, or all the (acceptable) objectives of the recipient, or some other standard, we may conclude that we cannot speak of a "best performance" without further explication. We could obviously not arrive at a single meaning tied to best performance until we settled on what "best performance" counted.[67]

E. Supplementary Directives

Professor Eskridge suggested a second variation on his original scenario; Georgia, worried about the effect of cholesterol on the children's health, instructs Kent to buy foods that an article says are low on cholesterol.

1. Faithful Performance

The precise relevance of Georgia's new instruction for her former soup-meat instruction is not straightforward. Since Kent could continue to buy soupmeat *and* buy the articles Georgia now wants, the significance of the new instruction for the old lies in its underlying reason. Georgia's expressed wish that her children avoid a lot of cholesterol is a strong reason not to buy soupmeat.

Two barriers exist to Kent's quickly concluding that he should cease buying soupmeat. First, Georgia has not said that he should stop. Perhaps she wants him to continue to buy soupmeat. Kent gathers, instead, that Georgia was not aware just how much cholesterol (beef) soupmeat contains. If Kent is an agent with substantial competence, he rightly matches his own reliable information with Georgia's expressed preference against cholesterol.

But even that judgment is not sufficient by itself for him to stop buying soupmeat. Beef in soup may have substantial nutritional value that offsets the danger of cholesterol. Kent can be confident his ceasing to buy soupmeat will fit Georgia's wishes, only if he assures himself that substitute purchases will not sacrifice the values of soupmeat. If he learns that chicken meat for soup has roughly the same value, he will perceive buying chicken as not at odds with the aims of Georgia's initial instruction.

2. Meaning

Just how should we conceptualize Kent's purchase of chicken meat for soup? Here a good bit turns on the word "soupmeat."[68] If Georgia and Kent have taken that word literally as any meat for soup, then chicken qualifies. Because Kent understood that Georgia originally wanted him to buy beef, the original instruction *implicitly* included a preference for beef, but he now buys the soupmeat that carries out Georgia's most recently expressed wishes. His interpretation of how to perform the first directive is colored by the reasons for the later directive. We might say that the *meaning* of the initial instruction has changed if we include implicit understandings, but otherwise it has not changed.[69]

The initial instruction looks different if we suppose that "soupmeat" has always meant, and continues to mean, "beef meat" for soup.[70] In that event, buying chicken is not "complying with" or "carrying out" Georgia's instruction to buy beef. The "meaning" of that instruction does not include buying chicken for soup. We might rather say, "Kent is doing the best he can to follow the *spirit* of Georgia's instruction, in the light of new facts."[71] Kent's purchase of chicken is not based on an interpretation of the original directive (taken by itself); his action is based on an interpretation of *all* relevant directives (or, perhaps more precisely, on an interpretation of the import of all relevant directives).

If Georgia and Kent assume that all instructions that continue in force are to be *interpreted* in light of all later instructions and their reasons,[72] then we might say Kent *is* interpreting and complying with the original directive (though self-consciously disregarding one of its terms). According to this view, the meaning of an instruction may shift as later instructions are forthcoming.[73]

Can we say that Kent is complying with the more abstract idea in Georgia's instruction to buy the best meat for soup, and with the abstract idea that her instructions should be interpreted to fit together?[74] *Perhaps*, but Georgia's instructions were specific, not abstract. However, this comparison tends to show that there is a no sharp line between when Kent complies with the original instructions though he no longer fulfills each of their specific terms and when Kent no longer complies with the instructions themselves, though he fulfills their broad spirit.[75]

We have so far assumed that the term "soupmeat" includes chicken or definitely excludes chicken. Matters might be less clear. The word "soupmeat" does not *literally* exclude chicken. Suppose, because of tastes, beliefs about health, and prices, people have long thought that the most desirable meat for soup is beef, and that "soupmeat" has come loosely to mean "beef."[76] New information makes beef seem much less desirable. Over time, this may shift the understanding of the term "soupmeat." The term "soupmeat" may quickly become more open in the specific meat(s) to which it refers. Kent's buying of chicken could be conceived, in part, as a kind of proposal that chicken should now count as "soupmeat." On this account, Kent offers a new interpretation of the meaning of Georgia's original directive, one he thinks she will endorse.

F. Radically Changed Conditions

The next changed circumstance in our example is rationing. Kent does not take Georgia's direction about the soupmeat as foreclosing his decision not to buy expensive meat, rather than other items of food. How are we to conceptualize his choice?

We can no longer talk of Kent carrying out Georgia's directive to buy soupmeat. Might we say, as we could with the purchase of chicken, that Kent is fulfilling the spirit of the directive? Yes and no. Kent's behavior *is in accord* with the spirit of the directive, to buy healthy food for children. But Kent would take it for granted that Georgia wants him to buy healthy food for her children.[77] Her instruction now looms as a possible obstacle to choice, one he reasonably disregards. While it is *not inaccurate* to say that Kent still acts in the spirit of the directive, conceiving the directive as *losing force* because of changed conditions is more illuminating.

This analysis confirms how blurry the line is between a person's *carrying out* a directive in changed circumstances and his regarding the directive as losing force.[78] Similarly blurry is the line between "interpretation of the spirit" of the directive and "disregard." If the aim of the directive had been something less obvious than healthy food for children, its rationale could continue to influence choice, even if none of its specific terms were followed.[79]

G. Lapse of Time and the Comparative Force of Judgments

Eskridge's story contemplates a substantial lapse of time during which Georgia is neither with her children nor communicating with Kent about their lives. We might imagine an earlier era when English parents go to India, leaving children with a housekeeper and other staff. In the most extreme and painful version, the parent dies after leaving instructions relating to the children. Even if the housekeeper continues to believe he should follow specific instructions for unchanged conditions, as time goes by and the parent is further removed, he will rely more and more on his own appraisals. One reason is the need, when it becomes impossible or unwise to follow the specific directives, to exercise judgment to carry out broad objectives the instructions reflect. Although Kent *might* do this by continuing to give overarching weight to what he thought Georgia would want in the circumstances, two more subtle changes also operate.

About many matters (although perhaps not diet), parents re-shift objectives for children as they interact with them and see them grow. Only in the broadest sense of "wanting what is best for them" do most parents maintain consistent objectives for children over time. An optimistic appraisal would be that parents learn more about what is good for their children as they learn more about their children. If Georgia is away for a long time, she is not on hand to do the learning; Kent is. Not only will his estimates about what Georgia *would want* become more unreliable, he will have increasing confidence in his own views, and declining confidence in Georgia's expressed or probable views.[80]

Relatedly, if Georgia is away for a long time, Kent and others who are present are likely to see raising the children as more and more *their* responsibility and less and less Georgia's. Similarly, people in Georgia's position are likely to feel that they have less right to dictate to those closer at hand; and sometimes the strength of their parental feeling dilutes with time. These patterns reinforce the tendency of the present housekeeper to give increasing weight to his judgment, and for that to be accepted by an absent parent.

These comments further illuminate the question of role. Someone in Kent's position will not have a standard conception of role that applies rigidly to all superiors at all times. His notion of role will shift as parents absent themselves or return to involve themselves more closely with their children.[81]

H. Abstract and Specific Purposes

With most directives, we can identify objectives ranging from the most specific to the most abstract. Roughly, we can think of directives formulated at very specific, middle range, and highly abstract levels. In our example, to what extent does the faithful housekeeper pay attention to abstract rather than specific objectives?

The soupmeat directive is very specific. Georgia made it specific because she expected Kent to fulfill it in a precise way. So long as conditions (and knowledge) do not change, Kent should do what Georgia has specifically requested, though even then his behavior will be restrained by implicit specific understandings and general objectives, for example, not buying spoiled meat. General objectives will guide his understanding of the directive in changed circumstances and signal when the directive's force has lapsed.

As a directive becomes more abstract, analysis becomes more complicated. Suppose Georgia tells Kent to buy meat that is "reasonably priced." One extreme among possibilities is that Georgia doesn't wish to waste money, but she leaves it to Kent to decide what is "reasonable." Another extreme is that Georgia has let Kent know exactly what she considers to be unreasonable pricing; both understand that "reasonably priced" is her shorthand for Kent's not paying more than specific prices for particular cuts of meat. As prices in general rise, Kent will have to exercise some judgment, but perhaps little more than if Georgia had set out an exact list of acceptable prices in the first place.[82]

Typically, people like Georgia and Kent will understand an instruction about "reasonably priced" not to embody either extreme. Kent is to be guided substantially by Georgia's opinions about reasonable prices, insofar as she has expressed these to him, but her expressed opinions don't cover every contingency. Kent is to exercise some independent judgment.[83]

These matters are relation-specific and context-specific. Suppose Georgia and Kent both recognize that Kent knows much more about meat prices than Georgia.[84] Kent may then take Georgia's opinions as only that, not restricting his own judgment, so long as he avoids wild extravagance.

Among these various alternatives, how would we decide what "reasonably priced" means in an instruction from Georgia to Kent? Unless Kent's task is to follow Georgia's wishes (even if not clearly expressed), we have no reason to privilege her sense of how he should understand what the phrase "reasonably priced" entails over his own. The "meaning" of the phrase should include their past relations bearing on what this phrase means *for them*, not assessed according to some general understanding.[85] The meaning here may depend on what they think it means, or, if they are divided, on what a reasonable understanding would be for this directive, by someone aware of previous exchanges between Georgia and Kent.

IV. CONCLUSION

What general lessons may be drawn from this examination of performance and meaning of informal instructions, and what relevance may these conclusions have for law?

I have focused largely on what can go wrong with authoritative informal instructions, situations when the speaker may have made a mistake, or the instructions do not clearly cover the action that should be taken, or conditions have changed, calling for different behavior from what the instructor envisioned. These situations raise questions about faithful performance and about what the instructions crucially "mean."

A central issue about performance is to what extent the person subject to the instructions should do what the instructor wants; how far he should follow the apparent import of the language of the instructions (if this diverges from likely intent); and how far he should use his own judgment. We have seen that when someone tries to follow informal instructions, the mental state intent of the person who gave them is very important, but often it is not the only guide to judgment. If an easy transposition to law were possible, we might suppose that this subjective intent would matter greatly, but would often not be the only guide to action.

One thing about which we can be sure is that no easy transposition from informal contexts to law is possible—as brief comments at the beginning of the chapter indicate. Our law contains very different kinds of norms. A common law rule is not the same as a disposition prescribed by an individual's will, and a rule that indicates how much of one's marginal income one must pay in federal income taxes is not the same as the highly general "compelling interest test" in constitutional law. It has rarely been suggested that interpreting common law rules comes down ultimately to discerning some individual's or group's subjective intent. Yet, some applicable legal rules seem at first glance not so different from instructions. These are the wills of individuals and orders or rules issued by single individuals who have the authority to dictate (within limits) what subordinates should do. Conceivably, a full theory about our system's legal norms would conclude that actual subjective intent has no role to play in determining performance, even for wills and individual directives, but that conclusion would be highly counterintuitive. In contrast, because of the difficulties of the concept of intent for multi-member bodies, because the officials who apply statutes must typically concern themselves with how those regulated understand the statutes, and because of the length of time between the adoption of statutes and performance of acts courts consider, the claim that subjective intent should not be central in *statutory* and *constitutional* interpretation is more immediately appealing.[86]

This chapter indicates a truth that is obvious upon slight reflection. The problem about how to determine relevant subjective intent exists *not only* when that intent is taken as *the* governing standard for action but also when that intent is taken as one relevant criterion for what should be done (and for what an instruction means). All the complexities I have explored about determining the intent that counts, as well as some additional problems, are relevant if subjective intent matters for performance in law.

In informal contexts, how the recipient thinks he can best perform instructions will depend partly on his sense of role, and that sense may vary from how the instructor sees their respective responsibilities. Perceptions of role may shift as time lapses from when an instruction is given. As conditions change and fulfillment of literal terms becomes impossible or unwise, exactly what the subordinate should do may shift. The opinion of a person giving an instruction *may* be more than "advisory" and less than "exclusionary." Although we can talk of "carrying out an instruction but not each detail," of "carrying out the spirit of an instruction but not its terms," and of "the instruction's losing force," the lines between these categories are not precise at the edges. These aspects of our analysis will prove to have relevance for understanding legal interpretation; but *how* they apply differs among branches of law and varieties of legal norms.

I have made five central points about the meaning of instructions. (1) In the absence of some overall theoretical structure that would yield more rigorous conclusions than reflective intuitions, we have no straightforward conception of the meaning that counts that applies comfortably in all instances. (2) What amounts to "literal meaning" is often debatable, since the degree of contextualization allowed for literal meaning is far from self-evident. (3) Ordinary understanding of instructions depends significantly on context, and particularly on shared assumptions of speaker and listener.[87] (4) Meaning does not always correlate perfectly with best performance (though one can, of course, stipulate that it does). (5) The meaning of an instruction, on many accounts, may change depending on the context of decision that is involved, on whether, for example, the context is an initial decision by the recipient of an instruction or review of the recipient's performance by someone else.

The lesson that the subject of meaning in law will not be simple may already have been obvious from writings about literary interpretation and related fields; but part of this chapter's rationale is that informal instructions are in most ways more like law than the kinds of texts on which we have focused in prior chapters. What our study shows us about the perplexities of meaning for imperative language, and about how meaning may diverge from best performance, have evident relevance for law.

A possible strategy to deal with these difficulties is to adopt a relatively simple approach to meaning and say that all other factors that performers of legal instructions and courts take into consideration is a question about something else, such as how practically to apply instructions, not an inquiry about meaning.[88] This strategy might produce a clarified sense of meaning, but it conflicts with the sense, within law, that people usually treat all the factors that go into interpretation and application as relevant to the meaning of the legal norm. Another strategy, the strategy that I find most sensible, is to acknowledge that meaning has many meanings, that a choice of one standard for what counts as "the meaning" comes down to a question of what will lead to desirable practical choices.

A final caution is warranted. We have consistently attended to instances that raise problems. As I have noted, the performance and meaning of instructions are often straightforward in context, leaving the recipient no important choice. As earlier chapters have suggested, and as we shall see in more detail in the chapters that follow, the same is true for law; in many instances, appropriate performance and meaning (though perhaps not the precise criteria for determining meaning) will be clear and will be congruent.

Notes

1 Perceptive modern treatments of rules in general are in Joseph Raz, *Practical Reason and Norms* (London, Hutchison and Sons, Ltd., 1975); Frederick Schauer, *Playing by the Rules* (Oxford, Clarendon Press, 1991). I use a different sense of "instruction" than the kind nonmandatory recipes or advice discussed by Schauer, at 3–4. In some respects, my discussion resembles Wittgenstein's sustained, if not systematic, examination of informal rules in Ludwig Wittgenstein, *Philosophical Investigations* §§138–242 (G.E.M. Anscombe trans., New York, MacMillan Pub. Co., 1953). On the nature of imperatives, see C.L. Humblin, *Imperatives* (New York, Basil Blackwell, 1987).

2 See Robert S. Summers, "How Law Is Formal and Why It Matters," 82 *Cornell Law Review* 1165 (1997).

3 It is conceivable that the relative formality of law will allow more definite conclusions for some matters than may be reached for informal instructions, but we will find that many of the problematic aspects of desirable performance and meaning carry over to a consideration of legal texts.

4 I assume that the person in authority is exercising his authority in a proper range, that, for example, the director of a play is not trying to make the play awful to get revenge on its main financial backer.

5 Thus, I do not include a very small child who may understand that he has been told never to cross the road, or talk to strangers, without apprehending why that is so.

6 Could we say that Cheryl actually carried out the instructions? I do not think so. Cheryl does what any player would ordinarily do, take a very easy shot. The coach's instructions to avoid shooting do not add to her reasons to do that. It is as if, at most, the coach had not spoken to this particular situation. (Unless on past occasions the coach had made clear that whenever she says "Don't shoot," she means "Don't shoot, except when you have a very easy shot, which you should take.") In an Appendix to Kent Greenawalt, "From the Bottom Up," 82 *Cornell Law Review* 994, 1037–38 (1997), I aim at more precision about situations in which a person self-consciously does not follow instructions.

7 Thus, Cheryl might say, "I knew you meant we should not take any shots at all, but I was sure I would make this one and that it would help the team win. So I went ahead." An "objective" may be put at different levels. If the objective is put

as "winning the game" or "making sure we don't lose the ball without scoring," Cheryl has tried to achieve the objective. If the objective is put as "keeping the ball from the other team as long as possible," she has not tried to do that.

8 Exactly which values will count as external will often depend on how narrowly or broadly one puts the objective of the instructions. See Schauer, note 1 supra, at 49, n. 13. See also M.B.W. Sinclair, "Law and Language: The Role of Pragmatics in Statutory Interpretation," 46 *University of Pittsburgh Law Review* 373, 388–89 (1985).

9 The concept of a "faithful performance" is not meant to imply that the recipient of instructions should necessarily carry out "the will" of the speaker. Indeed, this is not always what the person subject to instructions should do. Phrases like "desirable performance" or "best performance" might better avoid any implication that everything reduces to the wishes of the person in authority, but those terms present other difficulties. One can render a performance that happens to be desirable though one's motives have nothing to do with carrying out the instructions or fulfilling one's role. By "faithful performance," I want to signal the idea that a person is trying to be faithful to his responsibilities as the recipient of authoritative instructions he is attempting to carry out.

10 As Michael Moore notes in "The Semantics of Judging," 54 *Southern California Law Review* 151, 292 (1981), J.L. Austin talked of fact being "richer than diction." "A Plea for Excuses," 57 *Proceedings of the Aristotelian Society* 1, 21 (1956). Under Moore's "realist" approach to language, the meaning of words and phrases embraces the best understanding of concepts. But it is still true that at any point in time, our language does not actually mark clearly many subtle distinctions.

11 One might begin with an account of meaning—for example, drawing from the approaches of Grice (in Chapter 2) and Hirsch (in Chapter 3) and concluding that meaning is determined by the intent of the speaker—and then see how well that accords with what is appropriate performance. What one would learn fairly quickly is that no single straightforward account of meaning could cover everything that a recipient of instructions should take into account. One might, nonetheless, stick to a single version of meaning, conclude that meaning is only one component for practical choice by those subject to instructions, and comment on what besides meaning is involved. Nothing in this chapter indicates that this is an impossible task.

12 In a systematic account, one would need to compare all plausible candidates about meaning against all plausible versions of faithful performance, before one reached final conclusions about the "meaning" of instructions (or legal norms).

13 I employ the order of presentation that seems most fruitful, but I do not claim there is any necessary logical priority of performance over meaning. One criticism that might be mounted against my observations about both "faithful performance" and "meaning" is that a full account of either requires reference to an interpretive methodology. The critic would be right that recipients of instructions often employ (at least implicitly) strategies of interpretation; and that a final assessment of these matters involves measuring tentative judgments about performance and meaning against possible approaches to interpretation. My discussion proceeds on the assumption that much can be said about the performance and meaning of informal instructions without either conceptualizing common practice in terms of a theory of interpretation or recommending a particular interpretive theory for use. Indeed, illustrations of the sort I consider here can help provide the building blocks for descriptive and normative theories of interpretation.

14 "Proceedings of Law and Linguistics Conference," 73 *Washington University Law Quarterly* 191, 940–42 (1995). Professor Eskridge has employed a similar illustration using different names on other occasions.

15 Kent is supposed to shop for soupmeat on Monday and he is to go to Store X. The word "soupmeat" itself seems to leave more latitude for a range of choice than the other terms, but that range may have been narrowed, if Store X sells only one kind of meat as "soupmeat," or Georgia and Kent have previously agreed that they will use a certain kind of meat.

16 If those past dealings showed that Georgia meant a narrower idea of "soupmeat" than the general concept would include, Kent should buy the meat Georgia had in mind.

17 The instructions are not merely evidence of Georgia's mental state. Subordinates often do not have a responsibility to do what a superior wants (if, for example, they think an alternative is preferable) until they have been instructed to do so. Since Kent's awareness of what Georgia wants is not the equivalent of his being instructed, the instruction has an independent significance. The instruction is performative, see Max Black, *Models and Metaphors* 118 (Ithaca, N.Y., Cornell University Press, 1962); it alters Kent's responsibilities. Even if the subordinate does have a responsibility to carry out unexpressed desires, his duty to do a particular act will have greater weight if it is the subject of an instruction.

18 If we think of the reasonable listener as having all Kent's knowledge of Georgia, he will reach the same conclusion as Kent. If the reasonable listener is restricted to all past dealings of Georgia and Kent with respect to soupmeat, he may conclude that Monday really means Monday. The reverse possibility is that the reasonable listener may have more knowledge than Kent, say because Kent has just started to work for Georgia (and the reasonable listener is allowed information about past behavior of Georgia's that Kent lacks) or because, being none too bright, Kent has failed to draw inferences from Georgia's prior slips that a reasonable person would make. When we turn to "meaning," these discrepancies raise puzzles; but they are not of great importance for "faithful performance." Any actual recipient of instructions can only do the best he can with information he has (plus, further information quickly available at reasonable "cost").

19 When Kent thinks that Georgia has probably misstated her wishes, the most prudent or safe performance of his responsibilities as a servant might not be the course that is the most desirable in terms of her satisfaction (taking into account the likelihood of her satisfaction or dissatisfaction and the intensity of her feelings). Because Kent and Georgia have a common interest in continuing good relations, his taking the safer course of following her literal direction achieves some overall benefit; but if the instruction was very important, Kent might think he would serve Georgia best by taking a course of action that risks incurring her anger.

20 But see Moore, note 10 supra at 257, suggesting that a servant acts according to his perception of his master's wants.

21 Indeed, this illustration of Georgia misconceiving her responses to corrections of slips is one example of the subordinate not being bound to follow all unexpressed wishes of the superior.

22 Akeel Bilgrami has suggested to me that if I say "I am going towndown," the literal meaning obviously is "I am going downtown." That seems undoubtedly right if the term actually expressed is meaningless and the intended meaningful term is evident, as was the case with the title of Davidson's essay discussed in Chapter 2, the malapropism "A Nice Derangement of Epitaphs." Matters become more

debatable when the term actually expressed does have a coherent meaning in that context. One might wonder whether the "literal language" can demand something that is impossible; but a person could be instructed to fly, even if that is physically impossible, and a person could be instructed to shop at 3:00 A.M., even if it happens that no stores are then open. The phrase "3:00 A.M." does not involve the complexity of assigning a literal meaning to language that everyone understands has symbolic significance, such as "Look ere thou leap," mentioned in Chapter 4.

23 See Dennis Patterson, "The Poverty of Interpretive Universalism: Toward a Reconstruction of Legal Theory," 22 *Texas Law Review* 1, 14 n72 (1993), giving an example of someone who wants chicken noodle soup but says, "I would like to order minestrone soup." Paul Campos takes issue with Patterson's assertion that actual intention is irrelevant to the meaning of the statement. "This Is Not a Sentence," 73 *Washington University Law Quarterly* 971, 980–81 (1995).

24 The coach's aspiration could be more subtle. She might want the players to focus exclusively on avoiding shots (and keeping the ball from the other team), not attempting to get into position for any easy shots; yet, she might also hope that if a player fortuitously found herself in position for a very easy shot, she would have the good sense to take it. In tense conditions, good coaches do not want to give players too much to think about.

25 We might imagine how the coach would have responded had a player asked, "Do you mean we shouldn't even take a lay-up under the basket?" She might have said: (1) "Yes, don't take any shot"; (2) "No, if you are sure you can make an easy lay-up, go ahead;" or (3) "Hmm'n. I wasn't thinking of those. But, now that you've asked, you should [either (1) or (2)]."

26 The analysis here resembles that of Georgia's possible slip.

27 Here, however, judging which response is riskier is hard; a coach may say, "Of course I didn't mean you should pass up an easy lay-up."

28 For a defense of this basic approach, see Schauer, note 1 supra.

29 See the discussion of restricted quantifiers in "Proceedings of Law and Linguistics Conference," note 14 supra, at 825–99. Saying what words mean literally is often hard. A typical strategy for the defensive team in the basketball situation I have described is to foul, forcing the team with the ball to shoot foul shots. Cheryl's coach certainly does not mean that the team should not shoot its awarded foul shots (though many years ago that was an option). Does the literal meaning of "don't shoot" cover foul shots or only field goal attempts? I'd say the implicit limitation to field goals is so self-evident that the literal meaning covers only them. One attempt to draw the line between general background assumptions that figure in literal meaning and matters of particular context that do not is John Searle's *Expression and Meaning: Studies in the Theory of Speech Acts* (Cambridge, Cambridge University Press, 1979).

30 See generally William O. Poplin, "Law and Linguistics: Is There Common Ground?," 73 *Washington University Law Quarterly* 1043 (1995).

31 See, e.g., Campos, note 23 supra.

32 Even when the coach says after the fact what she meant, that does not give complete certainty. She may be lying, or have a lapse of memory, or shade the truth in subtle ways she does not recognize. A disappointed coach who did not advert to easy shots when instructing her players may tell a player who misses an easy shot, "I told you not to shoot!"

33 See, e.g., Philip F. Frickey, "Faithful Interpretation," 73 *Washington University Law Quarterly* 1085, 1088 (1995).

34 If we ask about the significance of language itself, detached from the special circumstances in which it is used, the relation of an ordinary and highly perceptive listener looks somewhat different. What much or all language means depends on general use (or general expert use in a field). About many simple terms taken by themselves, there may be no "most perceptive observer," unless it is someone who has studied the uses of others. Ordinary understandings determine meaning. However, with complicated instructions (as in I.R.S. regulations) and even sentences of ordinary complexity, a gifted reader may be better than a common reader at sorting out the implications of the language. See Robert S. Summers and Geoffrey Marshall, "The Argument from Ordinary Meaning in Statutory Interpretation," 43 *Northern Ireland Legal Quarterly* 213, 220–24 (1992).

35 One might say that "meaning" is determined by ordinary reasonable listeners, and that the more perceptive listener, with his superior insight about intent, acts contrary to the instruction's meaning or acts in accord with a special meaning; but these circumlocutions are confusing. Within a seminar Aaron Chait suggested that "meaning" should depend on a speaker's reasonable expectations about performance, given general and specific shared social practices, with the latter having priority. This approach lies close to one that makes a reasonable listener's understanding determinative.

36 It will, of course, not do to say that the best assessment is usually made inside the speaker's mind. Allowing that to count as the best assessment brings us extremely close to saying that actual intent determines meaning. For the assessment approach to be different, we must imagine the perspective of someone who does not have omniscient access to the internal workings of the speaker's mind.

37 From this standpoint, it may matter whether the recipients of the instructions are competent adults or children (though one might say the most perceptive child, say of 10, could perceive what a very perceptive adult could perceive). More generally, this problem raises the question of whether one thinks in terms of very perceptive real people, or superperceptive people, who are more perceptive than any actual human beings.

38 If the coach follows "don't shoot" with "I mean any shot," that amounts to, "don't take any kind of shot."

39 Cheryl will not care if the coach clarifies her wishes in the original time-out or a subsequent time-out. I assume the explanation reliably reflects the coach's original wishes. An unreliable and inaccurate explanation may supplement and alter the original instruction.

40 Indeed, if a single actor had to act on the instruction more than once, the instruction could have different meanings for him at different times.

41 A further development of reasons behind the instruction, though not focused on the particular problem the actor faces, could have a similar effect.

42 We might, however, still choose an option based on recipient understanding if it works much better for other situations, and we aspire to a uniform approach to meaning.

43 I refer here to the risk of generating a more hostile response if one guesses wrong. I have already mentioned that although one could try to accommodate this risk under a speaker's intent approach, such an accommodation is not fully satisfactory.

44 I assume the team has taken all its "times out," so stopping the game for clarification is not an option.

45 Of course, if the most astute observer takes into account the need for coordinated action, she interprets the instructions to bring her final judgment into line
with that of ordinary recipients. One might think of Cheryl as understanding that
the coach's overriding intent is that everyone perform the same play, which here
conflicts in application with her intent that the "logical" play be performed.

46 A further perplexity appears if four players realize that the fifth will misin-
terpret in a particular way, and they therefore act in the way that fits her actions.
In that event, we would certainly not say the instruction's meaning is in line with
the fifth player's misunderstanding; probably we would not say even that the best
performance follows her misunderstanding. Rather, we would say that the players
departed from the terms of the instruction to achieve the overarching aim of coordinated action. (We might run this conclusion backwards to say that the superior
listener, Cheryl, departs from the meaning of instructions whenever she tailors her
behavior to ordinary understanding, but that large extension of our problem of
one player's misunderstanding seems unwarranted.)

47 Conceivably, some particular approach to "meaning" may work best for all
practical affairs or those of a certain kind; but a sustained and complex argument
would be needed to support the case for any such approach.

48 Others who have discussed this problem with me disagree. I am assuming that
the precise time is not a central element of the instruction.

49 An unexpressed wish is a preference felt by Georgia but not conveyed (to
Kent). A hypothetical wish is one that would be felt if Georgia addressed the
circumstance. If Georgia has never expressed a wish to anyone, Kent will often
not know whether he is guessing about her unexpressed or her hypothetical feelings. However, since I am treating expressions to third parties not intended to be
conveyed to Kent as (relevantly) unexpressed, Kent may find out about feelings
not expressed to him.

50 I experienced such relations firsthand when I worked one summer on clay
tennis courts under the supervision of a professional, and one weekend when I
did some menial tasks at a greenhouse owned by the family of a close friend. In
neither instance did I have any basis to trust my opinion in opposition to the judgment of the person instructing me. We both understood this.

51 Needless to say, in-between possibilities are infinite, with the subordinate having more or less expertness than his superior, but with both having considerable
competence (or incompetence), or with significant variations in subdomains.

52 That category may cover the very easy shot under the basket.

53 By contrast, if God gives instructions, one supposes that human beings should
exercise the degree of judgment that God intends.

54 Further, he may not think that the "client" or director may alter the general
range of his discretion by a vague instruction to "Do whatever you think I probably want, even if I do not clearly say so."

55 This was suggested by Deborah DeMott at the Cornell Symposium.

56 See Stephen P. Garvey, "Are Housekeepers Like Judges?," 82 *Cornell Law
Review* 1059, 1041–42 (1997), discussing the "Not-Entirely Faithful Head-of-
Household." One may suppose that people in Georgia's circumstances can pursue
whatever objectives they want, short of harming their children, but often people
in authority have their own roles circumscribed to a limited range of purposes.

57 As we shall see in the next chapter, the law of agency generally does not allow
agents to take their own independent objectives into account.

58 Robert Cooter made this point at the Symposium.

59 See Joseph Raz, note 1 supra.

60 Frederick Schauer emphasizes this point in Schauer, note 1 supra. He responds directly to Raz in id. at 88–93.

61 This understanding of the instruction is possible only if we focus on Georgia and Kent, or upon a reasonable listener who knows enough about past relations between Georgia and Kent to add this to the words Georgia has spoken.

62 On this view, Georgia's instructions implicitly included a direction to choose necessary alternatives, and, thus, envisioned or authorized the choice of Store Y.

63 Notice that, under this conceptualization, Kent can conceive the instructions as having a meaning of which Georgia may be unaware. An approach that made speaker's intent, or a perceptive listener's understanding of the speaker's intent, crucial would require some emendation to incorporate this. The suggestion of William N. Eskridge Jr. and Judith Levi that some legal phrases be understood as "regulatory variables" is one way to accommodate this notion of changing meaning for altered circumstances. See Eskridge and Levi, "Regulating Variables and Statutory Interpretation," 73 *Washington University Law Quarterly* 1103 (1995), and Proceedings, note 28 supra, at 841–48, 945–52.

64 For example, Kent might find out indirectly what Georgia aimed to do with her communication to him, and still conclude that she had failed. An employee who recognizes that his boss *may* circumscribe his choices about dress or hairstyle may not regard himself as constrained absent explicit and clear instructions that restrict his liberty to decide for himself.

65 This is similar to how "realists" understand the meaning of natural, moral, and theory-laden terms, with "meaning" in accord with scientific reality or ideal choice. See e.g., Michael Moore, "A Natural Law Theory of Interpretation," 58 *Southern California Law Review* 277 (1985).

66 This comparison reemphasizes a point made earlier—that the phrase, "the meaning of an instruction," may reasonably be keyed more or less closely to the question of its appropriate fulfillment in the circumstances.

67 Perhaps appropriate objectives that are mutually accepted would be the right guide if one were trying to settle on a single standard of best performance that could determine meaning. One should probably count for this purpose objectives as to which one person (say, the speaker) is indifferent but accepts as guiding the other to some extent. (As Georgia might accept Kent's shopping at the store of his relative, if she has not directed otherwise.)

68 See Eskridge, note 14 supra at 943.

69 Alternatively, one might speak of the second directive as trumping an aspect of a first directive whose meaning remains constant.

70 We can put this alternative most pointedly if we assume that Georgia originally instructed Kent to buy beef for soup.

71 Kent is not disobeying Georgia's initial instruction, because Kent is assuming that the changed conditions eliminate its force in one particular; but Kent is not complying with the original directive either. The shift from beef to chicken differs from the shift from Store X to Store Y, because, unlike Store X, beef remains available, and many people continue to buy it for soup. Georgia meant beef and Kent understood that, yet he is buying chicken. Thus, it is harder to say that Kent is complying with the original instructions alone when he switches from beef to chicken than when he uses Store Y.

72 People might also want later instructions to be interpreted in light of earlier instructions, or earlier instructions that evidently remain in force.

73 Alternatively, one might regard the inquiry about meaning as narrower than all relevant steps in interpretation.

74 See generally David Brink, "Legal Theory, Legal Interpretation, and Judicial Review," 17 *Philosophy & Public Affairs* 105, 121–29 (1988) (discussing the role of abstract intent in determining meaning and purpose).

75 An intermediate example would be if Store X remains open, but has changed management and deteriorated. Shopping at Store X is not impossible—in that the example resembles the beef-chicken problem—but Store X (not only perceptions of it) has changed and is no longer the same Store X Georgia meant—in that the example resembles the burning down of Store X.

76 Of course, customers occasionally buy chicken and other meats for soup, but general usage has not included meats other than beef as "soupmeat."

77 When he bought chicken, he was still buying meat for soup regularly; absent the directive, he might not have given the children soup with meat. Georgia's instruction still influenced his choice. That is no longer true. Had she never uttered a word about soupmeat, he would still be buying the same non-meat items. I here disregard the possibility that the directive leads him to continue to buy items *for soup*.

78 Some directives may lose force permanently, because the conditions they envision will never reemerge. The soupmeat directive loses force only temporarily. When rationing ends, Kent should go back to buying chicken for soup.

79 Indeed, that could be true here if the first directive continued to influence Kent to buy ingredients *for soup*. Then, we could not speak simply of the directive losing force.

80 He might conceive a construct of what Georgia would want if she had been around and learned what he has about the children. But, his assessments of her actual mental state wishes at an earlier time or her probable wishes in the present (given her actual assumptions about the children) will carry less weight than they once did.

81 Georgia may undergo parallel changes in attitude.

82 I say *little* more, because if Georgia had set out the list, that might have reflected less confidence in Kent's judgments about rising prices than if she used the term "reasonably priced."

83 This (probably) does not mean that Georgia's opinions are merely guides that Kent is free to reject. If he thinks a particular meat is worth twice the price Georgia has said is reasonable, he is not free to exercise his own judgment and buy it.

84 She was once rich, and often told Kent to buy the best meat available, regardless of price. After suffering stock market losses, Georgia has decided to economize. She tells Kent to buy "reasonably priced" meat. She has always followed her expressed opinions about reasonable pricing with comments that Kent should trust his sense of when better quality warrants a higher price.

85 Were one to look only to general understanding, the phrase "reasonably priced" would be vague about the range of choice envisioned.

86 By complicating my examples in ways that bring them closer to many legal problems, Stephen Garvey shows how difficult it may be to fix on any intent that should be controlling. Garvey, supra note 56.

87 As Neil McCormick pointed out, we might think of the "locutionary" meaning of instructions (the behavior to which they refer) as depending in part on their "illocutionary" force (their function).

88 See, e.g., Kent Greenawalt, "The Nature of Rules and the Meaning of Meaning," 72 *Notre Dame Law Review*, 1449, 1461–76 (1997). A similar approach to the meaning of instructions is suggested early in this chapter.

Part II

INTERPRETING LEGALLY AUTHORITATIVE TEXTS OF PRIVATE INDIVIDUALS

In this part, we turn to the interpretation of written texts and oral communications that originate in private choices and have legal authority because the law confers that authority on them. The next chapter concerns the law of agency, when one person fulfills responsibilities for another under instructions. The two chapters that follow treat wills and contracts, respectively. Wills are written by, or for, single individuals who may choose how their property will be distributed after they die. Contracts involve language agreed upon by two or more persons or companies, containing the terms of transactions or relationships they regard as mutually beneficial. Chapter 10 cuts across three different areas of law, trusts, restrictive covenants for real property, and contracts. That chapter focuses on judicial decisions to move explicitly beyond the interpretation of authoritative language, and alter terms in order to reach more just or desirable results.

Three kinds of comparisons are important for these chapters. The first is internal. How do and should techniques of interpretation vary with the kinds of private texts (including oral "texts") that are involved, and when, if ever, should courts go beyond how a text should best be understood? The second comparison is with texts generated by public authorities, constitutions, statutes, and administration regulations. How much does it matter that those texts are meant to guide the behavior of many people over time and that they are issued by multiple authors? This comparison will be one focus of succeeding volumes. The third comparison is with the broad approaches to interpretation we have examined in the preceding chapters.

Chapter 7

The Law of Agency

I. INTRODUCTION

This chapter, which follows closely on our examination of informal instructions, examines the law of agency. That law sets the legal consequences when agents act on behalf of their principals with respect to third parties.[1] The general law of agency is less important than it once was, because more particular legal standards have been developed to deal with various kinds of relationships, but the way the law understands relations of principals and agents still holds great interest for our purposes. As Professor Deborah A. DeMott, the Reporter for the Restatement (Third) of Agency has written, "[T]he agent is heavily dependent on the principal's use of language and other signaling devices that the agent must interpret."[2]

The basic questions can be well clarified by a variation on the servant's instruction to buy "soupmeat" which played a central role in the last chapter. Suppose the servant reaches the grocery store and notices some expensive boxes of chocolate he thinks the children of his boss would like. He buys the boxes and charges them to the boss's account. Within the law of agency, we can identify three different inquiries. The first is how the servant should attempt to understand his shopping instructions for this occasion and his more general responsibilities to shop for the children's benefit. The second is whether, for legal purposes, the servant's actions should be regarded as within the range of authority that the master has conferred on him. One possibility—not the law, as we shall see—is that the servant would be required to make the best possible interpretation of what the master has said and done. If the servant in our example has fallen short, he would have to reimburse the master for the price of the chocolates. The third question concerns relations between the master (the principal) and the shopkeeper (the third party). Was the shopkeeper justified in relying on the servant's actions for charging the master's account if the master complains that the charge was unwarranted? In most agency cases, the third question turns out to be the primary legal concern. In some of these cases, but not most, a judge or jury must determine an agent's actual authority; and that question is the central one when the principal seeks a remedy against his own agent. The law indicates an answer to the first question, how the agent should interpret his principal's instructions, though that answer alone does not resolve actual cases.

An agent acts for a principal under the principal's instructions,[3] a concept central to the law of agency. In contrast to the focus of most agency cases, our primary interest lies mainly in how an agent should understand the instructions (and broader manifestations) of his principal and in how a person reviewing the agent's choice should decide if he acted appropriately. To grasp how the interpretation and application of instructions fits in the law of agency, we need a sense both of what kinds of relationships are ones of agency and of the law's distinction between actual and apparent authority. The recently adopted Third Restatement on Agency[4] will be our main guide.

II. AGENCY RELATIONSHIPS

Agency is a fiduciary relationship, which means roughly that the agent has a responsibility to act faithfully to serve the interests of the principal. The agent acts on behalf of the principal and subject to her control, both principal and agent having consented that the agent will act in this way.[5] Many agency relationships, unlike contracts, do not involve tangible benefits for both parties. A close family member or friend may serve as someone's agent without compensation.

Legal agents represent their principals with third parties. Thus, a lawyer is an agent of a client he represents, but an advisor or a doctor (in most respects) is not an agent. If a supervisor and a worker are both employed by General Motors, General Motors is the principal of both; the supervisor is not the principal of the worker.[6]

The principal's right to control is crucial for agency. If one person enlists another to produce a result, and leaves him completely free to determine how to carry out the task, the second person is not an agent, in the legal sense. We need not worry about the law's precise boundaries for agency relationships, so long as we recognize that many—but not all—situations in which a person with authority instructs a person who has a responsibility faithfully to perform *are* ones of agency.

The principal's right to control is a continuing one. Suppose P gives A instructions to govern a three year period of agency. Four months later, P gives instructions that require behavior at odds with what she previously told P to do. As an agent, A must follow the later instructions. This is true even if the first instructions are more favorable to A and *even* if those instructions are included in a contract between P and A. Rather than insisting on sticking to the earlier instructions, A must carry out P's later instructions and seek any redress by suing for breach of contract. A comment to the Restatement offers the illustration of an agent who is to buy coffee beans for a principal.[7] P has assured A he need not go abroad, and A's compensation has been calculated on that basis. When P later directs A to fly to Colombia to buy coffee beans, A may resign, or he may claim against *P* for his increased cost of performance; but he cannot simply refuse to obey *P*'s instruction.

III. ACTUAL AND APPARENT AUTHORITY

Although some cases directly involve a principal's disputes with her agent, the more common setting is when a third party seeks to hold the principal responsible on the basis of what the agent has done, and the principal claims not to be bound because her agent exceeded his authority. According to the law, the principal is bound to the third party if the agent had either actual authority or apparent authority.

Actual authority is authority that the principal *has conferred* on the agent. The precise range of actual authority involves how the principal's instructions and her other behavior are to be understood and what limits they impose for unexpected circumstances (a subject to which we shall return). Apparent authority exists when the third party reasonably assumes that the agent has authority. Frequently, both actual authority and apparent authority are present together. Since either kind of authority suffices for the third party to rely on what the agent has done, the existence of one of the two kinds becomes critical only if the other kind is (or may be) absent.

A long past but not forgotten irritating experience may provide an illustration of apparent authority in the absence of actual authority. After my car had broken down with an ignition failure at 10:00 P.M., a close friend and I managed to push the car to a garage, explaining the repair it needed. The man in charge said that no one could do the work that night, but someone would be available to do it the next day. When I showed up the next day, the garage manager told me they did not do such repairs. To my consternation, he refused to let me take the car without paying the overnight parking fee. My protest that I would never have left the car there had I not been assured about the repair fell on deaf ears, as did my explanation of why I reasonably relied on what the attendant had said. The attendant lacked actual authority to give me the assurance he did, but he probably had apparent authority, since I understandably took for granted that he was aware of what repair work the garage did and was supposed to convey that information to those who asked. Although apparent authority is created by a "manifestation" of the principal to the individual who relies on the agent's authority,[8] a person's placement by a business in a position with standard responsibilities is sufficient to make him an agent with apparent authority to do what those dealing with someone in such a position would expect.[9] Under the circumstances, the manager had no right to charge me the parking fee.

When disputes arise between third parties and principals, the exact boundaries of actual authority usually are not determinative, because the third party, who has assumed that the agent spoke for the principal, was not aware of exactly what has transpired between P and A. If the agent's authority is contested, the third party will usually find it simpler to establish apparent authority than actual authority. Yet actual authority is the more important topic for how to interpret instructions, because that authority involves the legal import of the principal's instructions for the agent himself, the person who directly interprets the instructions.

IV. INTERPRETING INSTRUCTIONS

According to Restatement commentary, the fiduciary relationship between an agent and his principal governs the way he interprets his instructions. He must do so "in a reasonable manner to further purposes of the principal.... An agent thus is not free to exploit gaps or arguable ambiguities in the principal's instructions to further the agent's self-interest, or the interest of another, when the agent's interpretation does not serve the principal's purposes or interests known to the agent."[10] In an illustration, the agent books his principal, an operatic tenor, into a concert hall without telling him that the hall has become acoustically unsound, because the agent wants to get a job with the hall's owner.

The rule that an agent may not try to serve interests other than those covered by his authorization extends to possible philanthropic acts. Commentary indicates that an agent should not, without specific authorization, give gifts and uncompensated uses of the principal's property or, more generally, engage in acts that do not promise economic advantage for the principal.[11]

How the law regards a version of an example drawn from the last chapter is not entirely clear. Store X, where A has been directed to buy soupmeat, has burned down. Given past relations with P, A rightly understands that P's instruction includes buying soupmeat elsewhere if Store X is unavailable. A knows that P has a slight preference for Store Y over Store Z, but A is confident that that preference is based on a mistaken judgment that quality and prices are less good at Store Z. A would like to shop at Store Z because its owners donate a part of their profits for poor relief. Assuming P has never indicated to A that he should be carrying out his responsibilities with an eye toward helping the poor, is A barred from shopping at Store Z, unless he informs P of the actual facts and gets her consent?[12]

One might say that if P does not suffer at all, given her own sense of what really matters (i.e., food quality and prices), A should be able to serve his own interests or worthwhile causes by shopping at Z. But we can easily perceive a basis for a stricter approach. Once an agent is encouraged at all to further his own interests or those of worthwhile causes, so long as he does not harm his principal's interests, his judgment about exactly what will satisfy his principal's interests may be skewed. He may convince himself, or hope he can convince others, that her interests did not suffer. Thus, we can see the point of a standard that an agent must always be guided by those interests of the principal he has been authorized to serve, *unless* he has informed her of what he would like to do and she has agreed.

If the agent must stick exclusively to the principal's purposes, it would seem to follow that the servant should not shop at Store Z, if he knows his boss has a slight preference for Store Y, and if he judges the food and prices at the two stores to be equal. Perhaps this is the best approach for such situations.[13] But the Store Z choice is not quite like a gift to a third party. The servant *is* carrying out the basic task he has been authorized to perform. It is a peripheral feature of shopping at Store Z that the poor will also benefit indirectly. The servant believes that his principal's actual interests will be served in exactly the same way and as well if he uses Store Z rather than Store Y. All that pushes him to Store Y is his knowledge of her slight preference for that. Suppose the servant is confident that his boss would be indifferent between Y and Z if she had more accurate information about the food quality and prices at the two stores. If it is impractical for him to communicate with her, or he is sure she would not want to be bothered by such a trivial decision, perhaps he should be able to go ahead and shop at Store Z.

I am not aware of actual cases in which the agent has claimed that the principal's tangible interests[14] were not at all adversely affected by a choice between two alternatives and the consideration that tipped the balance between the alternatives was a peripheral concern for public welfare that did not fall within the interests covered by the agency. I believe such a choice *should* be regarded as within an agent's authority, so long as the peripheral concern is a general good and not the agent's own welfare or particular interests.[15]

The rule that the agent must stick to interests he has been authorized to serve applies even when he might assist independent interests of the principal about which he is aware. *A*, a real estate expert, has been hired to bid on a parcel of land at an auction. Before the parcel is put up for sale, a ruby is auctioned. *A* happens to know that *P* has a collection of rubies and he also knows that the ruby is going to sell for a bargain price. *A* is confident *P* would want him to bid on the ruby for her. Nonetheless, *A* has no actual authority to do this; bidding on the ruby is too far removed from the authority *P* has conferred on *A*.[16] Of course, a ruby costs money. Paying for the ruby is different from achieving *P*'s interests that *A* has now been authorized to pursue and serving an independent interest of *P* without any sacrifice at all in terms of *P*'s resources[17] (or what *P* cares about). It is because of this difference that I believe the rule that the agent should not reach beyond the interests he is authorized to serve should be understood to be subject to a limited qualification.

How should an agent understand what his principal wants him to do? According to the Restatement, "[a]n agent has actual authority to take action designated or implied in the principal's manifestations to the agent and acts necessary or incidental to achieving the principal's objectives, as the agent reasonably understands the. . . manifestations and objectives. . . ."[18] The agent is to interpret *P*'s manifestations in light of "any meaning known by the agent to be ascribed by the principal. . . ." If the agent does not know any such meaning, he is to interpret "as a reasonable person in the agent's position would interpret the manifestations in light of the context. . . ."[19] His sense of *P*'s objectives should reflect *P*'s manifestations and inferences he can draw from the circumstances of the agency.[20]

We must remember that the law of agency joins a standard that should guide the agent with a standard that governs how a court (and presumably a fair-minded employer) should review what the agent has done. The latter standard determines actual authority. Application of that standard does not necessarily reflect what the reviewer takes as the *best interpretation* of the principal's instructions or wishes.

As we shall explore in more detail below, the agent is supposed to interpret instructions in light of the principal's wishes, estimated when the agent determines how to act.[21] He must act in accord with what he deems those wishes to be. The agent has actual authority if he acts according to his assessment of the principal's wishes reflected in her instructions *and* if his assessment is reasonable. Imagine two agents given identical instructions by the same principal. One agent honestly interprets them one way and the other agent in a different way. Both could have actual authority to do what they do, so long as both interpretations are reasonable.[22] But notice that an agent would not have actual authority if, despite being able to offer a reasonable interpretation to support his action, *his* honest belief about the principal's wishes did not fit this interpretation.[23] According to the Restatement commentary, an agent has actual authority to do an act if he reasonably believes "the principal has consented to its commission."[24] I shall return shortly to the notion of "has consented." As to "reasonably believes," the comment is explicit that the standard is subjective as well as objective. "Lack of actual authority is established by showing either that the agent did not believe, or could not reasonably have believed, that the principal's grant of actual authority encompassed the act in question."[25] The questions of actual and of reasonable belief are both for a jury in a jury trial. Because it will be a rare instance in which an agent admits that he did not believe he had authority to do what he did, and because it will be hard to establish that a reasonable belief was insincere, what typically will be in controversy is the reasonableness of an agent's claimed belief.

In various respects, agents can act beyond specific instructions or contrary to instructions. The overarching standard again is their honest assessment of the wishes of their principals within the range of the authority their principals have conferred on them. The law of agency thus provides a flexible response to changed information and changed external circumstances. Not only does the Restatement specifically refer to the agent's understanding when he "determines how to act,"[26] the comment draws a contrast with the law of contracts, for which interpretation focuses on the shared meaning at the time an agreement is made.[27]

Professor DeMott's discussion of this emphasis on the time of action bears an interesting relation to Gadamer's claim in Chapter 5 that new meaning is created with each application of a legal norm. DeMott writes that even if an instruction "taken as a linguistic artifact, raises no real doubt as to its meaning, the agent must always decide what to do in response." The agent faces "questions even when they would not conventionally be characterized as ones of interpretation."[28] In this passage, DeMott is explicitly employing a narrow sense of interpretation of instructions. So long as the agent is trying to discern the wishes of the principal in a broad sense, we may think of this as a form of interpretation, even if the import of a specific instruction, taken by itself, is not in doubt.

What if the principal intended to confer authority on the agent to perform the act he did, but the agent did not realize that? The rule is clear for circumstances in which the principal has attempted to communicate an authorization to act, but the agent has not received it. The agent does not have actual authority, because he has no basis to assume the authority has been conferred.[29]

Another kind of case has theoretical interest, if very little practical importance. *P* instructs *A*; *P* tells a friend she means the instruction to cover a certain act, and a reasonable agent would so conclude; *A* tells a coworker he does not think the instruction covers the same act, which he performs despite that opinion. According to the basic requirement that an agent must *believe* he has been authorized to perform an act, *A* does not have actual authority. But *P* clearly meant to confer that authority; *and* she communicated to *A* all she thought was necessary to that effect, *and* a reasonable person would have so understood the communication. *A* has performed the act on *P*'s behalf, and it turns out to be disadvantageous to *P*. Can *P* recover her losses from *A*? If *A* did not have actual authority, *P* can recover. But should *P* be able to disavow authority that she meant to confer and believed she had successfully granted to *A* by a communication that *A* did receive?[30]

I would think not. *P* should not be able to recover from *A* for an act she had every reason to believe she had fully authorized by a communication that *A* indisputably received.[31] If this conclusion is sound, another way actual authority could be conferred would be if (1) *P* explicitly intended to confer such authority, (2) *P* had successfully made a communication to *A* that would do that, and (3) *A* would reasonably have understood that such authority was conferred.[32]

When a principal and agent share an understanding of the principal's instructions, that determines what counts as the instructions, even if their shared understanding might differ from what the understanding of a reasonable person would be, and whatever would be ordinary customs and usages.[33] Customs and usages are generally relevant for determining what interpretations and actions by an agent are reasonable attempts to carry out the principal's wishes,[34] but it is these wishes that are to guide the agent.

Even an agent acting under fairly specific instructions will need to make certain judgments about larger objectives when he determines what actions not explicitly covered are necessary, usual, and proper to carry out the ends that are within his responsibility. This reference to needed means constitutes one kind of implied authority that is a standard part of actual authority.[35] Thus, if P authorizes A to buy a painting from S, and S lives in Paris, A can travel to Paris to deal with S.[36]

V. ACTING BEYOND THE TERMS OF INSTRUCTIONS

An agent must treat specific instructions in light of broad objectives in three other kinds of situations. On some points, instructions may be vague or ambiguous. An agent needs a sense of the principal's objectives to decide which among plausible courses of action he should take. In a second situation, the instructions authorize only certain acts by the agent, but circumstances arise that may justify the agent in performing other acts (beyond those necessary to perform the authorized acts). In the third situation, the instructions specifically forbid a certain action, but the agent may be justified in performing it anyway. We can lump these second and third situations as ones in which the agent acts beyond or in spite of his instructions.

One important caution about such situations is that the more formal and detailed P's instructions are, the harder A will find it to justify his not conforming,[37] although on occasion A may disregard terms of even formal instructions. A second caution concerns communication; as that becomes easier and faster, fewer and fewer situations will arise in which it is reasonable for an agent to go ahead without consulting his principal.[38] On a matter of importance, on which there might be any doubt, A can ask P whether it is all right to deviate from his instructions. Indeed, the requirement to consult one's principal can apply even to ambiguous instructions. When a man's instructions to his broker left it unclear whether the broker could place an order while trading was suspended or should wait until trading resumed, the court held that the broker took the risk of choosing the wrong construction if he acted without attempting to seek a clarification.[39]

One possible reason for an agent to deviate from instructions is that he is confident his principal did not really care about a minor detail in the instructions or does not mean to stick with one of its aspects over time. The former scenario is especially likely if P gives A detailed written instructions that follow a form. A may be confident, especially from past dealings, that P does not take every detail seriously. In that event, A might be justified in disregarding such details.[40]

If *P* gives oral instructions on the spur of the moment, *P* may say things that *A* is sure she will not wish to adhere to over time.[41] For example, in the heat of anger, an owner may tell a supervisor to fire a worker whose slip-up has cost some business. The supervisor may have had a number of experiences with the owner in which she has given such an instruction, only to retract it the next day. Although, in general, agents should assume that principals wish their instructions to be carried out, sometimes they reasonably believe their principals would wish them not to fulfill aspects of instructions. *A*'s disregarding part of what *P* says as a temporary aberration is hard to characterize as an interpretation of the meaning of what *P* has uttered on that occasion, although *A*'s selective disregard of a particular text can be cast as an interpretation of *P*'s entire course of behavior.

More interesting problems are presented by unforeseen circumstances. *P* directs *A* to reseed a park lawn by the end of the week. *A* learns that a hurricane is forecast for the midpoint of the planned reseeding. *A* has authority to postpone the reseeding.[42] Or, *P*, the owner of a golf course, adjacent to a parcel of land, authorizes *A* to bid $250,000 at an auction for the land. *A* learns at the auction that the only competitor for the land plans to build a cement factory that would seriously interfere with the air quality and the aesthetic atmosphere of the golf course, and could seriously hurt *P*'s business. *A*, unable to communicate quickly with *P*, would be justified in bidding $260,000 if that is necessary to prevent the parcel's falling into the competitor's hands.[43]

In each of these situations, *A* makes a highly reasonable appraisal of *P*'s interests, as reflected in *P*'s instructions and in *A*'s other knowledge of *P*'s concerns (a pleasing golf course) and of sensible practices (hurricanes interfere with effective seeding). This does not mean that having become an agent for one matter, *A* is free to represent *P* in every respect that he believes *P* will see as serving her interests.

The problems of deviations from instructions raise the question in just what sense an agent must reasonably believe a principal "has consented." In ordinary discourse, actual "consent" usually involves not just a mental acquiescence but also some manifestation of agreement (which could be a silent response to a question whether one has any objections). Actual consent usually requires that a person have considered a possibility, or at least that the possibility falls within a broad range to which she has consented.

What can we say about the reseeding and $260,000 purchase examples in this light? The possibility of a hurricane had not occurred to *P* when she conferred on *A* authority to reseed subject to a time limit. We might say that whenever anyone sets a time limit, it "goes without saying" that the time is somewhat flexible in relation to emergency situations. A proctor extends a three-hour limit on an exam if a bombing raid occurs in the middle of the test. It is not too much of a stretch to say that *P* has consented to *A*'s postponing the seeding to avoid hurricane interference. In an otherwise similar example not involving a time limit, the court held that a man was authorized to return from his fourteen-mile ride with a different doctor than his brother had instructed him to get to attend to his ill wife.[44] The doctor he had been told to get was unavailable. He reasonably hired an available doctor.

The $260,000 bid for the parcel is more complicated. P, wishing to use the parcel to add a driving range, has assumed that it will otherwise continue as farmland. She has failed to consider the possibility of the land being developed in a manner that would cause her golf course positive harm. When this possibility presents itself, A cannot be sure what P would wish him to do. Perhaps P would think the cement factory would never get built, or would fail quickly, or would not mar the atmosphere of the course; or perhaps P feels she is unable to raise more than $250,000 to buy anything right now. A must exercise his judgment in light of all the circumstances. It does not "go without saying" that P has conferred authority to spend the extra $10,000, although that amount is a small percentage of what she has explicitly authorized. P has not already consented. Indeed, we cannot even say that P wishes A to bid $260,000. All we can say, and all A can think, is that P would (probably) consent if the issue were put to her. A judges that bidding $260,000 fits best with the set of P's existing wishes concerning the golf course and her finances; what he concludes about P's attitude toward the specific choice at the moment he makes it is that it reflects P's hypothetical wishes (what she would wish) and would receive P's hypothetical consent (what she would agree to). (A might also conceive his choice as guided by P's highly probable future wishes, once P learns of the situation, and by her probable future consent.)

Places in the Restatement commentary make clear that this is sufficient. One formulation is that "the agent does not have actual authority to disregard instructions unless it is reasonable for the agent to believe that the principal wishes the agent to do so."[45] This language is broader than "has consented" because the agent may reasonably believe that the principal has relevant wishes that have not yet been expressed. Another passage indicates that the agent must interpret "instructions so as to infer, in a reasonable manner, what the principal would wish the agent to do in light of facts of which the agent has notice of at the time of acting."[46] The "would wish" clearly brings in circumstances in which the most accurate account would be that the principal would want and would consent to an action if she addressed the subject. Thus, a reasonable judgment about a principal's hypothetical consent can, even if mistaken, be sufficient for the agent to have actual authority.

All this does not mean, however, that an agent's reasonable guess about what the principal would probably want will as a matter of course give the agent actual authority. In one illustration, the Restatement says that a loan officer instructed to make no loans over $500,000 cannot go ahead and make a $1,000,000 loan he believes is highly secure. This example differs from the auction example in three important ways. The loan officer's instructions are specifically designed to curb his discretion to make such judgments (whereas the golf course principal had not conceived of the threat to her course); the extra amount of the loan is not just a small increment in what the officer was authorized to do; and a loan officer presumably has an opportunity to seek specific approval of his superiors before finalizing a bank loan. These variations bring us back to the basic notion that agents can disregard deliberate, seriously intended limits in their instructions only when circumstances are unforeseen and preclude further clarification from their principals.

VI. CONCLUSION

The law of agency deals with circumstances of the sort we explored in respect to informal instructions. Although the law's practical relevance mainly concerns when principals are liable to third parties with whom agents have interacted, it does set standards for how agents should understand instructions in light of the interests of principals. Agents must interpret instructions in light of what they convey about the principals' wishes; and agents may disregard the import of specific instructions if they are confident the principals would wish them to do so. The law of agency also establishes the relevance of reasonable but mistaken understandings on the part of agents and third parties.

These themes will occupy us in the remaining chapters of the book. For both wills and contracts, the relation between subjective understandings and reasonable understandings is a central problem; and for wills contracts, trusts, and restrictive covenants, interesting and important issues arise over when altered circumstances warrant deviation from what the original controlling texts require, issues that also pervade statutory and constitutional interpretation.

Notes

1 Deborah A. DeMott has compared the fairly narrow conception of legal agency with a broader sense in the literature of economics. "Disloyal Agents," 58 *Alabama Law Review* 1049, 1050–51 (2007).

2 DeMott, "A Revised Prospectus for a Third Restatement of Agency," 31 *University of California at Davis Law Review* 1035, 1039, (1988). She comments in "Disloyal Agents," note 1 supra at 1067, "The common law of agency has not always attracted the degree of academic interest that's warranted by its ubiquity as well as its theoretical interest and practical significance."

3 See Deborah A. DeMott, "Instructions and the Agency Relationship" (unpublished manuscript) 3–4.

4 American Law Institute, Restatement (Third) of Agency (2006).

5 According to the Restatement (Third) of Agency, §1.01, "Agency is the fiduciary relationship that arises when one person (a "principal") manifests assent to another person (an "agent") that the agent shall act on the principal's behalf

and subject to the principal's control, and the agent manifests assent or otherwise consents so to act."

6 Id., comments c and f.

7 Id., § 1.01, comment f, illustration 3.

8 Id., § 3.03, and comment b.

9 See id.; Harold G. Reuschlein and William A. Gregory, *The Law of Agency and Partnerships*, § 23, at 61 (2nd ed., St. Paul, Minn., West Pub. Co., 1990).

10 Restatement (Third), § 1.01, comment e.

11 Id., § 2.02, comment h.

12 One might wonder what practical importance the answer has, if any, if *P* could point to no damage to her interests. If *P* were otherwise bound to retain *A* for a period of time, she might nonetheless fire him for violating his duties as an agent.

13 Professor DeMott, note 3 supra, at 10–11, remarks that "*A* is not free to disregard what *A* knows about *P's* preferences" and, at 15, that "an agent always makes decisions about what to do or how to act that are relevant to the principal's interests."

14 I refer to "tangible interests" as roughly equivalent to the language of "economic advantage" in Restatement (Third), § 2.02, comment h, but the agent should also not be able to disregard nontangible interests perceived as such by the principal. Thus, *A* should shop at Store *Y*, if he knows *P's* preference is based on sympathy with the owner.

15 Such a situation seems different enough from those on which the Restatement commentary focuses so that I do not think its sweeping language should be taken to foreclose such a choice.

Were the agent able to further his own (selfish) interests on the theory that the principal cares about his welfare, that would invite too much compromising of the principal's interests. Thus, I am distinguishing serving philanthropic or public interests from serving the agent's own interests. I would limit the reach of philanthropic or public interests here to interests that either *A* is aware that *P* shares or that are very widely uncontroversial. A peripheral benefit to the National Rifle Association, the American Civil Liberties Union, or a particular religious denomination would not qualify in the latter category, since a principal might well not share an agent's belief about their contribution to the general good.

16 Id., § 2.02, comment e: "The relevant interests and objectives are those with respect to the agency and do not encompass other objectives or interests that a principal may have." See also Restatement (Second) of Agency, § 33, comment b, pp. 117–18 (1958).

17 This might be the situation if *A* knew *P* did care about poor relief but was wholly unaware that part of Store *Z's* profits go for that purpose and had never suggested that *A* further poor relief with her resources.

18 Restatement (Third) of Agency, § 2.02 (1).

19 Id., § 2.02 (2).

20 Id., § 2.02 (3).

21 Id., § 2.02 (1).

22 See id., comments c and f.

23 In the previous chapter, I raised the possibility of someone who thinks that one reasonable interpretation is slightly more probable than another reasonable interpretation, but who also thinks the instruction giver will be much more upset

if he wrongly acts on the first interpretation than if he wrongly acts on the second. This should be enough to constitute an honest belief in the second interpretation for the purpose of actual authority.

24 Id., § 2.02, comment e.

25 Id.

26 Id., § 2.02 (1).

27 Id., § 2.02, comment c.

28 DeMott, note 3 supra, at 5.

29 Restatement (Third) of Agency, § 2.01 and comment c. See DeMott, note 3 supra, at 16, citing Ruggles v. American Cent. Ins. Co., 114 N.Y. 415 (1889).

30 Notice that this issue could arise between a third party and *P*. *A* contracts with a third party on behalf of *P*, but the third party does not reasonably assume that *A* has authority to do this. Thus, apparent authority is absent, and *P*'s responsibility to the third party will depend on whether *A* has actual authority.

31 This issue presses on the assumption that all that matters are the agent's actual and reasonable beliefs. Here, what the principal actually and reasonably believes she has communicated might be a basis to preclude her dodging responsibility.

32 Whether the third condition should be required is arguable. Maybe it should be sufficient that *P* made a successful communication to *A* with a particular intention, even if a reasonable person would not have so understood it.

33 Restatement (Third) of Agency, § 2.02, comment e (shared, idiosyncratic understanding controls); comment f (regardless of contrary industry customs or practices).

34 The Reporter's note to § 2.02, cites some cases that, along with Restatement (Second) of Agency, required that a principal have notice of usages. What should be crucial is the agent's reasonable understanding of what the principal might know about industry practices.

35 Id. § 2.01, comment b; § 2.02, comment d. Given a division of cases among those that consider "necessity" in purely objective terms and those that make the agent's belief on that score relevant, (see Reporter's Notes to § 2.02), neither the text of § 2.02 nor the comments, see comment d, decisively resolve that question; but the general requirement that an agent believe he has authority would seem to preclude actual authority if the agent does not think an act is needed (and has no other reason to think it is authorized).

36 As this example indicates, "necessary" here is taken in a fairly generous sense to include acts one would expect, even if they are not absolutely required to carry out one's task.

37 Id., § 2.02, comment c, which indicates that a statement's formality "is relevant to, and often dispositive of, whether the agent could reasonably believe that the principal intended to consent to the agent's power to do acts beyond or other than those stated in the instrument."

38 See id., § 2.02, comment f.

39 R. Rowland & Co., Inc. v. Leahy, 561 S.W. 2d 115 (Mo. 1978).

40 Restatement (Third) of Agency, § 2.02, comment f.

41 DeMott, supra note 3, at 8–9.

42 Restatement (Third) of Agency, § 2.02, comment e, illustration 5.

43 Id., § 2.02 comment e, illustration 6. Professor DeMott, supra note 3, at 8, gives the example of a patrol told not to engage the enemy or take prisoners that happens to encounter the opposing general, unguarded. The patrol may

reasonably capture the general. (In this example, both those issuing orders and the patrol members are agents of the army (or the government), but the patrol's duties include obeying instructions of superior officers.)

44 Bartlett v. Sparkman, 8 S.W. 406 (Mo. 1888).

45 Restatement (Third) of Agency, § 2.02, comment f.

46 Id., § 2.02, comment g. See also id., § 2.02, comment f (agent "to determine with specificity what a principal would wish the agent to do...").

Chapter 8

Wills

I. INTRODUCTION

Among legal documents that courts interpret, wills are special in two respects. They are peculiarly unilateral; and their nominal authors are unavailable to testify about what they meant. Like typical instructions, wills issue from single persons who are exclusive authors from a legal point of view. In fact, lawyers and their staffs actually write many wills, and people often may not understand complex provisions that their wills contain;[1] still, the lawyers' main job is to carry out the wishes of testators as completely as possible, not to intrude their own views about who should receive property. Wills are unilateral in a way that ordinary instructions are not. Instructions are issued to a recipient, who has a crucial stake in how they are understood.[2] Most instructions create expectations and induce reliance, affording strong reasons to grant a recipient's perspective weight when someone reviews her performance, and we have seen that a recipient's reasonable understanding is typically decisive in establishing actual authority in the law of agency. Wills differ in significant degree. Unless a person has contracted to include particular dispositions,[3] she is free to alter her will up to the time she dies. Thus, no one can rely with confidence on the formulation of the will of someone who is still living. Further, when the potential beneficiaries of a will rely at all, they are much more likely to depend on what the writer says about what he has done in the will than on the will's actual language (which the potential beneficiary is unlikely to read). If a court's interpretation fails to correspond with the apparent meaning of a will's language, that will not typically defeat legitimate expectations developed before the writer's death.[4] Therefore, courts need not much concern themselves with expectations of possible beneficiaries that are developed before the writer dies and the final will is available to relatives.

The period between a will's being made public and its content being settled by a court is different. Someone then relying on the will's language might be disappointed by an interpretation that deviates from that, and uncertainty about how a court will interpret a will may interfere with transactions that depend on a beneficiary's receiving what he apparently has been given.[5]

When courts construe wills,[6] their writers are not available to say what they were trying to do (or how their wishes might have changed by the time they died). The formal requirements of wills and principles of their construction partly respond to the harsh fact of our mortality.

II. STANDARDS AND SOURCES OF INTERPRETATION

With wills, as with other legal documents, courts need standards for how to interpret and for what evidences of meaning to consult. Should they look to the general meaning of a will's language, at the writer's likely intent, or to a more subtle variation or mixture of elements? Should they take into account idiosyncrasies of the testator's background, her peculiar understanding of words, what she said orally she was trying to do? What weight should be given to changed circumstances that would likely alter the specific dispositions the writer of the will would want? This chapter grapples with these questions, preparing the way for comparisons with other domains of law.

A striking English case involving a married couple who died together at sea sharply poses many of these issues about wills.[7] Aware that he and his wife would be taking trips in the South Pacific from island to island in small ships, Dr. Rowland, using a printed form, and without consulting a lawyer, provided in his handwritten will that his wife would receive everything if she survived him, but in the event of her death "preceding or coinciding with" his own, his property would go to his brother and niece. Mrs. Rowland's will had similar language; if her husband did not survive her, her estate was to go to her niece.

The legal issue under the husband's will was whether his estate would go to his wife's niece or to his own relations. Given the circumstances of the wreck of the ship in which they were traveling, the Rowlands probably drowned very quickly or were eaten by fish.[8] If the deaths "coincided," his relatives would win. Otherwise, under a law providing that when the order of deaths is "uncertain," the younger person is presumed to have survived the older, Dr. Rowland's property would pass to his wife, and then on to her niece.[9]

What did "coinciding" mean in the will? All the judges in the Court of Chancery assumed Dr. Rowland used the word self-consciously, not that it was part of a will form to which he gave no attention.[10]

If we focus on what this word in the will means, we might look at usage by the broad community or usage by the doctor himself.[11] If the Rowlands consciously chose to use the term "coinciding," knowing that they would take many voyages together on small ships in the South Pacific, Dr. Rowland probably assumed that the term covered circumstances in which the two might be killed in a common wreck and died within seconds or minutes of each other[12]—what very likely occurred.

General usage is harder to pin down. In some contexts, to say that two events "coincided" is to say that they occurred simultaneously;[13] deaths separated by minutes do not occur simultaneously. But "coincide" is not always taken so narrowly. We might say that the reigns of two ancient monarchs coincided even though one began and ended one month before the other.[14] As we have seen in earlier chapters, people pay attention to the purposes for which words are used. Recognizing that the context was a will and that a wife dying minutes later could make no use of her husband's property, many people would say that two deaths "coincided" if they occurred from a common cause and within minutes of each other.[15]

A court taking Dr. Rowland's perspective, and assuming that he did focus on the word "coinciding," should conclude that he probably understood the word to cover deaths only seconds or minutes apart caused by a shipwreck. A court relying on general usage would have to decide how strictly "coincide" is generally understood, and the extent to which people using the word would take account of the circumstances in which the Rowlands made their wills and in which they died.

The majority of Chancery judges in *Rowland* adopted a standard of general usage that was strict. Justice Harman equated "coincident" and "simultaneous," and said that Rowland's relatives had presented no evidence that the deaths were "simultaneous."[16] Justice Russell took as the standard whether "the ordinary man would say that the two deaths were coincident in point of time or simultaneous."[17] For him, it mattered neither whether the Rowlands died by shipwreck in the Pacific or by rail or auto accident in England, nor what situations they foresaw when they wrote their wills.

Lord Denning disagreed sharply with his two colleagues. He contrasted his own approach with one favored in the nineteenth century, according to which judges inquired "what is the ordinary and grammatical meaning of the word 'coincide' as used in the English language?"[18] Under that approach, "coincide" would mean "simultaneous" and might not cover two people holding each other as a ship sank—an absurd result. The whole approach, he said, rests on a fallacy that a will's construction should depend on the meaning of a testator's words rather than on what he meant. For Denning, "the whole object of construing a will is to find out the testator's intentions," what meaning the words bore for him.[19] Dr. Rowland and his wife intended "coinciding" to have a wider meaning of "death on the same occasion by the same cause."[20] Judge Russell rejoined that this understanding of "coinciding" suggests a time element, but one so rough that it is quite uncertain.[21]

How should we evaluate the competing approaches in *Rowland*?[22] Each focuses on understanding at the time the will was written; like most interpretation of wills, each takes an originalist approach. The rule the majority adopts is convenient to administer, and will allow uniform construction of "coinciding" in wills, although the judgments of ordinary people are both more contextualized to circumstance and purpose and more divergent than the justices suppose.[23] According to their approach, very few deaths coincide, and language in wills about deaths coinciding will rarely be effective.[24]

The majority's approach possesses the merit of not requiring extrinsic evidence, but it turns out that Lord Denning's competing approach does not require much of that either. Denning looked at undisputed facts about the Rowlands' lives; his inference about Rowland's sense of "coinciding" is based on what a reasonable person in that situation would understand.[25] Although Denning did not rely on any disputed evidence about Rowland's own sense of "coinciding," a critic could complain that an approach that makes the writer's own sense determinative could draw judges into such evidence in future cases, unless judges impose limits on what they will consider—disregarding potentially debatable evidence about what a single individual understood by his words. [26]

Another problem with Denning's approach is its vagueness about what counts as "coinciding." Suppose Dr. Rowland died when the ship sank, but his wife swam to an uninhabited island with a fellow survivor, living two weeks before succumbing to her wounds. Dr. Rowland probably would not have conceived "coinciding" as comfortably covering that situation, instead understanding the term to include a time element briefer than two weeks.

In the actual circumstances of the case, a judge who used Rowland's probable desires as a guide would reach the same practical conclusion as one who adhered to the words in the will *as Rowland probably understood them*. But the island variation suggests how these two points of reference might diverge. If a friend had posed that variation in advance; Rowland might have said, "Since my wife would have no ability to use my property, I'd rather have it go to my relatives, not hers. But I see that our deaths wouldn't really coincide. Maybe I would need different language for that situation, but it is too remote to make redoing the will worthwhile."

If this would have been Dr. Rowland's response, what was his intention? When he wrote the will he had no narrow intention about the island scenario; he did not consider it. His understanding of the word "coinciding" was not broad enough to cover that possibility, but the overall purpose that led him to choose "coinciding" would have reached it. Were a court faced with such a two-week survival, victory for the husband's relatives would depend on the judges using a particular component of Rowland's intentions—his more general ones—to override his own sense of what the words he chose signified.

Our analysis of *Rowland* reveals a number of possibilities concerning both standards of interpretation and sources of evidence, possibilities that arise in other areas in which legal texts are interpreted. As to standards, courts might rely on: the general, or ordinary, sense of words and phrases, allowing greater or lesser attention to the context in which the words and phrases are used; established usages in localities or within subgroups; the sense of individuals situated as was the writer; the writer's own sense of the words he has employed; the writer's specific intentions for dealing with a situation; his broader purposes in disposing of his estate; or his hypothetical intentions about what he would have understood or wanted if he had focused on the situation.

If we could put aside all problems of evidence and convenient administration, there would be much to be said for trying to satisfy the testator's dominant wishes. But if the will is a result of compromise or agreement, we can see that it is the writer's *understanding* that should count, if that differs from his wishes. To concoct a bizarre hypothetical, suppose the Rowlands were aware just how narrowly previous decisions had interpreted "coinciding," and that Dr. Rowland suggested broadening that language to cover other situations in which the spouse who survives does not live long enough to use the other's property. Mrs. Rowland, also aware of the rule assuming survival of the younger, adamantly objected, reminding her husband of all the sacrifices she was about to make for him. He quickly dropped the proposed change, silently hoping a court would give an unexpectedly broad reading to "coinciding," if it ever came to that. If Dr. Rowland's subjective intentions were to matter, here it should be his understanding of what his words meant, not his hopes about what judges might do.[27]

Judges might pick one of the conceivable standards as an ultimate criterion for interpreting a will. In that event, inquiries under other standards might assist them in reaching a conclusion about application of the ultimate criterion. Thus, if Rowland's probable sense of his words was the ultimate criterion, a sense of his general purposes might help inform what he probably meant by "coinciding." Alternatively, judges might regard more than one standard as of final significance, somehow resolving instances in which the standards yield competing answers. For example, although one author has suggested that combining "internal and external standards yield[s] at best a forced and awkward fit,"[28] a court might decide that it had reasons to fulfill a testator's wishes *and* to give words their common meaning. In that event it would need to determine in individual cases in which answers under the two standards are not congruent which considerations carry more weight.

Figuring out whether a judge or scholar is thinking in terms of one ultimate standard or several is not always simple. Writing about the *Rowland* case, Michael Albery remarks that all three judges agreed that the "proper object of inquiry on construction of a will . . . is the objective meaning of the words as used by the particular testator."[29] That definitely sounds like a single ultimate standard. But Albery goes on to say that the factors determining interpretation of a crucial word are (1) its meaning as ordinarily used, (2) the context provided by the accompanying words of the will, (3) surrounding circumstances that help connect the will to the outside world, and (4) the inherent reasonableness of a possible interpretation.[30] The "objective meaning" turns out to be the meaning the law will ascribe, consisting of an amalgam of the factors the law treats as relevant.

According to a leading American treatise, "The primary purpose in construing a will is to determine the very disposition which the testator wanted to make, to determine if possible his actual intent rather than an intent presumed by law."[31] But the critical intention is that "expressed in his will when read in the light of surrounding circumstances and in view of the admissible evidence. . . ."[32] "The question . . . before the mind of the court is not what testator should have meant to do or what words would have been better for the testator to use, but what is the reasonable meaning of the words which he has actually used."[33] Courts cannot rewrite wills to conform to presumed intentions.[34] These various formulations point in different directions;[35] they settle neither the degree to which a court will accede to a testator's idiosyncrasies or correct her outright mistakes, nor what evidence they should consider. In wills, as in many branches of the law, "meaning" may come down to an awkward combination of relevant factors, although the movement in recent decades in the United States has been to give increasing emphasis to actual intentions of the testator.[36]

Whatever their standards of judgment they employ, courts might investigate every relevant source of evidence that could contribute to a decision under those standards, or they might impose limits. Courts have traditionally assumed that if the texts of wills have a plain meaning, they should not go beyond the texts; and more generally courts have refused to consider what testators said at the time they were trying to do or how they understood particular words they used in their wills.[37] The barring of evidence of testators' statements about their aspirations significantly restricts the field of information about their specific intentions.[38]

Why would anyone adopt such a restriction? A major reason is evidentiary unreliability.[39] Opportunities arise for outright fraud and honest disagreement about what the testator said at the time. A related rationale concerns predictability in the interpretation of the language of wills. Further, the status of wills has often been regarded as a reason to avoid external evidence. Crediting external remarks has been thought to violate the rule that a will's provisions cannot be overthrown by contrary dispositions, oral or written, outside the will (or to fall too close to a violation of the rule to be allowed).

When someone wants to dispose of her property by will, she must put her disposition in writing, sign the document, and have it attested by two or three witnesses; or (in many states) she must write the entire will in her own handwriting.[40] Given other devices by which people pass money when they die—designating beneficiaries in insurance policies, retirement funds, and some kinds of bank accounts without having the forms witnessed[41]—one may make a strong argument that will formalities should be relaxed. The Uniform Probate Code of 1993 reduces statutory requirements for execution and also gives courts a power to dispense with requirements if a proponent presents clear and convincing evidence of a testamentary intention.[42] Nevertheless most courts still apply requirements strictly. If, for example a signed document was undoubtedly meant to be a will but was not witnessed, most probate courts will not treat it as valid.

Will formalities are thought to serve at least five purposes.[43] One is evidentiary; the formalities help ensure that others can simply and confidently determine how a person wished to dispose of her property. The second purpose is cautionary. The ritual of making and signing a will, and having it witnessed, emphasizes to the writer the seriousness of what she does. A will is not a casual off-hand remark; it elicits careful deliberation and decision. A third purpose is self-protective. The formalities help guard against a person's being defrauded or unduly influenced into accepting a disposition she does not really want to make. Finally, the formalities serve two channeling functions. They allow courts to settle efficiently what disposition to make of an estate. And they help guide the wishes of those who consult lawyers or look at will forms to accomplish their objectives. In addition to providing precise language with clear legal effect, lawyers can suggest previously unconsidered contingent possibilities and legal devices to allocate control of property and minimize tax burdens.

A crucial question about interpreting wills is the import of the writing requirement. If we put aside various objective circumstances, such as divorce, that strongly suggest that a testator would not want to stick with key provisions of his will, we can quickly see why wills should not be open to challenge on the basis that their writers changed their minds between the time they made their wills and the time they died, as evidenced by oral statements.[44] Signed and witnessed documents are much easier to authenticate than claimed oral remarks by a person who has died.[45] The core of what is called the parol evidence rule is a principle of substantive law that other expressions will not be taken to supersede the terms of an authoritative written document.[46] A will cannot be superseded by either an oral expression or a writing that is not formalized in the way a will must be.

As Wigmore has emphasized, allowing evidence of what the testator *meant* in a will is not the same as allowing the will to be superseded; but many courts have taken the parol evidence rule to bar evidence of the writer's statements about what she meant to do with her will.[47] That a court is interpreting the will, not supplementing it, is clear if its inquiry is limited to what a testator aimed specifically to do with the language of his will—the inquiry in which Lord Denning engaged in *Rowland*.[48]

If we ask what purposes of the writing requirement might be compromised were external evidence about a testator's intention considered in respect to the will's interpretation, the answer is simplicity of administration and evidentiary reliability. The more courts need to consider, the more complicated the process of settling wills can become. Just how serious the risk of unreliability is depends heavily on the kinds of evidence involved; claims about oral comments made to prospective beneficiaries are susceptible to fraud and distortion to a degree that is neither true of more "objective" evidence of how a testator used terms in various contexts, such as letters, recordings, and diaries, other than his will,[49] nor of undeniable circumstances that might point to one intention rather than another.

In terms of the purposes of cautioning, self-protection, and guidance for the testator that will formalities serve, it does not matter significantly what techniques courts employ to interpret completed wills. For example, were courts to credit external evidence about what a writer meant in her will, that would not detract from the careful consideration testators would give to what they want to accomplish and how that can be done.[50]

One way to reflect on evidence courts should allow is to consider a radically inclusive approach suggested by Jane Baron.[51] Claiming that the law of wills pays too much attention to words and not enough to stories, she provides the example of her father's will, which left his "personal property" to her and the rest of his estate to his wife, Baron's stepmother. Did he mean by "personal property" only tangible items like chairs and tables, or also intangible property like stocks and bank accounts?

One might conceivably take Baron's proposal in a highly revisionist way, to allow the father's general wishes a kind of priority over the will itself, but it doesn't take too many conversations with members of the same family to realize that they can disagree sharply over a person's comparative affections. People represent themselves differently to different people, and perceptions of the same events vary widely. A judge could find it hard to build a composite story from the stories a daughter and her stepmother would tell about her father. If judges regarded wills as no more than helpful guides to wishes, their task would become nearly impossible, and the number of controverted cases would rise exponentially. Such a broad use of stories would undermine the choice someone has made to place his disposition in formal writing.

The more modest and plausible use of the father's story would be to illuminate what he meant by "personal property." The closer he was to his daughter, the more estranged from his wife, the more likely it was that he used the term expansively. Although the court's focus would remain on the will, the relevant evidence would be very broad. Even if contestants told the truth as they understood it, competing claims about comparative affection could be personally divisive, as well as troublesome for courts to evaluate. There is powerful reason not to admit such evidence of the father's general dispositions. Evidence drawn from the will itself and undisputed objective circumstances (such as the Rowlands' projected trip to the South Pacific) are less susceptible to distortion. If Baron could show that her father typically used the terms "personal property" to include stocks and bank accounts in his business dealings, that would give credence to the conclusion that he meant this broader notion in his will. The risk of admitting specific statements about the will's contents would depend on the kinds of statements involved. If her father wrote Professor Baron and her stepmother (with a copy to Baron) that Baron would receive his stocks, that would be highly reliable. Oral comments allegedly made to the person who would benefit would be unreliable.[52]

Leaving judges with a somewhat less rich picture of the aims of the testa-tor may be an acceptable price to pay for keeping out unreliable claims of oral statements and controverted and controversial testimony about the balance of someone's affections.

III. PLAIN MEANING, EXCEPTIONS, AND ALTERNATIVES

One possible approach to standards of interpretation and sources is to make everything depend on the apparent clarity of a will's language. When they find that a will has a plain meaning, judges have often barred any reliance on external sources to establish a different meaning.[53] Modern courts would not use this rule to bar evidence of local or trade usages, but a court faithfully applying the rule in a case such as *Rowland* would not consider evidence that would establish a writer's own special sense of words or his intent, unless the written words were ambiguous in context or vague in relation to some borderline situation.

Legal scholars of the last century did not look kindly on plain meaning rules, and leading scholars supported a focus on the intent of a will's author in preference to reliance on plain meaning.[54] Some scholars regarded plain meaning rules as incoherent or based on a logical error. Thus, Wigmore said that the plain meaning rule rests on the fallacy that "there is or ever can be *some one real* or absolute meaning."[55] Adam Hirsch has written that each of us has his or her own idiolect, that words can have multiple meanings, and that the plain meaning rule is "theoretically incoherent."[56]

Whatever may have been the misconceptions about language people may have entertained during the origins and development of the plain meaning rule, a defender of the rule need not assume that meanings are fixed and absolute. He may acknowledge that community sense deter-mines meaning, that meaning varies with social context, and that not everyone shares exactly the same meanings. All he need claim is that when certain words in a social context convey a meaning on which the vast majority of speakers of the language agree, that meaning is relevantly "plain."[57] In the law, meaning can also count as "plain" if legal tradition or legislation has established a definite, precise meaning for particular words such as "heirs" that does not depend on popular usage. One might con-ceive of a particular person's usage as so well established that the mean-ing of his words are plain even if others, even others in his circumstances, would not use words in that way. Such a personalized version of meaning is not considered plain meaning in the law of wills.

A plain meaning *rule* treats plain meaning as controlling, even if the speaker's subjective meaning may differ. When others rely on what a legal document says, giving substantial weight to the understandings of readers makes sense; but beneficiaries have only limited expectations based on the language of wills, and the main point of wills is to afford people wide discretion in how they wish to dispose of their property after death. Thus, while the reliance of readers is often a strong reason to follow plain meaning, that reason has little relevance for wills.[58] Any justification for privileging general meaning in wills over the intents of writers must lie instead mainly in the benefits of convenience, uniformity, and reliable evidence.

To evaluate those benefits, we need to look more closely at when evidence of individual meanings or intent is permitted or not permitted under the plain meaning rule,[59] and we also need to review some possible alternatives. The rule does not apply if a will is ambiguous—if the words as applied to external circumstances do not clearly convey one meaning rather than another. Most straightforwardly, words may be ambiguous on their face. Suppose T leaves "my most beautiful painting to my daughter Ann." The words taken by themselves do not signify which of a number of paintings is meant. Although historically, some courts refused to accept evidence to resolve such patent ambiguities,[60] regarding the terms as too indefinite to be applied, courts now will usually admit evidence to discern the writer's intent.[61]

Evidence has consistently been allowed to resolve latent ambiguities, apparent only when the language of the will is applied to the testator's property.[62] If T leaves "my diamond necklace," the direction is ambiguous if she owns two diamond necklaces. Evidence may show which necklace she meant.[63] Courts wanting to avoid unjust results will often stretch what count as ambiguities without explicitly abandoning the plain meaning rule.[64]

The crucial issue about plain meaning concerns claims about individual meanings, when no evidence of ambiguity exists except assertions about the writer's particular understanding. An example is a will that leaves property to "Mother." If the writer's mother is alive when his will is written, the word (barring some complication about a birth mother and adoptive mother) has a plain meaning, and it does not refer to the writer's wife. Under a plain meaning rule, the wife would not be able to show that her husband referred to her as "Mother."[65]

Suppose a widow offers disinterested witnesses that her husband always referred to her in this way. Might the husband not have realized that in his will, he should use precise words, not intimate terms of reference? A court might view the effort to get back to the husband's individual meaning as fraught with difficulty.

But is a total bar on evidence of idiosyncratic understanding a wise response? It may be better to indulge a strong assumption that words are meant in their ordinary sense, but to admit evidence of a different meaning, perhaps requiring the proponent of a special meaning to meet a high burden of proof. When one looks at the range of cases in which "plain meaning" can produce unjust results, this possibility gains in attractiveness. We can divide cases very roughly into those in which the testator has made an outright mistake and those in which the problem is less simple.

One form of outright mistake is that the language of the will, even as understood by the testator, definitely fails to accomplish his purpose.

Either he has made a slip in writing the will, or some failure occurs between his instructions to his lawyer and his signing of the will that both fail to catch.

Some wills omit clearly intended provisions. One provided that a daughter could receive a portion of the principal of Fund A (but not of Fund B) when she reached the age of forty, although other language in the will indicated that the aim was to allow her receipt of some of the principal of both funds. Extrinsic evidence showed that a typist had made an error.[66] In another kind of case, a husband and wife read their respective wills carefully, but each ends up signing the other's will.[67]

A somewhat different form of mistake involves terms with a precise legal significance and application that the testator does not recognize. Thus, one testatrix acting on her lawyer's advice designated her "heirs at law," apparently not realizing that at her death, her aunt might be her sole heir, with priority over her cousins.[68] In another case, the lawyer had used the term "heirs" after a woman had asked that the residue in her will go to her own blood relatives; in California the family of her late husband counted as half of her heirs.[69]

Relatedly, a testator may misunderstand legal consequences, in a way that does not depend on the meaning of a single term. In one case, a couple wanted their estates divided between their two families if neither of them or their children survived. Their lawyer wrote the wills to provide that the estates would be divided between the two mothers. The wife's mother, but not the husband's, survived the couple, who died with their children in a hotel fire. According to ordinary legal principles, the wife's mother would have taken everything.[70]

Some mistakes concern the external world to which the will applies. The writer may fail to benefit a child because she mistakenly believes he has died. Or she may make a mistake about how to describe a piece of property or about a name. In the instances or names, the writer often could not identify the mistake if he read his will very carefully, but he would recognize that he had picked the wrong name if the correct names of individuals or organizations were explained to him. If no one exactly fits a name in the will, courts will consider evidence to resolve the latent ambiguity, but what if the will perfectly matches an actual person or organization? One will contained a devise to Robert J. Krause (with his correct address); the testator did not know him, but Robert W. Krause was a long-time friend and employee.[71] In a more piquant case, Nasmyth, a resident of Edinburgh, left a legacy to the "National Society for the Prevention of Cruelty to Children."[72] It turned out that a society with just this name existed in London; the name of the analogous society in Edinburgh began with the word "Scottish." According to a handbook on legal construction, "a number of circumstances . . . rendered it highly probable that [he] would have preferred to extend his bounty to the Scottish society."[73]

Courts have strong reason to correct mistakes in wills. Nasmyth thought he had used the name of the society in Scotland; the California testatrix thought that her "heirs" were her blood relatives. Why should courts not give effect to words as the words are understood by those who write them, if there is powerful, acceptable evidence that their understanding deviates from general usage?[74] The result should be the same if a lawyer tells the testator that he is using words he won't bother to explain that will do the job the testator wants.[75]

If we focus on fair treatment for the testator, it also makes sense for courts to correct mistakes about exactly what words the will contains. If it is clear that the testator wanted the beneficiary to receive principal from Fund B, or to sign the will drawn up for himself, not his wife, or to leave money to his friend Robert W. Krause, a court should rectify the mistake. Courts *could* require evidence from within the will that a mistake has been made, as in the Fund B case, but sometimes external evidence can be reliable and powerful, as with the written donation to Robert J. Krause, even though nothing in the will itself sounds an alarm.[76]

A tentative conclusion that courts should correct evident mistakes does not resolve what standard they should employ in interpreting wills, what evidence they should consider that a mistake has been made, and what burden of proof they should place on the person who is urging the existence of a mistake. The approach most influentially urged in recent decades is that courts should inquire about the actual intent of testa-tors, that any evidence, or at least any evidence not barred by ordinary principles of evidence, should be permitted, but that the proponent of mistakes of fact or law should have to establish the mistakes by clear and convincing evidence.[77]

We shall look at three recent challenges to this combination of ele-ments, all of which agree that any strategy that fails to correct obvious mistakes in misguided. James L. Robertson offers an objective approach to interpretation, based on his experience as a judge on a state supreme court and heavily influenced by Oliver Wendell Holmes.[78] He urges that discerning the actual intent of a testator many years ago is commonly an impossible inquiry. Further, given the influence of various aids to inter-pretation that are external to the donor, it is "forced and awkward" to combine internal and external standards.[79]

In contrast to a major thesis of this book and much other writing about interpretation, Robertson suggests that the same objective approach can apply to all aspects of legal interpretation.[80] According to him, "We do and should seek circumstanced external meaning, not by invading the mind of the person who made the donative transfer, but by referring to the hypothetical, yet reasoned, intent of an external character, an imag-ined semi-sovereign donor ('SSD')".[81] A court should ask what the words would mean to a "normal hearer of English seeing them in the circum-stances in which they were spoken."[82] Robertson is open to courts con-sidering external evidence, including the lawyer's testimony in one of the "heirs" cases that the testatrix did not want her money to go to her one aunt rather than her twenty-five cousins.[83]

Just how Robertson's approach differs from an inquiry about subjective intent is elusive, in part because the range of evidence about circumstances that he would allow is not clear. As a hypothetical in which a court would not, and should not, deviate from the words of the will, he suggests an instance in which a father's will leaves a Chickering piano to one daughter (Maria) although he meant to leave it to another (Christina).[84] If Dad had written both daughters many times that Christina was to get the piano and Maria the painting, if the lawyer's notes reflected that intent, if Maria was an artist who despised piano music, a court employing an actual intent approach might decide that Christina should receive the piano. In principle this case does not seem different from the Robert Krause problem. Of course, people rarely leave money to strangers with names almost like those of good friends they fail to benefit, and people often leave pianos to daughters. But one can load the circumstances heavily so a gift to Maria seems highly implausible. If an external circumstanced approach would correct the gift to Robert J. Krause,[85] why could it not correct the gift to Maria?

And how are we to regard situations in which the testator uses terms in an unusual way? A normal speaker of English would not use terms in that way, but such speakers can understand from an enriched view of circumstances that another person is using terms in a nonstandard way.[86] If all circumstantial evidence is admitted, including evidence about the inclinations and idiosyncrasies of the testator, it is doubtful if a judge employing Robertson's objective approach would reach practical results different from one asking about actual intent. She would, of course, not admit to making an uncertain determination about probable intent; she would be able to say instead that she adopts the conclusion that the normal speaker of English who matched the will to circumstances would reach.

One suggestion that turns out mainly to concern evidence is what the author calls a "descriptive linguistics approach."[87] When courts look to extrinsic evidence, it should be for the meaning of words as the testator ordinarily uses them, not for his intent.[88] The evidence a court would admit about how a testator used language would not be subject to fraud, as might be a typical claim about intentions not reflected in the will itself.

Emily Sherwin has urged that using a standard of clear and convincing evidence for proof of testamentary intent by someone who has failed to comply with will formalities fails to achieve a rational compromise between formality and adjudicative justice.[89] Her basic argument is that a mistaken failure to recognize testamentary intent is as bad as a mistaken recognition of testamentary intent when it is absent. Using a standard of clear and convincing evidence, rather than the ordinary civil standard of preponderance of evidence, will result in a greater number of misjudgments. Sherwin does not herself extend her reasoning to issues of interpretation,[90] but her challenge should lead to a careful examination of possible reasons for a standard of clear and convincing evidence in that context.

One may think of such a standard partly as a caution against weighing certain kinds of evidence too highly. Some years ago, and perhaps up to the present, the Princeton philosophy department did not interview persons they were considering for appointments. The rationale was that the members recognized they would give undue importance to personal impressions. The heightened standard of proof might be a restraint on a judge giving too much weight to present testimony in relation to what can be discerned from the will itself. The standard can also operate as an exercise in tact. A judge need not say he thinks someone is probably lying, only that the proponent has failed to overcome the burden of producing clear and convincing evidence.

Perhaps most important, when claimed mistakes are at issue, misjudgments in one direction seem more tolerable than misjudgments in the other. If a testator or his lawyer has messed up, holding him to what the will actually conveys may be harsh; but it does not seem as bad as rewarding fraudulent claims of mistake. Many assertions of mistake that are not obviously correct are either actually true or the fruit of outright fraud. The clear and convincing evidence standard is a protection against fraud succeeding.

When measured against these various critiques, both an inquiry that focuses on actual intent, at least as to matters as to which the testator almost certainly had a definite intent, and a standard of clear and convincing evidence, seem appropriate.

Courts have commonly said that they can construe wills, but not reform them by adding new provisions. However, distinguishing construction from addition is hard to do when a name is substituted or a will the husband signed is given the terms of the will his wife mistakenly signed. Langbein and Waggoner argue persuasively that many American decisions have eroded any line between construction and reformation (or addition), and that courts should drop the pretense of "no reformation."[91] Rather, they should alter explicit terms when they have clear and convincing evidence that the terms do not reflect the intentions of the testator.

Although the courts' treatment of plain meaning and mistake has parallels in contractual and statutory interpretation, judges do not often suppose that legislators have made simple errors about the meaning of terms they have chosen for statutes.

How far should courts be guided by a testator's intent when something more complex than a mistake is involved? Courts will not alter specific language merely because it appears to be in some tension with a testator's overall objectives, judged from the body of the will or external evidence. Wills are not public regarding in the manner of statutes; their writers are free, within bounds, to be arbitrary or capricious. They need not be consistent in fulfilling purposes outsiders can identify. Judges have no occasion to substitute their judgment for what the writers have specifically provided.[92] However, if the clear general intent in a will is to provide equally for different branches for a family, and that conflicts with more specific language about a particular disposition, courts rightly seek to give effect to the paramount intention.[93] These situations usually arise when the testator has failed to foresee the contingency that actually occurs. Courts are particularly likely to alter specific dispositions if they would require taxes that the will could comfortably have avoided by other, better, language.[94] Mary Louise Fellows has sensibly proposed that courts should more broadly reform wills to achieve competent estate planning.[95]

It is conceivable that a writer's intent for a specific situation and his sense of his words may fly apart. Imagine that Dr. Rowland picked "coinciding," conceiving that it covered shipwrecks in which his wife and he would die together. In most circumstances, the two would die seconds or a few minutes apart. Dr. Rowland loosely assumed that the term would be adequate even if the deaths were a half hour apart, but if he had focused carefully on that question, he would have acknowledged that deaths a half hour apart do not coincide. Here, his specific intent about a situation would not fit his reflective sense of his own words, and yet he has not exactly made a mistake. In the absence of a mistake, a court is highly unlikely to have sufficient evidence to conclude that a writer's own sense of the words she uses fails to conform to the specific intent she had when she used the words.

A more frequent possibility is that a testator's general intent will seem frustrated by a specific disposition, even though the general intent is not directly provided in the will itself. One might view the Rowlands' circumstances in this way if the wife survived too long for the deaths to coincide (by any understanding), but not long enough for her to make any use of her husband's property.

Common calamities, in which the main beneficiary under a will is a victim of the same accident as the testator, survives hours or days longer, but is unable to make any use of the proceeds of the will, are one form of testamentary obsolescence, in which events somehow overtake (or probably overtake) what the will provides.[96] Other typical examples include divorce, killing of the testator by the beneficiary, and disposal of real property allocated to a beneficiary.

Instances like these may be dealt with by statutes or handled by judicial determinations whether the will should be reformed. Statutes may specify a number of days that a beneficiary must survive a testator to recover under the will and provide that a beneficiary who commits unjustified homicide may not take under the will (a rule usually justified on grounds of deterrence and desert, rather than likely testator preference). When the testator lives beyond the event in question, it often makes a difference how long he has failed to revise his will. The longer that period, the less likely a court will find that his existing will did not reflect his intentions at the time of death.

In one sense these kinds of circumstances pose issues about static or dynamic interpretation that exist in one form or another in every branch of legal interpretation. Many of the examples can also be viewed as pitting specific intentions against more general aims, one common aspect of arguments about dynamic interpretation.

Adam Hirsch has advocated that these situations be dealt with by default rules, which would apply unless the testator has indicated a contrary disposition.[97] He urges empirical research to reveal the attitudes and assumptions of most people, and suggests that at least some default rules for wills would better be based on what people assume will happen if they do not reform their wills rather than what they would want to have happen.[98] To use the example of divorce, if most people say they would prefer that a divorced spouse not recover under a will, but they believe a divorced spouse will recover unless the will is altered, the default rule would be to allow recovery (at least if a fair amount of time has passed). The basic idea is that if most people think it is necessary to change their wills to disinherit their former spouses, those who fail to change wills are likely to be those who do not want to alter things.

In addition to the problem of gathering the necessary empirical information, fully recognized by Hirsch, there are serious issues about categorization, since different segments of the population may well have different attitudes and assumptions. If one aspect of ignorance is about the existence of default rules and what is needed to avoid them, it is highly doubtful that all segments should be lumped together regardless of divergencies in expectations.

A different approach has been proposed by Pamela Champine.[99] She would have those making wills fill out a form in which they indicate explicitly whether courts are authorized to change provisions of their wills.[100] Champine is particularly concerned with the atypical testator who may not want his will changed although most people would prefer that. The more flexible the standards for change become, the more those testators may lose out. Getting explicit responses by testators about their openness to reformation would be helpful. Although one may doubt their ability to foresee and credit various kinds of events that may happen, the testators who have designated "no reformation" will be on notice they will have to alter their wills if they no longer are happy with dispositions they have provided.

IV. INTERPRETATION, GENERAL ASSUMPTIONS, AND PUBLIC POLICY

I have, thus far, largely omitted one significant topic, interpretation in light of general assumptions and public policies. Statutes constrain testators to a limited extent, requiring, for example, that spouses receive a substantial share; but beyond these restraints, various judicial, and statutory, principles of interpretation may affect how a will is construed. In circumstances of doubt, courts standardly interpret wills to do what most people would want and in a manner that reflects ideas of desirable distribution.

Courts assume that most people do not wish to disinherit their children and that they wish equality of distribution for heirs of equal degree.[101] If a will leaves the matter in doubt, it will be interpreted not to disinherit and to provide equality. These rules go beyond generalizations about likely wishes, they reflect what has been a social sense of desirable distribution.[102] Thus, it has been said, "Every reasonable construction in the will must be made in favor of the heir at law; and he can be disinherited only by words which provide that effect clearly and necessarily." [103]

In all areas of law, judges interpret in light of likely and appropriate behavior. Because of the freedom of the writers of wills, there may be less room for public policy to affect interpretation than elsewhere;[104] nonetheless, judges properly give some more weight to appropriate standards of behavior than a pure estimate of the testator's probable intentions might warrant. Thus, given the policy that caring for children is desirable, a court may construe an unclear will to do that, even if the balance of probabilities suggests that the testator wished otherwise.

The use of these standards of interpretation, among others, presents substantial questions about desirable policy and conceptualization. The concern about policy involves the atypical testator,[105] especially when he is a member of a minority who is at liberty to reject some prevailing assumptions, and does so. With various exceptions now in some jurisdictions, members of gay couples do not count as family; should a preference for family members over friends apply to an unclear will if the crucial "friend" and the testator have been a same sex couple for twenty years? If this problem gets sufficiently worked out so that gay couples can count as "married" for this purpose, there will remain couples (opposite sex and same sex) who choose to live together in a romantic relationship without formalizing their relationship. Such relationships have increasingly become socially accepted, and it may now seem unjust to treat the survivor worse than formal family members. In brief, while social norms can tip the balance on otherwise close questions, legislatures and courts need to be very careful not to permit outdated mores to hold sway, and to be attentive to what seems genuinely fair in individual circumstances.

The conceptual question concerns the status of these norms. Are they really aspects of interpretation or something else? They are undoubtedly included in interpretation in the broad sense I employ in this study, but that does not resolve whether they should be seen as a different kind of exercise from "ordinary" interpretation. Richard Storrow is sharply critical of the Restatement's abandoning of the distinction between determining an individual author's intentions (interpretation) and using construction to fill out the text when intentions can't be discovered.[106] However, so long as these general standards are employed on the basis that, in lieu of more direct evidence, the testator probably wanted to do what most people want, the distinction seems more of degree than kind. A judge relies on what most people want as one basis to infer what a particular testator probably intended. When judges employ standards based on public reasons in a way that goes beyond probable individual intentions, that is a different exercise from discerning, with whatever degree of confidence, what the individual had in mind.

In summary, among written documents with legal authority, the reasons for emphasizing writer's intent in some form are strongest for wills. In that respect, wills resemble a principal's instructions as an agent seeks to interpret them. In contrast with an agent considering instructions, the overarching focus for wills has been on the time they are written, although recent law has somewhat expanded the possibilities of reformation in light of changing circumstances. Thus, the typical interpretation rests on a form of originalism. Whether the reasons for such an originalist approach extend to other legal texts is one question we shall explore in the chapters that follow in this and subsequent volumes.

Notes

1 See James L. Robertson, "Myth and Reality—or Is It 'Perception and Taste'—in the Reading of Donative Documents," 61 *Fordham Law Review* 1045, 1073 (1993). Some complexities are introduced to minimize taxes. Most people wish to pay as little in estate taxation as they fairly can.

2 For some "instructions," matters are still more complicated. A search warrant is issued to guide police officers (who may themselves have written the warrant for judicial approval) while they are making a search and to provide notice to a homeowner about the search's appropriate limits. (Since homeowners rarely read warrants carefully and rarely are able to prevent excesses, exclusion of evidence is the main deterrent of abuse.)

3 Even if she has entered such a contract, she can change her will in a way that does not correspond with what she has agreed to. The change is effective, but her estate must meet her contractual obligations.

4 An important exception involves the wills of spouses, especially those in second marriages with children of earlier marriages. Each spouse may have legitimate expectations in what the will of the other provides, although it would not follow that a court should rely on the ordinary meaning of words rather than a different standard for discerning meaning.

5 See Robertson, note 1 supra, at 1074–76, on donative documents in general.

6 On the kinds of lawsuits in which provisions of wills are contested, see William J. Bowe and Douglas H. Parker, *Revised Treatise: Page on the Law of Wills*, §31 (Cincinnati, W.H. Anderson & Co., 1961), with 2004 Cumulative Supplement (subsequently cited as *Page on Wills*).

7 In re Rowland, [1963] Ch. 1 (Eng. C.A.).

8 Id. at 3.

9 Law of Property Act, 1925, 15 Geo5, c20, §184. The use of the word "uncertain" in the act might be regarded as affecting the degree of proof someone would need to offer to show the order of deaths. That is, even if the evidence showed that the younger person probably, but not to a high degree of certainly, died first or that two deaths coincided, it might be argued that the order was uncertain under the statute.

10 The facts leave unclear whether the Rowlands merely adopted standard language on a form or considered the words. It is extremely unlikely that they made

up the legal sounding phrase "preceding or coinciding." The fact that their wills were handwritten probably shows they were at least aware of the words, unlike many people who sign forms.

11 An intermediate possibility is usage by a special class of persons. See John Henry Wigmore, *Evidence in Trials at Common Law* §2458 (Chadbourne rev. ed., Boston and Toronto, Little Brown, 1981) (hereinafter cited as Wigmore), Wigmore also refers to usage by the parties to a bilateral act. If one thought of the Rowlands as agreeing on similar terms for their wills, one might think that the understanding of Mrs. Rowland should count.

12 If Rowland did not think about the term, perhaps it should be given the effect he would have assumed, had he thought about it. But it is hard to know what he would have thought, if he did not focus on the word. On reflection, he might have thought that the standard term was inadequate.

13 "Simultaneous" appears in many dictionaries as a synonym of "coincident."

14 One might resist this example on the ground that the reigns "coincided," except for the month at each end. On this view, a fairer test for whether two distinct events coincided is whether one might say that the deaths of John Adams and Thomas Jefferson, hours apart on the same day, coincided. I am inclined to think that "coincided" is fairly flexible, depending on the time period being considered. Thus, if one asks how far apart our first four presidents died, one might say that Washington died first by many years, that Madison survived by some years, and that the deaths of Adams and Jefferson coincided.

15 Some sticklers about language might say that the deaths did not exactly coincide in a strict sense, though they were very close. Even the sticklers would acknowledge that two deaths could relevantly coincide, even though an expert could tell us that one occurred a millionth of a second before the other. For example, after a bomb blast, an expert might be able to say that a person closer to the explosion died milliseconds before someone standing five feet further away.

16 1 Ch. at 14. Justice Harman, id. at 12, did accept the idea that a deviation from the ordinary meaning of words might be warranted if other language in a will or a testator's other expressions supported it.

17 He also argued that placement in the will of "coinciding" after "preceding" afforded a reason to construe it as dealing only with time. Id.

18 Id. at 8.

19 Id. at 10. As I shall subsequently explain, finding out a writer's intentions is not exactly the same as giving words the meaning they bore for him.

20 Id. at 11.

21 Id. at 18.

22 I put aside whatever force precedents may have had. The majority could claim that its stance followed earlier cases that had been very strict about when deaths "coincide." The court had refused to say that deaths coincided when a husband and wife clung to each other as a ship went down. Underwood v. Wing, [1854] Ch. 459, 4 De. G.M. & G. 633 (1855); Wing v. Angrave, (1860) 8 H.L.C. 183. Judges did find that the deaths of sisters from the same bomb were simultaneous in In re Pringle, [1946] 1 Ch. 124 (Eng. C.A.).

23 It is conceivable that understandings of "coinciding" differ in England and the United States or have changed significantly since the case was decided.

24 That Dr. Rowland could have used different language to cover the circumstance of death by shipwreck may also be urged in favor of the result, see Michael Albery, "Coincidence and the Construction of Wills," 26 *Modern Law Review* 353,

363 (1963), but it seems unfair to interpret his will in light of his failure to use an alternative a lawyer might have recommended.

25 Alternatively, one might say that judges should ascribe the meaning that a reasonable person in the situation would want and understand. In that event, whether Rowland himself paid attention to the language of his will would become irrelevant.

26 Michael Albery, note 24 supra, at 358, assumes that Lord Denning would not have allowed into evidence testimony about a conversation between the Rowlands about what they meant.

27 Perhaps a testatrix's hopes should prevail over her understanding if she misperceives the limits of what a will can do, she hopes her will can do more than she believes she has accomplished, she has managed to choose words that fit her hopes well, and it turns out those can be carried our consistent with the law of wills.

28 Robertson, note 1 supra, at 1053.

29 Albery, note 24 supra, at 358. What the judges disagreed about, he claims, is "the extent to which and the means whereby it is permissible to divert a word from its ordinary meaning." Id.

30 Id. at 358–60. Albery remarks that the weight attached to each ingredient is not "at the discretion of the court but is governed by well-established principles." Id. at 360. But these principles do not tell us that the various ingredients lead to some singular sense of meaning (nor, I think, do they give us a precise ordering of criteria), rather they tell us what the courts will count as the meaning.

31 *Page on Wills*, note 6 supra, §30, p. 2.

32 Id. at pp. 3–4.

33 Id. at p. 44.

34 Id. at 32.

35 As James Robertson sharply notes, note 1 supra, at 1065–66.

36 See American Law Institute, Restatement (Third) of Property (Wills and Other Donative Transfers) (2003), § 10.1: "The controlling consideration in determining the meaning of a derivative document is the donor's intention"; § 10.2: "all relevant evidence (of intention) . . . may be considered, including . . . extrinsic evidence."

See Pamela R. Champine, "*My* Will Be Done: Accommodating the Erring and the Atypical Testator," 80 *Nebraska Law Review* 387, 391–407 (2001), considering instances of claimed mistakes.

37 Thus, one way to understand *Rowland* is that if a term has a standard meaning, a court will not pay attention to any evidence that the writer probably intended a different meaning.

38 If evidence were barred only when the meaning is regarded as plain, a more precise way to view the approach would be that plain meaning is the controlling legal standard; only if that fails, do facts about the testator become legally relevant. This nuance of conceptualization is one indication of how thin the line can become between a narrow standard of interpretation (plain meaning controls) and a constraint on sources of evidence (no way to show testator's intention).

39 Scott J. Jarboe, "Comment, Interpreting a Testator's Intent from the Language of Her Will: A Descriptive Linguistics Approach," 80 *Washington University Law Quarterly* 1365, 1373–75 (2002), provides one account of modern justifications. Id. at 1371–73 recounts reasons for earlier English restrictions on external evidence.

40 See Adam J. Hirsch, "Inheritance and Inconsistency," 57 *Ohio State Law Journal* 1057, 1071 (1996) (twenty-nine jurisdictions).

41 For a discussion of will substitutes, see John Langbein, "Substantial Compliance with the Wills Act," 88 *Harvard Law Review* 489, 503–09 (1975); Nathaniel W. Schwickerath, "Public Policy and the Probate Pariah: Confusion in the Law of Will Substitutes," 48 *Drake Law Review* 769 (2000).

42 Univ. Probate Code §§2-502, 503. John H. Langbein earlier wrote favorably on a similar development in South Australia. "Excusing Harmless Errors in the Execution of Wills: A Report on Australia's Tranquil Revolution in Probate Law," 87 *Columbia Law Review* 1 (1987).

43 See John Langbein, note 41 supra at 491–98.

44 It would be comforting to suppose that since anyone can change her will, the will almost certainly reflects her wishes up to the time of death. But many people put off revising wills even if after their wishes have changed; and death overtakes some procrastinators. That many people fail to revise wills is the subject of frequent comment, but not often noted is the reality that thinking about our own death is disturbing for many of us, and one who is working on a will cannot help focusing on that inevitable occurrence.

45 I pass over situations in which an oral statement might be irrefutably authentic, as when a person sends a videotape to all family members.

46 Wigmore emphasizes that the rule is properly seen as one of substantive law, not evidence. Wigmore, note 11 supra, at §2400. If the rule is used to bar evidence of intent or of how a testator understood words that a court would consider relevant under its criteria of interpretation, then the rule operates as a genuine one of evidence.

47 See *Page on Wills*, note 6 supra, at §30, pp. 39–44.

48 The line between interpretation and supplementation becomes thinner if the testator's general intent, not revealed in the will itself but established by external evidence, is used to provide a specific disposition the testator did not conceive. The following chapter provides an example of how this line can become elusive in relation to a contract.

49 See Jarboe, note 39 supra, at 1388.

50 Similarly, a relaxation in will formalities does not deprive people of good reasons to do their wills carefully, see Langbein, note 42 supra, at 51; Emily Sherwin, "Clear and Convincing Evidence of Testamentary Intent: The Search for a Compromise Between Formality and Adjudication Justice," 34 *Connecticut Law Review*, 453, 466–68 (2002).

51 Jane B. Baron, "Intention, Interpretation, and Stories," 42 *Duke Law Journal* 630 (1992).

52 Ordinary rules barring hearsay evidence would reach some evidence of this sort, even without any special exclusion for the law of wills.

53 Wigmore, note 11 supra, at §2461.

54 See, e.g., id. at §2462; John H. Langbein and Lawrence W. Waggoner, "Reformation of Wills on the Ground of Mistake: Change in Direction in American Law?" 130 *University of Pennsylvania Law Reiew* 521 (1982); Joseph W. deFuria Jr., "Mistakes in Wills Resulting from Scrivener's Errors: The Argument for Reformation," 40 *Catholic Law Review* 1 (1990).

55 Wigmore, note 11 supra, §2462, citing Locke for the proposition that individuals signify different things by words.

56 Hirsch, note 40 supra, at 1116–21.

57 See, e.g., Oliver Wendell Holmes's reference to what "words mean in the mouth of a normal speaker of English, using them in the circumstances in which they were used . . . ." "The Theory of Legal Interpretation," 12 *Harvard Law Review* 417, 417–18 (1899).

58 *Page on Wills*, note 6 supra at §30, pp. 8–9, explains that courts are more liberal about construing intent in wills than in deeds and that American courts are more liberal than are English ones.

59 As Richard Storrow points out, extrinsic evidence is standardly used in will cases for purposes of identification, "Judicial Discretion and the Disappearing Distinction Between Interpretation and Construction," 56 *Case Western Law Review* 65, 73–77 (2005); but that need not detract from the meaning being plain.

60 Wigmore, note 11 supra, at §2472.

61 See, e.g., Andrea W. Cornelison, "Dead Man Talking: Are Courts Ready to Listen? The Erosion of the Plain Meaning Rule," 35 *Real Property, Probate and Trust Journal* 811, 819–20 (2001). Some courts will admit extrinsic evidence, but not evidence of the testator's intent.

62 Id., at 820–23.

63 This kind of uncertainty may be regarded as a separate category of "equivocation," a description that "fits two or more external objects equally well." Jesse Dukeminier and Stanley M. Johanson, *Wills, Trusts, and Estates* 437 (5th ed., Boston, Little Brown, 1995).

64 According to Andrea Cornelison, note 61 supra at 824, "the language of ambiguity largely has swallowed the plain meaning rule . . . ."

65 Arnold Duncan McNair, *The Law of Treaties: British Practice and Opinions: Part II, The Interpretation of Treaties*, c. 16, 175 (Oxford, Clarendon Press, 1938), refers to a will that said, "All for mother." In that case, Thorn v. Dickens, [1906] WN 54, the actual mother had died before the will was written. The court allowed evidence that "mother" was how he referred to his wife. Perhaps it could be relevant that this usage is not entirely idiosyncratic. Many husbands refer to their wives as "Mother" or "Mom" when talking to their children, and some address their wives directly in this way. Few would use these terms for their wives in a formal legal document, but in the actual case, the testator signed the three-word document the day before he died. Some courts maintain a personal use exception to the plain meaning rule. See Cornelison, note 61 supra at 825.

66 In re Estate of Dorson, 196 N.Y.S.2d 344 (Sur. Ct. 1959). The court allowed correction of the error.

67 In one New York case, the court admitted the will the husband signed to probate and reformed it in accord with the provisions his wife had actually signed. In re Snide, 418 N.E.2d 656, 437 N.Y.S.2d 63 (N.Y. 1981).

68 See Mahoney v. Grainger, 186 N.E. 86 (Mass. 1933). Answering criticisms that the court's ruling in favor of the aunt ignored crucial extrinsic evidence of the lawyer that the testatrix meant to benefit her cousins, James Robertson has defended the result as sound, given that the two cousins with whom she was "cordial and friendly" received specific legacies. Robertson, note 1 supra, at 1096–99.

I am not treating an idiosyncratic use of ordinary terms as a "mistake," so long as the terms reflect the writer's actual understanding and wishes, but one might say the writer is making a mistake in failing to adhere to general usage.

69 Estate of Taff, 133 Cal. Rptr. 737 (Ct. App. 1976). The court interpreted the will to carry out her intention. It noted that the trial court properly considered evidence to create an ambiguity and to resolve it. John Langbein and Lawrence Waggoner have remarked that "this way of stating the matter obliterates the fundamental distinction between ambiguity and mistake." Langbein and Waggoner, note 54 supra at 557–58. (It does not necessarily follow that the court would have taken the same approach if the will had used words that the testatrix herself would have realized did not accomplish her objectives if she had read the words over.)

70 In Engel v. Siegel, 377 A.2d 892 (N.J. 1963), the court followed the couple's intent and treated the mothers as representatives of the wider families.

71 In re Estate of Gibbs, 111 N.W. 413 (1961). The testator had apparently looked in the telephone book for his friend, and had put down the middle initial and address of the stranger. Believing that the proof established the mistake to a high degree of certainty, the court corrected it.

72 Michael Hancher, "Dead Letters: Wills and Poems," 60 *Texas Law Review* 507, 515 (1982).

73 The House of Lords gave the money to the English organization.

74 In the National Society case, there is a further argument that in context the title of the organization meant generally what Nasmyth assumed. Someone who says in New York that he is to get at dog at the S.P.C.A. means the American S.P.C.A. The National Society issue is more complicated because the title is in a formal document, and some people living in Edinburgh might choose to donate to the organization in England.

75 That is, it should not matter whether the lawyer says, "I've used 'heirs' to benefit your blood relatives," or, "I've used technical language to do what you wish."

76 I here treat this names case as one of a mistake about what words appeared in the will, but, if the testator did not know his friend's middle initial or address, one might say he chose the words he wanted and that his mistake was about the individual to whom those words referred. On my analysis, which of these two characterizations is preferable does not matter.

77 Restatement (Third) of Property (Wills and Other Donative Transfers) (2003), § 12.1 (document can be reformed to donor's intent if "clear and convincing evidence," including direct evidence that contradicts plain meaning of text, establishes mistake of fact or law). See Langbein and Waggoner, note 54 supra. Robertson, note 1 supra, at 1089, points out that these authors would impose a less exacting standard of proof for clerical errors.

78 Id.

79 Id. at 1053.

80 Id. at 1047.

81 See also Mary Louise Fellows, "In Search of Donative Intent," 72 *Iowa Law Review* 611 (1988), who suggests that courts "impute" intent. It is not clear how far imputed intent will ordinarily diverge from a probabilistic judgment about actual intent, although Fellows does say that testators do not have intents about matters they did not consider.

82 Robertson, note 1 supra, at 1076.

83 Id. at 1096–99.

84 Id. at 1061.

85 I am not certain Robertson would correct that gift; if he would not, his approach can be faulted on that ground.

86 An extreme illustration, mentioned in Chapter 2 on the philosophy of language, is when a listener realizes that the speaker misunderstands the meaning of a word in a language that is not the speaker's native tongue.

87 Jarboe, note 39 supra.

88 Id. at 1387.

89 Sherwin, note 50 supra.

90 But see Robertson, note 1 supra, at 184–85. Although rejecting a heightened standard of proof, Roberson, id. at 1102, says his approach would be inhospitable to claims of mistake based on the hearsay testimony of drafting lawyers about what testators wanted to achieve.

91 Langbein and Waggoner, note 54 supra at 566.

92 An exception involves the wills of people who have become incompetent. Then the argument is strong that courts should be able to reform their terms to carry out their objectives. See Fellows, note 81 supra at 621–26. Chapter 10 discusses the doctrine of *cy pres*, which authorizes explicit revision of the terms of trusts in changed circumstances.

93 See *Page on Wills*, note 6 supra, at §30, pp. 88–89.

94 The Restatement (Third) of Property (Wills and Other Donative Transfers) (2003) has an explicit provision, § 12.2, allowing wills and other donative documents to "be modified, in a manner that does not violate the donor's probable intention, to achieve the donor's tax objectives."

95 See Fellows, note 81 supra, at 613. She would afford people the benefits of competent planning even when their lawyers have failed to do so.

96 See Adam J. Hirsch, "Text and Time: A Theory of Testamentary Obsolescence," 86 *Washington University Law Review* 609, 618–20 (2009).

97 Id.

98 Hirsch treats his proposal as a possibility not previously recognized in the default literature, pointing out that information costs in learning legal rules are much more of a problem for wills than for the repeat players in contractual transactions, the usual subject for work on default rules. Id. at 634–35.

99 Champine, note 36 supra.

100 A sample form is at id., 461–62.

101 *Page on Wills*, note 6 supra at §30, pp. 111, 91.

102 Fellows, note 81 supra at 613.

103 *Page on Wills*, note 6 supra at §30, p. 111.

104 However, some contracts scholars argue that courts should give effect to what the parties wanted or would have wanted over any considerations of public policy they were at liberty to disregard.

105 See Champine, note 36 supra.

106 Storrow, note 95 supra.

Chapter 9

Contracts

I. INTRODUCTION

The law of contracts is a major part of modern private law, and the law's treatment of contracts is the subject of extensive scholarly attention in the United States. This chapter explores questions about contract interpretation similar to those concerning wills. How far should courts be guided by objective meaning, how far by the subjective intent of the parties? How general or contextual should objective meaning be taken to be? When should courts "write in" terms that parties have failed to supply—a power that is quite limited for wills—and how should they go about that task? If various contractual provisions point in different directions, should a court give each its apparent meaning, even at the cost of an unwieldy totality, or bend the language of some terms to make the whole contract work well? What evidences of meaning should courts allow?

Should courts assign meaning to contracts based on public policy, rather than the apparent significance of words or the intent of parties, if the explicit terms are unenforceable or seem to require actions that are permitted but generally disfavored, in the manner of disinheriting one's children?

How far should the answers to these preceding questions depend on the expressed or probable wishes of the parties about how courts should interpret? Should strategies of interpretation vary according to the nature of the parties and the contracts they have made?

A typical contract involves promises to perform reciprocal acts;[1] *A* agrees to sell his automobile to *B* for \$2,000, creating a legal duty on each to perform his undertaking. The usual remedy for a failure to perform is monetary damages that satisfy the other party's expectations,[2] but courts sometimes order parties to perform their specific promises instead. Contracts may be written or oral. Most important contracts are in writing, and judicial problems of interpretation usually arise over these. In modern times, people with oral contracts rarely are willing to undergo the expense of litigation. When courts do consider such contracts, they may lack an undisputed text, each person recalling the agreement in words that fit her own understanding of its substance.[3] Parties to a written contract agree to its text,[4] but the possibility arises of divergence between the text's general "objective" meaning and its contextual objective meaning, and between either of these objective meanings and a party's subjective understanding.

Beyond the obvious point that contracts, unlike wills, are subscribed to by at least two persons, contracts differ from wills in usually being performed without legal officials playing any role. In contrast to statutes and constitutional norms, contracts are formulated to achieve private objectives, not to set rules for public life. Although many contracts involve three or more parties, we shall concentrate on the common contract between two persons, or two companies, or one company and one person. Most of the discussion proceeds without distinguishing among kinds of contracts, although we shall examine some proposals by scholars that how contracts are interpreted should depend on their subject matter and on the sophistication of the parties, that, for example, prenuptial agreements should be regarded differently from sales contracts, and contracts between experienced business firms differently from contracts between individuals.[5]

This chapter does not touch, except in passing, on disputes over the content of the bargained terms of contracts, over whether parties have entered into contractual relations, and over whether contractual relations have been dissolved by subsequent events. The question of the existence of a contract is analogous to the question whether someone has made a valid will; but the answer to the question can be more complex and depends much less on formalities.[6] We will consider one kind of failure to make a contract—when interpretation of the terms of an intended agreement reveals a mistake that relieves the parties of their obligations. The next chapter addresses a set of questions about dissolution or judicial revision of terms because unexpected circumstances arise after a contract is formulated.[7]

II. BASIC ISSUES OF INTERPRETATION: OBJECTIVE V. SUBJECTIVE AND GENERAL V. CONTEXTUAL

We saw in connection with wills that if courts could reliably and easily know the specific intents of testators, fulfilling those intentions would be desirable, and we considered arguments that courts, nevertheless, should focus on general meanings of terms, because discerning particular intentions is difficult and because allowing individual understanding to trump objective meaning encourages sloppy drafting, creates temptations to lie, and engenders costly litigation. Placing a heavy burden of proof on someone who claims that a will was intended to have an application different from its apparent terms seemed a better judicial answer to these worries than imposing rigid restraints on evidence of what the testator intended by the terms of her will. Thus, a claimant might succeed if able to demonstrate convincingly that a testator understood the terms of her will in an idiosyncratic way or that she made a mistake in formulating the terms.

The analogous problems in contracts are similar but more complicated, because contexts may be richer and more variable, because the people involved may have had different understandings of what terms signified or different perceptions of what terms the contract contained, and because one party may realistically have been much more the author of terms than the other. Unlike the writer of a will, contractual parties are available to testify about what they intended, but when their relationship has frayed to the degree that brings them to court, each's report of what he believed is likely to be unreliable and self-serving.

The typical problem of ignorance about terms looks considerably different in contracts than it does in wills. The actual writer of a will, often a lawyer, is trying to carry out the desires of one person. Contracts involve bargains. Better terms for one side are worse terms for the other. Many contracts formed between large companies and individual purchasers (or users) are composed of forms that the individual must sign if she wishes to make a deal. Backs of forms may contain terms highly favorable to the company printed in small letters. Only an extremely conscientious (or compulsive) consumer reads through all these terms, let alone understands their significance; indeed it would often be irrational for the consumer to take the time and effort required to read and understand terms that are highly unlikely ever to make a difference. Courts and legislatures must decide whether such terms will have legal effect.

A related problem that arises for contracts, but not interpretation of wills, statutes, or constitutions, is that parties may believe their relations will not be governed by the terms of the written contract, but rather by principles of fair dealing.[8] Even a party aware of some unfavorable term may not believe her contracting partner will rely upon it. Suppose a salesman explains carefully that if you have a problem with the television set you are about to buy, the sales agreement provides you must seek redress from the manufacturer, not the store. You understand perfectly well but you still assume that if your television fizzles when you turn it on for the first time, the store will take it back and give you another. Your understanding of fair business practice differs from what you know are the written terms of your agreement. Whether judges should give effect to such understandings is a substantial question.[9]

Yet another difference between wills and some contracts concerns the wishes of their authors about techniques of interpretation. Each writer of a will is going to have her will interpreted only once. From her point of view, the best form of interpretation is the one which best promises to carry out the aims of her will.[10] For certain kinds of contracts, such as prenuptial agreements, the considerations are similar. But business firms that enter a large number of contracts in which they will be both buyers and sellers may well prefer a less expensive interpretive approach that will work best for them over the long run. If they suppose that they will be winners as often as losers when courts "get it wrong," they may prefer that courts interpret in an inexpensive, uncomplicated manner. Employing such an analysis, Alan Schwartz and Robert Scott argue that business firms dealing with each other should be able to get the standards of interpretation they want. Instead of seeking a "correct" approach to interpreting contracts, courts should treat the parties as sovereign about interpretation, adopting the "interpretive style parties [would typically] want courts to use when attempting to find the correct answer."[11] Most firms, the authors claim, will commonly prefer an objective "textual" approach that considers little, if any, extrinsic evidence.[12]

The fact that parties usually comply with contracts on their own can affect desirable methods of interpretation in litigated cases. If courts interpret particular terms in the same fashion, parties will be able to gauge more accurately how such terms will be treated; and this degree of predictability may reduce litigation. In this respect, systemic considerations like those that apply to standard form wills favor interpreting standard form contracts "objectively," so their terms will always mean the same thing. But it may be countered that parties will be more secure and less likely to litigate if they realize that will be held to ordinary trade usages and fair practices.

A. Objective and Subjective Elements

If we put aside system-wide concerns and ask what are the fairest and most desirable standards of interpretation for the parties to a contract, *and* we assume both that a court (with or without a jury) can accurately assess each party's understanding at acceptable expense and that the parties have not intended a form of interpretation that makes their specific understandings irrelevant,[13] the answer, across a range of cases, is a mix of objective and subjective elements.

A party's subjective intentions may diverge from the objective significance of contractual terms if the writing contains an error in one of the terms (or in punctuation), or the party is unaware of terms, or the party understands the terms differently from their most plausible meaning from an objective standpoint.

The error case is simple. S agrees to sell her painting to B for $1,000. When writing up the contract, S mistakenly adds an extra zero, so the contract reads "$10000". Because S is a new painter, whose work has no established market value, the error is not obvious from the face of the contract plus external facts (other than the parties' expressed intentions). If both parties agreed the painting was to sell for $1,000, fairness calls for that price, despite the mistake in the written contract.[14]

What if parties have different understandings of what the terms were meant to be, so that one party (honestly) thinks a mistake has been made and the other party (honestly) believes the written terms accurately reflect the agreement, or one party is ignorant of a term the other knows is in the contract? If the two parties are equally situated, if neither has an advantage in sophistication or bargaining power, a court ordinarily should enforce the written terms. Usually a person should be able to rely on a contract's terms without having to worry that the other party is under a misconception about what they are. Matters may be different when the terms are in form contracts and in fine print. Then a party who has written the form may be under some responsibility to meet likely misperceptions by the other about what the terms are. And even when parties are roughly equal, it may breach a requirement of "good faith" for one party self-consciously to gain an advantage based on its failure to remind the other party of a term that party is probably neglecting.[15]

In the more complex and interesting case, no one has made a mistake in writing down the terms of the contract, or neglected its terms, but at least one party understands the terms differently from what an objective reading would suggest. In a much rarer case, the parties have different understandings of some term, and neither understanding is more reasonable than the other.

Before we analyze these situations, we need to recognize nuances about "objective" understanding we have already reviewed for wills and instructions. Whereas a subjective approach is necessarily individual—its application depending on what specific persons (probably) believed—an "objective" approach may be more or less contextual. The "objective theory" of contracts is sometimes conceived as taking terms in a general way that abstracts from the details of any particular contractual relationship.[16] But if *the key* to an objective approach is a reliance upon external manifestations and events (understood not to include a person's mental states and his claims about those), an approach that asks what terms probably mean when used by people with the particular backgrounds and interactions of the parties can be "objective". That is, the terms would mean what a reasonable person aware of all the relevant circumstances would assume they mean in context. In the last chapter, we examined whether provision for deaths "coinciding" should have the same significance for any writer of a will or should be specially understood in the wills of a couple planning voyages on small boats in the South Pacific. The majority in *Rowland* came close to following an approach that was general as well as objective—"coinciding" meaning the same thing, and with similar applications, regardless of whose will is involved. But if one asked, "What would 'coinciding' probably mean to a young couple about to leave for the South Pacific and planning to take many voyages on small boats?", the answer would still be objective, not referring to the states of minds of any particular couple. Now, however, the objective standard would be highly contextualized.

In fact, exactly how to draw the line between what counts as objective and what counts as subjective is not simple. According to Corbin, "any meaning is an objective meaning if it is given to the word in any context by any person other than two contracting parties,"[17] but it is mistaken to suppose that a party can turn a claimed subjective understanding into an objective meaning by finding one other person who understands the terms in that way. Citing the treatise of Allan Farnsworth, David Slawson has written that the "objective theory of contracts . . . dictates that a contract shall have the meaning that a reasonable person would give it under the circumstances under which it was made, if he knew everything he should, plus everything the parties actually knew."[18] Insofar as this test makes relevant knowledge that the parties actually had which they had not revealed to outsiders and which outsiders would not reasonably have assumed, it introduces a subjective element into a test that is otherwise a contextualized objective one.

The most expansive notion of objective meaning may be any meaning revealed by external behavior, including conversations between the parties or involving the parties and third persons; but judges and juries are ill-suited to assess conflicting claims about what parties said in private. For practical purposes, I shall treat an inquiry as one about objective meaning so long as it is restricted to external manifestations, including customary practice, prior relations between the parties, memoranda about the contract itself, statements that were made to the other party before witnesses, and relations under the contract. If a party relies on a claimed state of mind that was not spoken, on an unrecorded oral conversation between the parties when no one else was present, or on a statement by her to a third person about what she had in mind, these count as assertions of her subjective understanding.

This brief analysis connects to four important points. (1) Once we recognize that an objective meaning can be contextual, we can see that the line between contextualized objective meaning and subjective meaning is blurry. Some judicial opinions framed in terms of objective versus subjective meaning could be reformulated in terms of how contextualized an objective meaning should be. (2) Whether, for practical purposes, a standard that is apparently subjective reaches beyond a contextualized objective approach depends heavily on just what evidence is allowed. Joseph Perillo has noted that in the late eighteenth and early nineteenth centuries when some judges and text writers suggested that the crucial inquiry concerned subjective understanding, parties were not allowed to testify.[19] Thus, the main sources of evidence needed to show that the parties' subjective understanding differed from a contextual objective understanding were unavailable. (3) The crucial practical question is which among many evidences about the meaning of contractual terms will be admitted, and what weight these various evidences will be given. (4) Finally, the chance of a discrepancy between the actual subjective understanding of both parties and the objective meaning of the terms they choose decreases as the evaluation of "objective" meaning becomes less general and more contextual. Even apart from circumstances when the parties are unaware of the written terms, we *can imagine* a situation of divergence between the parties' subjective understandings and the most contextualized objective understanding. A Canadian painter and an art dealer in New York who have always written sales contracts in dollars, meaning American dollars, are so discontented with U.S. foreign policy they decide to do a contract in dollars, meaning Canadian dollars; but the contract gives no indication of that and no outsider would guess at this particular method of protesting a country's foreign policy. The shared subjective understandings of the parties would differ from even a highly contextualized objective understanding of the term "dollars." Although we can conceive such situations, they will be very infrequent in real life.

Let me illustrate some of the issues I have raised with a fictional contract that a Croatian soccer star, Ivo Planić, signs to play for an American team, the Metro Stars, "during its season." Both Ivo and the Metro Stars representative who signs the contract understand that he will not be with the team during the weeks of training and exhibition games that precede the regular season. The team agrees to pay Ivo half of his salary even if he is injured before he joins it. During one of the last games of the European season, and after the Metro Stars has begun training, Ivo breaks his leg, precluding his playing for the American season. The team claims it owes him no money, because he breached the contract by not showing up at training camp. The judge concludes that the standard meaning of "during its season" includes training camp and exhibition games, but the judge also concludes that both parties understood the term differently on this occasion.[20]

In this circumstance, i.e., when the parties have had a common understanding (and putting aside any indications by the parties that *they* want a different form of interpretation), implementing that understanding is the fair approach. What other parties might mean when they employ the same terms is irrelevant.[21] Many modern courts do pay attention to the actual intent of the parties,[22] an approach straightforwardly provided under the Restatement (Second) of Contracts, Section 201(1), which says: "Where the parties have attached the same meaning to a promise or agreement or a term thereof, it is interpreted in accordance with that meaning."[23]

What reasons might a court have to interpret the term "during its season" according to what most people, or most people in the soccer business, or a reasonable person would understand? One might believe that figuring out what individual parties actually meant is too difficult, that adopting a generalized objective approach reduces incentives of parties to lie and that such an approach might even match actual intentions more often than an approach that seeks to determine individual understandings directly.[24] But let us assume here that the team president and Ivo told reporters after the signing that he would not have to report prior to the regular season. In that event, an uncontextualized objective approach could not reduce the likelihood of error about actual understandings of this particular contract term.

A court might, instead, rely on a conceptual argument that the meaning of a contract just does correspond with what its terms would convey in common usage or to reasonable observers. In what is sometimes called the classical conception of contracts, various writings may seem to reflect such a view. In one of his famous comments about contracts, Oliver Wendell Holmes suggested that the law does not concern itself with the actual mental states of individuals:

> "[N]o one will understand the true theory of contract . . . until he has understood that all contracts are formal, that the making of a contract depends not on the agreement of the two minds in one intention, but on the agreement of two sets of external signs—not in the parties having *meant* the same thing but on their having *said* the same thing."[25]

Learned Hand, one of our most distinguished appellate judges, put it colorfully:

> A contract has, strictly speaking, nothing to do with the personal, or individual, intent of the parties . . . . If . . . it were proved by twenty bishops that either party, when he used the words, intended something else than the usual meaning which the law imposes upon them, he would still be held . . .."[26]

This fully objective approach to the meaning of contractual language arose in the late nineteenth century in response to expressions that contracts require a "meeting of the minds."[27] Sweeping formulations of the objective approach may be understood as responsive to overstated notions about "the meeting of minds," and as attempts to render law more scientific,[28] rather than as refined evaluations of just when subjective intent should matter.

Any defense of an objective approach cast in terms of conceptual necessity would be misconceived. Earlier chapters have shown that interpreters, in general, face no logical compulsion to adopt an objective approach toward the meaning of texts. If two friends exchanging informal promises have a shared sense of meaning, they will be guided by that, not some objective meaning. The law of contracts could adopt the same perspective.

Holmes's objectivist stance was grounded in a utilitarian concern about a well-functioning legal system;[29] and those who now support a similar approach defend it on the basis that contracts will be better written and more economically or faithfully enforced if courts stick with objective meaning.[30] One might reasonably favor judges disregarding the possibility that both parties *shared* a meaning that deviates from a general one, if one thought that possibility was very infrequently realized.

We can conceive various approaches to deal with the problem of uncertainty about the actual subjective intentions of one or both parties. The simplest is to adhere to some form of general objective meaning in all (or almost all) circumstances. A second approach is to attend to "subjective understandings" or contextualized objective meaning only when an appraisal of common meaning leaves doubt, when that meaning is not plain. A third approach is to restrict the kinds of evidence courts may examine about subjective understanding, in order to assure that evidence is reliable, and to preclude any "end run" around the rule that oral understandings cannot supplant the provisions of integrated written contracts.[31] For example, courts might limit evidence to external manifestations other than oral conversations between the parties.[32] Finally, courts could be flexible and allow all sorts of evidence of subjective understandings but impose a heavy burden of proof on anyone who claims that both parties shared a meaning that varies from a general one. Unless that burden was met, a judge would follow the objective meaning. This last approach seemed the best for wills, and it might be best for contracts as well. However, before we can reach a thoughtful judgment about when evidence of subjective intentions should be admitted, we need to look carefully at how the plain meaning and parol evidence rules may affect contract interpretation. We also need to review the possibility that the most sensible approach to admitting evidence may vary according to the sophistication of parties and the subject matter of a contract. Also important is the particular version of "objective meaning" that might control, if courts do not inquire about the actual subjective intent of the parties. As I have said, if courts allow evidence of trade and local usages, *and* of various dealings between the parties, to establish a contextual "objective" meaning, the need to show subjective meaning will be much less frequent, because that meaning is much less likely to deviate from contextual objective meaning than from a general objective meaning.

Consider a case in which in 1937 a father, after a divorce, had agreed to pay his ex-wife $1,200 a year for his 10-year-old son "until" the son's "entrance . . . into . . . some college or . . . higher institution of learning beyond the completion of the high school grades," and then to pay $2,200 per year after his son's entrance to college for a period of that education but not for more than four years.[33] Upon completing high school in 1946, the son was immediately drafted into the army. Determining that the point of the trust agreement was to educate the son and provide maintenance for him while he was in his mother's custody, the court held that the father did not have to pay while his son was in the army. Only an exceptionally farsighted person in 1937 would have foreseen the son's induction in to the army; but some graduates of high school do work for a year or two and then enter college. Since these young people usually work at low paying jobs, a divorcing couple might or might not conceive that the father's obligation to contribute should continue during such a period. The more one understood about the father and mother—their expressed assumptions about children going to college immediately after high school, their backgrounds and levels of income, the father's comments about whether parents should be generous to children or encourage their self-reliance, the bitterness of the divorce—the more basis one would have to evaluate the significance of the agreed upon language for this circumstance.[34] One *might* regard a highly contextualized objective approach as an inquiry about how a reasonable person intimately familiar with both the father and mother, and the history of their relations, would take the language in their agreement.[35] There is no guarantee that the answer to that inquiry would fit what the parents actually had in mind, as revealed by their honest testimony at a trial or by their statements to each other about their intentions when the agreement was reached;[36] but the chance of a match would be much greater than if a court inquired only about the written language and what people in general who were using such a language would mean.

Whatever qualifications one might introduce for reasons of legal process and because the parties themselves may have wished to circumscribe the range of judicial inquiry, courts are faithful to the bargain parties actually struck if they give effect to their shared intended meaning over any opposed objective meaning.

B. Divergent Understandings

Matters become more complicated if the two parties do not share the same understanding. When one party's understanding squares with ordinary meaning and the other's does not, that understanding should typically be preferred. People should be able to assume that others take words in their ordinary sense; they should not be vulnerable to surprise claims that the words meant something special. This approach to situations when understandings diverge draws not only from systemic considerations but also fairness between the parties. As Melvin Eisenberg points out,[37] we can regard the approach as based on fault; the party with the less reasonable meaning is at fault for neither recognizing the other party's understanding nor informing her of his own understanding.

But this conclusion leaves open two important questions. Which should be dispositive: the *general* ordinary understanding or the understanding likely to exist among parties to this sort of contract? And might a court reasonably conclude that the party whose understanding fits a relevant objective one better should nevertheless lose because he bore more responsibility to have recognized the other's likely understanding or to have assured that the parties arrived at a shared understanding?

A variation on our soccer example, in which the team thinks "during its season" includes training camp but Ivo does not, can illustrate both issues. Suppose that in usage among people generally, "during its season" would usually be taken not to include training camp, but that within American sports contracts, including those of soccer leagues, "during its season" standardly includes training camp and exhibition games. Courts typically allow proof of trade and local usages, and these control even when the meaning is distinctively at odds with the popular meaning of terms.[38]

On behalf of a contention that his contrary understanding should control nevertheless, Ivo might offer two related arguments, one about meaning based on the objective circumstances of his situation, another about the responsibility to clarify possible misunderstandings.

Ivo was already under contract to play with a German team through the American team's exhibition season. Under an objective approach that looks only at the general meaning of terms and at common usage in a trade, this fact would be irrelevant. But the Metro Stars certainly had reason to learn of Ivo's existing contractual obligations, particularly since European players almost always accord priority to European competition. The team should have supposed that he would not have intended to break his German contract unless he explicitly, unambiguously said he would. The phrase "during its season" is imprecise enough to create doubt that someone signing a contract with that phrase, taken alone, would intend to break a conflicting contractual obligation. Thus, one might conclude that when a foreign athlete under contract to play abroad during a team's training camp and exhibition games signs a contract to play "during its season," the most reasonable meaning *in that context* is that "during its season" means only the regular season.[39] We see, as we did with the contract to support a son through college, that even if the controlling interpretation is to be objectively based on external circumstances, much depends on just how individualized is the context.

Ivo's related argument focuses on responsibility for any misunderstanding. The Metro Stars will contend that he should have been aware of the standard sense of the term "during its season" in soccer contracts, but he may respond that since he does not speak English well and because the team knew about his German contract, its representative should have told him precisely what "during its season" meant to it.[40] A judge might decide that the Metro Stars had much more reason to know of Ivo's meaning than he had to know of the team's meaning, even though the team's meaning comported with that in the industry.

The last century's history of contract law and scholarship suggests various approaches to divergent understandings. According to an objective approach that looks for the standard meaning of terms, the team would win. Recall that Hand talked about "the usual meaning which the law imposes upon [the parties]."[41] Such an approach leaves no room for argument that one party's unusual understanding should control.

The first Restatement, following Williston, employed a more complex objective approach to integrated contracts (those in which the writing is a final, complete expression of the agreement). The standard of interpretation was "'the meaning that would be attached . . . by a reasonably intelligent person' familiar with all operative usages and knowing all the circumstances other than oral statements by the parties about what they intended the words to mean."[42] This standard leaves us uncertain how to resolve Ivo's case. Much depends on just *how* individualized the relevant circumstances are taken to be. Would the "reasonably intelligent person" know of Ivo's contractual obligation with the German team and that virtually no European players would sacrifice the end of the European season for American training camp? (The Restatement section clearly bars consideration of oral statements about what the terms mean, but should a court allow evidence that the team and Ivo's did not discuss what "during its season" means?) If a judge did consider *all* the individual circumstances, he might well conclude that "during its season" meant only the regular season in this particular contract.

The Restatement (First) section on unintegrated contracts provided that "words or other manifestations of intention forming an agreement . . . are given the meaning which the party making the manifestations should reasonably expect that the other party would give to them."[43] This is yet another form of objective approach, but one that makes crucial a reasonable appraisal that a party who has formulated the disputed words would make of the other party's understanding. If the team developed the terms of an unintegrated contract having reason to know of a player's responsibilities to his German team, it could reasonably expect that he would take "during its season" in the narrower sense of "regular season" (especially since someone who had been playing in European competition would be in excellent condition).

The Restatement (Second) reflects Arthur Corbin's partly subjective approach to divergent understandings. Corbin suggested that a party should be able "to determine the operative meaning of the words of agreement by proving . . .that he so understood them and the other party knew that he did, or . . . had reason to know that he did."[44] In requiring someone like Ivo to show that he *did understand* "during its season" in the narrower sense (not that he reasonably would have done so), and in allowing him then to succeed if the team was (subjectively) aware of his understanding (whether or not it should have been), this approach relies on two subjective elements that the Restatement (First) disregarded. The Restatement (Second) provides that if one party actually knows the meaning attached by the other, that meaning prevails if the other does not know of the meaning attached by the first party (even if he had reason to).[45] Thus, if the Metro Stars knew how Ivo understood "during its season" and he was unaware of the team's contrary understanding, a court would adopt his understanding.

According to the Restatement (Second), the meaning attached by one party also prevails if that party "had no reason to know of any different meaning attached by the other, and the other had reason to know the meaning attached by the first party."[46] The spirit of this provision would support Ivo's claim that the team should have realized he did not plan to join it in training camp. But the section's literal language creates an obstacle to reaching this conclusion. Any party has *some* reason to learn the standard meaning of crucial terms, so Ivo had *some* reason to know the meaning the team might attach to the term indicating when he had to report for duty. In contrasting "no reason to know" with "reason to know," the Restatement does not explicitly address the situation in which each party has some reason to know the meaning attached by the other, but one of the two has a much stronger reason. (One would assume that "no reason" would include, at least, an extremely slight reason.) Our soccer example suggests that, when each party has failed to learn the other's meaning, *A* should prevail if *B* has substantially more reason to know *A*'s meaning than *A* has to know *B*'s meaning. In assessing reason to know, a court should take account of unequal bargaining power, imposing on the dominant partner a greater responsibility to learn than on the weaker partner, especially if the dominant partner chooses terms which the weaker party has little or no opportunity to contest or change.[47] In this way, a policy of fairness in contractual obligations would influence application of "reason to know."

The modern approach of Corbin, the Restatement (Second), and the U.C.C.[48] seems fairer to the individual parties in instances of divergent understandings than any alternative.[49] Until relatively recently, it seemed that this approach had largely won the day against the classical approach;[50] but it turns out not only that many courts continue to adhere to general meaning, some noted scholars defend that approach, at least for contracts between business firms.[51] They argue that attention to subjective understandings will lead to error and unduly burden both the courts and the parties themselves. We shall consider the possible roles of "plain meaning" and the parol evidence rule in establishing standards of interpretation and restricting forms of evidence, after we have examined another kind of situation courts occasionally face.

C. Divergent Understandings When There Is No Dominant Objective Meaning and Neither Party Is at Fault; and Vague and Incomplete Terms

What if the two parties attach different meanings to a provision, neither is more at fault than the other, and neither has greater reason to perceive the divergent understanding. Obligating either party to the understanding of the other would be unfair. The Restatement (Second) provides that if "(a) neither party knows or has reason to know the meaning attached by the other; or, (b) each party knows or has reason to know the meaning attached by other," there is no manifestation of mutual assent.[52] We might say that the agreement has no meaning in the crucial respect or that it had two meanings, between which the court will not choose.[53]

A classic case exemplifies this rule.[54] Two people contracted for a shipment of cotton from Bombay on the ship Peerless; the two had in mind different ships by that name that were leaving from Bombay on different dates, and neither party had reason to know of the existence of the ship that the other had in mind.[55] The court held that there was no contractual obligation.[56] The Restatement reflects the traditional assumption that when the *Peerless* conditions are satisfied, no contract exists. The exact rationale and breadth of the governing principle have proved puzzling.[57]

Before we engage some of the nettlesome issues, it helps to clarify two points about an appropriate approach and the Restatement. First, the Restatement covers situations in which two parties have different meanings and "each party knows or has reason to know the meaning attached by the other." This language might seem to put "knowing" and "having reason to know" on an equal footing. But if *A* knows what *B* understands, and *B* is ignorant of what *A* understands (though *B* has reason to know *A*'s understanding), *B* should prevail over *A* who is fully aware that *B* is harboring a different understanding and does nothing to straighten things out. This result is indeed provided by another Restatement section.[58]

The second "clarification," about "has reason to know," follows what we concluded about a party prevailing when it had no reason to know the other party's different meaning and the other party had reason to know of its meaning.[59] This section should be interpreted *not* to apply when each party (ignorant of the other's understanding) has *some* reason to know the meaning of the other, but one party has much more substantial reason to know than does the other. Thus, the soccer "contract" should not be a candidate for invalidation under this section, if the team had *much more reason* to know Ivo's understanding than he had to know the team's understanding.

One way of understanding a well-known case about the sale of "chicken" is in this light.[60] The term "chicken" might have meant chicken suitable for broiling and frying or have also included older, less valuable stewing chicken or "fowl." Judge Henry Friendly considered the term "chicken" ambiguous and explored various reasons to interpret it one way or the other in the contract. He resolved that the seller understood the term to include stewing chicken and that this coincided with *an* objective meaning. He apparently credited the buyer's claim that it intended to obtain broilers or fryers, but he did not need to settle that issue, because the buyer had failed to carry the burden of showing that "chicken" had been used in the narrower way. We might suppose that each party had some basis to perceive the ambiguity in "chicken" and to wonder what the other party was thinking, but that the buyer had *more* reason to be aware of the seller's understanding than the seller had reason to be aware of the buyer's understanding.[61]

Although the *Peerless* principle, when applied, has apparently always resulted in a determination that no contract has been formed, that consequence may not be called for if the misunderstanding is genuine but of trivial importance.[62] Imagine this variation on *Peerless*. The two ships, sailing from Bombay, are to arrive two days apart. *B*, the buyer, has understood "the Peerless" to be the first ship to arrive. After *B*'s agent in Bombay wires that no cotton was packed onto the first Peerless, *B* inquires of *S*, the seller, why she did not load the cotton. *S*, up to that moment planning to ship the cotton on the second Peerless, now realizes that she and *B* had different ships in mind. Because the price of cotton has risen substantially since she and *B* settled the contract price, she would like to walk away from the agreement. She wires *B* that the original misunderstanding about the ship precluded the existence of any contract. *B* responds that he is willing to be bound by *S*'s original understanding and to receive cotton on the second Peerless. After *S* refuses to ship any cotton, *B* seeks to enforce the contract, accepting *S*'s original understanding. Although the defect in this agreement is of the same nature as in *Peerless*, perhaps it should not stand in the way of enforcement by a party who is willing to accept an original understanding held by the other party.[63] If this is so, a *Peerless*-type misunderstanding could be seen as a serious defect in an agreement intended to be a contract, to be treated usually as vitiating contractual obligations, but sometimes as producing an interpretation of terms of an enforceable contract less favorable to the party who seeks enforcement.[64] In any event, *Peerless* cases are unusual instances in law in which courts decide that language which would normally carry authority and which the drafters intended to be specific is given no effect.

We now arrive at the central question of when a *Peerless* misunderstanding does exist. Parties to contracts often employ terms that neither understands very well and they often employ vague terms like "sufficient water," neither party having in mind a precise amount that is taken to be sufficient.[65] Courts undertake to interpret and apply such terms in a reasonable way, and they go further and supply terms that have been omitted altogether. The general idea is that if parties have meant to bind themselves to contractual obligations, courts should effectuate that purpose, even when judges may have to determine matters about which the parties have had no specific understanding.

There is some limit. Parties are not bound if the mutual undertaking is *too* vague.[66] For example, if W promises to work for E in return for E being "generous" to W, there would be no contract. However, courts are generally willing to interpret contractual provisions that are substantially vague, at least if the parties could not comfortably arrive at more specific measures for which performance could be verified;[67] and the U.C.C. and Restatement go very far in that direction.[68] In this respect, the law of wills is much stricter; courts are less willing to give content to vague terms. Insofar as one can defend the difference between wills and contracts, it has to do, on the one hand, with the legal formality of wills and with the predictability of the situations that may arise in the future, as compared with the informality of many contracts, and with the need for contractual relations to continue under unforeseeable changing external circumstances.

This account of differences, it must be admitted, is somewhat circular. A woman leaving most of her property to children with a life estate for her husband, might worry that all sorts of unpredictable events could affect just what share she would want each child to receive when her husband dies. Nevertheless, she must set out the shares when she writes her will. One obvious difficulty with leaving shares open is that she will not be around to make a later decision, and, if someone else is left to decide, under an instruction, say, to "distribute taking into account the characters of the children and their economic needs," too much will be unsettled.[69] Whereas the law has a policy against the writers of wills leaving so much undetermined in light of future contingencies, it has a policy favoring contractual flexibility to deal with changing commercial conditions.

Thus, the full point is more complicated than a simplistic idea that conditions facing will writers are more predictable than those facing contractors.

Courts have not commonly held apparent contracts to be invalid because of divergent understandings of terms, and this caution seems appropriate. William Young has argued persuasively that the typical application of *Peerless* should be when terms are equivocal or ambiguous, not when they are vague.[70] "Sufficient water" is a vague term. "The ship Peerless" or "a quart bottle" can be an ambiguous term, giving rise to two quite precise but different meanings.[71] Determining whether a phrase is vague rather than ambiguous is not always simple. "During its season" is at least somewhat vague; but if the expression has come to mean *either* (1) the complete season beginning with training camp *or* (2) the "regular" season of games that count in the standings, the phrase has become an ambiguous term with one of two precise meanings.[72] Similarly, as to "chicken," a general, somewhat vague, term could, in contracts for chicken to be eaten, come to mean either (1) chicken suitable for frying or broiling, or (2) chicken more broadly including stewing chicken.[73] As Young points out, many cases call for informed practical judgment; whether to apply the *Peerless* principle cannot be resolved by linguistic classification alone.[74] We will examine the courts' practice of filling in vague terms in more detail in a later section.

C. Plain Meaning and Parol Evidence Rules

Restrictive rules may bar certain kinds of evidence in contracts cases and they may preclude any external evidence if the meaning of the contractual language is regarded as plain. Modern courts standardly allow evidence about trade and local usages. However plain the ordinary language of a provision may appear, a party may show a contrary trade or local usage. What is at issue is whether a party can show more individualized contexts, including prior dealings between the parties, negotiations, and the course of performance, to overcome a meaning that appears clear if one looks only at the written text of the contract.

According to the parol evidence rule, an integrated written contract supplants and terminates any prior agreements; thus courts will not consider evidence of undertakings that may supplement the terms of an integrated written contract if one would expect such undertakings to be in the written contract.[75] Application of the bar on evidence of *supplementary* terms does not, in theory, turn on whether the written terms are clear.

A clear conceptual division would treat the plain meaning rule as about *interpreting* the provisions of contracts, and the parol evidence rule as about establishing what count as the controlling terms of integrated contracts; and Arthur Corbin consistently maintained that the parol evidence rule had nothing to do with interpretation.[76]

Two complications render matters less sharp. The first is that, as with regard to wills, courts have spoken, and continue to speak, with some frequency of the parol evidence rule as restricting evidence about the meaning of contractual terms.[77] When a court allows certain evidence, but not other evidence, to contravene apparent meaning, it may be awkward to speak of a plain meaning rule, which usually excludes all evidence. Many courts draw no clear distinction between a plain meaning rule and a parol evidence rule when it comes to interpretation.

The second, more subtle, point is this: the distinction between evidence about the meaning of language and evidence about supplementary terms can blur if parties are free to use language as they choose. Thus, a party may claim that an omitted term was "implicit" in the contract's language as a way to escape any bar on showing supplementary terms.

Consider a case in which the court gave effect to the literal language of a contract that provided that if a couple who owned property obtained a *bona fide* purchaser, another couple could "exercise their right to purchase said premises at a value equivalent to the market value of the premises according to the [tax] assessment rolls . . . ."[78] Nine years later, the surviving owner, who wanted to sell, received offers of $35,000 and $30,000. Her contractual partners then tendered the widow $7,820, twice the assessed value on the tax rolls.[79] The Pennsylvania Supreme Court said the meaning of the terms was plain, and therefore that intent was to be discovered only from the contract's express language; the trial judge had erred in admitting testimony that the formula was meant to serve as "a mutual protective minimum price . . . ."[80]

So long as Mrs. Steuart claimed that *in addition* to the terms of the contract, she and the McChesneys had agreed that they would pay a fair price in terms of actual market value, a court that had first decided that the contract was integrated would bar her testimony according to the parol evidence rule.[81] If she claimed, instead, that the term "the market value of the premises according to the [tax] assessment rolls" *embodied* an implicit assumption that the value on the assessment rolls would approximate half of market value (and that the county's failure to keep its rolls up to date meant that a condition for operation of the contract was not fulfilled), the claim would be one about how to interpret the contractual language, not about supplementing it.[82] In that event, a parol evidence rule that was strictly limited to evidence about supplementary terms would not prevent her testimony. Only a plain meaning rule, if applicable, (or a broader parol evidence rule that covers interpretation) would stand in her way. If Steuart claimed that the overall purpose of the contract was to assure a fair price between friendly neighbors, with no one seeking an economic advantage but rather with her and her husband trying to accommodate the desires of the McChesneys to buy an adjoining property, it might be hard to say whether the claim would concern supplementation or on an interpretation of the written terms that focuses on purpose. Yet the same actual conversations among the owners and their neighbors could give rise to any of these three claims. Here the difference between adding terms and interpreting terms would have more to do with legal ingenuity than substance. Thus, one might defend a parol evidence rule that covers interpretation as necessary to protect the force of the rule against claims of supplementary agreements.[83]

We can see how such a view might work in relation to reliance on preliminary documents leading up to an integrated contract. Such documents cannot establish independent terms of agreement that one would have expected to find in the final contract, but the documents can assist understanding of the terms of the final contract, showing what the parties were aiming to do or resolutions they rejected.[84] A ban on prior proposals to help interpret contracts might be justified as preventing deviations from the terms on which the parties finally agreed.[85]

In summary, the relation between the terms "plain meaning rule" and "parol evidence rule" can be confusing, both because courts often do not draw clear distinctions and because the border between claims of supplementation and interpretation is often blurred.

In the remainder of this section, we will focus on a rule that bars external evidence about meaning. If "the rule" is one that declares that "the plain meaning," if one can be found, is the legally relevant meaning, whatever the parties intended and whatever a more contextualized inquiry might reveal, then the rule is one of substantive law, not evidence. A genuine rule of evidence bars evidence that could help establish a proposition that is legally relevant.[86]

To speak of a "rule" as if all evidence is allowed or all evidence is barred is a considerable oversimplification. As Professors Schwartz and Scott explain, one may speak of a minimum evidentiary base "composed of the parties' contract, a narrative concerning whether the parties performed the obligations that the contract appears to require, a standard English language dictionary, and the interpreter's experience and understanding of the world." To this evidentiary base, courts have added "(1) the parties' practice under prior agreements; (2) the parties' practice under the current agreement; (3) testimony as to what was said during the negotiations; (4) written precontractual documents (memoranda, prior drafts, letters); and (5) [relevant] industry custom . . . ."[87] As courts admit more of these forms of evidence, they move toward a maximum evidentiary base that allows them to decide what, "all things considered,"[88] the parties intended—the evidentiary base favored by "contextualists." One way of characterizing this movement from a restricted minimum base toward a fuller one is as a shift from a formal to a substantive approach.[89]

A plain meaning rule bars evidence, not only of the parties' subjective understandings, but also of what a reasonable outsider would understand in light of the entire course of dealing of the parties. Indeed, in most cases discussing the plain meaning rule, the attempt is to introduce just such evidence of what the agreement meant "objectively" in context. Ross and Tranen write that, for contracts as well as statutes, "the real controversy is not whether to apply an objective or a subjective approach to meaning, but whether to consider evidence . . . that demonstrates in an objective way how the parties manifested their subjective intentions."[90]

A case in which a court distinguished between evidence of subjective understanding and of contextualized objective meaning is *Home Insurance Co. v. Chicago and Northwestern Transportation Co.*[91] The Seventh Circuit Court of Appeals had to decide if a provision in the contract limiting damages covered an accident between freight cars and commuter cars for which CNW was negligent. The court said it would admit "objective" evidence of ambiguity that a person familiar with "the context of the contract would know that the contract means something other than what it seems to mean" but would not admit "subjective" evidence of ambiguity about what the parties believed the contract means, "which is invariably self-serving, inherently difficult to verify and thus, inadmissible."[92]

Whether a rule should bar any evidence of how the parties did understand, or how a detached observer would understand, the terms of the contract is controversial.[93] The traditional or conservative approach allows evidence of actual subjective understandings or contextualized objective meaning only if the terms of the contract are vague or ambiguous. The Uniform Commercial Code, the Second Restatement, and many state courts have abandoned this restraint; they permit evidence of context that would lead a reasonable outsider viewing the contract to assign a meaning that was different from the standard meaning.[94] Under this liberal approach, Ivo could introduce his contract with the German team to show that he and the Metro Stars reasonably supposed that his contract with it covered only the regular season.

In the chapter on wills, we have reviewed and rejected the assertion that a plain meaning rule is actually incoherent. The force of the claim that, because all language is vague or ambiguous to some degree, meaning can never be plain, depends considerably on how "plain meaning" is to be understood, and particularly on how far an investigation of meaning considers at least some matters of context. A claim that meaning is plain, absent all reference to context, may indeed be incoherent about many communications, but meaning in certain familiar contexts is often clear. Suppose that for decades, "during its season" has, in contracts between athletes and American teams, included the entire season beginning with training camp. If one asks about the meaning of the phrase for American sports contracts in general, the meaning *is* plain.[95]

When one further particularizes context, meaning may become less plain. As Avery Katz writes, "what meaning is plain will be agent-specific and context-specific."[96] If one asks about the meaning of "during its season" in a contract with a foreign athlete who is already under contract to play elsewhere during the period of the training camp and exhibition games, the meaning becomes less obvious than if one asks about sports contracts in general. As the inquiry becomes further contextualized, the chances may increase that a meaning that seems plain, in general, will seem plain no longer, although sometimes the reverse will happen—that is, the richer, more specific, context will make meaning more plain.

As we have seen, as the inquiry about meaning becomes more contextualized, the chances that actual subjective understanding will vary from apparent meaning diminish significantly. If a judge is free to look at the social circumstances and past dealings of the parties, putting himself in the position of an extremely well-informed outsider, he is likely to discover any special or idiosyncratic meaning the parties shared. Once a judge initially determines that in the specific context a term most probably meant one thing, a party trying to show that she meant something different, *and* that either the other party agreed with her *or* that she should prevail over the party whose understanding fits what the court would expect, will carry an extremely heavy burden.

Putting aside convenience of administration, which some parties may desire, and the possibility that a restrictive rule will encourage better drafting of contracts and more faithful adherence to their terms, courts have no solid reason to refuse evidence that explains the full context of a contract. Should they bar evidence of subjective understandings that differ from what a contextual objective approach indicates about the meaning of terms? At the very least, courts should set a high burden of proof that a contract means other than what it seems to mean in context. Two reasons to bar such evidence altogether are the opportunity it presents for lying[97] and the slim chance that it will make a difference. In favor of admitting the evidence is the difficulty of winnowing out evidence of subjective understandings while allowing evidence of contextual objective meaning, and the judgment that if two parties have really shared a bizarre understanding, it should be recognized.[98]

Exactly how much evidence to admit of contextual objective meaning and of subjective understandings may well depend of the kind of contract involved. One article suggests that the complexity of a contract's provisions matters for interpretation but that no straightforward correlation exists between a contract's degree of simplicity and the liberality with which it should be interpreted.[99] Because the reasons why contracts are simple (or complex) differ significantly, so also does the appropriate interpretive response; the reactions of judges should depend on the reasons for simplicity (and complexity) they can identify.

III. PUBLIC POLICY AND INTERPRETATION: FAIRNESS TO THE PARTIES AND OTHER-REGARDING INTERESTS

Public policy considerations involving fairness between the parties or more general public interests can play a part in contractual interpretation and enforcement. Just how much part they should play is now controversial.

A. Unenforceability and Unconscionability

Most straightforwardly, public policy can bar the enforcement of contracts. Courts refuse to enforce agreements to commit criminal acts[100] or to engage in other undesirable behavior. For example, even in jurisdictions that allow private gambling, courts generally will not compel participants to pay gambling debts. In some instances, courts are able to save the rest of a contract and excise an offending term, but often an agreement that contemplates action that violates public policy is treated as invalid altogether. When that happens, the crucial decision is not about how to interpret the contract but whether to give it effect.

A major doctrine of unenforceability involves contracts that are "unconscionable," seriously unfair in how one party treats the other.[101]

Contractual terms may be "unconscionable" because one party lacked a reasonable chance to perceive and understand terms that seem unfair, or because the terms are unfair even if fully understood. Often the threads of informational failure and unfair terms are tangled. In *Williams v. Walker-Thomas Furniture Co.*,[102] the contract provided that if Williams failed to make a payment on the last appliance she had purchased on credit, the merchant could recover every item on which she had an outstanding balance, however slight. Whether Williams, a welfare recipient, understood the exact force of the crucial clause was doubtful, but even if she did, the merchant may have relied on unequal bargaining power to impose unfair terms on her.[103]

Here is an imaginary case of unfairness that does not involve an informational deficit. A woman with a boat discovers a wealthy man marooned on a remote island with adequate food and shelter. She says, "I'll save you, if you give me one half of your wealth; think about it as long as you want. I'll stop back every few days." After the man carefully weighs his options for two weeks, he accepts the terms. (According to a standard distinction between procedural and substantive unconscionability, one might think this agreement raises only a problem of substantive unconscionability; but unequal bargaining power is considered one form of procedural unconscionability, and the boater, as the only person aware of the man's situation, has unequal bargaining power.) At least in some circumstances, a well-informed, fully competent party who has rationally chosen to accept a bargain may still be able to claim unconscionability.[104]

Although the common consequence of a determination of unconscionability is nonenforcement of the entire contract or of the unconscionable term, a court may explicitly rewrite the terms of a contract to make them fair. UCC §2-302 provides that a court may "limit application of any unconscionable clause to avoid any unconscionable results."

The New Jersey Supreme Court was even more creative in *Vasquez v. Glassboro Service Association, Inc.*[105] Vasquez, a migrant worker from Puerto Rico living in quarters provided by a farm labor service organization, was discharged and was not permitted to remain overnight.

Represented by the Farmworkers Corporation, he claimed that he could not be deprived of his living quarters except by judicial process. Emphasizing the extreme inequality in the contract between Glassboro and Vasquez, the court concluded that, by failing to provide a reasonable time to find alternative housing, the contract was against public policy and unconscionable as sought to be enforced against Vasquez.[106] The court rewrote a term of the contract to assure workers a reasonable time to find other housing.[107] Rather than employing self-help, that is, simply putting workers out, the company had to proceed judicially to dispossess workers of housing, a course allowing judges to fashion appropriate remedies for stranded workers.

As far as interpretation is concerned, the more significant situations do not involve judges refusing to enforce terms or explicitly rewriting them, but reaching conclusions based on public policy and fairness that contractual terms do not mean what they seem to say. According to Section 203 (a) of Restatement (Second): "an interpretation which gives a reasonable, lawful, and effective meaning to all the terms is preferred to an interpretation which leaves a part unreasonable, unlawful, or of no effect . . . ."[108] Section 207 covering contracts that affect a public interest provides that in "choosing among . . . reasonable meanings . . . , a meaning that serves the public interest is generally preferred."[109] Comment c to Section 203 indicates that courts should not stretch too far to interpret contracts to make them lawful or reasonable.[110] They should choose such a meaning over an unlawful or unreasonable meaning when both are plausible; but they should not, in the guise of interpretation, adopt an implausible acceptable meaning over a plausible meaning that is not acceptable.[111] This comment states that "The search is for the manifested intention of the parties."[112]

The approach of interpreting contracts to be reasonable and consistent with the public interest bears interesting comparison with the effort of courts to interpret statutes so that they are constitutional. Just how far courts should strain ordinary meaning in that setting is controversial, but some important decisions give statutes otherwise implausible renderings in order to save them from invalidity, or even from constitutional doubt. Courts are hesitant to say that legislatures have acted invalidly, and declarations of invalidity of general statutes are of substantial moment. Saying that a private contract is unlawful carries much less practical import and involves no insult to a coordinate branch of government. Further, courts may explicitly substitute lawful for unlawful terms in a contract; they are more limited in the extent to which they can rework statutes.

What is more troublesome is whether in interpreting contractual provisions, courts should rely on public policies that parties could freely disregard if they did so by the explicit terms of the contract. A broad doctrine of interpreting contracts to be reasonable and in the public interest cannot be seen as simply a device to help carry out the likely intentions of the parties, because parties together may believe that their mutual advantage will be served by an agreement that fails to conform with the broad pubic interest, as a court will see it. In preferring a reasonable meaning to an unreasonable one, Section 203 of the Restatement (Second) signals that considerations of reasonableness should matter when competing interpretations are plausible, even beyond what fairness might indicate about the parties' intentions.[113]

One aspect of this encouragement of interpretation to yield a fair result is acknowledgment of a connection between degrees of assent and modes of interpretation. For many contracts, thinking of assent to terms as being equal is unrealistic. One party understands terms it has chosen; the other party signs on with little choice or understanding of many specific terms and with little awareness whether a better deal is "out there" somewhere. Generalizing from some examples, William Woodward has written, "[T]he smaller the contract and the more obscure or complex the term, the greater the chance that the nondrafter's true understanding of the deal—an understanding adequate to evaluate and 'price' the exchange—will deviate from what is in the writing."[114] By leaning toward an interpretation of terms that is fair, a court redresses an imbalance in assent to a degree. This reality suggests the more pervasive question how far courts interpreting authoritative language should take into account the conditions of its adoption, construing language in a manner that will compensate for imperfections in that process.

The rule that contracts that affect the public interests should generally be interpreted to serve the public interest has been mainly applied in cases dealing with public franchises and tax exemptions, discouraging courts from granting sweeping concessions to private interests that legislatures have not clearly provided. However, Corbin indicates that the rule is not restricted to such contracts,[115] and a recent article enumerates some other situations, including standard form contracts, in which the rule has been invoked.[116]

Some scholars have rejected public policy as an independent guide to interpretation over the range in which parties could freely contract.[117] Arguing that contract law should help parties carry out their aims, they urge that interpretation should follow what parties have probably (or probably would have) agreed to. In part, the idea is that sophisticated parties will simply need to expend more effort in writing terms if courts will use public policy to interpret vague terms to their disadvantage; in part the idea is that public policy is better served by independent branches of law, such as the law of marriage and divorce, environmental law, and labor relations law, than by judges trying to achieve public polices in interpreting contracts.[118] Perhaps it can be shown that for many kinds of contracts, interpreting in accord with public policy is unproductive or unnecessary or both, but we should not assume that because of some principle of autonomy,[119] contract interpretation in general should be free from the influence of public-regarding considerations when judges must choose between competing plausible readings of contractual terms. True it may be that parties can disregard some public policies, but so also can the writers of wills and legislators. If courts properly give weight to public policies in interpreting the texts of wills and statutes, they should not wholly disregard such policies when they interpret contracts.

IV. EXPRESSION RULES AND INTERPRETATION

Contractual interpretation is partly characterized by what Melvin Eisenberg calls "expression rules," which are narrower and may diverge in application from general principles of interpretation.[120] Eisenberg writes mainly about such problems in the law of offer and acceptance,[121] but he notes that expression rules also exist for the interpretation of contractual terms. For example, under a traditional rule about employment contracts that do not state a duration, a court will conclude that either party may terminate the employment at will, even if more general interpretive principles might yield a different understanding.[122] Another example may be the rule that insurance contracts are interpreted against the insurer. This specific rule carries forward a more general principle that contracts should be interpreted against the party that is more knowledgeable and controls and drafts terms. But if a medium-size insurance company gives pollution insurance to one of the country's largest corporations, whose representatives participate actively in drafting crucial language, the specific rule for insurance contracts would no longer be supported by broader principles of interpretation.

Relying on a discussion of John Rawls's, Eisenberg points out that an expression rule may be a maxim, a presumption, or a categorical rule.[123] A nonbinding maxim is loosely a *technique* of interpretation, of the kind familiar in statutory interpretation. A court need not reach the result to which the maxim points if the balance of reasons suggests a different result. A categorical rule must be followed, however strong the countervailing reasons.[124] A presumption lies in the middle; it is followed unless a party proves that an expression should have a different effect.

Eisenberg suggests that if the only concern were avoiding misguided decisions ("error" in whatever sense error is understood) that could support a maxim or presumption, but not a categorical rule; the reason is that sticking with a narrow rule does not make sense when one sees overwhelming reasons to proceed differently.[125] This leaves administrative justifications—convenience for judges and lawyers in settling disputes[126]—to explain why judges might adopt an expression rule that is categorical or creates a strong presumption. Thus, if courts want to adopt a uniform approach to the language of insurance contracts, and they know that insurers usually draft the language and impose terms on less knowledgeable insureds, they have an administrative reason to interpret language against insurers, whatever the actual relations of a particular insurer and insured.

V. FILLING IN TERMS

Although modern American courts interpreting written contracts do not typically disregard specific terms that seem in tension with the overall purposes of the contracting parties,[127] they will often provide content for indefinite terms and supply terms that the parties have omitted.[128] A common example is a contract that omits the time for performance; a court will require performance in a reasonable time. This power does not involve the court in changing a contract's explicit terms but in fashioning new ones. Yet, we do not find the same explicit power in the law of wills or in statutory and constitutional interpretation. Charles Goetz and Robert Scott describe a major shift from a traditional "presumption that the parties' writings and the official law of contract are the definitive elements of the agreement" to a law in which "evidence derived from experience and practice can now trigger the incorporation of additional, implied terms."[129]

Professor Scott, however, has claimed that the trend toward filling in incomplete terms has not gone as far as most scholars have supposed.[130] In a significant percentage of cases, courts will not enforce agreements that the parties deliberately leave incomplete, refusing to fill in terms that do not depend on events outside the contract and that could have been made specific, and whose performance could have been verified by the party to whom the obligations would have been owed.[131] Employing experimental analysis of behavior motivated by a sense of reciprocal fairness, as well as economic analysis of potential gains and losses to parties that deliberately leave unspecified terms such as the standards for a bonus, Scott claims that we can understand why parties rationally choose this course, depending on self-enforcement.[132] He further concludes that if the courts fill in such terms when parties bring such agreements to court, doing so could be socially inefficient.[133]

When courts do imply new terms for contracts, we can understand them as relying on four not always separable bases. One is the language of the express contract; thus, when an owner contracted to "transport" goods on his barge, the Supreme Court found an implied promise to supply the tug to tow the barge.[134] A second basis is the conduct of the parties. A third is standard usage in the trade. Finally, courts may imply terms that fit with legal policies.

Exactly how does this power to "fill in" terms relate to interpretation, and why do courts have this power for contracts? One technique that is used both for interpretation of ambiguities and for filling in omissions is to ask about a hypothetical bargain: what would the parties have agreed to had they specifically addressed this issue?[135] Courts often speak of an implied term, drawn from the provisions to which the parties have agreed. "Where there is tacit agreement or a common tacit assumption or where a term can be supplied by logical deduction from agreed terms and circumstances, interpretation may be enough."[136] In some instances, one may be hard put to say whether what is needed is a direct interpretation of existing terms or filling in of new ones.[137] Recall the case in which the father had promised to pay $1,200 per year for his son's upkeep "until" the son's entrance into college, and then $2,200 for his college years. The issue whether the father owed money for time his son spent in the army after being drafted could be understood as an interpretation of the significance of "until" in the context of the operative sentence in the agreement. But one might look at the agreement and respond, "The divorcing couple did not address the possibility of army service (or other work) between high school and college, so the question is how to fill in for this unforseen contingency." Even when a term is undoubtedly omitted, the court's exercise may not be so different from when it interprets an ambiguous term.

The Restatement (Second) adopts a different approach; as one of its comments explains, "where there is in fact no agreement, the court should supply a term which comports with community standards of fairness and policy rather than analyze a hypothetical model of the bargaining process."[138] One defense of this suggestion could be that courts cannot easily discern what parties would have done about matters they did not address; but administrative convenience also counts. If courts employ standards of fairness and policy to fill in omitted terms, perhaps they can treat similar contracts similarly, not worrying about what individual parties would have agreed to. This approach may have the further advantage that parties making contracts can rely on courts to supply "default" terms when negotiation of terms would be time-consuming and contentious, and unlikely to be relevant over the life of a contract, and the parties can inform themselves about what terms a court will supply, should unexpected circumstances require one.[139]

For courts that regard their job of "filling in" as drawing out the implications of the entire contract and deciding what term the parties themselves would have supplied, any distinction between discerning meaning and constructing meaning is blurred. But courts that rely mainly on standards of fairness and policy, apart from how those relate to the parties' likely intentions, have departed from trying to carry out just what the contractual language suggests that the parties wanted.

This subject is further complicated by the duty of good faith and fair dealing that contractual parties must assume.[140] Whether or not this duty is an independent source of contractual obligations, it can guide the way an agreement's terms are understood.[141] Judges who rely on that duty to fill in omitted terms may be seen as interpreting the entire contract.

Why are courts more willing to "fill in" terms in contracts than terms in wills or provisions for statutes? As we have noted, contracts are less formal documents than either wills or statutes. Parties making contracts rely on the willingness of each other to perform, and it may be desirable to have long-term contracts, relational contracts, that are both enforceable and leave some matters open as conditions change.[142] Further, because contracts are subject to negotiation, arriving at terms can be much more difficult for contracts than for wills. And, if a contract fails, the law typically does not have an alternative scheme of enforcement; if a will fails in some respect, the property goes to a residuary legatee or passes according to legal rules for intestate succession, thus reducing any need to "fill in."

Arriving at terms is even more difficult for statutes than contracts, but it is the business of legislators to adopt legislation. Legislators often assign wide discretion to administrative agencies. Courts will give content to vague phrases in statutes, as they will with contracts, and they must sometimes harmonize provisions that do not fit well together; but they do not commonly supply crucial terms legislators have consciously omitted.

In recent years, the role of the courts in respect to omitted terms and default rules[143]—rules that parties can bargain around if they choose[144]— has been the subject of scholarly attention and controversy. To oversimplify, some writers have strongly challenged the idea that courts should be active in creating default rules for construing contracts. Whether they are designed to promote efficient consequences that the parties would approve or to achieve justice between the parties or for the broader society,[145] such default rules are regarded as largely misguided.[146]

The efficiency challenge is complex, but its basic outline is straightforward enough. Default rules must be cast at a broad level of generality; contracts differ greatly. To promote efficient solutions, default rules must attain a wide acceptability; otherwise parties will simply circumvent them and they will have little effect. These default rules must also correspond with information that is available to parties and to courts. (A rule that keys damages to the difference between the contract price and market price satisfies this information constraint because the relevant facts can be known by the parties and a court.)[147] Given the variability in contractual relations, few default rules can meet the acceptability and information constraints.[148]

The challenge to default rules that are designed to reach just outcomes in particular cases or to promote socially desirable behavior, or both, may or may not rest on a principled philosophy about the justification for the law of contracts. For those who see contract law, and perhaps all of common law, as resting exclusively on considerations of efficiency, courts should have no occasion to deviate from efficient outcomes, unless the parties agree to that. Similarly, those who identify consent or autonomy as the key to contractual rights[149] might perceive the courts as unjustified when they swerve from trying their best to carry out the bargain of the parties.[150]

For those, like myself, who see contract law as one part of a law that should serve multiple values, the idea of having some default rules that reflect social considerations beyond the wishes of parties, and beyond the most efficient solutions to their individual relationships, is not objectionable in principle. It is not an answer to this perspective that the parties could have explicitly provided for the outcome the court deems less just. If they have failed to do that, there may be room for courts to consider broader social welfare in filling gaps or interpreting vague provisions. If parties to a contract are relying on legal enforcement and one party, at least, has sought that enforcement, with its attendant costs for the whole society, judges may reasonably say that as to matters the parties have left open, the court will strike a resolution that conforms with what is just between the parties or best for society at large.

Regrettably, perhaps, the dispute cannot be settled on the bases of broad theories about the law of contracts. An opponent of justice-serving default rules of interpretation and gap-filling may say that the general law of contracts—applied to parties only in the infrequent cases that get to court—is a very poor vehicle for trying to achieve social justice.[151] That aspiration is better achieved by discrete areas of law such as family law, labor relations law, environmental law, and consumer protection law. Further, default rules that fit social justice at the expense of the parties will be largely pointless since parties will bargain around them.[152] The power of this critique may depend on the sophistication of contractual parties, and on the possible influence of public opinion. It is strongest in respect to experienced parties who are familiar enough with the law of contracts to avoid default rules that may be to their disadvantage, and who do not worry that their avoidance may generate an adverse public opinion.

Were courts and state legislatures, perhaps affected by influential bodies like the American Law Institute, to cut back on the number of default rules, courts faced with contractual gaps of a sort previously filled by the rules would have to decide not to treat an incomplete agreement as a binding contract or to fill in the gaps without relying on default rules—presumably according to their best appraisals of the parties' objectives. The choice between these two alternatives should depend partly on the parties' intentions about interpretation and partly on the manageabililty of the task of gap-filling.

VI. EXPRESS TERMS AND OTHER FACTORS: REASSESSMENTS

The picture this chapter has presented, of express terms largely controlling the application of contracts, with complexities arising if terms are not clear, are vague, or are omitted, reflects a standard approach to the interpretation of contracts; but its accuracy and normative appropriateness can be challenged from both sides.

A convenient vehicle to examine the possibility that the text of contracts is less important than the standard approach supposes is an article by Eyal Zamir, whose central thesis is that the standard traditional account of the ordering of criteria to interpret contracts is actually inverted.[153] That is, he claims both that courts actually rely heavily on criteria that would be toward the bottom in standard treatments of bases of judgment; and that this "inversion" is desirable. One need not accept his thesis in full to wonder if text may be less central than one might assume from examining doctrines one by one, a suspicion that may be reinforced when one observes how often the courts appear to manipulate confusing doctrines to reach just results in individual cases.[154]

According to Zamir, in many legal systems contractual issues are supposedly resolved in an ordering that goes: express terms; parties' intentions deducible from the contractual documents, and the circumstances surrounding its making; indications from the parties' previous course of dealings; trade usages; statutory or judicial default rules; general principles of contract law such as good faith or the realization of reasonable expectations.[155] The hierarchy can be seen as involving a move from individual will to social values and from factual inquiry (about intentions) to normative evaluation.[156]

Although American doctrine has not been rigid in denying access to an inferior source if a superior source seems to provide an answer, nonetheless, something like a similar hierarchy has been presumed. That has been challenged by followers of Karl Llewellyn, who oppose any such hierarchy of sources; and the U.C.C. and Restatement (Second) emphasize the importance of implied terms, commercial context, trade usages, and ideas of fair dealing and reasonable expectations.[157]

Zamir argues that these are much more important than even the "Llewellyn position" acknowledges. Trade usages and ideas of fairness deeply influence how express terms are interpreted,[158] and their importance is greatly increased by obstacles to altering standard legal terms. Judges create some of these obstacles to assure that stronger parties have not taken advantage of weaker ones.[159] Expectations of the parties generate other obstacles; a party may hesitate to propose a term more favorable to her than the standard one, because she fears the other party may be put off, regarding her as someone who is sharply bargaining for unfair advantage.[160] Further, the manner in which parties behave during the course of performing a contract is often taken to waive terms in the written contract.[161]

Zamir contends that this actual emphasis on trade usage, fairness, and reasonable expectations not only can serve values of public welfare, fair dealing, reasonable (mild) paternalism, and efficiency (in countering the effect of imperfect markets and bounded rationality),[162] but may also reflect the intentions of parties, who often are not aware of specific terms, and, in any event, expect relations not to be rigidly dictated by express terms.[163] One way to conceptualize the reliance on some of these nontextual sources is that courts are interpreting practices of contracting parties more than the terms of their texts. Nothing Zamir says suggests that bargaining equals cannot control their relations by express terms if together they try hard to do so, but other factors clearly play a greater role in the law of contracts than in the law of wills.

The challenge from the other direction is that express terms continue to play a greater role than one would gather from the U.C.C. and the

Restatement (Second), that this is normatively desirable, and that a move back toward a textual approach to contracts that assumes that they are written in "majority talk" would serve the interests of the law of contracts as it applies to sophisticated parties dealing with each other.[164] One aspect of the challenge to the flexible standards of the Restatement and the U.C.C. is that the members of the bodies enacting them may have had interested reasons to prefer such flexibility.[165]

Part of the "anti-antiformalist" challenge against the flexible approach that derives from Llewellyn is that despite local customary trade practice, more general trade practices are necessary to make his approach work for national markets, and these are often absent.[166] Many scholars were surprised by Lisa Bernstein's discovery that within trade associations themselves, those resolving disputes tend to adopt textualist approaches, not to inquire about unwritten trade practices.[167] Although it does not follow that generalist judges should necessarily take the same posture,[168] the Bernstein findings at least cast doubt or the desirability of judges relying heavily on trade practices that may be reflected in a contract.

Most of the discussions about desirable interpretive strategies have been directed at the practice of courts, but Avery Katz has pointed out that in various ways parties can affect whether interpretation will be textualist or more encompassing.[169] Among the ways are how they write their contracts and how they choose those who will interpret them.

The particular questions about textualist emphasis that arise in contracts law do not replicate themselves exactly with statutes and constitutions; but one avenue for exploration of textualism in those domains is inquiry whether the disputes over contractual interpretation have relevance.

VII. SOME GENERAL REFLECTIONS ABOUT THE AWKWARDNESS OF "SINGLE INQUIRY" APPROACHES TO INTERPRETATION

We have seen in respect to contracts and wills that deciding just how courts should treat documents that are framed by private individuals and carry legal authority is fairly complex. Here we need not worry about the complications of having hundreds of authors or the survival of a text's mandatory force over centuries, yet courts and scholars struggle with the right balance of subjective and objective elements, and what looks right for wills does not look exactly right for contracts. This investigation of wills and contracts can provide a helpful comparative perspective when one turns to statutory and constitutional interpretation.

We can understand the awkwardness of trying to use a single inquiry approach to real meaning as it applies to the job of courts. With wills, if a legal rule gives a definite meaning to a term, judges will assume that the term carries that meaning (at least barring overwhelming evidence that the testator meant something different). Suppose the will says "heirs," and a disappointed relative claims that the testator meant the term in a way that does not correspond with strict legal usage. The court finds only modest evidence to support the position. It decides to give the term its standard legal significance without trying to resolve what the testator actually intended. A theorist who claims that meaning always depends on a writer's or speaker's intent might respond, "Perhaps the real meaning here was the loose colloquial sense of 'heirs'; but because there was not overwhelming evidence to this effect, the court used the standard sense, realizing that it was *either* carrying out the true meaning or displacing that meaning on evidentiary grounds." This *is* a possible conceptualization, but it is unwieldy. Saying that "the meaning in this will is the standard sense in the absence of overwhelming evidence of a contrary intent" is much cleaner.

The difficulties for the author's intent approach become even greater for contracts. Shall we suppose that whenever the parties have different understandings, there is no single meaning in the contract but two meanings at odds with each other?[170] On that view, what courts are doing is deciding which meaning will count legally, rather than determining what the meaning of the contract is. Yet those in the law typically suppose that courts are determining *the* meaning of contractual terms. And if judges are confident that at least one party adopted the more reasonable understanding, they need not resolve whether the parties shared that meaning or did not. The single inquiry, author's intent, theorist may have to say that according to the rules of contract law, courts often do not even take the initial step of deciding if there was one meaning or two; rather, they decide that *a* meaning will prevail whether shared or not.

Thus, in both wills and contracts, judges often do not even resolve step one of this form of single-inquiry approach: what is the real meaning or meanings? If judges do not resolve step one (i.e., meaning according to intent) and they adopt an interpretation of the text nevertheless, they will not know if, by adopting the meaning they have, they have adhered to a real meaning they have not taken the effort to discern or have displaced the real meaning in favor of something else. Nothing prevents a theorist from working out all these circumlocutions, but they begin to seem like the epicycles needed to explain how the sun circles the earth. Without working out all the details, we can surmise that other single-inquiry approaches to meaning will face similar difficulties. For law, the pluralist account, which acknowledges that courts consider many factors to resolve the meaning of authoritative legal texts is vastly more straightforward.

Notes

1 In some instances, one party performs an act to initiate contractual obligations, rather than making a promise. *A* says to *B* "If you wash my car tomorrow, I will pay you $10.00." *B* does not promise; but he washes the car.

2 If *B* refuses to pay *A* for the car, and *A* must sell it to C for $1,500, *B* must reimburse *A* with $500.

3 The words by which an oral agreement is reached may have less intrinsic significance than the words of a written contract. According to 2 Samuel Williston, *The Law of Contracts* (New York, Baker, Voorhis, 1920) §606, at 1165, "In an ordinary oral contract . . . the minds of the parties are not primarily addressed to the symbols which they are using: they are considering the things for which the symbols stand." See the summary in Mark C. Movsesian, "Are Statutes Really 'Legislative Bargains'? The Failure of the Contract Analogy in Statutory Interpretation," 76 *North Carolina Law Review* 1145, 1160 (1998).

4 It is possible, of course, that all copies of a written contract may be lost or destroyed. In that event, the text may be in dispute. And even when a text is undisputed and available, parties may disagree whether they have reached a supplementary understanding.

5 See Alan Schwartz and Robert E. Scott, "Contract Theory and the Limits of Contract Law," 113 *Yale Law Journal* 541 (2003). See also Robert Childres and Stephen J. Spitz, "Status in the Law of Contracts," 47 *New York University Law Review* 1 (1972) (arguing that courts take categories of contracts and parties into account sub silentio in deciding whether to use the parol evidence rule). For one response to the approach of Schwartz and Scott, see Juliet P. Kostritsky, "Plain Meaning vs. Broad Interpretation: How the Risk of Opportunism Defeats a Unitary Default Rule for Interpretation," 96 *Kentucky Law Journal* 43 (2007–08).

6 It is often critical whether the parties have committed themselves by making an offer and an acceptance; determining that issue may involve interpretation of what each has said that is not fundamentally different from interpreting the content of undoubted contractual commitments. Melvin A. Eisenberg, "The Responsive Model of Contract Law," 36 *Stanford Law Review* 1107, 1116–27, and especially note 31 on p. 1117 (1984) (suggesting that a parallel analysis applies, whether one is talking about interpretation to determine whether a bargain has been concluded or about interpretation of an admitted bargain).

7 A related question involves alterations of terms by the parties themselves. Suppose that *B*, responding to *A*'s assertion that the terms have become highly impractical for him, agrees to new terms. When *A* then performs, and *B* sues to get the benefit of the original bargain, a court must decide if the new terms are legally binding. Judges often sustain new arrangements by the parties even though they would not by themselves have relieved either party from its original obligations. Schwartz and Scott, note 5 supra at 613–14, suggest that business firms should be able to write contracts that block modifications.

8 See Eyal Zamir, "The Inverted Hierarchy of Contract Interpretation and Supplementation," 97 *Columbia Law Review* 1710, 1765–66 (1997). Peter Linzer, "The Comfort of Certainty: Plain Meaning and the Parol Evidence Rule," 71 *Fordham Law Review* 799, 806, note 33 (2002), notes a lease he signed that required window curtains to have a white backing; he relied on the manager's assurance that "they don't enforce that rule," but, as a contracts teacher, realized he was depending on the landlord's grace. One can imagine an analogy involving administrative or legislative regulations: a person subject to the regulations assumes that their strict terms will not be enforced, and practice supports that assumption.

9 According to Arthur L. Corbin, "The Interpretation of Words and the Parol Evidence Rule," 50 *Cornell Law Quarterly* 161, 181 (1965), assertions that the

written words do not manifest an actual understanding are not "interpretation" of the written words. A claim of that sort may be one for reformation or some other remedy. Id. at 174–75.

10 More precisely, the degree of risk of serious failure would be relevant. Also, the projected cost of litigation could count, but not many testators would choose what would otherwise be a less desirable strategy of interpretation to save their estate money that would otherwise go for litigation costs.

11 Schwartz and Scott, note 5 supra at 569.

12 Id. at 544–49, 584–94. Avery Katz has suggested the difficulty of generalizing about the interpretive strategy parties will want courts to use; the traditional scholarly approach "founders on a lack of information about the likely consequences of formal and substantive modes of interpretation." "The Economics of Form and Substance in Contract Interpretation," 104 *Columbia Law Review* 496, 538 (2004). See also William J. Woodward, "Neoformalism in a Real World of Forms," 2001 *Wisconsin Law Review* 971, 973, 991–1004, who urges both that the needed empirical evidence for a move toward formalism is lacking and that such an approach could have counterproductive effects on the behavior of many parties.

13 See Eric A. Posner, "The Parol Evidence Rule, The Plain Meaning Rule, and the Principles of Contractual Interpretation," 146 *University of Pennsylvania Law Review*, 568–73 (1998), discusses parties who fear that judges will err or that litigation will become too expensive, and consciously desire that courts not undertake inquires about their subjective understanding. See also Schwartz and Scott, note 5 supra, at 584–90.

14 Melvin A. Eisenberg, "Mistake in Contract Law," 91 *California Law Review* 1575, 1610 (2003), writes of mistranscriptions as mistakes that do "not affect the terms of the bargain." These fall within a broader category of what he calls mechanical errors for which a party should obtain relief, except insofar as the other party relied reasonably. Id. at 1589–1611.

15 See Market Street Associates v. Frey, 941 F. 2d 588 (7th Cir. 1991), in which Richard Posner wrote an opinion indicating that a party with a right to buy property at a bargain rate if the lessor did not negotiate about a loan could not intentionally proceed with a hope and expectation of the lessor's ignorance of that term of the contract. See generally Robert Summers, "'Good Faith' in General Contract Law and the Sales Provisions of the Uniform Commercial Code," 54 *Virginia Law Review* 195 (1968).

16 Eisenberg, note 6 supra, at 1108–10.

17 Corbin, note 9 supra, at 170. Whether Corbin would include an instance in which no outsider uses a term in a particular way, but C understands that A and B, the contractual parties, do use the term in this way, is unclear.

18 W. David Slawson, "The Futile Search for Default Rules," 3 *Southern California Interdisciplinary Law Journal* 29, 38 (1993), citing E. Allan Farnsworth, *Contracts* §9 (2d ed. 1990).

19 Joseph M. Perillo, "The Origins of the Objective Theory of Contract Formulation and Interpretation," 69 *Fordham Law Review* 427, 435–36, 443–44 (2000).

20 I do not discuss just whose understanding counts for a large firm, or for anyone who is represented by a lawyer, a problem that resembles somewhat the discerning of legislative intent in statutory cases. But if people choose to have lawyers represent them in contract negotiations, they are ordinarily bound to the lawyers' understandings.

21 See, e.g., E. Allan Farnsworth, "'Meaning' in the Law of Contracts," 76 *Yale Law Journal* 939, 949 (1967).

22 Melvin Aron Eisenberg, "Expression Rules in Contract Law and Problems of Offer and Acceptance," 82 *California Law Review* 1127, 1133–34 (1994); Farnsworth, note 21 supra. But see Posner, note 13 supra, at 534–40, reporting that some courts continue to apply what he calls a "hard" version of the parol evidence rule, according to which they exclude extrinsic evidence of prior negotiations and rely on the writing, unless the writing on its face is incomplete or ambiguous or a party claims a bargaining defect such as fraud or mistake.

23 §201(1) (1981). This approach differs from the more objective one of Restatement (First) (1932). For integrated contracts, its standard was "the meaning that would be attached . . . by a reasonably intelligent person" knowing the circumstances. §230. For unintegrated contracts, the meaning was that "the party making the manifestations should reasonably expect that the other party would give to them . . . ." §233.

24 In Steuart v. McChesney, 444 A.2d 659, 662 (Pa. 1982), the Supreme Court of Pennsylvania noted that the plain meaning rule "has been supported as generally best serving the ascertainment of the contracting parties' mutual intent."

25 O.W. Holmes, "The Path of the Law," 10 *Harvard Law Review* 457, 464 (1897). Perillo, note 19 supra at 474–76, provides an account of Holmes's role in developing the objective theory. According to Perillo, Holmes followed the lead of some counts in adopting an objective approach. Holmes propounded a similar objective approach to virtually all branches of law. Citing Holmes's *The Common Law*, Eisenberg remarks that for some proponents of the classical model, it may "have reflected a broader program in which a single norm could generate all legal rules: Actors must conform their activity to the conduct one could reasonably expect of the average person." Eisenberg, note 6 supra, at 1108–09.

26 Hotchkiss v. National City Bank, 200 F. 287, 293 (S.D.N.Y. 1911). Hand's quote does make an exception for "cases of mutual mistake or something else of the sort," but that apparently refers to mutual mistake about the subject of the contract, not about the significance of terms. Lawrence Friedman has written, "Pure contract law is blind to details of subject matter and person . . . . Contract law is an abstraction—what is left in the law relating to agreements when all particulars of person and subject matter are removed." *Contract Law in America* 20–24 (Madison, University of Wisconsin Press, 1965).

27 Allan Farnsworth traces this subjective theory back to 1551, Farnsworth, note 21 supra, at 943, and notes that it accorded well with the 'will theory' of contracts which attained hegemony in the nineteenth century . . . ." Id. at 945. Farnsworth goes on to say, "No responsible authority seems ever to have suggested that the process of interpretation deals only with those terms on which there was a meeting of the minds at the time of agreement." Joseph Perillo, note 19 supra, emphasizes the objective elements in contract interpretation from the earliest times, and notes that the inability of parties to testify before the mid-nineteenth century undercut the practical relevance of comments that subjective understanding was the guide to meaning.

28 See Eisenberg, note 6 supra, at 1108.

29 Eisenberg, id. at 1110, remarks that "despite its formal de-emphasis of policy, the classical school's philosophical, psychological, and jurisprudential assumptions seem to have reflected an extremely strong premium on certainty."

30 Charles J. Goetz and Robert E. Scott, "The Limits of Expanded Choice: An Analysis of the Interactions Between Express and Implied Contract Terms," 73 *California Law Review* 261, 307 (1985), write that "[t]hrough the revised rules of the Uniform Commercial Code and the Second Restatement the 'contextualists' have succeeded greatly in reducing the exclusionary potential of the interpretive process,"; they suggest, "Rigorous application of the plain-meaning rule reduces interpretation error by encouraging more careful choices of clear, predefined signals." Id. at 311-12. See also Posner, note 13 supra, on judicial application of the parol evidence rule in some circumstances in which the parties themselves might wish to avoid the use of external evidence of their understandings; Schwartz and Scott, note 5 supra.

31 The third and second approaches could be combined; courts might restrict the occasions for evidence of intentions and the kinds of evidence they will entertain, or they might admit more evidence in some circumstances than in others. One version of a restriction on kinds of evidence is the bar that existed two centuries ago on parties testifying. See note 19, supra.

32 Under this approach, a party who had not spoken previously could not make a claim well after signing about what he really understood at the time. Such a rule could seriously reduce the possible significance of subjective elements in contract interpretation, because parties who suppose that their understandings are shared may have no occasion when their contract is signed to explore potential differences.

A comment to the Restatement (Second) may support this approach. The comment is to the innocuous Section 200, which provides, "Interpretation of a promise or agreement or a term thereof is the ascertainment of its meaning." Comment b says that "the intention of a party that is relevant to formation of a contract is the intention manifested by him rather than any different undisclosed intention." Most straightforwardly, the comment says that a party cannot claim an undisclosed intention that conflicts with an intention that he manifested. If Ivo had said at the time that contract was signed, "I understand I will have to be there at training camp," he could not later claim that he harbored a different, secret, intention about the terms to which he agreed. But suppose he then said nothing about how he understood "during its season." Is he later barred from claiming that his understanding was the regular season? I do not think the comment is meant to have this consequence. It seems mainly about intentions to enter into contractual relations, cautioning that parties will be bound to manifested intentions that they may secretly not have embraced.

33 Spaulding v. Morse, 76 N.E.2d 137, 138 (Sup. Jud. Ct. Mass. 1947).

34 This highly contextualized approach might extend beyond dealings between the parties to aspects of the parties revealed by behavior toward others. Especially insofar as such behavior was included, an objective appraisal might conclude that the two parties would assign different meanings to the terms. A recent article reports empirical evidence that interpreters of contracts are likely to overestimate the degree to which their own interpretation of language is commonly shared. Lawrence Solan, Terri Rosenblatt and Daniel Osherson, "False Consensus Bias in Contract Interpretation," 108 *Columbia Law Review* 1268 (2008).

35 If the inquiry concluded that these people would not have considered the option of work before college, a court would have to decide what treatment of the unforeseen circumstance of compulsory military service would best fit their objectives. If the inquiry concluded that the couple had considered ordinary work

but not army service, a court would still have to decide how it should treat army service.

36 Farnsworth, note 21 supra, notes that with many provisions of detailed contracts, there is no subjective intent. A court then has to interpret them objectively or assign a meaning that fits broader purposes the parties subjectively had in mind.

37 Eisenberg, note 22 supra, at 1131–32. See also Randy E. Barnett, "A Consent Theory of Contract," 86 *Columbia Law Review* 269, 303 (1986), explaining why, according to a consent theory of contract, people should be able to rely on "objectively ascertainable assertive conduct . . . ."

38 Thus, in the lumber industry, two packs of a certain size were regarded as 1,000 shingles. A contract to deliver 4,000 shingles could be fulfilled by delivery of 2,500 shingles in eight such packs. Soutier v. Kellerman, 18 Mo. 509, 510–12 (1853).

39 A party who is not part of a trade is not commonly held to trade usages that differ from common usage unless it is proved "either that he had actual knowledge of the usage or that the usage is so generally known in the community that his actual individual knowledge of it may be inferred." Frigaliment Importing Co. v. B.N.S. International Sales Corp., 190 F.Supp. 116, 119 (S.D.N.Y. 1960), quoting 9 Wigmore (3d. Ed., Boston, Little Brown, 1940) §2464.

40 The persuasiveness of this argument might depend partly on whether Ivo was advised by an American lawyer; if so, perhaps he should not be able to complain that he personally didn't know the meaning of crucial terms. This possibility raises the general problem of how to deal with claimed divergencies between what a party's lawyers do, or should, understand and what a client understands. We saw one aspect of this issue with wills. One must worry about perverse incentives. If clients can benefit by not understanding what their lawyers do, they have an incentive not to become fully informed. But if clients are locked in to what their lawyers understand, they may have a (slight) incentive not to consult lawyers. Unless a lawyer has made an outright mistake in formulating the terms of a contract, a party should probably be bound by the understanding of his or her lawyer, and that indeed is the prevailing law.

41 See text accompanying note 26 supra. (I am assuming that "the usual meaning" would be contextualized enough to take into account standard usage in the industry.)

42 Internal quoted language is from Restatement §230. The rest is summary by Farnsworth, note 21 supra, at 959.

43 Restatement §233. Perillo, note 19 supra at 454–56, recounts the development of similar approach by the utilitarian theologian William Paley. (Farnsworth, note 21, at 946, note 40, says that an exception to §233 dealing with situations when a party manifests his intention "ambiguously" and the other party believes it to bear one meaning and has no reason to know it may bear another, may swallow up the rule. It seems to me that the conditions of the exception are met in fewer circumstances than Farnsworth supposes and that, in any event, its treatment is largely consistent with the underlying rule, except that it does make relevant the subjective understanding of the party to whom the manifestation is given.)

44 Arthur Linton Corbin, 3 *Corbin on Contracts* §538, at 59–61 (Rev. ed., St. Paul, West Pub. Co., Minn., 1960).

45 Restatement Second §201 (2) (a).

46 Id. §201 (2) (b).

47 One might focus on which party can learn the other's meaning at lower cost, or on which party has more experience in the market, standards that would not always track greater bargaining power.

48 See U.C.C. §§1–205, 2–202, 2–207, 2–302 (2003).

49 At least this is true so long as one assumes that the parties have not intended a more objective form of interpretation, see note 13 supra, and one also assumes that the court's role is to give coherent content to the terms of the contract, not to strike some intermediate accommodation in such situations—splitting the difference as it were.

50 See, e.g., Stephen P. Ross and Daniel Tranen, "The Modern Parol Evidence Rule and Its Implications for New Textualist Statutory Interpretation," 87 *Georgetown Law Journal* 195 (206-7) (1998).

51 See Schwartz and Scott, note 5 supra.

52 §20(1).

53 Corbin, note 9 supra at 169, writes of "more than one objective meaning."

54 Raffles v. Wichelhaus, 159 Eng. Rep. 375 (Ex. 1864). The case is discussed at length in William F. Young, "Equivocation in the Making of Agreements," 64 *Columbia Law Review* 69 (1964). Farnsworth note 21 supra, analyzes five hypothetical variations.

55 In the actual circumstances, one might better have concluded that each party had reason to wonder if both agreed on the same ship. See Eisenberg, note 6 supra, at 1123–24.

56 See Young, note 54 supra.

57 See id.

58 See §201 (2). One can imagine an argument, based on the difficulty of a judge's deciding if one party really did know what the other understood, that knowing and having reason to know should be treated the same, but that approach would yield an unfair result when one could be confident that one party was ignorant and the other was not.

59 See discussion in text following note 46 supra.

60 Frigaliment Importing Co. v. B.N.S. International Sales Corp., 190 F. Supp. 116 (S.D.N.Y. 1960).

61 However, in a subsequent opinion, Judge Friendly indicated that the case might best be understood as an application of the *Peerless* rule, with recovery denied because the buyer had failed to establish an obligation on behalf of the seller. See also Marvin A. Chirelstein, *Concepts and Case Analysis in the Law of Contracts* 85–88 (4th ed. New York, Foundation Press, 2001).

62 However, William Young tells us that the principle's application does not depend on the importance of the term involved. Young, note 54 supra, at 621, n.10.

63 More precisely, a party in the position of B would be able to accept the understanding of S, when that understanding is no less favorable to S than B's original understanding (though less favorable for S than treating the "contract" as void). One argument against this result is that B should not be in the position of having a free choice whether to accept S's understanding or treat the apparent contract as a nullity. Marvin Chirelstein, note 61 supra, at 36–38, suggests that the actual parties in *Peerless* were making different "bets" on the times of a favorable market price for them. Were the ships to sail and arrive two days apart, that feature of the original case would be missing. Perhaps courts would require S to perform according to some standard of unjust enrichment without holding the contract itself to be binding.

64 Another possibility is a judicial construction of terms that compromises a difference in understandings.

65 Young, note 54 supra, at 629.

66 Id. at 628.

67 An article by Robert Scott that surveys cases involving indefiniteness concludes that many courts still do hold agreements unenforceable when parties choose to leave unspecified measures of performance that could be specified at low cost. Robert E. Scott, "A Theory of Self-Enforcing Indefinite Agreements," 103 *Columbia Law Review* 1641 (2003).

68 See U.C.C. §2–204(3) (2002); Restatement (Second) of Contracts, §33 (2).

69 If the women left all her property to her husband outright, he could make a subsequent judgment about a desirable distribution to children, but she might not trust his judgment about that, and under present estate tax law, she might thus forfeit significant tax advantages of a life estate.

70 Young, note 54 supra, at 626–28. Eisenberg, note 6 supra, at 1123, n. 45, says that the question is whether "two parties gave different but equally reasonable meanings to the same expression," I do not think Eisenberg disagrees with Young as much as he seems to think. If both parties realize a term is vague, they will understand it will have to be filled in later. Even if they have somewhat different, equally reasonable, ideas about the range of application, a court appropriately does the job of filling in. Eisenberg's comment is a helpful caution that the *Peerless* doctrine should not apply if terms are somewhat ambiguous or equivocal but one meaning is much more likely than the other.

71 Id. at 627. "Quart bottle" may be either a bottle that can contain a quart of liquid or a bottle that displaces a quart of liquid. Ambiguity may be created by syntax, the significance of "and" or "or," the placement of a comma, as well as by uncertainty about what words mean. See Farnsworth, note 21 supra, at 954.

72 Young makes this point about a contract calling for delivery of egg coal. Young, note 54 supra, at 629.

73 It was apparently agreed in the *Frigaliment Importing Co.* case that "chicken" did not include cocks or old roosters.

74 Id. at 641–47.

75 One formulation is that a term is "not such as might naturally have been omitted;" another formulation is that a term "would certainly have been included."

76 See 3 Corbin, note 44 supra, §579 at 412–13. Michael L. Boyer, "Contract as Text: Interpretive Overlap in Law and Literature," 12 *Southern California Interdisciplary Law Journal* 167, 171–78 (2003), compares the text-centered view of Williston, which Corbin challenged, as analogous to the New Criticism in literary theory; he sees Corbin's own approach as like literary theories that accord more weight to author's intent. He believes such comparisons are illuminating, but does not suggest any easy transition from a desirable form of literary interpretation to sound legal interpretation.

77 See, e.g., Posner, note 13 supra, at 568–70. It used to be thought that parol evidence could resolve latent ambiguities, ones not evident from the text itself but revealed by external facts (as in the *Peerless* case), but should not resolve patent ambiguities, evident from the text itself. Given the reality of the contextualization of linguistic usage, this is not a clear distinction in practice and it no longer plays a significant role in contracts discussions. Farnsworth, note 21 supra, at 960–61. Peter Linzer writes of the parol evidence and plain meaning rules as "conjoined like Siamese twins." Linzer, note 8 supra at 801. The two rules could be conjoined in

that the application of the plain meaning rule would trigger application of the parol evidence rule, but the conflation of the two rules is more thorough than that.

78 Steuart v. McChesney, 444 A. 2d. 659, 660 (Pa. Sup. Ct. 1982).

79 The practice was to set assessment value at half market value, so this was the amount apparently contemplated by the contract's literal terms.

80 Id. at 661.

81 However, many courts would admit this testimony as bearing on whether the written contract was integrated. The obvious possibility of an unfair price under the literal terms of the contract might be taken to suggest that the contract did not embody the full understanding of the parties.

82 Alternatively, the owner might have asserted that courts should adopt an "interpretive presumption that express terms supplement rather than trump the contractual context . . . ." Goetz and Scott, note 30 supra, at 313. On this view, the contract would include standard assumptions one would make about fair and reasonable terms, unless they were explicitly disavowed.

83 John D. Calamari & Joseph M. Perillo, *The Law of Contracts* §3.9 at 148 (4th ed., St. Paul, Minn., West Group 1998), have written, "The very same words offered as an additional term that are rejected because the court deems the writing to be a total integration, can be offered as an aid to interpretation of an ambiguous written term. Able courts look at both proffers of evidence as governed by the 'parol evidence rule.'"

84 It is not always easy to establish whether a proposed resolution was rejected or carried forward, but the same is true about prior legislative proposals; and that fact has never been thought to make prior drafts useless as legislative history.

85 Although worries about this problem may be lessened to some degree because interpretation is generally up to the judge, not the jury, factual disputes that bear an interpretation may be resolved by jurors. See Farnsworth, note 21 supra, at 962. William C. Whitford, "The Role of the Jury (and the Fact/Law Distinction) in the Interpretation of Written Contracts," 2001 *Wisconsin Law Review* 931, shows not only that jurors often resolve contests over contractual interpretation but that, according to a standard understanding of the line between legal and factual issues, they should. One reason to bar external evidence is distrust that jurors will fairly decide factual issues that such evidence raises. Richard A. Posner, "The Law and Economics of Contract Interpretation," 83 *Texas Law Review* 1581, 1603–06 (2005), suggests that judges relying on their "best guess" about efficiency or commercial sense in interpreting ambiguous terms avoids subjecting parties to the vagaries of jury determinations.

86 For example, if Ivo's belief about what "during its season" meant was legally relevant, and a court refused to consider what he told reporters, the preclusion would rest on a rule of evidence. This conceptual distinction between rules of law and rules of evidence has limited practical import. If most evidence that might show that subjective understandings differ from objective ones is barred, the consequence will be a law of contracts that gives these subjective understandings little significance. See Perillo, note 19 supra at 435, on the relation between the exclusion of party testimony and an ostensible subjective approach to meaning.

87 Schwartz and Scott, note 5 supra, at 172. This is a quibble, but I think it is a bit misleading to treat an interpreter's experience and understanding as an aspect of an evidentiary base. No doubt, it is part of her informational base, but she does not typically consider it as evidence (though she might treat some isolated personal event like evidence).

88 See Katz, note 12 supra at 498.

89 See id. at 497–98.

90 Ross and Tranen, note 50 supra at 216–17.

91 56 F.3d 763 (7th Cir. 1995). See Goetz and Scott, note 30 supra, at 307.

92 56 F.3d at 768. See also Judge Posner's earlier opinion in AM International, Inc. v. Graphic Management Associates, Inc., 44 F.3d 572 (7th Cir. 1995). On this division, public comments to reporters made by both parties together at the time of signing might be classed as "subjective," but they would not involve the problems that evidence about subjective understandings would typically involve.

93 See generally Farnsworth, note 21 supra at 952–65. See also Pacific Gas and Electric Co. v. G.W. Thomas Drayage & Rigging Co., 442 P.2d 641 (Cal. 1968), a famous opinion by Roger Traynor indicating that the key issue, citing Corbin, was how the writers understood their words, but, as Peter Linzer has noted, Traynor required that extrinsic evidence "prove a meaning to which the language of the instrument is reasonably susceptible." 442 P.2d. at 644, discussed in Linzer, note 8 supra, at 822–23.

94 See Restatement (Second) §§201–203. These sections also make relevant actual subjective understandings. An intermediate approach is to require vagueness or ambiguity before external evidence may be introduced as to meaning but to be very generous about the minimum necessary to surmount the threshold of vagueness and ambiguity. According to William C. Whitford, note 85 supra, at 935, the main contention is among objective approaches, but "A few commentators still advocate inquiry into the existence of a subjective meeting of the minds as the first step in any interpretive process."

95 That is the meaning according to what Schwartz and Scott, note 5 supra at 570–72, call "majority talk." They have in mind ordinary understandings in the population generally, but I do not think it stretches their purpose too much to include understandings that are near universal for narrower settings, such as sports contracts.

Of course, meaning can evolve over time, but right now the phrase "during its season" has a standard, widely understood, significance.

96 According to Katz, note 12 supra at 521, "for a given audience or interpreter, plain meaning corresponds to the interpretation associated with the interpreter's ordinary or zero-cost context—that is, the context that the interpreter can apply with minimal work." This definition either rejects or neglects what I believe is a crucial feature—that a plain meaning must be "plain" or obvious.

97 The worry about lying is increased when jurors resolve relevant factual matters. See Whitford, note 85 supra at 943–44. Jurors may reward a sympathetic party by crediting an implausible story. Similar risks also attend some claims about contextual objective meaning.

98 See Posner, note 13 supra at 553–55, who reviews various factors that would bear on rational decisions about how strictly to apply the parol evidence rule, and the treatment of Schwartz and Scott, supra note 5, of contracts involving business firms.

99 Karen Eggleston, Eric A. Posner, and Richard Zechhauser, "The Design and Interpretation of Contracts: Why Complexity Matters," 95 *Northwestern Law Review* 91 (2000).

100 People who agree to commit criminal acts have already committed the crime of conspiring. Such prosecutions raise the interesting question of *just how* the terms of agreements in writing should be understood for the purpose of criminal

liability. Modern criminal law adopts a primarily subjective approach in which it is the understanding of the defendant that counts. He would be exonerated if his understanding is innocent, even though "objective" understanding and the understanding of other participants contemplates criminal behavior. (A more complex question is raised if the particular defendant thinks he is agreeing to acts that are, in fact, criminal, even though an objective interpretation and the understanding of other participants covers only noncriminal behavior). A special wrinkle concerns agreements with mixed criminal and speech elements, as in United States v. Spock, 416 F 2d 165 (1st Cir. 1969), discussed in Kent Greenawalt, *Speech, Crime, and the Uses of Language*, 208–09, 266–67, 335–36 (New York, Oxford University Press, 1989).

101 See generally Melvin Eisenberg, *Basic Principles of Contract Law*, Ch. 4 (forthcoming) (New York, Oxford University Press). We can distinguish unconscionability (terms that are unfair in their origin) from frustration (the purpose behind the contract is destroyed after the contract is made) and impracticality (satisfaction of one's party's obligations has become impossible or very difficult). I reserve discussion of frustration and impracticality for the following chapter, which deals with explicit judicial alterations of terms that are legally binding at the outset.

102 350 F.2d 445 (D.C. Cir.1965).

103 The court of appeals remanded the case for a determination if the terms were unconscionable. The suggestion that they were is controversial. It is argued that if merchants in poor areas cannot impose such terms, they will not make products available on credit. Marvin Chirelstein, note 61 supra at 82–84, argues persuasively that the arrangement was particularly coercive.

104 That this is proper would be obvious *if* the other party is refusing to do something she has a legal duty to do. But I am assuming in my illustration that the woman with the boat could, legally, drive by *and* not bother to inform anyone. (Of course, one could respond she would have a moral duty not to act in that way.)

105 83 N.J. 86, 415 A.2d 1156 (1980).

106 Id. at 104, 415 A.2d at 1165–66.

107 Except in concerning fairness between the parties and in correcting an original flaw in the contract, this judicial authority is not so different from the court's power to implement *cy pres* in trust cases, which we shall address in the chapter to come.

108 This language covers all instances in which one possible interpretation would make a contract unenforceable. See Zamir, note 8 supra, at 1722–24. We should understand "unlawful" in Section 203 as including agreements that would be legally unenforceable, such as to pay gambling debts, as well as agreements to do what is independently unlawful. The main idea of "reasonable" in the section concerns relations between the parties, but an agreement contrary to another public policy may also be unreasonable.

109 Section 207. The rule this section expresses has, comment a tells us, been used to interpret grants of public franchises and tax exemptions.

110 "If a term or contract is unconscionable or otherwise against public policy, it should be dealt with directly rather than by spurious interpretation."

111 It is worth noting that the party toward whom possible unreasonable terms are disadvantageous may be better off if the contract is so construed and then declared unenforceable, than if the contract is interpreted favorably enough toward her so that it is enforceable.

112 By contrast, comment a to section 207 about contracts that serve the public interest says that that rule "rests more on considerations of public policy than on the probable intention of the parties." Considering this rule one of "construction," Corbin, note 9 supra, at 170, wrote, "The interpretation of a written contract is the process of determining the thought that the users of the words therein intended to convey to each other." When a court relies on public policy to oppose the probable aims of the parties, it is no longer interpreting in this sense.

113 Zamir, note 8 supra, at 1722–23. However, comment c to Section 203 does say, "The search is for the manifested intention of the parties."

114 Woodward, note 12 supra at 990.

115 Corbin, note 44 supra, §550.

116 Zamir, note 8 supra, at 1723–24. A concern that a public agency may be "captured" by private interests that receive franchises and exemptions is not present when purely private parties contract.

117 See, e.g., Schwartz and Scott, note 5 supra, at 594, suggesting that in contracts between business firms, courts should facilitate efforts of the parties to maximize their joint gains.

118 Anthony T. Kronman, "Contract Law and Distributive Justice," 89 *Yale Law Journal* 472 (1980), demonstrates that contract law cannot disregard issues of distributive justice, but he does not concentrate on interpretation of contracts between parties who could disregard such considerations.

119 See generally Barnett, note 37 supra.

120 Eisenberg, note 6 supra.

121 An example is a rule that a qualified acceptance terminates an offer. According to the ordinary understanding of people who deal with each other, a qualified acceptance—S says "I'll sell you this car for $8,000;" B says "I'll buy it for $7,500"—would not necessarily terminate the original offer. A rigid rule to that effect deviates in result from what application of more general principles would suggest.

122 Eisenberg, note 6 supra, at 1143.

123 Id. at 1135–41.

124 Although a categorical rule can be used to interpret a contract, it is hard to characterize the rule itself as involving interpretation in any ordinary sense, since the rule prevails over all regular standards for discerning meaning.

It may help to distinguish two situations. In one, the categorical rule dictates a result, unless there is an explicit contractual provision that requires a result contrary to the one the rule would produce. In another, the categorical rule provides a measure according to which various interpretive claims are judged. If the rule is that provisions will be construed against the insurer, nevertheless the language of a contract may be so favorable to an insurance company that it would win the case even if interpretation is against it. One might think of a categorical rule that interpretation be against the insurer as like a presumption that the insurer should lose if the language is not clear.

125 Although an expression rule may serve some noninterpretive policy, Eisenberg claims that such a justification "is likely to have only limited weight," because the justification conflicts with "the object of facilitating the power of self-governing parties to further their shared objectives through contracting." Id. at 1143. Of course, insofar as an expression rule serves a strong public policy that courts are willing to put aside only if parties are very clear about their intent to do so, the weight a policy justification supplies could be considerable.

126 Eisenberg suggests that an administrative justification can have only a limited weight in settling the content of a rule, because disputes need to be settled properly, based on the parties' understandings and public policy. Id. at 1143–44. Perhaps this is another way of saying that an expression rule must usually correspond with general principles of interpretation.

127 See, e.g., Steuart v. McChesney, 444 A.2d 659 (Pa. Sup. Ct. 1982), discussed in text accompanying notes 78–83, supra. Since a provision is likely to favor one party at the expense of another, courts are hesitant to say a provision consciously adopted by both parties is to be disregarded in light of an overall purpose.

128 According to Restatement (Second) §204: "When the parties to a bargain sufficiently defined to be a contract have not agreed with respect to a term which is essential to a determination of their rights and duties, a term which is reasonable in the circumstances is supplied by the court." As a Note in the 2003 Columbia Law Review indicates, all courts in the United States are generous in filling in the terms of sales contracts, covered by the Uniform Commercial Code. Some remain restrictive in dealing with service contracts. The Note argues for a flexible approach to all kinds of contracts. Nellie Eunsoo Choi, "Contracts with Open or Missing Terms Under the Uniform Commercial Code and the Common Law: A Proposal for Unification," 103 *Columbia Law Review* 50 (2003). Robert E. Scott, note 68 supra, at 1657–61, defends the traditional practice of nonenforcement for some indefinite agreements.

129 Goetz and Scott, note 30 supra, at 274. For an account of the general jurisprudential assumption of Karl Llewellyn, the major draftsman of the U.C.C., that law lies in patterns of practice rather than in explicit rules, see Richard Danzig, "A Comment on the Jurisprudence of the Uniform Commercial Code," 27 *Stanford Law Review* 621 (1975).

130 See Scott, note 68 supra, at 1642–44.

131 Id. at 1642–44, 1657–61.

132 Id. at 1661–85. For a skeptical view about the possible merits of a formalist approach for actual contractual relations, see Woodward, note 12 supra. Woodward is particularly critical of proposed reforms of the U.C.C. that would require courts to stick more closely to the explicit terms of forms. Id. at 991–93.

133 Scott, note 68 supra at 1685–92.

134 Sacramento Nav. Co. v. Salz, 273 U.S. 326, 329 (1927), discussed in 3 Corbin, note 44 supra, §561.

135 David Charny, "Hypothetical Bargains: The Narrative Structure of Contract Interpretation," 89 *Michigan Law Review* 1815, 1816 (1991). Charny points out just how complicated are the questions why a hypothetical bargain may matter and how one should understand the bargain. In determining how individual or general and how ordinary or idealized one believes judges should make hypothetical bargainers, one may well be influenced by the theory of justification for enforcing contracts that he accepts, Id. at 1820–79.

136 Comment c to Restatement (Second) §204.

137 According to Richard Craswell, "Contract Law, Default Rules, and the Philosophy of Promising," 88 *Michigan Law Review* 489, 505 (1989), "While it is perhaps more common to speak of 'interpretation' in cases where parties attempt to resolve an issue but do so with insufficient clarity, and to speak of applying default rules in cases where the parties made no attempt to address an issue, the principle is much the same in either case." A helpful note on psychological premises underlying the idea of "tacit assumptions" in the context of changed

circumstances is in Lon L. Fuller and Melvin Aron Eisenberg, *Basic Contract Law* 720–23 (6th ed., St. Paul, Minn., West Pub. Co., 1996). Robert Scott's treatment of non-enforcement of incomplete agreements, see note 68 supra at 1692–93, suggests that examination of the entire agreement may suggest the parties intended nonenforcement, or at least did not unambiguously intend enforcement. This is an example in which interpretation of the entire scope of an agreement can be involved in deciding whether or not a legally binding contract exists.

138 §204, Comment d. But see Scott, note 68 supra, on why courts should not always supply "fair" terms if the parties have chosen to leave terms indefinite. 3 Corbin, note 44 supra, §561 says that when terms are implied because of legal policy, that does not involve "true interpretation."

139 Reliance on highly specific contexts can undermine to a degree the value of having standard legal provisions, which parties can assume unless they direct otherwise. Goetz and Scott, note 30 supra, at 273–80. Although the standard assumption has been that default terms should largely be guided by what most parties would want, Ian Ayres, "Preliminary Thoughts on Optimal Tailoring of Contractual Rules," 235 *Southern California Interdisciplinary Law Journal* 1, 6 (1993), has suggested that using terms the parties would probably not want could be a helpful technique to force them to deal with issues explicitly. See also Ian Ayres and Robert Gertner, "Filling Gaps in Incomplete Contracts: An Economic Theory of Default Rules," 99 *Yale Law Journal* 89, 91–95 (1989).

140 See Restatement (Second) §205; U.C.C. §1–203. This is a duty that parties cannot bargain around.

141 Howard O. Hunter, *Modern Law of Contracts* 8–19 (Rev. ed., Boston, Warren, Gorham & Lamont, 1993). (Mel Eisenberg says (orally) there are three schools of thought. The dominant one may be that the duty is not an independent source of contractual obligations. I am assuming that all schools agree that the duty can guide how terms are construed by courts.)

142 See Ian MacNeil, "Contracts: Adjustment of Long-Term Economic Relations under Classical, Neo-classical, and Relational Contract Law," 72 *Northwestern Law Review* 854 (1978); Charles J. Goetz and Robert E. Scott, "Principles of Relational Contracts," 67 *Virginia Law Review* 1089 (1981). Elizabeth S. Scott and Robert E. Scott have suggested that marriage should be viewed as a relational contract. "Marriage as a Relational Contract," 84 *Virginia Law Review* 1225 (1998). For a skeptical view of competence of courts to define and enforce the terms of such contracts, see Eric A. Posner, "A Theory of Contract Law Under Conditions of Radical Judicial Error," 94 *Northwestern Law Review* 749 (2000).

143 Randy E. Barnett, "The Sound of Silence: Default Rule and Contractual Consent," 78 *Virginia Law Review* 821, 823–24 (1992), remarked on "an almost imperceptible shift" in rhetoric from "gap filling" to "default rules."

144 Alan Schwartz, "The Default Rule Paradigm and the Limits of Contract Law," 3 *Southern California Interdisciplinary Law Journal* 389, 390 (1993).

145 See id. at 390–91, distinguishing problem-solving, equilibrium-inducing, information-forcing, normative, transformative, and structural default. W. David Slawson, note 18 supra, has criticized the concept of default rules as too broad (embracing all areas of law as to which parties can surrender rights by agreement) or unhelpfully narrow.

146 See Schwartz, note 144 supra; Schwartz and Scott, note 5 supra, at 547.

147 Schwartz, note 144 supra, at 392.

148 Ian Ayres, note 139 supra, discusses the comparative merits of rules and standards as default rules.

149 See, e.g., Barnett, note 37 supra, at 269–71.

150 Richard Craswell, note 135 supra, suggests that promisory and autonomy theories are little help in determining how to fill in substantive terms; but those theories seem to point toward respect for the parties' aims. Barnett has responded to Craswell, note 143 supra at 875–94. See also Jody S. Kraus, "Philosophy of Contract Law," in *The Oxford Handbook of Jurisprudence and Philosophy of Law* 687, 687–90 (Jules Coleman and Scott Shapiro, eds., Oxford and New York, Oxford University Press, 2002), on how theorists may think terms should be filled in.

151 See Schwartz and Scott, note 5 supra at 545–46; Schwartz, note 144 supra, at 419.

152 Id. at 418–19. Omri Ben-Shahar, "A Bargaining Theory of Default Rules," 109 *Columbia Law Review* 396 (2009), argues that courts in filling in missing terms should mimic what the parties would have bargained for, choosing terms favorable to the stronger party. In id. at 411–12, he explicitly rejects a fairness approach. Apart from other reasons not to try *only* to mimic the bargain that would have occurred, I think it is relevant that the party with greater bargaining power may want to avoid an explicit bargain to cover an issue because such a bargain would take too much effort or provoke resentment that could affect subsequent relations. If such a party gets the benefit of not explicitly bargaining, it would be odd to simply grant it also what it would have gotten had an explicit bargain occurred.

153 Zamir, note 8 supra.

154 Skepticism about doctrines of interpretation is a major theme of Marvin Chirelstein, note 61 supra.

155 Zamir, note 8 supra, at 1712.

156 Id. at 1718–19.

157 Id. at 1713. However, Restatement (Second) of Contracts §203 (b) orders in weight express terms, course of performance, course of dealing, and usage of trade.

158 Id. at 1721–27.

159 Id. at 1738–44.

160 Id. at 1756–57.

161 Id. at 1736.

162 Id. at 1777–1802.

163 Id. at 1771–76.

164 See Schwartz and Scott, note 5 supra. In a recent article, Jody S. Kraus and Robert E. Scott, "Contract Design and the Structure of Contractual Intent," 84 *New York University Law Review* 1023 (2009), argue that courts traditionally have taken an approach that emphasizes the intended ends of contracts, but that this approach, influenced by traditions of equity, is largely misguided. Courts instead should focus on the means on which the parties agree, which the text displays.

165 Alan Schwartz and Robert E. Scott. "The Political Economy of Private Legislatures," 143 *University of Pennsylvania Law Review* 595, 597 (1995).

166 David Charny, "The New Formalism in Contract," 66 *University of Chicago Law Review* 842, 45 (1999).

167 See, e.g., Lisa Bernstein, "Private Commercial Law in the Cotton Industry: Creating Cooperation Through Rules, Norms and Institutions," 99 *Michigan Law Review* 1724, 1735–37 (2001).

168 Avery Katz, note 89 supra at 526, points out that industry tribunals may be formalist partly because the judges are already expert and do not need external information that might help a generalist judge.

169 Id. at 508–12.

170 On the author's intent approach, it will not do to say that the real meaning is the one that is the more reasonable.

Chapter 10

Judicial Alterations of Textual Provisions

Cy Pres and Relatives

I. INTRODUCTION

Having seen in the last two chapters that judges may correct mistakes in wills and revise terms of contracts they find unconscionable, we will now examine judicial responses to claims that conditions have changed radically from the time that a text was written. These exercises bear some resemblance to an agent's decision whether he should depart from a principal's specific instructions if doing so will better serve the principal's overall purposes within the scope of the agent's responsibility. We will focus especially on instances when courts acknowledge they are going beyond interpretation of controlling terms and they explicitly authorize consequences different from those provided for in the privately created texts they are considering. The chapter's main emphasis is on *cy pres* in the law of charitable trusts, but it also covers efforts to alter restrictive covenants on real property and to escape obligations because the purposes of contracts have been frustrated or their performance has become impossible or impractical.

According to a doctrine traditionally called *cy pres*, judges reform provisions of charitable trusts when their fulfillment has become impossible or impractical.[1] This technique differs from how courts treat changed conditions in statutory and constitutional interpretation. When a straightforward reading of a statutory or constitutional provision would yield a highly impractical result, judges typically interpret the provision not to mean what it seems to say. Judges do not say they are reaching a resolution at odds with the meaning of the authoritative provision.[2]

We shall be interested in five overarching and interrelated questions: Why does the law of charitable trusts have a doctrine of *cy pres*? What are the circumstances in which it is employed? Does the doctrine deserve extension, or retraction? To what extent is the application of *cy pres* a product of interpretation; in what respects does it reach beyond interpretation? How similar are related doctrines in other areas of law?

II. THE RATIONALE FOR *CY PRES*

The term *cy pres* derives from the Norman French *cy pres comme possible*, roughly translatable as "as close as possible."[3] Cy *pres* authority, initially developed by chancery, perhaps in an effort to save gifts to religious bodies,[4] falls within a court's equitable powers. The need for a modern doctrine of this sort arises to a large extent from special features of many charitable trusts. The trusts have no termination point; the persons who have created them may have died, and, even if they are alive, neither they nor any other individuals have authority to rewrite the terms. By contrast, political bodies may repeal or revise statutes and constitutional provisions. Contracts are for a limited time; and the parties may alter their terms. With simple wills, courts distribute property, and that is the end of it. Although many wills do create private trusts for family members, these trusts are subject to the Rule Against Perpetuities,[5] which precludes trusts of indefinite duration (on the grounds that allowing indefinite control by a testator would be unfair to the survivors and socially undesirable).[6]

Conditions that underlie the creation of charitable trusts can change radically. What the terms require, such as maintaining a public park for whites only, may become illegal. Or they may support research about a disease that has been eradicated. Judges must reform the terms of such trusts or allow the property to revert to family members (or be transferred by "gifts over" to private individuals or charities.) If fulfilling a trust's terms is neither illegal nor impossible, only highly impractical, judges may decide to continue to enforce the original terms, but they may determine instead that an alternative is much more sensible.

The dominant rationale courts express for reforming the terms of charitable trusts "when it becomes impossible, impracticable, or illegal to comply with the settler's expressed intent given changed conditions,"[7] is that this aids in carrying out the important objectives of the creator. So understood, the doctrine of *cy pres* functions as a way to give effect to a settlor's major purposes by disregarding and altering detailed instructions that stand in the way of achieving those purposes. One can also understand the doctrine of *cy pres* as loosening the "dead hand of the past" over modern expenditures of charitable resources. Scholars believe that judges often mask the second rationale with expressed fealty to the first.[8] A view about the desirable scope of *cy pres* depends on evaluating the comparative significance of these two rationales and the capacities of judges to implement them without making the law too uncertain and unpredictable.

A doctrine that parallels *cy pres* applies to administrative provisions of trusts: a court may approve deviations from these when compliance is impossible or illegal, or when "owing to circumstances not known to the settlor and not anticipated by him compliance would defeat or substantially impair the accomplishment of the purpose of the trust."[9] The "substantially impair" language allows courts to deviate from administrative provisions more easily than from substantive provisions under *cy pres*. Donors may well care less about administrative details, such as the physical location of a charitable institution, than the substance of their trusts; but dividing substantive concerns from administrative ones is not always simple,[10] and judges may manipulate the categories to reach results they want. These difficulties underlie one argument for relaxing the requirements for *cy pres* reformations in order to bring them into line with the standards for administrative deviations.

III. TERMS OF APPLICATION – THE PROBLEM OF INTENT

In addition to requiring that the purpose of a trust have failed or become impractical, courts have applied *cy pres* only when they have found that the donor had a general charitable intent—an intent to benefit charity that reaches beyond the specific terms of the trust. If the point of *cy pres* is courts doing the best they can to carry out the intentions of the creator of a trust, and judges could confidently assess a creator's state of mind, requiring a general intent would make perfect sense. Suppose two different people create trusts to benefit an organization engaging in cancer research. After some years, the organization dissolves. *A*, who wished mainly to finance cancer research in an effective way, would have rather had her money go to another organization than revert to family members. *B*, who wished to aid the organization only because close friends were running it, would have rather had his money revert.

Both the requirement that creators of trusts have had a general intent and the standards used to discern that intent have become controversial. Critics worry that the particular standards are either too rigid or are so flexible that judges have sweeping discretion to find a general intent or not, producing decisions that are impossible to square with each other.[11] One objection to the requirement itself is that in circumstances when a donor has failed to indicate clearly in the text what he wished to happen if the specific terms of his trust could no longer be carried out, judges will find it impossible to determine if he had a general intent. Another objection is that the requirement emphasizes the creator's intent to the exclusion of using resources in a socially valuable way. When courts manipulate findings of general intent to serve broader social objectives, their possibly desirable results are purchased at the cost of clarity in the law and wasteful litigation.

In the standard approach to *cy pres*, the perspective of the creator matters not only for whether any shift in original terms is warranted, it also guides a court in determining two other questions. Donor intent can bear on the degree of impracticality that would warrant employing *cy pres*. Suppose two donors have given art collections with conditions for display that now interfere significantly and equally with maximum public enjoyment of the collections. If the first donor was obviously aware that her conditions would seriously limit public viewing, and the evident impetus of her gift was more to perpetuate her name than to benefit the public, a judge could be confident that she would want her conditions followed even if the public inconvenience became greater than she anticipated. If the second donor set conditions that she thought would benefit the public and changes in circumstances made them counterproductive in that respect, a judge would conclude that she would want the conditions terminated.

Donor intent could also guide what dispensation of resources is close to the original. If two donors give money in trust for a local medical facility that proves wholly unnecessary, one might have preferred that her money go to another (non-local) medical facility, the other that her money go for nonmedical local charities.

The most straightforward alternative to relying on donor intent would be for courts candidly to acknowledge that they make decisions about *cy pres* in light of the desirable uses of social resources. But such an approach raises questions about fairness to the creators of trusts and about the ability of courts to determine effective uses of social resources. These worries can be met to some degree, but only to some degree, by placing wide-ranging discretion in the trustees who control trusts to decide when resources should be diverted from their originally prescribed uses.[12]

The way in which a finding about general intent affects the application of *cy pres* is well illustrated by a trust created in 1861. A man left money to trustees to create public sentiment that would end Negro slavery and to aid fugitive slaves.[13] Once slavery was abolished, and the terms of the trust could no longer be carried out,[14] the court, instead of giving the money to the heirs, directed that the trust fund support welfare and educational work for freed blacks in New England.

Judges often treat the crucial question about general intent as a hypothetical one. "If the testator had known that it would not be possible to follow the express terms of his trust, would he have wanted the funds to go to a similar charitable purpose or to revert to his heirs?"[15] Answering such a question may not be simple. Suppose the donor of a trust to help end slavery was a legalist who was deeply offended by the notion of slaves who lacked basic legal rights, but hardly cared about other forms of discrimination. What such a donor would have wanted under changed conditions he did not address may be hard to gauge.

Just what evidence can a court bring to bear to try to answer the question about a donor's intent? This issue brings us back to the discussion in the chapter on wills about what evidence a court will consider to discern a testator's intent.[16] If a court followed a strict "four corners" rule and limited itself to what a will (or other instrument creating a trust) provided, it would have to ask whether a person who wrote such a will would be likely to have a general intent. Instead, courts usually consider undisputed surrounding circumstances, such as gifts a person made to charities during his lifetime.[17] However, evidence about what the donor said is generally not admissible.[18] The evidence, taken as a whole, may allow judges to make an individualized judgment about a particular donor, but there is no guarantee they can answer the crucial hypothetical question confidently.

Evidence of intent here plays a somewhat different role than it does in typical wills contests. In those, the language of the will (or the language plus undoubted objective circumstances) establishes a presumptively correct result. If judges stick with the will's language unless evidence of a contrary intent is overwhelming, allowing such evidence does not turn the interpretation of wills into a swearing contest about intent, with highly uncertain results. For *cy pres*, the issue about intent arises only when carrying out the terms of the trust has become impossible or impractical, and the will itself (or other instrument creating the trust) does not clearly indicate what should be done in the circumstances. The court must decide what to do about changed circumstances that the language of the will has not addressed. Unless judges establish general presumptions favoring continuation of charitable activities or favoring reversion to heirs, they have no presumed result against which evidence of a contrary intent would contest. Rather, they have to estimate what, on balance, the testator's intent was, or would be. Thus, in *cy pres* cases, allowing broad evidence of intent, including evidence of the donor's comments, could introduce considerable uncertainty about how to resolve cases. Since only courts can grant *cy pres* relief, and *cy pres* applications must, therefore, be reviewed by courts, uncertainty about the law's application is not as likely to affect private behavior and the amount of litigation as does uncertainty in some other areas,[19] but uncertainty is still undesirable. One way for courts to minimize it would be to adopt a stance of promoting charitable purposes, declining to find a general intent only if the evidence that a donor did not have such a intent was very strong.

Even a judge who considers evidence extrinsic to the will may end up with little sense of a particular testator's specific intent; she may have to fall back on what most people of that type would want. Would *a person* who donates money for poor relief want that money to continue being used for that purpose? If judges must so categorize testators, that may open the door to arbitrariness in how they determine their classifications.[20] Sometimes the classification will be fairly simple—the donor wanted to finance effective cancer research. But should a judge classify a woman who has donated money to build a local hospital that turns out not to be needed, as someone who is interested only in local medical services or is mainly interested in local improvement more generally, or is mainly interested in medical services more generally?[21]

The possible complexities of discerning intent are well revealed by a case that twice reached the Supreme Court. Senator Bacon left money to establish a public park in Macon, Georgia, to be used by white women and children. After the Supreme Court held that public parks could not be segregated by race,[22] Georgia courts had to decide whether to establish an integrated park or void the gift, and return the money to Bacon's heirs.[23]

How should the Georgia courts have resolved this question?[24] Had Senator Bacon been a rabid segregationist or a Southern liberal who felt constrained by irrational community feelings to have the park segregated by race, discerning his relevant intent would be easy. The heirs should receive the property of the segregationist;[25] the park donated by the liberal should be integrated. Regrettably, Senator Bacon was not so conveniently classifiable. In his will he declared himself not to be influenced by any "want of consideration for the Negroes," but "without hesitation," he declared his opinion that the "two races" should not use "recreation grounds" in common.[26] The Georgia courts returned the property to Bacon's heirs, considering the limitations to white users to be "an essential and indispensable part" of Bacon's plan.[27] Richard Posner has criticized the result, because we have no indication Senator Bacon wanted mainly to foster racial segregation; and he likely would have preferred an integrated park to no park.[28]

In truth, we don't know what Bacon would have thought, but even putting the counterfactual question raises a deeper question about how one assesses the intent of someone long dead for circumstances in which legal contexts and social mores have shifted radically. Suppose, as a member of the elite, Senator Bacon could not imagine whites and blacks together in an integrated park, and would *then* have chosen no park over a racially integrated park. But social opinions have changed greatly in the meantime, and virtually all members of the white elite now accept integrated public parks without qualm. (This generalization was, in reality, less accurate in the late 1960s, the time of the case, than it is now.) If we ask how Bacon, with most of his characteristics unchanged, would now feel about racially integrated parks, we might conclude that "had he lived to see this day," he would almost certainly have accepted them. If the Georgia judges had reconstituted the donor to make his opinions shift with changes in dominant opinions, or, using a more direct approach, had disregarded his unwillingness to benefit all parts of the citizenry together as historically conditioned and contrary to a modern understanding of democratic values, they might have emphasized his general intent to create a park for residents. Few courts have been willing, at least explicitly, to reconstitute donors' preferences in this manner.[29]

I have explored some tangles about intent, but my main point is that in many cases deciding whether a relevant general intent exists will be difficult. A court may be reduced to asking what a rational person who makes the gift would have wanted.[30] If the issue involves an effective use of funds, or satisfying broad objectives after a particular organization dissolves, the "rational donor" works well. A rational donor approach does not simply collapse into judges approving whatever uses of funds they think valuable. A judge who believes that money is much better spent on medical research than art understands that a "rational donor" to an art museum has a different scale of priorities.

However, in some cases, a rational donor approach, honestly applied, may not prove very helpful. In a controversial California case that was eventually settled, a woman had established a trust to be used for the needy and for other charitable purposes in wealthy Marin County, California.[31] The value of the interest in an oil company that she donated had risen from $7 million when she died to $400 million at the time of the suit. The foundation holding the Buck trust sought to invoke *cy pres* to spend the benefits throughout the Bay Area. Professor John Simon argued that the donor would have wished her trust to have a wider scope if she had been aware of its magnitude, because that would reflect how "major American philanthropists" make their gifts. But without knowing more about Mrs. Buck as a person, whether she disliked urban areas or the liberal flavor of San Francisco, we can hardly assess what she would have wanted if her gift turned out to be much larger than she had any reason to guess.

One device courts have used to discern intent is to look for various signposts. A major signpost is whether a will provides that if its terms can no longer be implemented, the assets are to be transferred by a "gift over" to private persons or to some other charity.[32] The essential idea is that if the donor thus explicitly includes a gift over, he has considered and provided for the circumstances of the trust's terms being frustrated. The crucial issue about gifts over is whether they should be viewed as precluding *cy pres*, or only as matters for judges to take into account.

Here one must initially draw an important distinction: the conditions specified for the gift over may or may not themselves be satisfied. In a 1978 case, the testator's will established a trust in favor of a particular Unitarian church he had helped found, with a "gift over" to "support Unitarian education at Harvard and the poor of McLean Asylum . . . ."[33] The gift over was to take effect "if the [church] changes its religious tenets and cease[s] to inculcate a 'Liberal Religion.'" After the church dissolved, courts had to decide whether to enforce the gift over or apply *cy pres* in favor of the general Unitarian-Universalist Association.

Unitarians do not believe in the divinity of Jesus or in the Trinity, and they tend to emphasize the human potential for good, rather than the inevitability of sin. The donor evidently feared reversion to a more orthodox congregationalist version of Protestantism out of which Unitarianism developed; if the local church ceased to inculcate a "liberal religion," the money would go elsewhere. We cannot be sure what the donor would have wanted had he foreseen dissolution of the local church. In such an instance, the sensible approach would be to use the "gift over" as relevant evidence about the donor's attitude, but *not* as a conclusive basis by itself to deny *cy pres*.[34]

On the other hand, had the original will provided a gift over if the local church dissolved, the very event that happened, the gift over should be a nearly conclusive basis to deny *cy pres*.[35] So long as donor's intent remains a central aspect of *cy pres*,[36] such a gift over should be less than conclusive *only* if the circumstances in which the specified event happens are radically different from those the donor imagined, so that his words fail to provide a reliable basis on which to answer the hypothetical question of what he would have wanted done. For example, even had Senator Bacon provided a gift over to relatives in the event that public parks could no longer be segregated, judges *might* have responded that desegregation in the 1960s has a far different social significance than desegregation in the 1880s (or that courts should not give effect to a racial attitude that is now regarded as malign).

Another "signpost" used by courts has been a presumption that if the testator has left the "bulk" of his estate to charity, he would want the money to continue in that way rather than revert to individual heirs. This signpost for whether a creator has a general intent to assist one kind of charity is no help at all if a gift over is to a different charity, because the resources will continue in charitable use whether or not *cy pres* is employed. Even when money will otherwise revert into private hands, the "percentage" approach is hardly a very reliable sign of whether a donor has a general intent.[37] When someone donates a high percentage of her estate to charity, that is *some* indication that she would not like to see all the money revert to family members of a succeeding generation; but a person who leaves ninety percent of her estate to family members, confident that she has provided for them adequately, may also care a great deal that the ten percent remains in charitable use.

IV. THE DESIRABLE BOUNDARIES OF *CY PRES*

The two crucial questions in relation to *cy pres* are whether courts should find the circumstances of its application generously or restrictively and whether they should focus primarily on the donor's intent or the common good. When issues about *cy pres* were first raised in the United States, courts were wary of perpetual trusts, concerned particularly that property left to religious organizations deprived heirs of their due and took resources out of commercial life.[38] Such attitudes led to a restrictive approach to *cy pres* modifications.[39] By the second half of the nineteenth century, judges regarded charitable trusts more favorably, acknowledging their substantial contribution to social life.[40] It is now widely assumed that charities play a very positive role in American society, and some scholars have called for a presumption of saving a charitable gift.[41]

One aspect of a thoughtful judgment about the benefits of the doctrine of *cy pres* concerns the family members who do not receive the property that a donor leaves to charity. Most money given to charitable trusts is donated by wealthy people who leave considerable assets to immediate family members.[42] When issues of *cy pres* arise, family members known to the testator may all have died. If remote descendants, like Senator Bacon's scattered heirs, receive a reversion, it will come as a kind of windfall.

One who thinks that charitable trusts are highly desirable will oppose a restrictive version of *cy pres* that frustrates the likely wishes of donors that their charitable purposes be accomplished. But this judgment leaves open how far courts should presume unrevealed wishes, and how far they should rely on a donor's presumed wishes rather than estimates of the common good. A crucial aspect of both inquiries is what issues courts can appropriately resolve.

Let us first consider a case in which many of the conditions for a generous application of *cy pres* were comfortably met, although the New York court resolved not to alter the terms of the trust.[43] The case differs from the examples we have been considering in treating a trust unlike those for typical charities, but the same principles of *cy pres* were applicable. A request was made to change the terms of competition for America's Cup races, which had been established in three successive deeds of gift by members of the New York Yacht Club who had won the cup in England in 1851. The third and current deed of gift was made in 1887 by the sole surviving member of the original group. According to its terms, most conditions for holding the races favored the host club, but a challenging club could name the size of yacht to be used, with a length at the water-line of not less than sixty-five or more than ninety feet. Together the clubs could agree to set conditions that varied from those prescribed in the deed of gift. In the years preceding 1987, clubs involved had generally agreed upon conditions for the races, including preliminary competitions among potential challengers from various countries and among potential defenders for the host country. The racing yachts, a type called the international twelve-meter class, were smaller than the minimum size specified in the deed of gift; and in 1956 the deed was revised by a court to allow a minimum length at the water line of forty-four feet.[44]

After the San Diego Yacht Club won the Cup in 1987, it envisioned a multinational regatta for the cup in 1990 or 1991;[45] but, before it announced its plans, New Zealand's Mercury Bay Boating Club made a challenge, for 1988, according to the third deed of gift, proposing ships that were ninety feet at the water line. When the New Zealand club sued to have its challenge accepted, the San Diego Club asked the court to amend the third deed of gift to conform with the practices of recent Cup competitions. Criticizing the San Diego Club for refusing to negotiate with the challenger, the New York court refused to amend the deed of gift, finding that the donor's purpose could still be carried out under the terms of the trust.[46]

Alex Johnson and Ross Taylor argue that a court should have reached a different conclusion under *cy pres* doctrine as it has developed; they also use the case to mount a general critique against limitations upon *cy pres* relief.[47] Specifically at stake was how rigorous the condition of impossibility or impracticality should be. Allowing ninety-foot ships and single nation challenges is not literally impossible, but the yachting community has developed a relatively broad consensus about how best to carry on this international competition. An isolated club should not be able to throw a temporary monkey wrench in these practices by making a single challenge with an unorthodox ship size, and refusing to budge.[48] The donor of the third deed of gift could not have foreseen how the procedures for international competitions would develop; he had an overarching aim, we may assume, to promote healthy international competition.[49] Thus, faithfulness to the donor's overall aims and attention to the common good both suggested that a change in the gift's terms was appropriate under New York law.[50]

In this yachting conflict, a judge could find a sufficiently concrete and objective standard of common good. Fair and healthy international competition may be vague as a principle, but its application here was straightforward enough. One country's club should not get a large advantage over others simply by filing a document at the propitious time and turning what has become (by consensus) a multinational competition into a single country challenge. Nor should one club be able to dictate a size of boat at odds with a standard practice.

What if we somehow knew that George Schuyler, the donor of the Cup, had a substantial preference for large ships and single country challenges?[51] Would application of *cy pres* still be appropriate? I think the answer is "yes," for two important reasons. First, the international yachting community has reached a consensus that smaller ships and multinational competition are desirable. Since America's Cup races can occur only yearly, or every other year, the multinational approach gives each country a fairer opportunity to succeed than does a series of single challenges. Given the general use of twelve-meter yachts in other competitions, it is somewhat less expensive to have similar boats used for the America's Cup, rather than a special breed of large boat.[52] Second, Schuyler's "investment" was donating a cup, whose monetary value had been dwarfed by the expense and effort involved in running, and participating, in the competitions. It would be odd to have Schuyler's investment dictate Cup practices, against the judgments of virtually all those now involved in the competition.[53] A court that deals with an objective standard of common good and a minimal investment of the donor should appropriately consider that good as more important than a donor's uncertain intent.

Drawing on scholarship about relational contracts and dynamic statutory interpretation,[54] Johnson and Taylor argue that the terms of trusts should be viewed flexibly to achieve their broad objectives and "to promote the maximum and efficient use of resources."[55] The authors may overstate the strength of the analogies to relational contracts and dynamically interpreted statutes,[56] both of which differ significantly from trusts in need of *cy pres* relief. Relational contracts are negotiated; settlors of trusts are able to choose their own terms. Judicial creativity with long-term contracts is mainly to fill in terms and make vague terms more concrete, not to supplant existing terms with alternatives. Statutory interpretation, even of a dynamic sort, involves the construal and application of terms the legislature has provided, not an explicit deviation from prescribed terms in favor of alternatives. Still, Johnson and Taylor have a powerful point: because charitable trusts have a public character and are for public benefit,[57] as time passes, judicial evaluation of the public good should increasingly matter in comparison with donor's intent.

Regrettably for a sweeping favoring of public good, reasons to respect the donor's intent are often stronger than in the yachting example. Simple evaluation of the public good is not always possible, and saying just how public good should weigh in relation to likely intent is far from straight-forward. The donation to a local Unitarian church, with a gift over for Unitarian education at Harvard and for the McLean Asylum if the church ceased to inculcate a "liberal religion," provides an illustration. After the local church dissolved, the court enforced the gift over instead of employing *cy pres* in favor of the national Unitarian-Universalist Association. The argument against the decision is that benefiting the national body of Unitarian worshipers seems to come closer to the donor's intent than enforcing the gift over. But among Unitarians, as is true for other churches with a congregational form of governance, primary authority lies with the local church, and dominant theological views may differ significantly.[58] Whatever the precise relations were between the local church and more inclusive bodies when the donor made his gift, the donor must have been aware that local churches sometimes cease thriving and dissolve. Perhaps his failure to make a gift over to any larger church organization shows that he did not want his money to go there. We cannot know for certain. And a guess in that respect might require estimates about a Unitarian's attitudes that a court would rightly hesitate to make.

A judge trying to resolve what to do in such an instance faces troubling questions both about how to respond to a donor's uncertain intent and about how to assess the desirable use of social resources. A court that is guided by the donor's wishes and concludes that he would want the gift over would comfortably direct the money to Harvard and the McLean Asylum. But suppose a judge determines: "*Probably* the testator would want the money to go to the Unitarian-Universalist Association, but he could have provided that and failed to do so." To generalize from the example, should a court apply *cy pres* based on the testator's probable but uncertain wishes, or should it enforce a gift over, or allow reversion to heirs, unless it is highly confident that application of *cy pres* is what the testator would want?[59] A preference for charity over reversion to indi-viduals could resolve some cases, but that would not help when a gift over is to another charity.

Let us now bring "common good" into the equation, supposing (contrary to fact) that the entire gift over was to the McLean Asylum. "Common good" can matter both for decisions *whether* to apply *cy pres* and for deci-sions about *how* to apply it. How is a court to decide whether money is better spent for the Unitarian-Universalist Association or for the poor relief provided by the McLean Asylum?

Part of this problem relates to religion. People differ wildly in their estimates about the value of religion writ large, and of various religions. In our legal order, in which church is separated from the state, courts cannot decide *which* religions deserve support.[60] Courts, as organs of the state, cannot even compare the value of religious organizations in general with the value of aid to the poor. Thus, comparisons of common good, independent of the testator's intent, should not figure in decisions whether to apply *cy pres* in favor of a religious group or enforce a gift over to another charity.

The difficulty with decisions about religion is still more extensive. According to the Supreme Court's interpretation of the religion clauses of the federal constitution, secular courts cannot determine which changes in doctrines and practices are fundamental; they cannot determine when a religion ceases to be "liberal."[61] Thus, not only are many judgments about common good out of bounds when religion is the subject, so also are some judgments about applying the specific terms of trusts themselves.

Problems about common good are not restricted to religion. Suppose a trust is created to fight polio, which is then largely eradicated; the court considers *cy pres* in favor of an organization directed against another childhood disease rather than enforcing a gift over for the McLean Asylum. A court should not decide whether money to cure disease contributes to the common good more than assistance to the poor.

These perplexities should not lead us to extreme skepticism about any criteria of the common good.[62] On many occasions, standards of efficacy will be relatively objective. Among two charities doing similar work, one that delivers a much higher percent of its income to needy beneficiaries is better serving the common good than one whose income goes almost entirely to administrative personnel. And the standard of fair and healthy international competition provided a viable criterion of common good for the America's Cup. Courts may also say that serving a donor's broad charitable purposes is socially preferable to having money go to private individuals only remotely related to him.

Although modern courts have found a general charitable intent rather easily and have relaxed the requirement that applying the trust's terms must have become impossible, they have neither eliminated the role of general intent nor substituted "common good" for "donor's intent" as their guide. [63] A resurgence of belief in individual rights, especially rights of property, may be one reason courts have not moved further in the direction of using common good as their main criterion, but increasing skepticism about the capacity of courts to determine the common good may also be at work. A standard of faithfulness to a donor's broad intentions, as difficult as it is sometimes to apply, allows judges to avoid explicit determinations about common good they are ill suited to make.

The sharpest issue about a common good approach arises when a fairly objective judgment about common good conflicts with the highly likely wishes of a donor, whose resources continue to sustain the charitable activities.[64] The claim that the donor's wishes should prevail flows from her ability to dictate the terms of the trust in the first instance. The counter argument is that courts better pursue common good than defer to the probable wishes in modern circumstances of someone who died long ago. Since courts usually act only when trustees apply to deviate from the terms of the trust, they need not make their own judgments about common good from scratch; they can give weight to the judgments made by trustees.[65]

One can offer instrumental and inherent arguments that courts should not lightly disregard donors' intent. The instrumental argument is that if potential donors come to believe they will not be able to control the disposition of their charitable gifts, they will not make the gifts.[66] This argument is weak, at least if *cy pres* is limited to situations in which the donor's preferences have not been clearly stated in the trust document. Even if courts candidly stated that the donor's intent does not matter when other conditions for *cy pres* are satisfied, donors could largely protect themselves by covering multiple contingencies in their original grants or by assigning their trustees broad discretion.[67] The effect on donations would probably not be significant were courts to give greater weight to common good, both because most donors could protect their specific aims by dealing explicitly with various contingencies[68] *and* because charitable donations offer tax advantages.[69]

The inherent argument for attending to the donor's intent is that it deserves to be followed for its own sake, even at some sacrifice of the common good. That intent would be followed if explicitly implemented by the will's terms, and perhaps judges should follow it if they can infer it.

Both the inherent and instrumental arguments for paying attention to the donor's intent have *some* force; *cy pres* should definitely not become an inquiry exclusively about common good. *However,* the comparative power of donor's intent to control assets should diminish slowly over time, and it should be weaker when the conditions he has prescribed are directly aligned against some public policy,[70] rather than merely requiring a less than optimal use of resources.[71]

The relaxation in requirements of impracticality and general charitable intent recommended by some authors is a good idea. Evaluations of "common good" should often play a part in decisions about *cy pres*; but some such evaluations are beyond judicial authority, and "common good" should not altogether displace donor's intent.

VI. SERVITUDES AND EASEMENTS IN REAL PROPERTY LAW

According to a doctrine that resembles the trusts doctrine of *cy pres*, when use of real property is subject to a restriction, or servitude, that can no longer be accomplished because of a change in conditions, a court may terminate the servitude. The Restatement (Third) of Property also provides that a court may modify a servitude to permit its purpose to be accomplished.[72]

When covenants run with the land, owners have agreed to subject their properties to a common restriction. In *El Di Inc. v. Town of Bethany Beach*,[73] the agreement was that no one would sell alcohol on their premises. In this quiet town formed in large part by the Christian Missionary Society of Washington, D.C., the development company had sold land with restrictive covenants prohibiting the sale of alcohol and restricting construction to residential cottages. Most of the original purchasers undoubtedly welcomed a "dry" environment.

Once signed, valid covenants, passing with the land to bind each new owner, are not easily undone.[74] The necessary unanimous agreement is hard to achieve. If courts were unable to provide relief, when changing social conditions render a restriction pointless, a single beneficiary could refuse to release his fellow property owners or demand an exorbitant price for doing so.

In *El Di*, the Supreme Court of Delaware pointed out that Bethany Beach had become a popular summer resort; that in the central district the restriction against commercial buildings had broken down, restaurants allowed patrons to bring in their own alcoholic beverages, and alcohol was sold not far outside the restricted district. The court also accepted the claim of Holiday House that it could better control drinking if it sold alcohol rather than allowing "brown-bagging." The court concluded, over two dissenters, that "the business uses, the availability of alcohol in close proximity to this section [of the town], and the repeated use of 'brown-bagging' render the originally intended benefits of the covenant unattainable . . . ."[75]

El Di is an easy case to understand but a difficult one to resolve. The court writes as if "brown-bagging" is virtually indistinguishable from the sale of liquor, but that is at best a dubious assumption;[76] and the Court of Chancery, the fact finder, had determined that the community had not changed so drastically that the restrictive covenant was purposeless. A comment to the Restatement notes that few appellate courts considering changed conditions have terminated servitudes.[77] The comment also notes that the justifications for the changed conditions doctrine lie in both the parties' implied intent and public policy, the same justifications that support the *cy pres* doctrine. Outmoded restrictive covenants definitely reduce the value of land and prevent its efficient use. Those who originally agreed to such covenants would not want their continuance if they lacked any point whatsoever. But *El Di* suggests problems, ones that in various respects look different from their close cousins in trusts law.

Is the implied intent of the parties a complete fiction or does it bear a powerful relation to what the parties would have wanted if they could have foreseen the changed conditions? With *cy pres* it is definitely the latter. People donating money to charity want it used productively; most would wish their money well spent even if the specific beneficiaries differ from those they imagined. Original parties to a restrictive covenant would care whether family descendants would lose a quality of life they have sought to protect, and would be burdened by outmoded restrictions, but do the original parties care much what happens to property values and the local quality of life decades after their land is sold to strangers? Probably not. The connection of the original participants to later owners is more remote than the analogous connection in *cy pres*.

If we did ask what the original participants would have wanted in *El Di*, we run directly into attitudes about alcohol. In 1900, many religious groups and individuals regarded alcohol as a tremendous evil; religious groups were, after all, the main impetus behind national prohibition, adopted two decades later. The original signers might have been appalled by "brown-bagging," but they would have preferred that to the sale of alcohol if they thought sales would further increase alcohol consumption.

Although modern concern about use of alcohol may generally lack the degree of moralism characteristic of those who once favored prohibition, given the havoc alcohol wreaks in the lives of our citizens, as alcoholism destroys individuals and families and drunken drivers kill, we cannot blithely suppose that wanting one's own small community to be as free from alcohol as is reasonably possible has become irrational. If we guessed about the attitudes of the original signers, we might well conclude they would have agreed with the dissent in *El Di*. The majority opinion represents what most present property owners prefer better than what the original signers would have wanted in modern conditions.

This whole inquiry casts doubt on the contemporary significance of the views of long dead original signers. The attitude of present owners who have purchased restricted property seems more relevant. Did a substantial number want to preserve what their covenants guaranteed,[78] or would the great majority of rational modern owners have believed that the restriction has lost its point? The more resolution of these cases turns on the needs of modern owners rather than implications about the aims of the original signers, the less it involves interpretation of the original agreement in any sense.

Scholars have emphasized how important the changed conditions doctrine is to economic welfare,[79] and one might best justify *El Di* on that basis. But this defense raises a question about evaluating public welfare similar to that we reviewed in connection with *cy pres*. Who can say whether increased land value and convenience in access to liquor outweighs the symbolic value and modest practical restraint of not allowing sales of liquor? At least if one focuses on a single geographical community, comparing these values is hard.[80] Reasonable landowners could prefer a "dry" environment, even at the cost of some monetary value for their own property.[81] Comparison is more straightforward when the benefit of the servitude is mainly economic, and its cost now definitely outweighs its benefits.

With only modest support in decided cases, the Restatement provides that courts may modify servitudes rather than terminate them, so long as modification does not increase the burden on the restricted estates.

The Restatement also provides that compensation may be given for a loss of benefit. Courts able to modify restrictions and compensate have much more power to achieve an equitable resolution than if they must simply continue or terminate a restriction.[82] But one may worry that such a power will bring about more frequent interference with vested rights by judges who lack adequate standards to determine just what losses various parties should suffer. Closely similar questions arise in respect to instances of frustration and impracticality in contracts, discussed in the next section, but courts may have a greater need for this broader authority in respect to restrictive covenants, because of the larger number of interested parties and the longer periods over which the covenants extend.

Conservation servitudes supported by state subsidies and entered into with state agencies present some special features. In return for a covenant to keep land for farming, a property owner may receive tax breaks and other benefits. Suppose future development renders continued use of the land for farming undesirable, and the owner seeks to end the servitude. Since the owner has received significant benefits, he should, if successful, be required to take alternative conservation measures or pay damages to the government. Whatever may be true in instances of privately negotiated servitudes, the courts should certainly have powers of modification and compensation when conditions render unsuitable restrictions aimed at conferring a public benefit.[83]

VII. FRUSTRATION AND IMPRACTICABILITY IN CONTRACT LAW

In the law of contracts, doctrines of frustration and impracticability deal with changed conditions. A practical question these doctrines raise is whether courts should rewrite obligations or limit themselves to deciding whether one party has an excuse to avoid performance. A theoretical question is the familiar one whether relevant approaches should be regarded as based on interpretation or something beyond interpretation.

In instances of frustration and impracticability, performance of one party's obligations has become extremely expensive in relation to the benefit he may acquire. The classic cases in which the point of a contract was frustrated after its formation[84] involved the renting of rooms from which to view a coronation parade, which was canceled because of the King's illness.[85] The courts held that those who rented the rooms did not have to pay money that had not come due at the time the parade was canceled. The courts did not allow the renters to recover money they had already paid.[86]

To many, it seems fairer that in cases of frustration, people unable to enjoy the fruits of what they have bargained for should recover what they have already spent; and indeed in England this approach has now supplanted that of the Coronation Cases.[87] However, Andrew Kull has defended what he calls the "windfall" approach of leaving losses where they are.[88] He claims that the payment schedule reflects the parties' own sense of who should be taking the risk that some catastrophe will spoil the purpose of the contract, that placing the entire burden of loss on one party rather than the other is itself unfair, and that courts have no means to allocate the burden of loss fairly. For Kull, having rooms with a good view on the parade route was a valuable asset, of which the owners should not have been totally deprived. Whatever appeal Kull's approach has for this setting depends on the parade not being rescheduled, as in fact this parade was. With a rescheduled parade, the owners can recoup their original losses. It is unfair for renters to pay twice to watch a parade that takes place only once.

The Restatement provides that a party's remaining duties to render performance are discharged when the purpose of a contract is frustrated.[89] It does not by itself provide for recovery of money or efforts already expended, but it does not preclude such measures, which might be required under separate principles of restitution.[90]

Impracticability occurs when one party's performance becomes very difficult. S contracts to sell liquor to B, and the government then forbids the sale of liquor. Or S promises to deliver goods in Poland, but the Germans then invade Poland, making delivery extremely dangerous. The Restatement formulation, closely parallel to that on frustration, applies when a party's performance is made impracticable . . . by the occurrence of an event the non-occurrence of which was a basic assumption on which the contract was made . . . ."[91] Again, only discharge is provided, not recovery for efforts already expended.

The crucial questions about impracticability are these. How far should such cases be governed by some account of the parties' probable intent? Do courts have adequate means to decide when performance becomes impracticable? Should a decision be limited to excusing nonperformance, and possibly granting recovery for efforts already expended, or should a court feel free to rewrite the contract's obligations to achieve an equitable distribution of loss between the parties?

The origin of the doctrine of impracticability lay in cases in which performance had become impossible.[92] A rents out a dance hall to B for a date a month from the making of the contract. One week later the dance hall burns down, without either party being at fault. A does not have an obligation to B to supply the hall or to pay B damages for whatever loss B suffers. As an opinion in an old English case put it, "[I]n contracts in which the performance depends on the continued existence of a given person or thing, a condition is implied that the impossibility of performance arising from the perishing or the person or thing shall excuse the performance."[93] A's relief from performance follows from a determination that he has not expressly assumed the risk of impossibility.

The development of modern doctrine involves movement from cases in which performance is impossible to ones in which it has become prohibitively costly.[94]

Under a modern approach to claims of impossibility or impracticability, a court's initial inquiry is whether the parties explicitly or implicitly allocated the risk in their contract. If the contract to deliver goods to Poland had been signed after journalists had written that a German invasion of Poland was imminent, and if the seller said he would deliver only for $30,000, triple the ordinary cost, a court would infer that the seller was taking the risk that the Germans would invade. At this initial stage of analysis, then, the court is interpreting the whole contract, deciding what the parties intended, or reasonably would have intended, about the distribution of risk.

The cases became interesting, and difficult, once the court decides that the particular risk is not addressed by the contract itself. A famous example involved a contract by Alcoa to process aluminum for fifteen years under a price set in relation to the Wholesale Price Index.[95] Because of a sharp rise in the cost of petroleum, Alcoa stood to lose more than $60 million from the time it sought relief to the time the contract would end.

Among the standards courts and scholars have suggested for deciding how the risk of loss should be allocated are (1) magnitude of loss or harshness, (2) foresight of the risk, (3) foreseeability of the risk, (4) capability to bear the risk, (5) fairness to the parties, and (6) continuity of contractual relationships. The Restatement formulation makes the critical assessment for allocating the risk of loss (7) an inquiry into whether the contract was founded on a basic assumption that a circumstance would exist (such as a peaceful Poland), the nonexistence of which causes the hardship. This "basic assumption" approach undoubtedly draws in some of the other inquiries.

How many of these standards involve interpretation of the contract in some sense? When judges ask about what risks the parties did foresee, they are asking, at least in part, how these parties would explicitly have allocated the risks if they had had to do so in advance. They would probably have allocated the risk to the party who would suffer less in bearing it. Thus, if the risk was foreseen, the party who suffers less would not get an excuse.

Foreseeability, that is *reasonable foreseeability*, does not directly concern the actual knowledge or intent of the parties.[96] The question of what reasonable parties would have intended turns on who could better bear the risk, and is largely a question about hypothetical actors seeking to maximize efficiency. That approach may be defended as desirably promoting economic efficiency; however, given the difficulty judges face in deciding in individual cases who would have been the better risk bearer, and the uncertainty that standard thus introduces, judges using it in these sorts of cases may not actually promote efficient outcomes.[97]

The concern with continuity of contractual relationships fits with a view that many parties want to establish a relationship of trust over time with their contractual partners—they enter into relational contracts.[98] A focus on continuity could involve interpretation in a broad sense if a court tried to discern from a contractual relationship whether those particular parties highly valued continuity over time.

The "basic assumption" approach, in principle, reflects the understanding of the parties, but whether it does so in reality will depend on how a court decides what the basic assumptions of the contract were. How does a court determine that, although Alcoa was undoubtedly risking some rise in the price of oil, a basic assumption of the contract was that rises would be moderate and not extreme?

When judges base decisions on magnitude of loss, harshness, and fairness to the parties, they focus mainly on what is fair to the parties *now*, given unexpected conditions, rather than on how best to interpret what the parties have undertaken. In summary, some of the possible bases for resolution of impracticability cases are a kind of extension of interpreting the language of the contract and the parties own intentions; others are more candidly focused on equities and efficiencies under present circumstances.

If one focuses on equity in present circumstances, it seems to make sense to allow the court to rewrite contractual obligations, rather than merely excusing performance or requiring performance. That is what the court undertook to do in *Alcoa*, restructuring the price schedule in a way that would be fairer. *Alcoa* has apparently not had a wide influence, involving as it did a sharp departure from existing doctrine.[99] More importantly perhaps, critics worry that the case requires judges to perform a task for which they are ill suited, and that it marks a regrettable deviation from the general rule that parties should work out their own obligations. The *Alcoa* approach to rewriting contractual obligations, which perhaps most closely resembles *cy pres* among contractual remedies, has a weak foothold in the case law, but the Restatement (Second) provides that in cases of impracticality and frustration, if the application of other rules cannot avoid injustice, "the court may grant relief on such terms as justice requires, including the protection of reliance interests."[100]

Concerns about judicial role and the autonomy of contractors have led courts to be very hesitant to excuse performance when that has become costly but not impossible. Interestingly, most of the Restatement's illustrations are ones in which parties are not relieved of performance that has become much more expensive than they anticipated. Cases in which shipping costs rose sharply because the Suez Canal was closed during a war are representative. Parties who had agreed to carry goods for a certain price, expecting ships to go through the canal, did not receive any excuse or financial relief when it turned out that ships had to take the much longer route around the Cape of Good Hope.[101]

VIII. CONCLUSION AND ANALOGOUS STATUTORY AND CONSTITUTIONAL PROBLEMS

This chapter has considered various doctrines in the law of trusts, property, and contracts according to which courts may refuse to enforce or may alter terms that were valid when originally formulated. We have seen that in approaching such cases, judges rely on various combinations of probable intent and an evaluation of public good. We have identified some of the difficulties that surround such efforts, ones that resemble similar perplexities in the law of wills about when to alter provisions because of changed circumstances.

What should courts do when the terms of statutes and constitutions seem to fit badly with modern conditions? Is something like a specific *cy pres* doctrine appropriate? As we shall see in subsequent volumes, courts have resisted any such explicit approach, although interpretations do sometimes change with changing conditions. Two important questions are whether such adjustments are warranted and whether courts should explicitly acknowledge that they are rejecting or deviating from what the terms of authoritative texts created by legislative bodies require.

Notes

1 In modern parlance, the doctrine is sometimes referred to as approximation.

2 One exceptional circumstance in which judges may explicitly reach a resolution that is at odds with the meaning of a statute is when the statute violates the Constitution; a court may reform the provisions to eliminate the objectionable feature. See Welsh v. United States, 398 U.S. 333, 344–45 (1970) (Harlan, J. concurring). Justice Harlan contended that the statute governing eligibility for treatment as a conscientious objector unconstitutionally included religious objectors and excluded nonreligious objectors. Rather than invalidate all exemptions, the Court, he claimed, should extend the class of persons made eligible. For a case employing this approach to extend benefits provided by statute to families with an unemployed father to families with an unemployed mother, see Califano v. Westcott, 443 U.S. 76 (1979).

3 George Gleason Bogert & George Taylor Bogert, *The Law of Trusts and Trustees* §431, at p. 95 (Rev. 2nd ed. Repl. Vol., St. Paul, Minn., West Pub. Co., 1991).

4 See id. at pp. 97–98, but the authors note that a similar notion existed in Roman law and now exists in civil law countries.

5 According to the common law rule, any interest had to be certain to vest, if at all, within the life of some person alive at the testator's death, plus twenty-one years. See George T. Bogert, *Trusts*, §50, p. 189 (6th ed., Hornbook Series, St. Paul, Minn., West Pub. Co., 1987); C. Ronald Chester, "Cy Pres: A Promise Unfulfilled," 54 *Indiana Law Review* 407, 421 (1979). Many states have modified the common law rule in various ways, but they retain the basic idea of preventing individual trusts of indefinite duration. For ways in which a rule against perpetuities does apply to charitable trusts, see Bogert, *Trusts*, at §68, pp. 251–54.

6 A need for reformation can arise with individual trusts. In Donnelly v. National Bank of Washington, 179 P.2d 333 (Wash. Sup. Ct. 1947), a trust created for a

young man to go to college and law school specified that no payments were to be made after 1945. In 1942, having finished a year of law school, Donnelly was drafted; he was not discharged until 1946. The court ordered payments to continue. The case is discussed in Jonathan Macey, "Private Trusts for the Provision of Private Goods," 37 *Emory Law Journal* 295, 300–01 (1988).

7 Alex M. Johnson and Ross D. Taylor, "Revolutionizing Judicial Interpretation of Charitable Trusts: Applying Relational Contracts and Dynamic Interpretation to *Cy Pres* and America's Cup Litigation," 74 *Iowa Law Review* 545, at 562 (1989), citing Restatement (Second) of Trusts §399 (1957).

8 Ronald Chester, for example, in "*Cy Pres* or Gift Over? The Search for Coherence in Judicial Reform of Failed Charitable Trusts," XXIII *Suffolk University Law Review* 41, 43 (1989), writes of courts "cloaking their decisions in . . . poorly understood and often outdated rules . . . ."

9 Johnson and Taylor, note 7 supra at 565–66, quoting Restatement (Second) §381, comment a. See Bogert, *Trusts*, §147, p. 519.

10 Johnson and Taylor, note 7 supra, at 566, speak of the distinction as "indeterminate."

11 If one looks through a summary of relevant cases, see Bogert and Bogert, note 3 supra at pp. 134–57, one finds contrary decisions on facts that appear closely similar.

12 This is proposed by Ron Atkinson, in "Reforming *Cy Pres* Reform," 44 *Hastings Law Journal* 1112, 1142–47 (1993). According to present law, it is only the courts, rather than the trustees, that have authority to determine when an application of *cy pres* is justified. See Bogert and Bogert, note 3 supra, §435 pp. 129–31. Of course, if the creator formulates her original purposes in very broad terms, the trustees have wide discretion under the original trust. Thus, someone might create a trust to "promote the arts" or "support medical research," leaving it to the trustees to decide how funds may best be spent. And a settlor may confer on trustees explicit discretion to deviate from more specific terms.

13 Jackson v. Philips, 96 Mass. (14 Allen) 539 (1867).

14 This conclusion assumes that the terms referred to slavery within the United States and to people whose present status was as fugitive slaves. This is the assumption in Chester, note 5 supra, at 413. (One could aim to create sentiment to eliminate slavery in other locations in the world, and one could aid people who had formerly been fugitive slaves.)

15 See Vanessa Laird, "Phantom Selves: The Search for a General Charitable Intent in the Application of the *Cy Pres* Doctrine," 40 *Stanford Law Review* 973, 978 (1988).

16 See id. at 979.

17 See Bogert and Bogert, note 3 supra, at 142–43.

18 Id. at 136–37. However, if the donor is alive, he may testify about the nature of his intent.

19 For example, uncertainty in how contract cases will be resolved may affect the extent to which parties carry out contractual obligations and choose to bring contract issues to court.

20 See Laird, note 15 supra at 980.

21 As I have put the case, the court must decide whether the donor has a general intent and, if so, whether a local recreational facility or medical assistance in the neighboring town is closer to the original gift. The example in the text is a variation on In re Will of Neher, 279 N.Y. 370, 18 N.E. 2d 625 (1939).

22 Evans v. Newton, 382 U.S. 296 (1965).

23 This issue shows, among other things, that the question about general intent can be one in relation to a particular alternative use rather than all alternative uses. If Bacon had been an unbending segregationist, he would not have had a general intent to further any integrated facilities, but he might have had a general intent to promote uses beneficial for whites only. Thus, if a small park became unsuitable because a factory was built next to it, Bacon's general intent might have reached an indoor swimming pool for whites only.

24 I put aside here any possible argument that a park once committed to the public could not be withdrawn because the conditions of use are unconstitutional.

25 However, one *might* think that attitudes that are opposed to present ideas of justice should be given little or no weight.

26 Evans v. Abney, 396 U.S. 435, 445–46 (1970).

27 Evans v. Abney, 165 S.E 2d 160, 163 (Sup. Ct. Ga. 1968), aff'd, 396 U.S. 435 (1970).

28 Richard Posner, *Economic Analysis of Law* 482 (3rd ed., Boston, Little Brown, 1986). Jonathan Macy disagrees, believing that, although Bacon's primary intention may not have been to maintain racial restrictions, it was far from clear that he would have preferred a desegregated park to having his heirs take the property. See Macey, note 6 supra, at 304–05.

29 In In re Certain Scholarship Funds, 575 A.2d 1325, 1328 (N.H. 1990), the New Hampshire Supreme Court, dealing with a charitable trust whose limitation to "protestant" boys was unconstitutional (given administration by a public high school board), approved an adjustment to eliminate that condition, remarking that the trial court found no indication that the settlors "would not have responded to the changes in attitude experienced by society since the creation of these trusts."

30 See Posner, note 28 supra, at 482–83; Chris Abbinante, "Protecting 'Donor Intent' in Charitable Foundations: Wayward Trusteeship and the Barnes Foundation," 145 *University of Pennsylvania Law Review* 665, 697 (1997).

31 The case is discussed in Laird, note 15 supra, at 980–86. The litigation is summarized in a later collateral proceeding. Estate of Buck, 35 Cal. Rptr. 2d 442, 443–45 (Ct. App. 1994).

32 Another signpost is whether the donor has made gifts to many charities.

33 First Church of Sommerville (Unitarian) v. Attorney General, 376 N.E. 2d 1226 (Mass. 1978).

34 See Chester, note 8 supra, at 45–70.

35 This is how courts regard the fulfillment of such conditions. But see Home for the Incurables of Baltimore City v. University of Md. Med. Sys. Corp., 797 A.2d 746 (Md. 2002), in which the court excised a now illegal discriminatory condition rather than proceeding to an alternative beneficiary.

36 One might argue that *cy pres* should depend dominantly on social desirability, that donor's intent should recede greatly in significance as years pass. On that view, gifts over would lose some of their power as a reason not to employ *cy pres*.

37 See Matthew B. Perkins, "The Cy Pres Doctrine in the 1980s: The Case for Charitable Favoritism," 10 *Probate Law Journal* 163, 174 (1990).

38 See Chester, note 5 supra, at 408–10.

39 These concerns, of course, had no direct bearing when a failure of the initial terms of the trust would result in a gift over to a different charity, rather than a reversion to private hands, but one might approve a strict general rule

about altering terms as the best way to get property into the hands of private individuals.

40 See Chester, note 8 supra, at 61; Perkins, note 37 supra, at 176.

41 Of course, some of their salaries, like mine, are paid by private universities that rely heavily on charitable gifts.

42 See generally John J. Havens et al., *Charitable Giving: How Much, by Whom, to What, and How? The Nonprofit Sector: A Research Handbook* 542, 544–58 (2nd ed., New Haven, Yale University Press, 2006).

43 See Mercury Bay Boating Club v. San Diego Yacht Club, 76 N.Y. 2d 256 (1990); Johnson & Taylor, supra note 7. For a more recent America's Cup case, see Golden Gate Yacht Club v. Société Nautique de Genève, 12 N.Y.3d 248, 907 N.E.2d 276 (2009).

44 Havens, note 42 supra, at 553.

45 Its failure to announce before winning the cup what the conditions would be for the next defense of the cup apparently opened the door for the problems that followed.

46 Havens, note 42 supra, at 558.

47 See id.

48 The court gave considerable weight to the effective use of mutual consent to sidestep the conditions set out in the terms of the gift. Of course, a provision for mutual consent does not assure that an unreasonable challenger or defender will compromise, but if the defending San Diego Club had been unreasonable in this instance, it may have ill behooved it to claim that the original terms had become "impractical" because they permit such unreasonable failures to agree.

49 Insofar as the deed of gift seemed to favor the host country, one might think that one objective of the donor was to benefit the New York Yacht Club, but that objective is not one anyone would want to admit, and its relevance at this point in time, with the Cup elsewhere, would be slender in any event.

50 The New York statute requires that literal compliance with the terms of the trust become "impracticable or impossible", but Johnson and Taylor summarize the New York decisions as construing the statutory terms "broadly to optimize the use of charitable trust assets in light of changed conditions." Id. at 563. If one thought that the basic problem in the dispute was unresponsive behavior by the San Diego Club, one could believe that the ability of competitors to agree on conditions had so far protected all those who acted reasonably.

51 For such preferences to be highly significant, he would need to have been aware of racing with smaller ships and of multinational competitions of the kind that have since developed around the America's Cup. In those, competitors are paired singly against each other until a single challenger for the Cup and a single defender emerge.

52 However, one may argue that, given the vast amount of money spent designing America's Cup yachts, it would be fairer for ordinary races to have a different class boat than that used in the America's Cup.

53 One could, of course, say, "If modern competitors don't like Schuyler's conditions, let them set up their own different competition." Such a view slights the significance of tradition in sporting competitions.

54 Havens, note 42 supra, at 569–88.

55 Id. at 547.

56 They write of a charitable trust as "in some respects the prototypical relational contract," an agreement between the settlor and society that sets up

quasi-contractual relations of trustee and beneficiaries and of trustees and settlor. Id. at 571–72. The authors emphasize the public character of trusts as making them analogous to legislation. Id. at 579–84.

57 Id. at 582–85.

58 Unitarians reject the traditional Christian doctrine of the Trinity, but vary greatly in regard to their conceptions of God.

59 If a judge thinks that the writer did not foresee circumstances, he is asking about a probable hypothetical intent, about what the donor would have wanted.

60 See generally, Kent Greenawalt, *Religion and the Constitution, Vol. I, Free Exercise and Fairness* 261–89 (Princeton, Princeton University Press, 2006), and *Vol. II, Nonestablishment and Fairness* (2008). As recently as 1987, Bogert, *Trusts*, §57, p. 219, expressed doubt about attempts to create trusts for Islam and "other oriental religions." It also indicated that courts might not approve as charitable a purpose to challenge religious views. Id at p. 220. Modern free speech jurisprudence, with its rule against viewpoint discrimination, would require that promotion of atheism be treated equally with promotion of religion (though intellectual promotion of either kind might be distinguished from activities of worship).

61 See Greenawalt, *Free Exercise and Fairness*, note 60 supra.

62 Iris J. Goodwin, "Ask Not What Your Charity Can Do for You: *Robertson v. Princeton* Provides Liberal-Democratic Insights into the Dilemma of *Cy Pres* Reform," 51 *Arizona Law Review* 75 (2009), argues that *cy pres* is appropriate to protect a neutral regime of rights, but not to resolve issues about greater goods. I believe the capacity of courts to resolve issues about common good depends heavily on just what competing goods are involved and how well they will be served by alternative dispositions. A 1939 student note reflecting a legal realist approach remarked upon "the highly desirable trend of the courts toward disregarding the specific fulfillment of the donor's design in favor of the interests of public welfare." Note, "A Revaluation of *Cy Pres*," 49 *Yale Law Journal* 303, 322 (1939), discussed in Chester, note 5 supra, at 409–10. In one New York case, land had been given for a memorial hospital, which the town proved unable to build and maintain, medical needs having been met by a hospital in a neighboring town. In re Will of Neher, 279 N.Y. 370, 18 N.E. 2d 625 (1939). The court allowed the town to use the land for a memorial administration building. See Chester, note 5 supra, at 415.

63 Ronald Chester explained in 1979, "Courts may be reluctant to assume a direct role in reallocating charitable funds for public purposes precisely for fear of taking one more step toward the obliterating of individual will in an increasingly socialist world." Chester, note 5 supra, at 418.

64 I mean to distinguish this situation from that involving the America's Cup, for which the contribution of the original donors had become marginal.

65 Rob Atkinson, note 12 supra, at 1142–47, would solve the *cy pres* problem by giving virtually unfettered authority to trustees. Whether that is a wise resolution, one needs to keep in mind that a trustee judgment in favor of *cy pres* usually precedes judicial judgment authorizing reformation, and that trustees might feel constrained by a donor's wishes beyond what would be legally enforceable on them were they given more authority to dictate deviations. See id. at 1126–27. See also Rob Atkinson, "The Low Road to *Cy Pres* Reform: Principled Practice to Remove Dead Hand Control of Charitable Assets," 58 *Case Western Law Review* 97 (2007). On the typical lack of enforcement against trustees who exceed the

terms of trusts, see Stephanie Strom, "Donors Gone, Trusts Veer from Their Wishes," *N.Y. Times*, Sept. 29, 2007, at A1.

66 See Macey, note 6 supra, at 313–14.

67 How potential donors would react if courts relied frequently on unexpressed but probable broad intentions to deviate from the strict terms of grants is unclear. In id., Macey argues in favor of straightforward rules that donors can rely on.

68 If donors lost all power to prescribe conditions that a later court might find no longer serve the public interest, the incentive to set up trusts might decrease.

69 However, these advantages will alter significantly if estate taxes are sharply reduced or eliminated, as the law recently provided for the future.

70 A donor's wishes could contravene public policy not only in the manner in which resources are distributed but in a reason for a distribution that would be innocuous in itself. A donor might prefer aiding the fewer poor of Marin County rather than the greater number of poor in the Bay Area, but a court probably should not rely for this conclusion on strong evidence that the donor was a racial bigot who would not have wanted money to go to other parts of the Bay Area in which a substantial percentage of the population is nonwhite.

71 One might say that yachting is a luxury, and that if a donor wanted ninety-foot boats and single country challenges, no one would be hurt. Countries need not participate if they choose not to. Efficiency is more important for medical research and poor relief.

72 §7.10. The formulation in the Restatement covers two traditional doctrines: a changed-conditions doctrine for covenants and a frustration of purpose doctrine for easements.

73 477 A.2d 1066 (Del. 1984).

74 There are, however, limits on the kinds of covenants that will be enforced. Covenants must "touch and concern" the land; land owners cannot impose restrictions that have nothing to do with the upkeep and use of property. State courts might have employed this doctrine to bar racially restrictive covenants on ownership and use. In Shelley v. Kraemer, 334 U.S. 1 (1948), the Supreme Court ruled that judicial enforcement of such covenants was "unconstitutional." See Carol Rose, "*Shelley v. Kraemer* Through the Lens of Property," in Gerald Korngold and Andrew P. Morris (eds.), *Property Stories* 169 (New York, Foundation Press, 2004).

75 447 A.2d, at 1070.

76 Based on my limited experience, more liquor and more hard liquor gets drunk in restaurants that sell alcohol than in restaurants that allow brown-bagging; and beach communities that prohibit the sale of liquor remain more sedate than neighboring communities that are "wet." Time spent in Atlantic City and Ocean City, N.J. (before gambling was allowed in Atlantic City) and in Wildwood and Cape May, N.J. provides the basis for my opinion about beach communities.

77 §7.10, comment a. The test is stringent: relief is granted only if the purpose of the servitude can no longer be accomplished.

78 It might be argued that any present owners had waived their rights by accepting commercialization and "brown-bagging." But the covenants gave no explicit right to stop "brown-bagging," and owners might reasonably have objected to the sale of alcohol but not commercialization.

79 See Michael A. Heller, "The Boundaries of Private Property," 108 *Yale Law Journal* 1163 (1999).

80 One might suppose that *total* liquor use will not be affected and that society as a whole does not benefit if use in one small enclave is reduced and use elsewhere increases.

81 It is a question in modern property law how far restrictions may legitimately protect non-economic values.

82 If courts can distribute financial benefits among competing parties, their power to rewrite original agreements may be even greater than it is in regard to *cy pres*.

83 Jeffrey A. Blackie, "Note, Conservation Easements and the Doctrine of Changed Conditions," 40 *Hastings Law Journal* 1187 (1989). Nancy A. McLaughlin, "Rethinking the Perpetual Nature of Conservation Easements," 29 *Harvard Environmental Law Review* 421 (2005), suggests that principles of *cy pres* should be extended to conservation easements.

84 The Restatement (Second) §265 puts it: "a party's principal purpose is substantially frustrated without his fault by the occurrence of an event the non-occurrence of which was a basic assumption on which the contract was made . . . ."

85 See Krell v. Henry, [1903] 2 K.B. 740; Chandler v. Webster, [1904] 1 K.B. 493 (C.A.).

86 In id., the court made it clear that someone renting a room not only could not recover money already paid, but had to pay money owed (but not paid) before the parade was canceled.

87 See Fibrosa S.A. v. Fairbairn Lawson Combe Barbour, Ltd., [1943] A.C. 32 (H.L.). The court allowed a Polish buyer to recover payments made for machines a defendant was to supply, after the German invasion rendered performance of the contract impossible. The Law Reform (Frustrated Contracts) Act, 1943, 6 & 7 Geo. 6, ch. 40, allowed for the recovery of benefits conferred.

88 Kull, "Mistake, Frustration, and the Windfall Principle of Contract Remedies," 43 *Hastings Law Journal* 1 (1991).

89 §265. There is a qualifying phrase: "unless the language or the circumstances indicate the contrary"; but "the contrary" apparently is "no discharge."

90 See Fowler v. Insurance Company of North America, 155 Ga. App. 439, 270 S.E.2d 845 (Ct. App. 1980).

91 Section 261. Interestingly, Mrs. Steuart in Steuart v. McChesney, 444 A.2d 659 (Pa. Sup. Ct. 1982), discussed in Chapter 9, might have argued that the failure of the county to keep its property assessments up to date was the nonoccurrence of an event whose occurrence was a basic assumption of the contract.

92 See Sheldon W. Halpern, "Application of the Doctrine of Commercial Impracticability: Search for the Wisdom of Solomon," 135 *University of Pennsylvania Law Review* 1123, 1131–32 (1987).

93 Opinion of Justice Blackburn, in Taylor v. Caldwell, [1863] Queen's Bench, 3 Best S. 826.

94 According to comment d to §261 of the Restatement, "Performance may be impracticable because extreme and unreasonable difficulty, expense, injury, or loss to one of the parties will be involved."

95 Aluminum Co. of America v. Essex Group, Inc. 499 F. Supp. 53 (W.D. Pa. 1980).

96 However, one might infer probable foresight from foreseeability. One might also believe that a party has a responsibility to deal with foreseeable risks in the contract.

97 See Halpern, note 92 supra, at 1157–65.

98 See, e.g., Ian MacNeil, "Contracts: Adjustment of Long-Term Economic Relations Under Classical, Neoclassical, and Relational Contract Law," 72 Northwestern University Law Review 854 (1978).

99 See Halpern, note 92 supra, at 1126, 1175–77.

100 §272.

101 See Transatlantic Financing Corp. v. United States, 363 F.2d 312 (D.C. Cir. 1966), in which it was claimed that taking the longer route added $44,000 beyond the contractual price of $306,000.

Chapter 11

Conclusion and a Comparison

In the previous chapters, we have looked at the basic components of legal interpretation. We have explored how other disciplines might bear on legal texts, and what constitutes desirable performance and the meaning of informal instructions. We have also examined the various components— some agreed upon, some controversial—that are aspects of interpreting texts (and oral communications) created by private individuals but enforceable in law.

In this concluding chapter I offer a few general observations about how these efforts relate to what will follow in subsequent volumes, and I compare my conclusions with those of an outstanding Israeli judge and jurist, Aharon Barak, who has offered a general, comprehensive theory for the interpretation of legal texts.[1]

Although we have considered some controversial issues about the interpretation of wills and contracts, these pale in significance with disagreements about statutory and constitutional interpretation, which touch the core of the role of judges within a liberal democratic political order such as ours. As I have already suggested in the chapters on other disciplines, general theories of interpretation may seem to have special importance for an understanding of broad legal norms designed to carry force over many generations, norms typically found in constitutions and in some statues. For such norms, the role of the interpreter takes on an evident centrality that is not present for highly specific rules that have been recently formulated.

Although at this point in history, how judges should interpret the common law is less controversial than how they should interpret constitutions and statutes, the historical development of that law over time and the fact that it is not exactly textual interpretation (despite the importance of previous judicial opinions) present their own interesting questions about interpretation. There is serious disagreement among scholars about how to conceptualize common law interpretation and about the relevance of various techniques that it involves, such as reasoning by analogy. General theories of interpretations may provide insights on these subjects.

Subsequent volumes will pursue these various inquiries, asking how far statutory, constitutional, and common law interpretation resemble and do not resemble the forms of legal interpretation we have studied here, and also asking how far other disciplines shed light on actual and desirable performance in these three domains.

Among the topics this book has touched on is the question of whether the fundamental nature of human communication can tell us how legal interpretation should proceed. My skepticism on this score is further developed in subsequent volumes. A powerful argument can be made that the subjective intentions of the writer of a will should be controlling for interpretation; that argument is much less strong in respect to statutes and constitutions. Indeed, in respect to these texts, enacted by collective bodies, there is a perplexing question whether the whole concept of intention makes sense, and if so, how that concept should be conceived. I will contend that intentions of enactors are relevant, although not dispositive, for statutory and constitutional interpretation, but defending that contention is not simple.

In connection with agency, wills, and contracts, we have inquired how far the content of specific provisions should dictate results if they seem to conflict with more general purposes. That turns out to be a crucial concern about statutes and constitutions. And, as the last chapter suggests, the extent to which interpretation should respond to developments after an authoritative text is enacted is especially important when texts survive over time.

In each domain to which we have given attention, one overarching issue is whether judges should employ a single interpretive standard or a number of standards. If the answer is a number of standards, should these be arranged in a hierarchical ordering, or given weight in some looser fashion? If the exclusive test was "how an ordinary reader would understand the text," or "what the writer intended," there would be a single uniform standard. The "plain meaning rule" admits multiple standards but in a hierarchy. A judge does not look at subjective intentions of writers if the meaning is plain, but if the meaning is not plain, the judge turns to external evidence of what the parties intended. If judges take into account both the ordinary meaning of a text and what the writers probably intended without a clear ordering, they are considering multiple standards without a decisive ordering. These issues arise, and are sharply contested, for both statutory and constitutional interpretation.

For those publicly created texts, as for those created by private parties, two complications about standards of interpretation are highly important. The first, as we saw in the wills chapter, is that judges or scholars may announce what purports to be a single standard of interpretation, but that standard itself may be composed of diverse elements with no clear ordering among them. The second complication concerns the distinction between subjective standards (what actual people had in mind) and objective standards (what a reasonable writer or reader would understand). In subsequent volumes, I will suggest various ways in which this distinction is much less sharp than it appears at first glance, but one of those ways has been developed in the chapters on wills and contracts. The more an "objective" inquiry includes the particular circumstances, or context, in which a text is written, the closer it will come to capturing the probable subjective intentions of those who wrote the document.

A question that I have mentioned, and resolved for the purposes of this book, is what constitutes legal interpretation. I have used a broad understanding. The same question pervades statutory and constitutional interpretation, with debates over the appropriateness of judicial creativity and "judicial activism."

In the remainder of this chapter, I explore the positions I have taken in relation to one comprehensive theory of legal interpretation, that of Aharan Barak. I have chosen his theory in particular because, in contrast to Ronald Dworkin, the most influential writer on that subject in Anglo-American jurisprudence,[2] Barak devotes substantial attention to wills and contracts.

In evaluating my theoretical approaches, it is helpful to see how they coincide with and diverge from Justice Barak's. Contrary to what might initially appear, what our approaches share is far more important than what divides them; and I thus take Barak's experience at the highest level of judging (as Chief Justice of Israel's Supreme Court) and his impressive command of the concepts of an extensive range of legal systems as providing significant support for most of the practical conclusions in the preceding chapters, and in those that will follow. After sketching broad areas of agreement, and noting some disagreements about practical and conceptual subjects, I address forms of conceptualization by Barak that do not distinguish his approach as sharply from mine as may first appear.

In developing his theory of "purposive interpretation," Barak urges that judges consider a mixture of factors that are subjective (what the writers of a text really intended) and objective (what a reasonable person would do, what the underlying values of the legal system recommend).[3] The exact combination of factors and the weight judges should assign each depends, among other things, on the general area (wills or contracts, statutes, or constitution), on the kind of text (specific or general), on relations of parties (negotiated contract or contract of adhesion), and on the time that has passed (new or old text).[4] Courts should be guided by presumptions, such as that parties have used language in a natural and ordinary way, and that they aim for a just outcome.[5] External sources of evidence about subjective intent should be generally admitted, although internal evidence from the text may be more reliable.[6]

For both wills and contracts, the subjective intent of the writer(s) is crucial, indeed achieves a "rule-like status,"[7] but courts should recognize a multiplicity of subjective purposes.[8]

In considering relevant factors, judges should aim for coherence, trying to achieve a synthesis or harmony if possible. Thus, if evidences of subjective intent point in opposite directions, judges should choose the intent that fits with reasonable behavior and the deep values of the legal system.[9] A court's approach to interpretation should be holistic, not proceeding by separate independent stages according to which one reaches a later stage only if an earlier stage is indecisive.[10]

Each of these practical proposals of Justice Barak's fits with the views developed here.

In respect to strategies of interpretation, Barak suggests that desirable interpretation depends on the system that is involved.[11] Legal interpretation differs from aesthetic interpretation,[12] and interpretation within a totalitarian legal system differs from that within a democracy. Although general hermeneutic theory can teach lessons,[13] it cannot resolve what legal interpretation should be like.[14] Many canons of interpretation reflect natural use of language,[15] and answers to legal questions are often clear.[16]

In various chapters, I have also claimed that a strong relation exists between natural use of language and understanding in law, that legal answers are often clear, and that one needs to make normative political and moral judgments to assess desirable interpretive strategies in law.

On some other points, my position is definitely or possibly at odds with that of Justice Barak. He apparently welcomes all kinds of evidence about subjective intent and proposes a standard of preponderance of evidence for evaluation.[17] We agree that external evidence should be allowed even when textual meaning appears plain, but I am more open than Barak to the exclusion of some forms of evidence that may be highly unreliable and create a temptation to fraud,[18] and I believe that a heightened standard of proof may sometimes be desirable for evidence that would overcome the apparent force of binding language.[19]

Barak's emphasis on purpose seems, by itself, to give priority to general aims over specific, or concrete, intentions. In American discussions, purpose, as he recognizes, often is contrasted with narrower intentions,[20] and *some* of what he writes, as well as his labeling of his theory as "purposive interpretation," appears to do so. [21] Although his treatment of both wills and contracts affords a high priority to how parties meant to resolve particular issues, when the resolution is clear, Barak's focus on general objectives, as contrasted with narrow ones, is substantial. I am more hesitant than he is to generalize about when judges should rely on higher levels of abstraction.

In a subject that will be relevant for succeeding volumes, Barak comments almost in passing that one cannot attribute a subjective intent when the legal text is a referendum.[22] But, however difficult it may usually be, we can conceive some issue that is unresolved by the text but is so central to campaigns for and against passage that one could be confident what resolution most of the positive voters in a referendum intended.[23]

In various passages, Barak indicates that it does not matter whether judges begin at more concrete or more abstract levels,[24] or start with presumptions about subjective purpose or objective purpose,[25] yet for some issues, one starting point will be natural and another awkward.[26]

My differences with Barak extend beyond these practical matters to certain conceptualizations. The two most important of these are what counts as interpretation in a narrow sense and the exact division between subjective and objective purpose.

Barak posits that *in law* real interpretation must fit within the semantic meaning of the text;[27] when judges fill gaps, resolve contradictions, correct mistakes, and change language to prevent absurdity, they perform some non-interpretive tasks. These exercises require special doctrines to justify them.[28] Matters are much more complicated than Barak acknowledges, as we can see in respect to mistakes.

Barak extends the notion of semantic meaning, by saying that writers of wills and contracts can create their own semantic meaning. They can even call black "white" and white "black."[29] Thus, in respect to the designation of Robert. J. Krause in a will discussed in Chapter 8, if the testator had always thought (mistakenly) that his best friend had the middle initial of J, the will could be "interpreted" to refer to Robert W. Krause. If the testator put "J" as the middle initial without thinking, although aware on any reflection that his friend's middle initial is W, he made a mistake.[30] It does not make sense to say that the second scenario requires a special doctrine for judicial action, whereas the first does not.[31] Both involve legal interpretation.[32] I reach similar conclusions about genuine absurdity (which may be regarded as a form of mistake) and some gap filling.

To understand how much any theory of interpretation depends on subjective, as contrasted with objective, elements, we need to know how the theory divides those elements. At its central core, subjective factors concern what actual people did (or probably did) intend or believe. In his division of subjective and objective purpose, Barak apparently places people's hypothetical intent on the objective side,[33] based partly, it appears, on the absence of evidence of such an intent. But we often have substantial evidence about what a particular person would have thought about an issue she did not consider. On some previous occasion, she may actually have focused on and resolved what is essentially the same issue. Alternatively, given her general habits of mind and emotion, we may be confident she would be inclined in one direction, not another. To draw a trivial analogy, if a sports fan is away on a wilderness trip and out of contact with others or has died and the team she has long rooted for makes it to the World Series (against a team she has long detested), we could be pretty sure who she *would* be rooting for if she was aware of the competing teams. That is a hypothetical intention about which we can be highly confident.

In truth, when one evaluates unexpressed intentions, one cannot be sure if they are actual (though undisclosed) or hypothetical. In the example of Dr. Rowland's will, we are uncertain after the fact whether he *did* think about how "coincide" should be understood or *did not* think about it but *would have conceived* a relatively broad sense. So long as the focus is on a particular human actor, or a group of actors, an inquiry about hypothetical intent better falls on the subjective side of the division between subjective and objective.

Another distinction that can matter for interpretation is between "specific" and "abstract." Barak generally treats more abstract levels as those concerning substantive propositions that are more general (a presumption in favor of wills including family members is more abstract than a conclusion that the language of a particular will probably implies that each child should receive a painting).[34] Barak also employs a different sense of abstract, treating the inquiry about a reasonable person as more abstract than one about actual people, even when the substantive question being addressed is precisely the same.[35] While neither sense of abstraction is misguided, we must be careful not to conflate the two completely different kinds of moves from more specific to more abstract.

Central questions that will occupy us in the next volume include the comparative responsibilities of legislators and courts. Barak comments that subsequent legislation does not interpret earlier legislation.[36] The coverage of clear provisions of new statutes does not depend on whether legislators are interpreting old laws or self-consciously revising them; but it is entirely possible that many legislators may have been be moved to act because of how they have interpreted an earlier law. Barak's language here may reflect his view that judges are the authoritative interpreters of legal texts, but that does not mean they are the only interpreters; and, indeed, other government actors have some serious interpretive responsibilities. One appropriate basis for a statutory revision is a belief by legislators that judges have misinterpreted the original statute; and if judges discern this belief, that may affect how they construe vague or ambiguous passages in the two laws.

Having explored a large range of agreement and some discrete points of apparent disagreement, I now reach what are by far the most crucial matters for understanding the relation of Barak's work to my own. That concerns the aspiration for a comprehensive systematic theory of interpretation. Barak's "purposive interpretation" is such a theory that covers all legal texts.[37] At first glance, that conception seems very different from my approach, which is particularistic, hesitant to embrace any general theory given the wide diversity of legal texts that courts consider. But are we really very far apart?

Barak suggests multiple elements of both subjective purpose and objective purpose. Even if we adopt my suggestion that the hypothetical intent of actual persons should be seen as an aspect of subjective purpose,[38] Barak's objective factors still include what a reasonable person would understand by the language of the text in its context, what broader purposes a reasonable person would conceive as underlying the text, how a reasonable person would understand that kind of legal instrument, and what are the basic values of the legal system.[39] The "ultimate" purpose, the purpose normatively constructed by judges as determinative of meaning, involves the best combination of subjective and objective purposes.[40]

Justice Barak recognizes that a substantial degree of weighing of values will be needed, and he offers various recommendations for how that weighing should be done.[41] Acknowledging that judges will often have a hard task assigning appropriate weights and will sometimes have to exercise discretion to choose between two legally permissible alternatives,[42] Barak remarks that his approach "is not based on a single, clear criterion for resolving" the difficult question about how to settle on ultimate purpose.[43]

One question about Barak's approach is his acceptance of judicial discretion, a subject I have hardly mentioned in this book, beyond a brief treatment in Chapter 2 in the discussion of vagueness. For the most part, Barak seems to take relevant discretion as existing if judges must make a choice, if reasonable judges and lawyers will disagree about the better choice, and if a choice either way will be regarded as legally acceptable. By these criteria, everyone agrees that judicial discretion exists. Whether in some deeper sense judges lack discretion[44] is of limited importance for interpretive strategies. Those explore how judges do and should try to resolve issues,[45] not whether difficult issues have, in some complex sense, correct answers that we can only struggle to determine and never ascertain with confidence. When I address that thesis in subsequent volumes, I shall draw a vital distinction between right answers about results (usually either-or) and right answers about ideal legal formulations (among many, possibly scores, of conceivable alternatives).[46]

What I wish to emphasize here is that range of difference between Justice Barak and myself resembles disagreement over whether a glass is half full or half empty. Justice Barak offers illuminating proposals for how various factors should be understood and weighed; many of these proposals strike one as clearly sound once one perceives them,[47] others are debatable and deservedly controversial. He may have a greater degree of confidence than I do about how judges should weigh various factors over a wide range of legal texts; but for him, as for me, matters come down to a weighing of various kinds of factors without any simple formula, a weighing that is and should be radically different for different kinds of legal texts. When it comes to resolving particular cases and how much weight to give to various factors across a range of legal texts, Barak's approach is not markedly more determinative than my own. We agree that judges should aim for a kind of consistency, but that only a modest amount can be said about precise degrees of importance of competing considerations when relevant factors do not line up in the same direction.

In understanding this volume and those to follow, readers should be aware of my sense that the approaches I suggest do not differ drastically from any comprehensive approach that is actually plausible, that is, any comprehensive approach that recognizes all the nuances and variations among legal texts and legal issues.

Subsequent volumes will explain many reasons that statutory and constitutional interpretation (and common law interpretation as well) differ greatly from the interpretation of privately created documents with legal authority, and from each other. These volumes will explore the implications of those reasons for how legal interpretation within these major domains of common law systems should proceed.

Notes

1 Aharon Barak, *Purposive Interpretation in Law* (Princeton, N.J., Princeton University Press, 2005).
2 I have occasionally noted positions of Dworkin's in this book, and in later chapters we will look at the major aspects of his theory.
3 Barak, note 1 supra, at 85–203. See also Aharon Barak, *The Judge in a Democracy* 122–76 (Princeton, Princeton University Press, 2006). In this book, Justice Barak devotes some attention to the common law, id. at 15, 89, 97, 155–63.
4 Barak, note 1 supra, at 118, 128, 183–84.
5 Id. at 46–48, 117, 138, 140, 182. These presumptions are not rigid rules; they can be rebutted by sufficient evidence. Id. at 46–48.
6 Id. at 146, xiv, 88, 120, 186–89, 326–27.
7 Id. at 122–23. For contracts, that intent needs to be mutual, but it is enough that one party should reasonably have been aware that the other party had a particular intent. Id. at 21.
8 Id. at 117–18, 182.
9 These deep values should be drawn from the perspective of the legal community, not a judge's idiosyncratic sense of how things should be. Id. at 39. See Barak, note 3 supra, at 91–106.
10 Barak, note 1 supra, at xii, 74.
11 Id. at 30–36.
12 Id. at 111.
13 Id. at 57, 230–32.
14 Id. at 220. Legal interpretation is distinctive both because of the special role of the judge and because of law's social aims. Id. at 59–60, 221–23. In any determination about desirable legal interpretation, the appropriate role of the judiciary is very important. Id. at xvi.
15 Id. at 8.
16 Id. at 7. Barak focuses on legal outcomes as contrasted with the precise principles that judges may draw from a legal text.
17 Id. at 309–11, 132.
18 An example would be what a testator told his daughter about his degree of affection for her stepmother.
Barak welcomes without qualification Jane Baron's proposal, discussed in my Chapter 8, that judges should listen to "stories" to decide testator's intentions.
19 Our divergence over standards of proof may be partly explained by a feature of American law that Barak does not discuss—the fact that some crucial findings about intent may be made by jurors—but my acceptance of constraints would go somewhat beyond his even were judges always the ones to estimate subjective intent.
20 Id. at 127.

21 In one passage, he comments that the "concrete (consequentialist) intention may influence the judge as a source of information about abstract purpose—and no more." Id. at 127–28. He misleadingly puts this position as giving concrete intention "as much weight as abstract intention." This phraseology is misleading because normally when one phenomenon is relevant only as evidence of another phenomenon, and the latter is what really matters, we do not speak of equal weight.

22 Id. at 119, 130.

23 I assume that the relevant intent here is that of voters (perhaps including, as I shall explain in the next volume, those who voted against as well as in favor) and that the relevant kind of intent would be similar to the intent of legislators for statutes.

24 Id. at 150.

25 Id. at 113–14, 203. These comments fit Barak's sense that interpretation is holistic, comprising a kind of hermeneutic circle, in Gadamer's image.

26 Indeed, Barak's own treatment of wills and contracts suggests that subjective intention or purpose is the natural starting point for those.

27 Id. at xiii, 18–19.

28 Id. at 63–66.

29 Id. at 307, 309–11.

30 An intermediate possibility is that the lawyer looked in the telephone book on the day the testator made his will and asked if Robert J. Krause is his closest friend, and the testator answered "yes," not paying attention to the middle initial.

31 The intermediate scenario falls somewhere between but is probably closer to the first than to the third (since at the crucial moment the testator really thought J was the right initial).

32 A somewhat puzzling claim made by Barak, likely drawing from Gadamer, is that no text is plain until interpreted. Barak, note 1 supra, at xii, xv. Perhaps he means only that judges should be willing to consider evidence that could affect how even the plainest appearing text should be treated. But he may mean that any use of language, even "Please pass the salt," must be interpreted for it to be plain; if so, he is assigning a very broad scope to interpretation. If no text is plain without it, we would need to recognize that no judicial interpretation and instructions can themselves make a course of action plain for officials who carry out rulings, since only the interpretations of these officials can make judicial language plain.

33 Id. at 36, 121. In other passages, Barak seems to treat the relevant hypothetical intent as one about a reasonable author. Id. at 148–49; Barak, note 3 supra, at 148.

34 See Barak, note 1 supra, at 113–14.

35 Id. at 150–51.

36 Id. at 247.

37 Id. at xi, 74.

38 See text following note 33. On Barak's own categorization, the hypothetical intent of actual people is yet another element of objective purpose.

39 Id. at 148–79.

40 Id. at xiii–iv, 182–203.

41 For example, a more important value should count more heavily than a less important one. As a rough generalization this is uncontroversial, although it also matters how deeply the two values are implicated in the particular context. Barak also discusses weighing and balancing in note 3 supra, at 164–76.

42 Barak, note 1 supra, at 53–55.

43 Id. at 183.

44 The leading American denial of discretion has come from Ronald Dworkin, who has claimed that within the law there really is a correct answer to each legal issue, however hard it may be to identify it, with "the law" including morally best answers on issues as to which narrower legal sources are indecisive. See Ronald Dworkin, "Judicial Discretion," 60 *Journal of Philosophy* 624 (1963); *Taking Rights Seriously* (rev. ed.) 333–45 (Cambridge, Mass., Harvard University Press 1978); *Law's Empire* (Cambridge, Mass., Harvard University Press 1986). My responses are in "Discretion and Judicial Decision: The Elusive Quest for the Fetters That Bind Judges," 75 *Columbia Law Review* 359 (1975); *Law and Objectivity*, 207–28 (New York, Oxford University Press, 1991). The chapter in the book contains some thoughts about the limits of reassurance the correct answers thesis in a complex form would give to ordinary people. Id. at 226–27.

45 Barak, note 1 supra, at 208, does sometimes write as if judges appropriately recognize they are making a choice as to which there is no correct answer in law.

46 My simple claim is that a denial of "discretion" is more plausible if the choice is between two alternatives than if the choice is among scores of reasonable alternatives.

47 For example, he points out that autonomy of the will reflected in the law of wills and contracts fits with modern democratic notions of human dignity.

Index

A

Abortion, 115, 125, 165, 169–70

Abraham (Hebrew Bible), 131

Abstract versus contextual
interpretation
contract interpretation, 256–73
generally, 7, 9, 14, 334
informal instructions, interpretation
of, 182, 185–93, 203–06
literary interpretation, 67
philosophy of language, 33–38

Actual authority of agents, 218–26,
229n30, 229n35

Administrative decisions, 8, 36–37, 42,
56n122, 113–14, 281, 286n8

Aesthetic interpretation, 155, 67–68,
98n43, 175n42, 178n115, 332

Affirmative action, 1–2, 7

Agency, interpretation and
acting beyond terms of instructions,
211n57, 224–27
actual authority, 218–26, 229n30,
229n35
apparent authority, 218–20
best interpretation standard, 222
choice between alternatives in interpreting instructions, 221–22
definition of agency, 227n5
fiduciary relationship, 218, 220
overview, 217–18, 227
principal's right to control, 218–19
reasonableness in interpretation
of instructions, 220, 222–23,
229nn31–34
specific versus general
provisions, 330
time of action, relevance of, 223
unforeseen circumstances
and, 225–27
vague or ambiguous
instructions, 224

Aggadot (Jewish narratives), 123,
143n73, 144n74

Albery, Michael, 235, 250n24,
250n26, 250nn29–30

*Aluminum Co. of America (Alcoa) v.
Essex Group, Inc.* (1980), 318–19,
326n95

Alexandria School, 131

Alston, William, 53n57

Ambiguity
agency, interpretation of vague or
ambiguous instructions in, 224
contract interpretation, 292n71
informal instructions, interpretation
of, 189–93
faithful performance, 189–90,
207n9
meaning, 190–93
vagueness and, 56n126, 57n136
wills, interpretation of, 253n69

American Law Institute, 113, 282

America's Cup, 309–10, 312,
323nn51–52

*AM International, Inc. v. Graphic
Management Associates, Inc.* (1995),
294n92

Analogies
between legal and non-legal interpretation, 3, 4, 14, 22–23, 63, 68,
70–71, 92–95, 98n54, 104n151,
107, 110, 112, 135–36, 292n76,
323–24n56,
constitutional interpretation
analogy, 111–13, 140n19,
148n194, 320
relation between analogy and
syllogism, 128–29
religious use of, 127–29, 132

Animal Farm (Orwell), 72

Anthropology, 96n4, 166

Antioch School, 131